Analysing Policy:
What's the problem
represented to be?

To Stephen, Angie, Anne W. and Anne F.

Analysing Policy:
What's the problem represented to be?

Carol Bacchi

Copyright © Pearson Australia (a division of Pearson Australia Group) 2009

Pearson Australia
Unit 4, Level 3
14 Aquatic Drive
Frenchs Forest NSW 2086

www.pearson.com.au

Acquisitions Editor: Joanne Stanley
Project Editor: Kathryn Munro
Associate Editor: Jessica Sykes
Production Coordinators: Chris Richardson and Barbara Honor
Copy Editor: Abigail Nathan
Proofreader: Bree DeRoche
Copyright and Pictures Editor: Emma Gaulton
Indexer: Lisa Knowles
Cover design by Natalie Bowra
Cover photograph from Getty Images
Typeset by Midland Typesetters, Australia

Printed and bound in Australia by The SOS Print + Media Group.

1 2 3 4 5 13 12 11 10 09

National Library of Australia
Cataloguing-in-Publication Data

Author:	Bacchi, Carol Lee.
Title:	Analysing policy: What's the problem represented to be?
Edition:	1st ed.
ISBN:	9780733985751 (pbk).
Notes:	Includes index.
	Includes bibliography.
Subjects:	Policy sciences—Evaluation.
Dewey Number:	320.6

Pearson Australia is a division of

Contents

Preface

This book offers students a way to analyse policy. It should be stated at the outset that it does not offer a conventional form of policy analysis. Indeed, this is a most unconventional book about policy. It is best described as a poststructural approach to policy analysis. What this means will be made clear in due course. Stated simply, the intent is to dig deeper than usual into the meaning of policies and into the meaning-making that is part of policy formulation. As Beilharz (1987, p. 393) put it some years ago, 'the object becomes that of seeking to understand policy better than its authors'.

I developed the methodology introduced here, called 'what's the problem represented to be?', in an earlier book (Bacchi 1999). My specific task in that book was to examine how such an approach could provide insights into the ways in which women's inequality has been understood in Western policy interventions, and the implications for feminist theorists. The positive reception the approach received both in Australia and overseas led me to develop it further and to show how it can be applied more widely. While the starting place for analysis is public policy in Australia, the focus on methodology and application means that the approach is easily adaptable to other settings. This is also the case due to an explicit intent to understand national policies within broad international contexts.

The book has been designed for ease of application. Chapter 1 lays out the steps in the approach in a straightforward, 'how to do' fashion. The hope is that students can begin to use the approach right away, should they wish to do so. Chapter 2 provides the theoretical background to the key concepts in the approach. Chapters 3 and 4 apply the approach in a systematic way, while Chapters 5 through 10 develop a more integrated form of analysis. Terms that appear in bold are explained in the Glossary. A supplement to the text, containing hyperlinks to key references, is downloadable from the publisher's catalogue (www.pearson. com.au/Catalogue/Browse.aspx).

The book has an underlying and unifying argument. It offers a 'what's the problem represented to be?' approach to policy analysis as a counter to the current enthusiasm in both education and in public policy for 'problem *solving*'. This argument gets an airing in the Introduction, and runs as a sub-theme through to Chapter 10, where it is more thoroughly discussed. The message of the book, put briefly, is that, to offer new dimensions in thinking about how governing takes place, it is imperative to shift the focus from 'problem' *solving* to 'problem' *questioning* – interrogating the ways in which proposals for change *represent* 'problems'.

REFERENCES

BACCHI, C. 1999, *Women, Policy and Politics: The Construction of Policy Problems*, Sage, London.

BEILHARZ, P. 1987, 'Reading Politics: Social Theory and Social Policy', *Australian and New Zealand Journal of Sociology*, vol. 23, no. 3, pp. 388–406.

Acknowledgements

Because the 'what's the problem represented to be?' approach has been tested and refined over the past ten years, many people need to be acknowledged. In particular I am indebted to the feedback and support provided by my colleagues Joan Eveline, Chris Beasley and Carol Johnson. In addition I learned a great deal from discussions with undergraduate and postgraduate students who have worked with the approach. Angelique Bletsas, Zoe Gill and Zoe Gordon merit special mention. Exchanges with scholars around the globe and opportunities to offer courses and lectures based on the approach in Umeä, Copenhagen and Aalborg assisted greatly in its development.

Special thanks are owed to Angelique Bletsas for editorial suggestions and for coming up with an abbreviated name for the 'what's the problem represented to be?' approach to policy analysis. My research assistant, Anne Wilson, contributed significantly to the final product, hunting down elusive references and discovering new, relevant material. Anne also read the entire manuscript, checking references and spelling consistency. In addition I wish to thank the staff of Pearson Australia, in particular Joanne Stanley, Kathryn Munro, Abigail Nathan and Lisa Knowles, for their support and advice. I am also indebted to Mitchell Dean, Pat Armstrong and Anette Borchorst for the time and consideration they put into producing their generous endorsements. Thanks also go out to the outstanding group of reviewers whose careful commentary on the proposal significantly contributed to this first edition: Susan Keen, University of NSW; Sarah Maddison, University of NSW; Jeannette Taylor, Murdoch University; Sue Goodwin, University of Sydney; Megan Allesandrini, University of Tasmania; Kate Driscoll, RMIT; Marty Grace, Victorian University; Andrew Parkin, Flinders University; Greg Marston, University of Queensland; and Marilyn Palmer, Edith Cowan University. And, as always, eternal gratitude to my son, Stephen, for his patience and encouragement, and for his artistic suggestions.

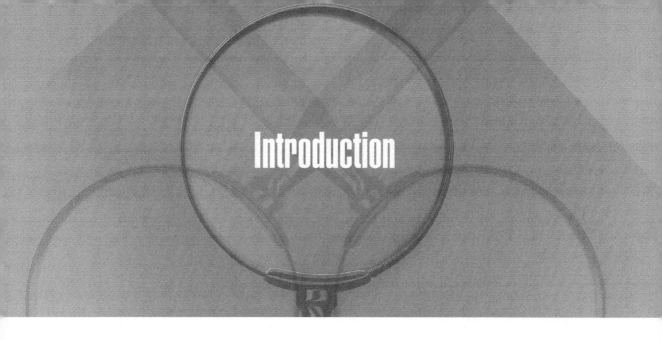

Introduction

The approach to policy introduced in this book – called 'what's the problem represented to be?' – takes nothing for granted. Indeed, the very idea of 'policy' becomes a subject for interrogation. As Miller and Rose (1990, p. 3) contend, the whole notion of 'policy' fits within a particular understanding of the role of government. It is this role I intend to explore. In addition, as Shore and Wright (1997) insist, policy has an undeniable cultural dimension. It takes shape within specific historical and national or international contexts. In this sense it is appropriate to think about policy in anthropological terms, as a cultural product. This way of approaching 'policy' – asking questions about its sources and how it operates – is part of a larger project: to understand how governing takes place, and with what implications for those so governed.

A brief elaboration is required. In asking how governing takes place the aim is to understand how order is maintained, and how we live within and abide by rules. The concern with public policy, therefore, includes but extends beyond laws and legislation to encompass 'a general understanding of societal administration' (Dean and Hindess 1998, p. 17). Laws or legislation are taken as starting points for asking questions about how governing (**governance**) in a broad sense occurs on a daily basis. Of particular interest are the roles of experts and professionals in this process.

The term 'policy' is generally associated with a program, a course of action. *Public* policy is the term used to describe *government* programs. There is an underlying assumption that policy is a good thing, that it fixes things up. Policy *makers* are the ones who do the fixing. The notion of 'fixing' carries with it an understanding that something needs to be 'fixed', that there is a *problem*. This presumed 'problem' can be, but does not need to be, explicitly elaborated. That is, most government policies do not officially declare that there is a problem that the policy will address and remedy. Rather this is implicit in the whole notion of policy – by their nature policies make changes, implying that something *needs* to change. Hence, there are *implied* 'problems'. It is at this level that a 'what's the problem represented to be?' approach intervenes. It makes the case that it is important to make the 'problems' implicit in public policies *explicit*, and to scrutinise them closely.

To accomplish this task six questions are posed, followed by a directive to apply the set of questions to one's own policy suggestions (see below). Question 1 creates the starting point for analysis by asking 'what's the problem (of whatever subject is being discussed) represented to be?' within a particular policy or policy proposal. This first question is straightforward – if a government proposes to do something, what is it hoping to change? And, hence, what does it produce as the 'problem'? For example, if training courses are offered to women as part of a policy to increase their representation in better paid occupations or in positions of influence, the 'problem' is represented to be women's *lack* of training.

Subsequent questions (2 through 6) probe deeply into this proposal for change, inquiring about rationales for the proposal, deep-seated presuppositions underpinning the proposed change, possible silences in the understanding of what needs to change, and the effects that are likely to accompany this particular understanding of the 'problem'. Continuing our example, training schemes for women assume that women's lack of training explains their absence from positions of influence. This proposal rests on some deep-seated assumptions about the nature of work and the nature of 'skill'. In this specific proposal little attention is paid to the kinds of work made available, the other demands created by caring commitments, the cultural assumption that women will undertake those caring commitments, and so on. Hence, it is at least possible that, with this understanding of the 'problem', little will change.

The directive to apply the set of questions to one's own policy suggestions signals the need to recognise that any policy proposal we put forward may well reflect deep-seated cultural assumptions. Hence, that proposal may contain silences and have unintended deleterious effects. Requiring self-scrutiny of this kind is unusual in policy analysis and marks the approach recommended in this book as distinctive.

As we shall see, the presumption that the purpose of policy is to *solve* 'social problems' remains a grounding premise in most conventional approaches to policy analysis. By contrast, showing that policies by their nature imply a certain understanding of what needs to change (the 'problem') suggests that 'problems' are **endogenous** – created within – rather than **exogenous** – existing outside – the policy-making process. Policies *give shape* to 'problems'; they do not *address* them.

It is necessary to explain the particular understanding of the word 'problem' in a 'what's the problem represented to be?' approach because of the many ways in which we use the term in everyday speech. The word 'problem' has two common usages. It is used either to describe something that is difficult to deal with, as in a *problem* child, or to refer to a puzzle or challenge that needs to be 'solved', as in 'problem solving'. Sometimes these meanings are combined, as in 'there is a need to *solve* the binge-drinking *problem*'. The word 'problem' in a 'what's the problem represented to be?' approach means something quite different. It refers simply to the kind of change implied in a particular policy proposal. Using the same example of training schemes for women, a policy that recommends training courses for women implies that the 'problem' (or the cause of their under-representation) is women's lack of training.

It is important to clarify this point because of the tendency, both in the media and in the sociological tradition of studying 'social problems' (Ritzer 2004), to talk about a range of social conditions as 'social problems'. For example, both the government and the media in Australia (and elsewhere) are currently paying a good deal of attention to obesity and binge-drinking, especially among the young, as 'social problems'. By contrast, a key premise in a 'what's the problem represented to be?' approach to policy analysis is that it is unwise and inappropriate to think that 'problems' somehow exist in the world in the way these discussions suggest.

This proposition does not mean to imply that there are not a full range of troubling conditions that ought to be dealt with. However, calling those conditions 'problems' or 'social problems' fixes them in ways that need to be interrogated. Even those who wish to contest a particular understanding (or construction) of a 'social problem' – asserting, for example, that binge-drinking is a result of a Western drinking culture rather than a result of the behaviours of 'irresponsible' young people – often still assume that at some level a 'problem' (of binge-drinking, drug addiction, welfare dependence, etc.) exists. By contrast a 'what's the problem represented to be?' approach challenges this presumption. It directs attention to the ways in which particular representations of 'problems' play a central role in how we are governed.

Another way to put this is to say that policies are problematising activities. Osborne (1997) makes the case that government cannot get to work without first problematising its territory. His particular topic is health policy, but it is possible to generalise this insight. In fact, Osborne is making the same point as the one I make at the outset: policies 'claim' to 'fix' things; hence, by their nature they assume the existence of a 'problem' that needs 'fixing'. It follows that the ways in which issues are problematised – how they are thought about as 'problems' – are central to governing processes. In effect, we are governed through problematisations rather than through policies. Therefore, we need to direct our attention away from assumed 'problems' to the shape and character of problematisations. These ideas are developed in Chapter 2.

To study problematisations it is useful to open them up for analysis by 'reading off' (or identifying) the implied 'problem' – what is seen as in need of 'fixing' – from the plan of action that is proposed (the policy or policy proposal). It is possible to do this because what we propose to do about something indicates what we think needs to change ('the problem'). This characterisation of the 'problem' is the place to start in order to understand how an issue is being understood. I call this implied 'problem' – described by Dean (1999, p. 102) as the 'problem space of rule' – a *problem representation*.

A problem representation refers to the understanding of the 'problem' implied in any policy or rule.

What's the problem represented to be?: An approach to policy analysis

1. What's the 'problem' (e.g. of 'problem gamblers', 'drug use/abuse', domestic violence, global warming, health inequalities, terrorism, etc.) represented to be in a specific policy?
2. What presuppositions or assumptions underlie this representation of the 'problem'?
3. How has this representation of the 'problem' come about?
4. What is left unproblematic in this problem representation? Where are the silences? Can the 'problem' be thought about differently?
5. What effects are produced by this representation of the 'problem'?
6. How/where has this representation of the 'problem' been produced, disseminated and defended? How could it be questioned, disrupted and replaced?

Apply this list of questions to your own problem representations.

An expanded version of the approach is available at the end of Chapter 2.

The concept of **problematisation**, which grounds this analysis, has been developed by a number of political theorists and with somewhat different emphases. Chapter 2 examines some of these contributions more closely, and describes how the approach in this book is located in relation to them. For the time being it is adequate to engage the commonsense understanding of problematisation as how something is put forward (or represented) as a 'problem'. In this process, problematisations necessarily reduce complexity (Osborne 1997, p. 175). That is, by positing an issue as a particular sort of issue, a range of factors must be simplified. Only part of a story is being told. As a result it is critically important to interrogate the **problem representations** that lodge within public policies in order to see what they include and what they leave out.

Because problematisations, and the problem representations they contain, reduce complexity, they can be described as framing processes (see Entman 1993). However, the methodology introduced in this book is different from sociological framework theory in several ways. While framework theory in the main is interested in framing processes as either innate cognitive functioning (Moscovici 1984) or as the conscious shaping of arguments to win supporters (Benford and Snow 2000), the focus in a 'what's the problem represented to be?' approach is on the ways in which *problematisations are central to governing processes.*

Put briefly, the argument is that, in order to understand how we are governed, we need to examine the problem representations that lodge within policies and policy proposals. Rather than accepting the designation of some issue as a 'problem' or a 'social problem', we need to interrogate the kinds of 'problems' that are presumed to exist and how these are thought about. In this way we gain important insights into the thought (the 'thinking') that informs governing practices.

To summarise the two key premises put forward so far:

1. We are governed through problematisations.
2. We need to study problematisations (through analysing the problem representations they contain), rather than 'problems'.

Before we proceed further it is useful to try a couple of activities to establish these points.

The space of rule

With a classmate or on your own, construct a list of the different government policies that impact on your life from the moment you get out of bed in the morning till the time you go to sleep at night, or even overnight. Ask yourself, to what extent is your life rule-regulated? Note: there is no implication here that it could be otherwise but that it is important to reflect on the shape of the rules we take for granted.

The shape of rules

Take one of the laws or rules you identified in the first Activity and consider how it assumes a particular kind of 'problem' that needs to be 'fixed'. For example, speeding laws presume that there is a problem of safety that needs to be addressed. While this might appear to be obvious and uncontroversial the goal is to see how each rule or law produces an implicit understanding of a 'problem', of what needs to change.

From the Activities above a couple of things become clearer. First, rule or governance is a complex and ever-present activity. And second, rules presume or imply kinds of 'problems'.

There is a level of commonsense to the proposition that rules or laws presuppose particular understandings of a 'problem'. After all, how you feel about something determines what you think should be done about it. For example, if you feel that Aboriginal living standards are abhorrent, you want certain things to occur. You may call for an increased police presence in certain Aboriginal communities; you may suggest that a greater proportion of the health budget be directed to Aboriginal health; you may campaign for reconciliation.

The approach to policy introduced here says that your specific proposal reflects (and hence reveals) how you understand the 'problem'. If you call for an increased police presence in Aboriginal communities, you understand the 'problem' as a law and order issue. If you recommend that a greater share of the health budget be directed to Aboriginal health, you consider the 'problem' to be a matter of inadequate resources directed to Aboriginal health. If you support reconciliation, in your view the 'problem' of Aboriginal living standards involves deep levels of symbolic and institutional harm.

The next proposition that needs to be defended is that problem representations matter. It should be clear with the example above about Aboriginal living standards that whatever you recommend will have a range of effects. It is less clear what these effects will be. Indeed the 'best way' to understand the 'problem' is completely unclear.

The questions that form a 'what's the problem represented to be?' approach offer a way through this conundrum. As Chapter 1 explains and elaborates, their goal is to assist in understanding in some depth the bases and implications of particular representations of 'problems'.

I need to stress that this approach does not involve a conventional form of policy evaluation. There is no intention of attempting to *measure* Aboriginal living standards, through comparing infant mortality rates, for example, and on this basis to declare a particular policy a success. The kind of analysis introduced in this approach works at another level entirely. The goal is to probe the premises that underpin particular problem representations. Put simply, it is essential to think deeply about the assumptions and presuppositions that lie behind and shape selected policies. It is also essential to consider the implications that flow from these presuppositions and how particular forms of rule have come to be.

An example is useful here. Shapiro (1981, p. 186) offers an analysis of a 1972 Australian policy statement on Aboriginal health in the Northern Territory. To explain the high incidence of child mortality, the policy paper identified the 'semi-nomadic life of some of the Aborigines' as a contributing factor (McMahon 1972 in Tatz 1972, p. 3). Here the 'problem' is represented to be Aboriginal people's way of life and the solution, by implication, was for them to change their lifestyle. A 'what's the problem represented to be?' approach to policy analysis directs our attention to the deep-seated presumption in this Report about desirable and undesirable lifestyles. It also stresses the significance of reflecting on how such a representation of the 'problem' has implications for the ways in which Aboriginal people are portrayed and the accompanying impact on race relations in Australia. In addition, this example of policy indicates the close intermeshing of the medical profession and medical technologies in Australian governance.

Shapiro notes that a social scientist ('not under contract to the government') offered an alternative representation of the 'problem': 'instead of emphasis being placed on Aboriginal failure to assimilate to our norms, it should rather be put on our failure to devise strategies that accommodate to their folkways' (Tatz 1972, p. 15 in Shapiro 1981, p. 187). The proposal here locates the 'problem' in the inflexibility of Australian health services at the time rather than in the 'recalcitrance of the Aborigines' (Shapiro 1981, p. 187). This problem representation carries very different implications for what needs to change – if the 'problem' is the mode of delivery of the medical system, this is what needs to change.

A more recent example illustrates very similar themes. A Report on diabetes 2 (*Science News* 2008) stresses that this form of diabetes is preventable. Diabetes 2 is called a 'lifestyle' disease because of its association with obesity. The Report goes on to emphasise the high prevalence of diabetes 2 among Aboriginal and poor populations. The implication, as in the Report examined by Shapiro, is that these populations have things to 'fix up' in their lifestyles. Again, there are assumptions about desirable ways of living, and intimations that targeted groups bear some degree of responsibility for the diseases they acquire, and indeed even some responsibility for their premature demise.

Turning to a completely different area of policy Shapiro (1992, p. 99) reflects upon the 'problem' of traffic congestion. He notes that the common policy 'response' is to 'address' the 'problem' with practical suggestions such as overpasses, underpasses, tram lines, freeways, etc. Shapiro asks us to think about what follows if we broaden our analysis to think about traffic congestion as a middle-class 'problem', produced by people who have enough money to purchase one or more cars, and the funds to fuel them. In this view traffic congestion is not simply something to be *reduced* in amount, but something to be *rethought*. The kind of analysis Shapiro offers here can easily be transferred to recent concerns about carbon emissions and global warming, and certainly complicates attempts to blame newly industrialising countries for the phenomenon.

A 'what's the problem represented to be?' approach to policy analysis provides a systematic methodology for teasing out the kinds of insights offered in these examples. It creates the opportunity to question taken-for-granted assumptions that lodge in government policies and policy proposals by interrogating (problematising) the problem representations it uncovers within them. In this sense, it is a critical mode of analysis.

'A critique does not consist in saying that things aren't good the way they are. It consists in seeing on what type of assumptions, of familiar notions, of established, unexamined ways of thinking the accepted practices are based' (Foucault, 1994, p. 456).

> The goal of a 'what's the problem represented to be?' approach to policy is to problematise (interrogate) the problematisations in selected government policies, through scrutinising the premises and effects of the problem representations these problematisations contain.

A 'what's the problem represented to be?' approach offers both a novel way of thinking and a new way of analysing policy. As a way of thinking the approach mounts a challenge to the current dominant intellectual paradigm that focuses on *solving* 'problems'. While it might appear to be fairly uncontroversial to talk about solving 'problems', it can be argued that this particular approach to knowledge and practice can be identified as a specific governance project in recent decades. In tune with this project, a dominant paradigm in current public policy, as we shall see in several chapters, is to discover 'what works', what will *solve* 'problems' (i.e. 'evidence-based policy'). Our schools and universities meanwhile are intent on producing students as 'problem-solving' subjects (see Chapter 10). Hence, in the current climate, it seems almost heresy to suggest that we need to shift our focus from how to *solve* 'problems' to consider how particular proposals imply certain understandings of 'problems', understandings that may need to be put in question. The significance of this challenge, the guiding purpose of the book, is discussed briefly here.

According to Cox (1986) problem-*solving* approaches are by their nature conservative. This is because the idea that there are just a few 'problems' that need to be 'addressed' creates the impression that societies are generally functioning well and, hence, that not much needs to change. In Cox's words (1986, pp. 208–9) problem-solving theory:

> … takes the world as it finds it, with the prevailing social and power relationships and the institutions into which they are organized, as the given framework for action. The general aim of problem-solving is to make those relationships and institutions work smoothly by dealing effectively with particular sources of trouble … Indeed, the purpose served by problem-solving theory is conservative, since it aims to solve the problems arising in various parts of a complex whole in order to smooth the functioning of the whole. This aim rather belies the frequent claim of problem-solving theory to be value-free.

Deleuze (1994) is equally critical of 'problem solving'. He objects to the implicit assumption that 'problems are given ready-made, and that they disappear in the responses or the solution'. He describes the logic within 'problem solving' as 'a social prejudice with the visible interests of maintaining us in an infantile state'. Countering this position, Deleuze (1994, p. 158) argues that we remain 'slaves so long as we *do not control the problems themselves*, so long as we do not possess *a right to the problems*, to a participation in and management of the problems' (emphasis added). By demanding a 'right to the problems' Deleuze draws attention to the critical importance of deciding what is a 'problem' and how it is to be understood.

A 'what's the problem represented to be?' approach shares the concerns of both Cox and Deleuze. It suggests that shifting one's perspective from assumed 'problems' to the ways in which 'problems' are represented constitutes a claim to 'participation in and management of the problems' (Deleuze 1994, p. 158). As a result, this shift in focus opens up new forms of political thinking and assessment, and new ways to envisage relations of rule. A case is made for a new paradigm, 'problem-*questioning*' rather than 'problem-*solving*'. More will be said about this new paradigm and about the political implications of a 'what's the problem represented to be?' approach in Chapters 2 and 10.

Given the prevalence of the 'problem-solving' paradigm in current approaches to education and public policy, it is necessary to retrain our minds, to encourage us to start asking the new questions associated with the approach introduced in this book. A useful place to practice this novel way of thinking is media reports. That is, the media is notorious for putting a particular 'slant' on issues. Hence, we are not surprised to find that newspaper reports offer particular understandings of a 'problem'.

To help us practice the approach as a way of thinking, see the Activity on 'Reading the Media'.

Reading the media: 'Melbourne's nightlife should be vibrant, not violent'

'When the architect of Victoria's drinking laws voices grave concern at what his reforms have led to, you know there is a problem. When the Australian Hotels Association calls for a freeze on all new bars and nightclubs in Melbourne's centre, it is clear there is a serious problem. And when a senior policeman refers to the CBD's [Central Business District] party precincts as "alcohol-fuelled bedlam" that has led to frightening violence, injury and death, there is no question that the situation has spun dangerously out of control and that something has to be done to help create order and responsible serving and consumption of alcohol.' (Editorial 2008)

- In this account, what interpretation is offered of the causes of 'excessive' alcohol consumption? What is the 'problem' represented to be?
- Consider the assumptions upon which this interpretation rests, possible gaps in the understanding of the 'problem', and possible effects that could accompany the particular focus of this interpretation.
- Consider if, in your view, 'binge drinking' is a problem?

As a way of thinking (differently), the 'what's the problem represented to be?' approach is useful in a number of settings and for a variety of tasks. As in the Activity on 'Reading the Media' it assists us to sort through the kinds of explanations put forward in media reports. We can also use this way of thinking to examine politicians' statements about particular policy objectives. For example, South Australia's Health Minister, John Hill (in Kelton 2007), has been quoted as saying, 'Up to 50 per cent of diseases are determined by lifestyle choices. We need to get the message across to individuals that they are their prime life giver, not doctors'. In this case, when we ask 'what's the problem represented to be?', the 'problem' is fairly easily identified as lifestyle choices (see Chapter 6). We can also use a 'what's the problem represented to be?' approach (as a way of thinking) to analyse academic theories and academic texts. The argument here is that, since all theories posit forms of explanation, they necessarily contain implicit problem representations that demand scrutiny. In this vein Chapter 5 applies a 'what's the problem represented to be?' approach to criminal justice theories, while Chapter 6 applies it to the range of theories underpinning health policies. Chapter 10 rounds out the exercise by subjecting theories about policy formulation to a 'what's the problem represented to be?' analysis.

As a form of policy analysis (rather than just a way of thinking differently), a 'what's the problem represented to be?' approach allows us to explore the shape of 'problems' within public policies, the major task in this book. Since, as we saw in the Activities on the previous page, public policies affect every dimension of our lives, the ways in which 'problems' are constituted (or shaped) carry all sorts of implications for how we live our lives on a day-to-day basis. It is important to make this point because the language of problem *representation* can lead readers to think that we are dealing only at the level of ideas or impressions, whereas, in point of fact, the ways in which policy 'problems' are represented in public policies translates into real, lived experience. In this sense, problem representations take on lives of their own. As an example, consider the 1996 Western Australian 'three strikes' legislation, referred to as mandatory sentencing (see Activity).

The 'three strikes' legislation

In 1996 the Western Australian Government introduced and passed the *Criminal Code Amendment Act (No. 2) 1996 (WA)* (Government of Western Australia 1996). The new law made the following changes:

- ■ it created a separate offence for home burglary, increasing the maximum penalty to 18 years imprisonment from 14 years for other types of burglary;
- ■ it increased the penalty for burglary committed in circumstances of aggravation to 20 years imprisonment;
- ■ it imposed a mandatory minimum term of at least 12 months imprisonment or detention for both juvenile and adult third time convicted home burglars.

- **Considering the kinds of changes made, what's the 'problem' of criminal offence represented to be in this legislation?** *(see Chapter 5)*

- **How do mandatory gaol terms constitute the 'problem' of home burglary?**

- **How does this change in the law affect citizens' lives?**

It is also important to emphasise that, in a 'what's the problem represented to be?' approach to policy analysis, the focus is not on the *intentional* shaping of issues. Reflecting back on our politician's (Minister Hill's) comment, it is commonplace to talk about politicians as persuaders, as users of rhetoric. Hence, we are often faced with the conundrum of asking if they *really meant* what they said, or if the issue was being shaped *deliberately* to influence opinion. Perhaps Minister Hill was just trying to deflect attention from a blow-out in the health budget, for example. Also, many scholars are concerned to identify *gaps* between the terms of a specific policy and what is *actually* delivered. The suggestion here is that declared commitments in some policies are empty promises, that there was no *intent* to deliver on them.

Scholars interested in these sorts of questions might well find it interesting to talk about how a particular 'problem' is being represented. However, a 'what's the problem represented to be?' approach to policy analysis is not concerned with *intentionality*. Rather, the task is to identify *deep conceptual premises* operating within problem representations. The point, in other words, is not to identify some 'promises' as *empty*, but to draw attention to the assumptions and presuppositions that *made it possible* to make those 'promises' and to develop those policies.

This distinction helps to highlight what is meant by characterising the approach to policy analysis taken in this book as *digging deeper than usual* (see Preface). The examples earlier that identified the presuppositions about Western civilisation that lodge in proposals to get Aboriginal peoples to change their lifestyles, and the taken-for-granted acceptance of car ownership (private property) that lodge in traffic 'management' plans, are the kinds of deep conceptual premises targeted by the approach. To repeat the claim made in the Preface, the goal is to understand policies *better than* policy makers.

Clearly, the conceptual premises identified here — presumptions about the nature of civilisation and the sanctity of private property — are deeply engrained in Western culture and in our times. To work at this level of analysis, therefore, requires that we recognise that none of us stands fully outside such premises. For this reason, it is vitally important that we, as researchers or as concerned citizens, undertake to apply the full set of questions in the approach to our own policy suggestions and the problem representations these imply. To subject one's own problem representations to critical scrutiny in this way involves a form of *reflexive* research practice, a topic pursued in subsequent chapters.

> 'It would not behove me, of all people, to claim that my discourse is independent of conditions and rules of which I am very largely unaware.' (Foucault 1973 in Simons 1995, p. 90)

A 'what's the problem represented to be?' approach to policy analysis is innovative in several ways.

First, while the subject matter in the book (selected policies, media reports, academic studies) is derived mainly from Australian sources, with a few examples from other countries, primarily Western industrialised countries, the methodology is introduced in a way to encourage its application in other contexts. Indeed the approach has the specific aim of challenging national/international boundaries. Asking 'what's the problem represented to be?' provides a new way to think about comparing social and political developments across space and time. We shall see, for example, how some key problem representations in criminal justice, immigration, health and education policies appear in a number of settings. Indeed, it is useful to think of some of these ideas as 'travelling ideas' (Sahlin-Anderson 1996) – or more precisely as travelling problem representations – whose journey needs to be tracked. The approach also encourages forms of cross-cultural and cross-national comparison to tease out distinctions among problem representations. That is, it is much easier to identify the shape and contours of a specific problem representation within one's own country or region through examining how the issue may be represented differently elsewhere. As an example it is useful to ask (as we do later) why there is no equivalent of Repetition Strain Injury, a recognised medical complaint in Australia, in the United States.

Second, while the chapters appear to align with conventional policy areas (e.g. welfare, education, health), the analysis encourages us to think about links *across* areas, from welfare to crime, from welfare to health, from crime to immigration, etc. Indeed, the analysis in the book highlights important cross-cutting themes, such as an emphasis on making citizens responsible for ever-enlarged aspects of their lives, and an emphasis on risk in governing discourses.

Third, as mentioned earlier, the approach marks the terrain for study – governance – as broader than government. It therefore increases the purview of analysis beyond the state to include other 'governing' parties, such as professionals and social scientists.

The scope of a 'what's the problem represented to be?' approach

The approach institutes three 'cross-border' moves:
- challenging national/international boundaries;
- challenging policy 'specialisms', e.g. education policy, foreign policy;
- extending the purview of analysis beyond the state to include the full array of professionals and agencies involved in governing.

Because it is tedious to keep repeating 'what's the problem represented to be?' (as I am sure you have already discovered), a shortened form – WPR approach – is introduced. I caution against describing the approach as a 'What's the problem?' approach, as it is crucial to emphasise that the task at hand is *not* trying to identify *real* problems. Rather the task is to focus on how 'problems' are *represented*.

Chapter 1 outlines the steps to take in applying a WPR approach to policy analysis. It specifies the questions to ask and indicates what each question is designed to probe. The theory underpinning the approach is offered in Chapter 2, along with a more careful explanation of how a WPR analysis differs from other approaches to policy studies and policy analysis. While it is unusual to place the theory chapter second, I believe it is possible to apply the approach, introduced in Chapter 1, without immersing oneself in complicated theory. Indeed, it is the simplicity of the approach that I think recommends it for wide application. Cross-references (from Chapter 1 to Chapter 2) alert students to places where they may want or need some elaboration of particular theoretical premises.

Chapters 3 and 4 apply the six questions, and the accompanying directive to apply the questions to one's own problem representations, systematically. Subsequent chapters (5 through 10) develop a more integrated form of analysis, with parenthetical references to **Q1** (Question 1) or **Q2** (Question 2), for example, to indicate when a specific question has been applied. Chapter 10 brings together the insights generated in the book into the current status of the 'problem-solving paradigm' and the implications that follow for research practice.

To summarise, a WPR approach to policy analysis rests on three key propositions:

1. We are governed through problematisations.
2. We need to study problematisations (through analysing the problem representations they contain), rather than 'problems'.
3. We need to problematise (interrogate) the problematisations on offer through scrutinising the premises and effects of the problem representations they contain.

REFERENCES

BENFORD, R. D. & SNOW, D. A. 2000, 'Framing Processes and Social Movements: An Overview and Assessment', *Annual Review of Sociology*, vol. 26, no. 1, pp. 611–39.

COX, R. W. 1986, 'Social Forces, States and World Orders: Beyond International Relations Theory', in *Neorealism and its Critics*, ed. R. O. Keohane, Columbia University Press, New York.

DEAN, M. 1999, *Governmentality: Power and Rule in Modern Society*, Sage, London.

DEAN, M. & HINDESS, B. 1998, *Governing Australia: Studies in Contemporary Rationalities of Government*, Cambridge University Press, Cambridge.

DELEUZE, G. 1994, *Difference and Repetition*. Trans. P. Patton, Columbia University Press, New York.

EDITORIAL 2008, 'Melbourne's Nightlife Should be Vibrant, not Violent', *The Age*, 23 February, p. 8.

ENTMAN, R. M. 1993, 'Framing: Toward a Clarification of a Fractured Paradigm', *Journal of Communication*, vol. 43, no. 4, pp. 51–8.

FOUCAULT, M. 1973 [1966] *The Order of Things: An Archaeology of the Human Sciences*, Vintage, New York.

FOUCAULT, M. 1994 [1981], 'So is it Important to Think?', in *Power: Essential Works of Foucault 1954–1984*, vol. 3, ed. J. D. Faubion, Trans. R. Hurley & others, Penguin, London.

GOVERNMENT OF WESTERN AUSTRALIA 1996, *Criminal Code Amendment Act* (No. 2), Attorney-General's Department, Policy & Legislation Division, <www.justice.wa.gov.au>, accessed 21 October 2008.

KELTON, G. 2007, 'Stay Healthy – Hill's Cure for all Ills', *The Advertiser*, 20 June.

MCMAHON, W. 1972, Statement by the Prime Minister on: *Australian Aborigines: Commonwealth Policy and Achievements*, Government Printer, Canberra.

MILLER, P. & ROSE, N. 1990, 'Governing Economic Life', *Economy and Society*, vol. 19, no. 1, pp. 1–31.

MOSCOVICI, S. 1984, 'The Phenomenon of Social Representations', in *Social Representations*, eds R. M. Farr & S. Moscovici, Cambridge University Press, Cambridge, UK.

OSBORNE, T. 1997, 'On Health and Statecraft' in *Foucault, Health and Medicine*, eds A. Petersen & R. Bunton, Routledge, London.

RITZER, G. ed. 2004, *Handbook of Social Problems: A Comparative International Perspective*, Sage, Thousand Oaks.

SAHLIN-ANDERSON, K. 1996, 'Imitating by Editing Success: The Construction of Organizational Fields' in *Translating Organizational Change*, eds B. Czarniawska & G. Sevón, Walter de Gruyter, Berlin.

SCIENCE NEWS 2008, 'University of Queensland (14 January 2008) Type 2 Diabetes Explosion Predicted, *ScienceDaily* 14 January 2008, <www.sciencedaily.com>, accessed on 14 July 2008.

SHAPIRO, M. J. 1981, *Language and Political Understanding: The Politics of Discursive Practices*, Yale University Press, New Haven & London.

SHAPIRO, M. J. 1992, *Reading the Postmodern Polity: Political Theory as Textual Practice*, University of Minnesota Press, Minneapolis.

SHORE, C. & WRIGHT, S. 1997, 'Policy: A New Field of Anthropology', in *Anthropology of Policy: Critical Perspectives on Governance and Power*, eds C. Shore & S. Wright, Routledge, New York.

SIMONS, J. 1995, *Foucault and the Political*, Routledge, New York.

TATZ, C. 1972, 'The Politics of Aboriginal Health', *Australian Journal of Political Science*, vol. 7, no. 1, pp. 3–23.

Introducing a 'what's the problem represented to be?' approach to policy analysis

Chapter 1

The approach to policy analysis introduced in this book challenges the commonplace view that policy is the government's best attempt to deal with 'problems'. In this conventional understanding of public policy, governments are seen to be *reacting* to fixed and identifiable 'problems' that are exogenous (outside) the policy process. Hence, the focus of analysis is limited to competing ways of 'solving' policy problems. The terms in which specific policy problems are understood are left unexamined.

By contrast, a 'what's the problem represented to be?' (WPR) approach offers a different way to think about policy. It suggests that, if you look at a specific policy, you can see that it understands the 'problem' to be a particular sort of 'problem'. Policies, therefore, constitute (or give shape to) 'problems'. Hence, rather than *reacting* to 'problems', governments are *active* in the creation (or production) of policy 'problems'. There is, however, no suggestion that this is an exercise in manipulation or misrepresentation. Rather, it is a necessary part of making policy. That is, because all policies make proposals for change, by their very nature they contain implicit representations of 'problems'. If, for example, you send police and troops into outback Aboriginal communities in 'response' to a report on child sexual abuse in those communities, you are 'implying' that the 'problem' is a matter of inadequate law enforcement (see Chapter 5), and hence constituting it as such.

Further, how the 'problem' is represented, or constituted, matters. This is because the way in which the 'problem' is represented carries all sorts of implications for how the issue is thought about and for how the people involved are treated, and are evoked to think about themselves.

It is not new to draw attention to the constructed character of 'problems'. There is a large literature that focuses on the social construction of 'social problems' (see Bacchi 1999, Chapter 3). However, the suggestion that public policies *constitute* policy 'problems' in specific ways adds a new dimension to these considerations. It highlights the creative or productive role of government in shaping particular understandings of 'problems'. The next chapter will clarify the novelty of this contribution by comparing it with other approaches to policy studies and policy analysis. It will also provide the theoretical underpinnings of the approach. In this chapter we look at what the approach involves, the questions that form its content, and the purposes behind each question.

A WPR approach to policy analysis consists of six interrelated questions and a directive to apply these questions to one's own problem representations. For convenience, the approach is summarised in the chart below.

What's the problem represented to be?: An approach to policy analysis

1. What's the 'problem' (e.g. of 'problem gamblers', 'drug use/abuse', domestic violence, global warming, health inequalities, terrorism, etc.) represented to be in a specific policy?
2. What presuppositions or assumptions underlie this representation of the 'problem'?
3. How has this representation of the 'problem' come about?
4. What is left unproblematic in this problem representation? Where are the silences? Can the 'problem' be thought about differently?
5. What effects are produced by this representation of the 'problem'?
6. How/where has this representation of the 'problem' been produced, disseminated and defended? How could it be questioned, disrupted and replaced?

Apply this list of questions to your own problem representations.

*An expanded version of the approach is available at the end of Chapter 2.

Each question will now be elaborated, clarifying just what is sought in each case and how the questions interconnect.

QUESTION 1: WHAT IS THE 'PROBLEM' (E.G. OF 'PROBLEM GAMBLERS', 'DRUG USE/ABUSE', DOMESTIC VIOLENCE, GLOBAL WARMING, HEALTH INEQUALITIES, TERRORISM, ETC.) REPRESENTED TO BE IN A SPECIFIC POLICY?

The opening question is a clarification exercise. As the Introduction explains, a WPR approach builds on the premise that, since all policies are problematising activities, they contain implicit problem representations. The argument here is that, since how you feel about something determines what you suggest doing about it, it is equally true to say that looking at what is proposed as a policy intervention will reveal how the issue is being thought about. I have spoken about this basic proposition as a form of commonsense. The Introduction offered activities to practise this way of thinking differently.

This way of thinking differently challenges the all-too-common tendency to describe policy makers as 'problem solvers', as if 'problems' sit outside the policy process, waiting to be addressed and 'fixed'. By contrast a WPR approach recommends 'working backwards' from concrete proposals to reveal what is represented to be the 'problem' within those proposals.

A practical example is useful here. Consider: a gymnasium decides to put water-timers on showers to cut down on water bills. This decision forms the policy under consideration. The water-timers turn off the water source after three minutes of showering. The policy (the water-timers) constitutes the 'problem' as 'excessive' showering, which implies 'indulgent' consumer behaviour. A WPR approach starts with the policy – the water-timers – and works backwards to elucidate the problem representation – 'indulgent' consumer behaviour.

Child care offers a useful policy example of this process. Consider each of the following 'responses' to child care and how it represents the problem.

Child care: policy options and problem representations

Policy option 1: A cash rebate is offered when both parents are engaged in paid labour.

Problem representation: Child care is a *labour market* 'problem'. It is judged to be a 'problem' when both parents, including the primary care giver (most often the woman), are engaged in paid employment.

Policy option 2: Means-tested subsidies are made available to assist with child care expenses.

Problem representation: Child care is a *welfare* 'problem'. Parents with inadequate 'means' are to be assisted.

Policy option 3: Vouchers are given to families to spend either on family day care or on institutional care, or as a subsidy for a parent (most often a mother) who stays at home.

Problem representation: Child care is a 'problem' of *family choice*. Members of families are given the chance to 'choose' how they wish to handle caring responsibilities. The option exists to allow primary care givers, usually women, to continue in this role for a specific, usually low, amount of money.

Policy option 4: Operating grants go to child care centres from public funding.

Problem representation: Child care is a matter of *public responsibility*, akin to primary and secondary education.

Policies, of course, are often complex, combining a range of proposals. Hence, there might well be more than one problem representation within them. The different kinds of representations in any one policy may conflict and even contradict each other. The task of identifying problem representations, therefore, needs to be recognised as a challenging one.

> The goal of Question 1 in a WPR approach is to identify implied problem representations in specific policies or policy proposals.

One way to simplify the task is to see how funds are targeted within a proposal. This certainly assists in identifying dominant problem representations. For example, as we shall see in Chapter 4, the Howard-led Coalition government spent many times more money on attempts to reduce the use of so-called 'illicit' drugs than on reducing consumption of 'licit' drugs such as alcohol, producing the drug 'problem' as largely to do with 'illicit' drugs. The following Activity provides an opportunity to reflect on how the National Youth Suicide Prevention Strategy represents the 'problem' of youth suicide.

National Youth Suicide Prevention Strategy 1995/97

The strategy allocated funds in the following manner:
- $12 million to enhance counselling services
- $3 million to parenting programs
- $2 million to the education and training of professionals
- $1 million for research activities

(Parliament of Commonwealth of Australia 1997, p. 2)

- **Consider how these proposals (funding and allocations) represent the 'problem' of youth suicide.**
- **What is the dominant problem representation?**

Policies are usually located within a web of related or interconnected policies that need to be considered as part of your analysis. A section at the end of this chapter elaborates practical guidelines for applying the approach.

QUESTION 2: WHAT PRESUPPOSITIONS OR ASSUMPTIONS UNDERLIE THIS REPRESENTATION OF THE 'PROBLEM'?

Once we have identified the implied problem representation/s (or perhaps the dominant problem representation) in a specific policy, the real work begins. That is, little is achieved in saying simply that, if you propose to do 'such and such' (in a policy), you must assume that the 'problem' is 'such and such' (e.g. if you introduce training programs for women, you must assume women lack training). Rather, we need to start thinking about the understanding that underpins identified problem representations. What is assumed? What is taken-for-granted? What is not questioned?

Question 2 begins this task, asking which presuppositions or assumptions underlie an identified problem representation. The term 'presuppositions' (or assumptions) in Question 2 refers to background 'knowledge' that is taken-for-granted. It includes epistemological (see **epistemology**) and ontological (see **ontology**) assumptions. Through examining presuppositions, therefore, we can identify the conceptual premises (**conceptual logics**) that underpin specific problem representations.

A key point needs to be made here. The kind of analysis recommended in Question 2 does not elicit the assumptions or beliefs *held by policy makers*. We are not interested in attempting to identify biases, for example. Rather the task is to identify the assumptions and/or presuppositions that *lodge within problem representations*.

To some this may appear to be a fine distinction but it is an important one. This is because the level of analysis encouraged by a WPR approach goes beyond what is in people's heads to consider the *shape* of arguments, the forms of 'knowledge' that arguments rely upon, the forms of 'knowledge' that are necessary for statements to be accorded intelligibility. The question becomes not why something happens but how it is possible for something to happen – what meanings need to be in place for something to happen (see Doty 1993). With Foucault (1973) we are interested in what could be thought, what it is possible to think.

> The goal of Question 2 of a WPR approach is to identify and analyse the conceptual logics that underpin specific problem representations. The term 'conceptual logic' refers to the meanings that must be in place for a particular problem representation to cohere or to make sense.

This kind of analysis includes a search for deep-seated cultural values – a kind of social unconscious – that underpin a problem representation, Here we are working at the level of basic or fundamental worldviews, akin to Foucault's (1973) notion of **epistême** (which he later replaced with the term 'archive'; Sawyer 2002, p. 437). Hence, the goal of Question 2, as an exercise in Foucauldian **archaeology**, is to uncover the (assumed) thought that lies behind specific problem representations.

For example, the *National Youth Suicide Prevention Strategy* is based upon a particular understanding of individual psyches associated with nineteenth and twentieth century psychology. The child care option that focused on 'family choice' contains deep-seated

assumptions about both the nature of family and about individual agency. These are the
sorts of presuppositions that need to be teased out for reflection and analysis. Thinking back
to Shapiro's (1992, p. 99) comments on the 'problem' of traffic congestion, the culture of
consumption that underpins this 'problem' rests upon basic liberal notions about individuals
as property-owning creatures and about the right to privacy. More obviously, the Report
that suggested that Aboriginal peoples adopt 'settled' lifestyles rests upon premises about the
value of Western 'civilisation' (see the Introduction for both of these examples).

Access to reproductive technologies

In July 2000 the Federal Court in Victoria ruled that the *Victorian Infertility Treatment Act 1995
(Vic)* (Government of Victoria 1995) that limited ART (Artificial Reproductive Technology) to
married and heterosexual de facto couples breached the *Federal Sex Discrimination Act 1984
(Cth)* (Australian Government 1984). The then Prime Minister, John Howard, announced plans
to amend the Federal legislation to allow states to restrict IVF procedures to married women
or those women living in heterosexual de facto relationships. He declared: 'This issue primarily
involves the fundamental right of a child within our society to have the reasonable expectation,
other things being equal, of the care and affection of both a mother and a father' (Gordon and
Farrant 2000).

- **Which presuppositions underpin Howard's statement?**
- **What is the 'problem' represented to be?**

For this Activity see Smith 2006 and Johnson 2003.

There are patterns or 'styles of problematisation' in the ways in which 'problems' are thought
about (i.e. in the conceptual logics) across a range of policies. Scholars associated with the
study of governmentality (e.g. Dean 1999; Rose 2000) call these patterns **governmental or
political rationalities** (or sometimes 'modes of governance', 'regimes of governance', or
'modes/diagrams of rule'). Rationality, as used here, has no connection with the common
understanding of rationality as being rational or wise. Rather it refers to the kind of thinking
that lies behind, or the rationales for, particular styles of governing. These are the 'mentalities'
referred to in the concept of 'govern-mentality' (see Chapter 2).

   Those involved in studying governmental rationalities (mentalities) tend to categorise them
differently. As an example, Walters (2001) identifies four different ways in which unemployment
has been thought about in Western democratic states: neo-liberal, neo-social democratic and
communitarian strategies of government, and a strategy of criminalising the poor (see Chapter 4).
For Walters, therefore, there are four distinct govern-mentalities. By contrast, because Rose (2000,
p. 12) emphasises common premises in neoliberal and neo-social modes of governance, he captures
both within the umbrella form of governmental rationality he calls 'advanced liberalism'.

The position adopted in this book emphasises the simultaneous coexistence of various forms of rule, which are often hybrid (see Chapter 2). Hence, it places more emphasis on identifying key underlying premises within modes of rule (Question 2) and the effects of those premises on those who are governed (Question 5) rather than on attaching labels to those modes of rule or creating ideal types. However, it remains an important task to recognise imbalances in the influence of different 'styles of problematisation'. As we shall see throughout the book, a current dominant style of problematisation creates individuals as primarily responsible for their lives.

Clearly, identifying deep-seated cultural premises and values within problem representations, the primary goal in Question 2, is a challenging task given that we are all immersed in the 'knowledges' and perceptions of our age. This is why a WPR approach emphasises that the questions it encompasses need to be applied to our own problem representations, as is stated at the end of the list of questions. This part of the approach is elaborated towards the end of this chapter.

There are, happily, forms of analysis to assist in this challenging task of uncovering deep-seated presuppositions. A starting point is to recognise that policies are elaborated in **discourse**. More attention is paid to this difficult concept in Chapter 2. At this stage it is adequate to think about discourse as meaning systems. Discourse is more than language. It encompasses the assumptions, values, presuppositions and accompanying signs that I have called conceptual logics. So, while it is clear that policies are expressed in language, we wish to dig deeper into the ways in which meaning is created through particular language uses. Policy is about meaning creation and our task is to identify how meaning is created. To this end, it is useful to engage in a form of discourse analysis, identifying and interrogating the binaries, key concepts and categories operating within a policy. Let us look briefly at each of these recommended forms of analysis.

Binaries

A good deal of public debate rests on binaries or dichotomies. Consider as examples: nature/culture, public/private, national/international, mind/body, male/female, economic/social, licit/illicit, responsible/irresponsible, legal/illegal. A binary assumes an A/not-A relationship. That is, what is on one side of a binary is considered to be excluded from the other side. In addition, there is a hierarchy implied in binaries. One side is privileged, considered to be more important or more valued than the other side. Invariably binaries simplify complex relationships. Hence, we need to *watch where they appear in policies and how they function to shape the understanding of the issue.*

The goal, as above, is to reveal the operation of conceptual logics that may act to constrain or limit our understanding of an issue. For example, an implied civilised/uncivilised dichotomy underpins many policies around Aboriginal issues. The child care policies we examined briefly, rest upon a distinction between 'private' remedies (the parent, most often the mother, at home) and 'public' solutions (publicly funded child care). We shall see the licit/illicit binary at work in drugs/alcohol policies (Chapter 4), and the responsible/irresponsible binary in a range of policies, including alcohol and gambling policies (Chapter 4), welfare policies (Chapter 3) and health policies (Chapter 6).

Key concepts

Policies are filled with concepts. 'Health' is a concept, as is 'welfare'. Concepts are abstract labels that are relatively open-ended. Hence, they are hotly contested. People fill them with different meanings. Disputes over the meaning of key concepts are related to competing political visions. A great deal is therefore at stake in the meanings assigned to concepts. For example, we shall see in Chapter 6 that, in health policy, it matters a great deal if you think about 'health' as general wellbeing rather than as the absence of disease.

I specify that concepts are *relatively* open-ended because some concepts are so solidly grounded in history and culture that it is difficult to recognise their constructed nature. Many concepts, like equality, liberty, youth, unemployment, participation and democracy, for example, appear to have clear-cut and obvious meanings, until we probe more deeply. Moreover, specific meanings of concepts are embedded deeply within governmental practices, complicating attempts to contest them.

'Nurturing Commonwealth Youth'

'The Commonwealth's future lies in the hands of its youth. They are the inheritors of fundamental values in promoting respect for diversity, economic and social development, democracy and good governance, and are a major resource in support of these values. The challenge is to enlist the enthusiasm of youth for the Commonwealth in the new century ... Youth volunteering, mentoring, leadership education and enterprise development schemes will facilitate the transfer of much needed skills and knowledge for development across the Commonwealth.' (CHOGM 2002, p. 10)

- **Identify key concepts that have contested meanings in this government proposal.**
- **Consider how 'youth' are represented in this passage (see Chapter 3).**
- **What is the 'problem' of 'youth' represented to be?**

For this Activity see Bessant 2004.

Given the contested nature of concepts, one task is to identify key concepts in problem representations and to see which meanings are given to those concepts. For example, in considering a child care tax rebate (see Activity on 'Child care'), how is the notion of work or labour understood? Are domestic tasks and caring for children and others considered to be a form of labour? Should they be? How would this shift in understanding alter the representation of the 'problem'?

Categories

Categories are concepts that play a central role in how governing takes place. Some examples would be: age categories, zoning categories, disease categories, gender and sexuality categories. Here we look more closely at *people* categories because of their centrality to governing processes. Consider, for example, the categories 'youth', 'single mothers', 'the homeless', 'tax-payers', 'students', 'welfare dependents', 'citizens'. The task here, as with binaries and key concepts, is not to accept these categories as given but to see how they function to give particular meanings to problem representations.

This approach to people categories accepts Hacking's (1986) claim that people are 'made up'.

'Were there any perverts before the latter part of the nineteenth century? According to Arnold Davidson [1990], "The answer is NO...Perversion was not a disease that lurked about in nature, waiting for a psychiatrist with especially acute powers of observation to discover it hiding somewhere. It was a disease created by a new [functional] understanding of disease." Davidson is not denying that there have been odd people at all times. He is asserting that perversion, as a disease, and the pervert, as a diseased person, was created in the nineteenth century. Davidson's claim, one of many now in circulation, illustrates what I call making up people.' (Hacking 1986, p. 222)

Along lines similar to Hacking, Foucault (1979) notes that 'homosexuals' did not exist before the end of the nineteenth century. Like Hacking regarding 'perversion', he is not saying that same-sex activities did not take place before then, but that the category 'homosexual' (and correspondingly 'heterosexual') had not yet been created. In other words, merely engaging in same-sex activities is not what constitutes individuals as 'homosexual'; rather, the category reflects a way of organising behaviours and people that has not always existed across space and time.

The creation of people categories has significant effects for the ways in which governing takes place, and for how people come to think about themselves and about others. We examine these effects more closely when we look at Question 5 below.

Categories, particularly people categories, are created through measurement, highlighting the important role played by measurement techniques such as censuses and surveys in governing. Question 3 pursues the role of such governmental techniques or mechanisms.

A discourse analysis such as the one introduced here has two goals: the first, already introduced, is to reveal underlying assumptions and preconceptions in problem representations; the second goal, to identify and reflect upon silences, is taken up in Question 4. Before we undertake this task, we need to reflect upon how particular representations of problems come to pass.

'Discovering' bikie gangs

On 7 May 2008 the South Australian Upper House passed the *Serious and Organised Crime (Control) Act 2008 (SA)* (Government of South Australia 2008). The legislation allows the Attorney-General to declare 'bikie gangs' illegal organisations. Control orders can be placed on members of these gangs, restricting whom they mix with. Under section 35 a person could go to gaol for five years for associating with someone under a control order six or more times a year, even if that person has committed no crime. The day before the legislation was introduced in the House of Assembly, Premier Mike Rann told the House that 'These are the toughest anti-outlaw bikie gang laws that we can find anywhere in the world where these groups operate' (Kanck 2008).

- **What does it mean to make bikie gangs 'declared organisations'?**

- **How does the creation of bikies as a collective entity facilitate governance objectives?**

- **Are there reasons to be concerned about the creation of some people categories?**

QUESTION 3: HOW HAS THIS REPRESENTATION OF THE 'PROBLEM' COME ABOUT?

There are two interconnected objectives in this question. One is to reflect on the specific developments and decisions (the non-discursive practices) that contribute to the formation of identified problem representations. The second is to recognise that competing problem representations exist both over time and across space, and hence that things could have developed quite differently. To achieve this perspective we draw on Foucault's genealogical theory, discussed at greater length in Chapter 2.

If you think for a moment about what it means to conduct a **genealogy** of your family you will get the basic idea of what it means. With genealogy, we begin our analysis in the present and ask how we have got here from there. We look back in time to trace 'roots', the 'descent' of our family. What we often find are surprises. There is not a clear path of descent with predictable outcomes; rather there are twists and turns, even the occasional skeleton in the closet.

So, too, when we seek to trace the 'history' of a current problem representation, we need to follow the twists and turns rather than assume, as often happens in conventional historical accounts, that current practices and institutions, and the ways 'problems' are understood, are the inevitable product of 'natural' evolution over time. The goal of genealogy is to upset any such assumptions about 'natural' evolution. By identifying specific points in time when key decisions were made, taking an issue in a particular direction, we can see that the problem representation under scrutiny is contingent and hence susceptible to change. Genealogy therefore has a *destabilising effect* on problem representations that are often taken for granted. It also provides insights into the power relations that affect the success of some problem representations and the defeat of others (see subjugated knowledges in Chapter 2).

An example here is abortion policy. For a good deal of the nineteenth century in Western democracies abortion was a common method of birth control. So, when did it become a legal 'problem', subject to criminal law? In Britain it was not a crime for a woman to abort herself until the 1861 *Offences Against the Person Act 1861 (UK)* (UK Statute 1861). This legislation was promoted by medical practitioners who were emerging as a profession in this period and who wanted to clamp down on unregistered practitioners (Bacchi 1999, Chapter 8).

From this example we learn that it is not necessary for abortion to be considered a legal 'problem'. It can be 'thought' differently. We can also identify some of the influences behind its creation as a legal 'problem'.

Genealogies like this one direct us to find out how a 'problem' took on a particular shape. The focus is on process — on how something came to be. There is also recognition of the need to attend to differential power relations where some groups have more influence than others in ensuring that a particular problem representation 'sticks'. Attention therefore is directed to a range of non-discursive practices including, in the abortion case, the rules that gave medicos institutional authority in this domain.

> The purpose of Question 3 of a WPR approach is to highlight the conditions that allow a particular problem representation to take shape and to assume dominance.

In Question 2 above, we considered the importance of people categories as part of governance. The techniques associated with the creation of people categories, such as censuses and surveys, form part of the non-discursive practices that allow specific problem representations to gain dominance. To *govern* it is necessary to *know* (Rose 2000, p. 209). Hence, people are counted and surveyed. Hacking (1986, p. 222) refers to an 'avalanche of numbers that begins around 1820'. He also points out that official statistics were obsessed with '*analyse morale*', 'the numerical analysis of suicide, prostitution, drunkenness, vagrancy, madness, crime, *les misérables*'. Hacking's concern is not the usual one about 'damned lies' and statistics, but that statistics create knowledge *of a particular kind*.

It follows that, when we see statistics invoked as a part of, or as a defence for, a particular policy, we need to ask — why these statistics and not others? Who gets counted? How do they get counted? How does their counting feed into the specific policy and its implied problem representation?

'Discovering' exnuptial birth

The Australian Bureau of Statistics 2007 report on 'Births' notes the following:

'In 2006, 67% of births were to mothers who were married (marriage in this publication refers to a registered marriage unless otherwise indicated). Exnuptial births accounted for the remaining 33% of births, although many of these births may have been to mothers in de facto relationships. The proportion of exnuptial births has been increasing since the 1950s, and has risen sharply over the last two decades' (ABS 2007, p. 13).

- **What is the governmental interest in births? In exnuptial births? Why are these figures collected?** *(see Chapter 7)*
- **How do these figures play a role in 'making up people'?**

Other techniques associated with the development of specific policies affect the way in which the 'problem' is represented. For example, a case-management approach to dealing with the unemployed produces the 'problem' as an *individual's* ability or inability to fit into a labour market. Mechanisms like this one may also affect people's perceptions of their place in society. As Rose and Miller (1992, p. 200) describe, 'Making people write things down, and the nature of the things people are made to write down is itself a kind of government of them, urging them to think about and note certain aspects of their activities according to certain norms'. The ways in which governmental mechanisms encourage the production of governable political subjects is pursued in Question 5, under subjectification effects.

To this point a methodology has been offered which: identifies problem representations within specific policies (Question 1), analyses their conceptual underpinnings (Question 2), and examines their origins, history and mechanisms (Question 3). We turn now to reflecting on gaps and silences in designated problem representations.

QUESTION 4: WHAT IS LEFT UNPROBLEMATIC IN THIS PROBLEM REPRESENTATION? WHERE ARE THE SILENCES? CAN THE 'PROBLEM' BE THOUGHT ABOUT DIFFERENTLY?

This question allows us to begin exploring the critical potential of a WPR approach to policy analysis. As stated in the Introduction, the underlying intent is to problematise the problematisations on offer by subjecting the problem representations they contain to critical scrutiny. One way to do this is to consider **limits** in the underlying problem representations. A key intervention here is to ask – what fails to be problematised? The failure to examine the contribution of rampant consumption to the 'problem' of traffic congestion is one example. The failure to examine the inadequacies of medical service delivery in the case of Aboriginal health 'problems' is another example. The argument here is not simply that there is another way to think about the issue but that specific policies are constrained by the ways in which they represent the 'problem'. The objective therefore is to bring into discussion issues and perspectives that are silenced in identified problem representations.

> The objective of Question 4 of a WPR approach is to raise for reflection and consideration issues and perspectives silenced in identified problem representations.

The discourse analysis performed in Question 2 is helpful here. Since, as mentioned, binaries simplify complex experience, it is possible to indicate where this simplification distorts or misrepresents certain issues. As an example, it is common in liberal democracies to suggest that governments need to limit their activities to the so-called 'public' sphere, leaving people's 'private' lives untouched. However, governments intervene in everyday living arrangements all the time, both by what they do and by what they do not do. For example, the lack of good publicly-funded child care might well have an influence on decisions within families about having children. Hence, the public/private dichotomy mystifies relationships between governments and individuals/families (Olsen 1985).

This kind of analysis usefully draws attention to tensions and contradictions in problem representations, again highlighting limitations or inadequacies in the way the 'problem' is being represented. For example, a policy that suggests that diabetes 2 is a lifestyle disease and that then (simply) observes its prevalence amongst Aboriginal people and across poor populations seems to miss the obvious observation that something else is going on, unless of course Aboriginal people and poor people are simply deemed unable to make 'good' lifestyle choices.

'Discovering' binge drinking

Consider the following description of the Rudd government's *National Binge Drinking Strategy*: 'Binge drinking among young people is a community wide problem that demands a community wide response, including a new emphasis on young people taking greater personal responsibility for their behaviour' (Rudd 2008).

- **In your view, what is the 'problem' of binge drinking among young people represented to be in this description?**

- **What, in your opinion, fails to be problematised?**

'Discovering' healthy habits

Consider this initiative of the Rudd Labor government, described as part of its 'new approach to prevention' in health policy: 'Parents will be provided with a *Healthy Habits for Life Guide*, which will provide practical, accessible tips on their child's health and development at a critical stage of their young lives' (Roxon 2007).

- **In your view, what is the 'problem' of ill-health represented to be in this proposal?**

- **What, in your opinion, fails to be problematised?**

Because genealogies (Question 3) draw attention to competing problem representations (those that were not taken up), they assist in the task of identifying silences in those problem representations that gain institutional endorsement. Cross-cultural comparisons can also help us to realise that certain ways of thinking about 'problems' reflect specific institutional and cultural contexts and, hence, that problem representations are contingent. For example, there is no equivalent of Repetition Strain Injury (RSI), a widely recognised medical complaint in Australia, in the United States (Bammer and Martin 1992). Putting aside the possibility that Americans do not suffer from muscle strain due to repetitive forms of work, this kind of discovery prompts us to ask how something becomes a 'problem' in one situation and not in another. Which institutional factors allow RSI to gain recognition as a 'problem' in Australia? Which institutional factors prevent this from happening in the United States? In each case we want to highlight the conditions that allow particular problem representations to take shape and to assume dominance, whilst others are silenced.

'The Iceland Controversy'

The collection of comprehensive biometric data on Icelanders, undertaken post-1998, produced a highly polarised debate. A plan in Britain to collect similar kinds of data attracted very little attention. According to Pálsson and Rabinow (2006) a key factor was that, in the two countries, there was a different relationship between physicians and parliament in the regulation of human research. In their view, there was no protest in the UK because there the 'funders of research, the managers of the data base and the regulators can be in the same institutions' (Kaye and Martin 2000 in Pálsson and Rabinow 2006, p. 100). They conclude that, in order to understand 'divergent problematizations', 'it is not the issues alone that are at stake but a specific historical, political and economic conjuncture in which an issue becomes a problem' (Pálsson and Rabinow 2006, p. 94).

QUESTION 5: WHAT EFFECTS ARE PRODUCED BY THIS REPRESENTATION OF THE PROBLEM?

Question 5 allows us to continue our critical analysis. A WPR approach to policy analysis starts from the presumption that some problem representations create difficulties (forms of harm) for members of some social groups more so than for members of other groups. There is no suggestion, however, that these difficulties form a standard and predictable pattern. This is the very reason we need to interrogate the problematisations on offer, including our own (through scrutinising the problem representations they contain), in order to see where and how they function to benefit some and harm others, and what can be done about this.

In order to perform this kind of assessment we need to direct attention to the effects that accompany specific problem representations. As mentioned in the Introduction this form of assessment does not refer to the standard policy approach to evaluation with a focus on 'outcomes'. Indeed, as we shall see in Chapter 6 and elsewhere, a WPR approach puts in question the premise of evidence-based policy that lies behind such measurement approaches to evaluation. Effects, as understood in a WPR approach, are much more subtle in their influence and rely for their understanding on a number of theoretical perspectives, including poststructuralist discourse psychology and feminist body theory (see Chapter 2).

> 'My general theme isn't society but the discourse of true and false, by which I mean the correlative formation of domains and objects and the verifiable, falsifiable discourses that bear on them: and it's not just their formation that interests me, but the *effects in the real* to which they are linked.' (Foucault 1978, p. 55 in Bernauer 1992, p. 144; emphasis added.)

For our purposes here it is adequate to identify three, interconnected and overlapping kinds of effects that need to be 'weighed up':
1. Discursive effects: effects which follow from the limits imposed on what can be thought and said;
2. Subjectification (or 'subjectivisation') effects: the ways in which subjects and subjectivities are constituted in discourse;
3. Lived effects: the impact on life and death (Dean 2006).

We proceed to consider each briefly in turn.

> The goal of Question 5 of a WPR approach is to identify the effects of specific problem representations so that they can be critically assessed.

Discursive effects

There are clear links here with Questions 2, 3 and 4, which identify deep-seated assumptions and presuppositions within problem representations, the discourses which give expression to these, and the silences these discourses contain. The proposal is a simple one. If some options for social intervention are closed off by the way in which a 'problem' is represented, this can have devastating effects for certain people. The fact that traffic congestion is conceived of as a matter of inconvenience and/or interruption to the operation of business practices, closes off consideration of certain citizens' lack of access to cars (and/or the petrol to fuel them). Portraying child care as a necessity for women engaged in paid labour (through a rebate) closes off consideration of the child care demands placed on other women. Making child sexual abuse in Aboriginal communities a law and order issue (by sending in troops) closes off consideration of the connections between colonisation, living standards and white supremacy. In each of these examples, identified problem representations and the discourses which frame them make it difficult to think differently, limiting the kinds of social analysis that can be produced. In a WPR approach this form of silencing is an effect that needs to be closely monitored.

Subjectification effects

The concept of subjectification is a tricky one. Basically the idea is that we become subjects *of a particular kind* partly through the ways in which policies set up social relationships and our place (position) within them. This setting up of social relationships takes place within discourse.

Another way to say this is that discourses make certain **subject positions** available. And, when such a position is assumed, a person tends to make sense of the social world from this standpoint, all the while being subjected to the full range of discourses constituting this position. Hence, who we are – how we feel about ourselves and others – is at least to an extent an effect of the subject positions made available in public policies. While this proposal may be disconcerting, the suggestion that policies such as child-care policy or its lack, for example, modify our behaviours and our thoughts about when to start a family seems fairly uncontentious.

A particular issue that requires scrutiny when we turn to subjectification effects is the way in which the problem representations within policies often set groups of people in opposition to each other – a dynamic Foucault (1982, p. 208) calls **'dividing practices'**. Think, for example, about the unemployed *versus* the employed, 'problem gamblers' *versus* 'recreational gamblers', 'binge drinkers' *versus* 'socially responsible drinkers'. Following Foucault's argument, this stigmatising of targeted minorities serves a useful governmental purpose, indicating and encouraging desired behaviours among the majority. More will be said about this important subjectification effect in subsequent chapters.

In addition, representations of 'problems' usually have built into them implications about who is responsible for the 'problem'. One task, therefore, is to bring these implied attributions of responsibility into the open so that we can consider whether or not we believe that responsibility is being sheeted home appropriately, and what effects follow from particular attributions of responsibility.

In many instances, for example, dividing practices create members of targeted groups as themselves (responsible for) the 'problem'. Thinking back to Question 4, we need to consider what is silenced in this representation of the 'problem'. Fulcher (1989), for example, makes the case that the discourse surrounding education policy and disability constitutes disabled children as the 'problem', distracting attention from the disabling structures which shape the possibilities of their lives. She also notes that representing the disabled as the 'problem' allows government 'responses' to be seen as benevolent, generous and compassionate, reinforcing existing power relations. Similar things could be said about the ways in which a range of policies create targeted groups – for example, welfare recipients, single mothers, Aboriginal parents, and 'illegal' immigrants – as the 'problem'.

Going further, it is necessary to reflect upon the impact of such problem representations on the people who are targets of the policy. For example, does being constituted a 'problem' influence how those called 'disabled' feel about themselves? As another example, in dominant understandings of affirmative action, recipients are described as beneficiaries of 'preferential treatment'. In a society that prizes initiative and frowns upon dependence, members of targeted groups are therefore often deterred from supporting the reform (Bacchi 2004; see Chapter 8). This has the effect of reinforcing the social status quo. The political implications that accompany how subjects are constituted within problem representations, therefore, deserve a good deal of attention.

Due to the subjectification effects accompanying problem representations – the ways in which they influence how we feel about ourselves and others – it is often difficult to stand back from them in order to think about and interrogate them. We reflect on this dilemma shortly.

> 'The subject is either divided inside himself (sic) or divided from others. This process objectivizes him. Examples are the mad and the sane, the sick and the healthy, the criminals and the "good boys".'
> (Foucault 1982, p. 208)

Lived effects

The concept of lived effects directs attention to the *material* impact of problem representations. How 'problems' are represented directly affects people's lives. If access to resources depends upon one's location within welfare categories, for example, the premises underpinning the grounds for categorisation can mean lack of food and/or inadequate housing. Along similar lines, the quarantining of welfare payments of those families called 'dysfunctional' can produce emotional and material distress for those families. The notion of lived effects thereby highlights the way in which policies create representations of problems that have effects *in the real* by materially affecting our lives.

Question 5 Summary

Because a WPR approach makes the case that problem representations impact unevenly on different groups of people, the kind of analysis of effects described here forms a crucial part of the methodology. The overall goal is to be able to say which aspects of a problem representation have deleterious effects for which groups, and hence may need to be rethought. There is also the intention of providing a means to consider the long-range impact of policy interventions in terms of social change. The following sub-questions should be considered an integral part of Question 5:

■ What is likely to change with this representation of the 'problem'?
■ What is likely to stay the same?
■ Who is likely to benefit from this representation of the 'problem'?
■ Who is likely to be harmed by this representation of the 'problem'?
■ How does the attribution of responsibility for the 'problem' affect those so targeted and the perceptions of the rest of the community about who is to 'blame'?

Approaches to drug education

The syllabus for the New South Wales Drug Education classes states that many health problems:

Can be associated with the lifestyles adopted by individuals, particularly with respect to drug use, accidents, diet, physical activity, sexual activity, as well as a number of other high risk behaviours. Because of their association with certain behaviour patterns, many modern diseases are therefore largely preventable depending on the choices made by individuals. (NSW Board of Studies 2001, p. 7 in Stanton 2005, p. 51)

• **What is the 'problem' of drug use represented to be in this statement?**

• **What effects does the representation of the 'problem' produce? Consider discursive effects, subjectification effects and lived effects.**

For this Activity see Stanton 2005.

QUESTION 6: HOW/WHERE IS THIS REPRESENTATION OF THE 'PROBLEM' PRODUCED, DISSEMINATED AND DEFENDED? HOW COULD IT BE QUESTIONED, DISRUPTED AND REPLACED?

This question builds on Question 3, which directs attention to practices and processes that allow certain problem representations to dominate. At this stage in the analysis it is appropriate to think about the means through which particular problem presentations reach their target audience and achieve legitimacy. Foucault (1991, p. 60) asks, 'What individuals, what groups or classes have access to a particular kind of discourse? How is the relationship institutionalized between the discourse, speakers and its destined audience?' The role of the media in disseminating and supporting particular problem representations ought to be considered here (see Chapter 10).

The question of possible resistance also needs to be addressed. On this issue it is important to recognise that discourses are plural, complex and, at times, inconsistent. In a sense, therefore, discourses can be seen as 'assets' or resources for re-problematisation. See Chapter 2 for more on this topic.

> The goal of Question 6 in a WPR approach is to pay attention both to the means through which some problem representations become dominant, and to the possibility of challenging problem representations that are judged to be harmful.

APPLY THE LIST OF QUESTIONS IN A WPR APPROACH TO YOUR OWN PROBLEM REPRESENTATIONS: THE NEED FOR REFLEXIVITY

At the end of the list of six questions, there stands a deceptively simple directive to 'apply this list of questions to your own problem representations'. Here we reflect briefly on what this means.

Several times already it has been mentioned that we need to subject our own problem representations to a WPR analysis (i.e. apply the six questions). Self-analysis or **reflexivity** of this kind is necessary because we are immersed in the conceptual logics of our era and because who we are, as just considered under Question 5, is at least in part shaped through the very problem representations we are trying to analyse. As a result, we have to accept that, as researchers, we have work to do in ensuring that we do not simply buy into certain problem representations without reflecting on their origins, purposes and effects. Chapter 2 reflects in more detail on the political stance this perspective entails.

PRACTICAL GUIDELINES

The approach to policy analysis introduced here encourages a sceptical stance toward claims to 'knowledge', and aims to disrupt taken-for-granted 'givens' wherever they are found. This is clear in Question 4 about identifying silences and considering alternative ways of conceptualising 'problems'. Some practical guidelines are needed to ensure that the approach is not employed in an overly simple, and hence counter-productive, manner. Four issues are considered here: text selection, complexity, context and 'nesting' (the way in which problem representations are embedded within each other). Each will be considered in turn.

Text selection

The kind of text selected for examination is fairly open-ended. Generally, it is wise to find a specific piece of legislation or a government report as a place to start. However, it is often, even usually, necessary to examine related texts, including such things as parliamentary debates, ministerial pronouncements, related government reports and media statements, to build up a fuller picture of a particular problem representation. Note also that, given the focus in the book on governance conceived broadly, it is possible to apply the approach to institutional policies, as we did in the last Activity on the NSW Education Department.

Given the almost endless variety and numbers of texts that could be selected, it needs to be recognised that choosing policies to examine is itself an interpretive exercise. That is, you will already be involved in analysis when you select a policy or policies for examination. Your choices will reflect your particular interests and/or topical concerns.

Often you will choose policy texts in order to develop a particular argument. For example, in Chapter 7, I examine a policy directed to increasing the Australian birth rate alongside a policy on long-stay immigrant visas, a somewhat unusual combination. The objective here is to encourage reflection on the 'thought' involved in governing Australia's population.

Complexity

Policies often contain tensions and contradictions. There is seldom a single voice lying behind them. As with text selection, therefore, it is important to recognise the interpretive dimension of the analytic process. Be careful not to distort documents when choosing particular segments to support an interpretation. Acknowledge contesting positions within a document when they are apparent.

Context

To understand your selected policy you need to have a solid understanding of the background to the issue/s you are considering. You also need to see how specific issues fit into wider debates. To assist with this task it is important to consider the web of policies, both historical and contemporary, surrounding an issue. One reason this is so important is because context matters – what you deduce about the specific case you study will reflect the circumstances affecting it. Note that the task of 'filling in' context is never simply a descriptive exercise, however, since reflections on context are themselves interpretive. Indeed, in many cases it is necessary to pay attention to how a context, for example, 'globalisation', is itself represented.

Nesting

It is important to note that the questions in a WPR approach are not intended as a one-off exercise. Rather, they require repeated application due to the ways in which problem representations 'nest' or are embedded one within the other. For example, competing approaches to reform in the area of girls and education are grounded in different views of both the 'problem' of 'women's inequality' and of the 'problem' of education more generally (Bacchi 1999, Chapter 6). In health policy the term 'health' itself requires reflection and interrogation. Similarly, it is important to consider the kind of 'problem' that 'prevention' is represented to be in health policies described as 'preventive' (see Chapter 6). Applying a WPR approach to policy allows you to probe all these levels of problem representation. Therefore, when you first identify a problem representation by 'working backwards' from a policy, it is important to check if there are key terms or topics within that problem representation that themselves need to be subjected to a WPR analysis.

The best way to appreciate and gain confidence with the approach is to practice it yourself. Hence, I encourage you to have a try. You might, however, feel the need to see the methodology at work. If this is the case, Chapters 3 and 4 apply the approach systematically, making them easy to follow. A more integrated form of analysis is available in Chapters 5 through 10. The goal in each case is to illustrate what an application of the approach looks like, not to suggest that my analysis is in any sense comprehensive or correct. You may produce a very different analysis of the same or related material.

SUMMARY

This chapter has introduced you to a WPR approach to policy analysis through a step-by-step overview of each of the questions in the approach and its goals. It is hoped that this method of introduction will allow you to trial the approach without further ado. Those who wish elaboration of the theoretical premises and politics grounding the approach should turn to Chapter 2. Those who wish to see the methodology applied can dip into any of Chapters 3 through 10. The proviso above – to apply the set of questions repeatedly – indicates and supports the overall objective, to dig deeply into the meaning-creation involved in public policy.

REFERENCES

ABS (Australian Bureau of Statistics) 2007, *3301.0 Births 2006*.

AUSTRALIAN GOVERNMENT 1984, *Sex Discrimination Act*, Attorney-General's Department, Commonwealth of Australia Law, <www.comlaw.gov.au>, accessed 16 October 2008.

BACCHI, C. 1999, *Women, Policy and Politics: the Construction of Policy Problems*, Sage, London.

BACCHI, C. 2004, 'Policy and Discourse: Challenging the Construction of Affirmative Action as Preferential Treatment', *Journal of European Public Policy*, vol. 11, no. 1, pp. 128–46.

BAMMER, G. & MARTIN, B. 1992, 'Repetition Strain Injury in Australia: Medical Knowledge, Social Movement, and De Facto Partnership', *Social Problems*, vol. 39, no.3, pp. 219–37.

BERNAUER, J. W. 1992, *Michel Foucault's Force of Flight: Toward an Ethics for Thought*, Humanities Press, New Jersey.

BESSANT, J. 2004, 'Mixed Messages: Youth Participation and Democratic Practice', *Australian Journal of Political Science*, vol. 39, no. 2, pp. 387–404.

CHOGM [Commonwealth Heads of Government Meeting] 2002, *Report by the Commonwealth High Level Review Group to Commonwealth Heads of Government*, Commonwealth High Level Review Group, Coolum, <www.thecommonwealth.org>, accessed 5 July 2008.

DAVIDSON, A. 1990, 'Closing Up the Corpses', in *Meaning and Method*, ed. G. Boulos, Cambridge University Press, Cambridge.

DEAN, M. 1999, *Governmentality: Power and Rule in Modern Society*, Sage, London.

DEAN, M. 2006, 'Governmentality and Powers of Life and Death' in *Analysing Social Policy: A Governmental Approach*, eds G. Marston & C. McDonald, Edward Elgar, Cheltenham, UK.

DOTY, R. L. 1993, 'Foreign Policy as Social Construction: A Post-Positivist Analysis of U.S. Counterinsurgency Policy in the Philippines', *International Studies Quarterly*, vol. 37, no. 3, pp. 297–320.

FOUCAULT, M. 1973 [1966] *The Order of Things: An Archaeology of the Human Sciences*, Vintage, New York.

FOUCAULT, M. 1978, '*Table ronde du mai 1978*', in *Dits et Écrits, IV*, 1980–88.

FOUCAULT, M. 1979, *The History of Sexuality, Volume I, An Introduction*, Trans. R. Hurley, Allen Lane, London.

FOUCAULT, M. 1982, 'The Subject and Power', in *Michel Foucault: Beyond Structuralism and Hermeneutics*, 2nd edition, eds H. Dreyfus & P. Rabinow, University of Chicago Press, Chicago.

FOUCAULT, M. 1991 [1968], 'Politics and the Study of Discourse' in *The Foucault Effect: Studies in Governmentality*, eds G. Burchell, C. Gordon & P. Miller, University of Chicago Press, Chicago.

FULCHER, G. 1989, *Disabling Policies? A Comparative Approach to Education Policy and Disability*, The Falmer Press, East Sussex.

GORDON, M. & Farrant, D. 2000, 'Howard sparks IVF storm', *The Age*, 2 August.

GOVERNMENT OF SOUTH AUSTRALIA 2008, *Serious and Organised Crime (Control) Act*, South Australian Consolidated Acts, <www.austlii.edu.au>, accessed 20 October 2008

GOVERNMENT OF VICTORIA 1995, *Victorian Infertility Treatment Act*, Victorian Consolidated Legislation, no. 63, <www.austlii.edu.au>, accessed 20 October 2008.

HACKING, I. 1986, 'Making up People', in *Reconstructing Individualism: Autonomy, Individuality and the Self in Western Thought*, eds T. Heller & C. Brooke-Rose, Stanford University Press, Stanford, California.

JOHNSON, C. 2003, 'Heteronormative Citizenship: The Howard Government's Views on Gay and Lesbian Issues', *Australian Journal of Political Science*, vol. 38, no. 1, pp. 45–62.

KANCK, S. 2008, Supplementary Question in the Legislative Council, 7 March, <http://sa.democrats.org.au>, accessed 5 July 2008.

KAYE, J. & MARTIN, P. 2000, 'Safeguards for Research Using Large-scale DNA Collections', *British Medical Journal* vol. 321, no. 4, pp. 1146–49.

NSW BOARD OF STUDIES 2001, *Years 7–10 Personal Development, Health and Physical Education Syllabus* (no. 2001195), Sydney.

OLSEN, F. 1985, 'The Myth of State Intervention in the Family', *University of Michigan Journal of Law Reform*, vol. 18, no. 4, pp. 835–64.

PÁLSSON, G. & RABINOW, P. 2006, 'The Iceland Controversy: Reflections on the Transnational Market of Civic Virtue' in *Global Assemblages: Technology, Politics, and Ethics as Anthropological Problems*, eds A. Ong & S. J. Collier, Blackwell, London.

PARLIAMENT OF COMMONWEALTH OF AUSTRALIA 1997, House of Representatives Standing Committee on Family and Community Affairs, *Aspects of Youth Suicide: Summary Report of a Seminar*, May, <www.aph.gov.au>, accessed 14 August 2007.

ROSE, N. S. 2000, *Powers of Freedom: Reframing Political Thought*, 1st edition 1999, Cambridge University Press, Cambridge, UK.

ROSE, N. & MILLER, P. 1992, 'Political Power Beyond the State: Problematics of Government', *The British Journal of Sociology*, vol. 43, no. 2, pp. 173–205.

ROXON, N. 2007, Speech, Tackling Childhood Obesity in Australia Summit, Sydney, 11 December, <www.accessibility.com.au>, accessed 6 July 2008.

RUDD, K. 2008 'National Binge Drinking Strategy', Media Statement, 10 March 2008 <www.alp.org.au>, accessed 6 July 2008.

SAWYER, R. KEITH 2002, 'A Discourse on Discourse: an Archaeological History of an Intellectual Concept', *Cultural Studies*, vol. 16, no. 3, pp. 433–56.

SHAPIRO, M. J. 1992, *Reading the Postmodern Polity: Political Theory as Textual Practice*, University of Minnesota Press, Minneapolis.

SMITH, J. 2006, 'Governing the Mother: Access to Reproductive Technologies' in *Analysing Social Policy: A Governmental Approach*, eds G. Marston & C. McDonald, Edward Elgar, Cheltenham, UK.

STANTON, B. 2005, 'School Drug Education in New South Wales: Moral Panic and the Individualisation of Youth Drug Use', *Social Alternatives*, vol. 24, no. 4, pp. 50–54.

UK STATUTE 1861, *Offences Against the Person Act*, Parliament of the United Kingdom and Ireland, <www.cirp.org/library/legal/UKlaw/oap1861/>, accessed 20 October 2008

WALTERS, W. 2001, 'Governing Unemployment: Transforming "the Social"?', in *Rethinking Law, Society and Governance: Foucault's Bequest*, eds G. Wickham & G. Pavlich, Hart Publishing, Oregon.

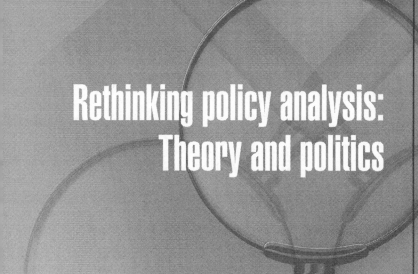

Rethinking policy analysis: Theory and politics

Chapter 2

As we saw in the Introduction, a WPR approach involves three key propositions:

1. We are governed through problematisations.
2. We need to study problematisations (through analysing the problem representations they contain), rather than 'problems'.
3. We need to problematise (interrogate) the problematisations on offer through scrutinising the premises and effects of the problem representations they contain.

It is now time to explore each of these proposals in greater depth. In the process we distinguish between a WPR approach to policy analysis and other approaches, and explore the meanings of key theoretical terms, including **governmentality**, **power**, subjectivity and reflexivity.

PROPOSITION 1: WE ARE GOVERNED THROUGH PROBLEMATISATIONS

The locus of study for a WPR approach is broader than in most other approaches to policy studies and policy analysis. This scope is best captured by the idea that we are interested in how rule takes place, in how we are governed. This broad focus on 'rule' means incorporating, but also looking beyond, the state in order to identify other forms of influence on governing conduct. We are trying to understand how society is managed, and with what repercussions for different groups of people, including 'citizens' and those positioned outside 'citizenship'. Government in this broader understanding is 'not a definite and uniform group of institutions' but 'an inventive, strategic, technical and artful set of "**assemblages**" fashioned from diverse elements' (Dean and Hindess 1998, p. 8). A particular focus is indirect influences, including the role of experts, 'that link the conduct of individuals and organizations to the objects of politics' (Miller and Rose 1990, p. 1).

Clearly, looking beyond the state to understand how governing occurs in this broad sense makes a WPR approach significantly different from most forms of policy analysis, which by their nature and focus ('public policy') presume that the state should be the primary site for study. The kind of analysis introduced in this book keeps the state as an important player – as is clear in the use of specific state policies as the entry points for reflection – but the state is conceived of as only *one* player in the general administration of societal relations. The other players, as we shall see below, include the full panoply of professional groups, such as doctors and social workers, and of groups which influence the shape of governing knowledges, including social science researchers. This kind of analysis, therefore, poses a challenge to conventional distinctions between the state and civil society.

It is also important to distinguish this perspective from studies that talk about network governance (e.g. Marcussen & Torfing 2006), or about the influence of experts on public policy. In a WPR approach we are focusing on the *knowledges* through which rule takes place, and the influence of experts and professionals *on and through these knowledges*, rather than examining their direct role as participants in political processes (e.g. as members of lobby groups).

> '[M]y problem is to see how men [sic] govern (themselves and others) by the production of truth' (Foucault 1991a, p. 79).

This shift in focus has much to do with the work of Michel Foucault (1926–1984). Foucault is particularly concerned with the way in which the thinking which informs government altered towards the end of the eighteenth century. This was due, in his view, to the growth of population. Expanding numbers of people, considered here within national borders, and the growing complexities of social relationships posed new challenges to governments. Securing the life and health of population/s became a social imperative, a kind of social unconscious, within government.

Foucault coins the term 'governmentality' to talk about different forms of rule. He uses the term in two ways. At a more generic level, he uses it to identify different rationalities or mentalities of rule (govern-*mentalities*), the different kinds of thinking associated with particular approaches to government. At a more substantive level, he uses the term to refer to the form of rule that emerged in the late eighteenth century, that which focused on population.

Foucault compares the kind of power associated with this population-focused form of governmentality with other forms of power, principally with sovereign power and with disciplinary power. He describes sovereign power as a mentality 'where the problem is how to perpetuate one's rule over a given territory and its subjects' (Walters and Haahr 2005, p. 9), and where the 'privileged instruments' are law, violence and pageantry. Disciplinary power targets *individual* bodies and uses the techniques of surveillance and **normalisation** 'to produce useful, calculable subjects' (Walters and Haahr 2005, p. 10). By contrast, governmentality operates at the level of population and utilises such means as social and economic policy to ensure security and order.

'One of the great innovations in the techniques of power in the eighteenth century was the emergence of "population" as an economic and political problem; population as wealth, population as manpower.' (Foucault 1979, p. 25)

This focus on population coincides with the emergence of political economy, a form of knowledge that 'rendered visible' the population 'both as an object and an end of government' through statistical measurement (Gunn 2006, p. 709). The economy comes to be seen as a thing apart from the state and as increasingly self-managing. To govern effectively, the government has to work through the economy to ensure the health and security of the population. This concern translates into *a need to know* about the full range of people's activities, particularly those such as sexual behaviours that impact directly on the numbers and health of the population.

'It was essential that the state know what was happening with its citizens' sex, and the use they made of it, but also that each individual be capable of controlling the use he made of it. Between the state and the individual, sex became an issue, and a public issue no less; a whole web of discourses, special knowledges, analyses, and similar injunctions settled upon it.' (Foucault 1979, p. 26)

The need to know about populations helps to explain the 'avalanche of numbers' (Hacking 1986, p. 222; see Chapter 1) produced in the eighteenth century and continuing to today, which involves counting death rates, birth rates including nuptial and exnuptial birth rates, divorce rates, abortion rates, diabetes rates and unemployment rates among many others. The use of 'rates' of measurement is significant. It indicates that individuals on their own are considered to be less important than *proportions* of phenomena within a national or sub-national population. In this sense a 'population' is treated as a singular, organic body, described by Foucault (1979, p. 139) as a 'species body'. In Chapter 7 we examine the baby bonus as a governmental technique targeting population.

Exnuptial births revisited

As noted in Chapter 1, the Australian Bureau of Statistics keeps records of, among many other things, the proportion of births in Australia that are 'exnuptial' (outside of registered marriage).

The following pattern is recorded:

1986	16.8% of births were exnuptial
1991	23.0%
1996	27.4%
2001	30.7%
2002	31.3%
2003	31.6%
2004	32.2%
2005	32.2%
2006	32.7%

(ABS 2007, p. 23)

- **How do the statistics collected above illustrate Foucault's line of reasoning about governmental concern with sexuality and with population?**

Importantly, Foucault is not saying that governmentality *replaced* sovereignty or discipline as forms of rule. Rather, he speaks about a triangle of rule, *including* sovereignty, discipline and government (governmentality) (Foucault 1991b, p. 102). In addition, he is particularly interested in the ways in which forms of rule intersect. For example, he speaks about two poles 'around which the organization of power over life was deployed' (Foucault 1979, p. 139): biopower (or **biopolitics**), which looks at society in its entirety as a ('species') body, and anatomo-politics (or discipline), which targets individual bodies. He concludes that the form of power of the modern state, which he calls the 'normalizing state', is essentially concerned with the control over life that can be exercised either individually through discipline or at a societal level through forms of regulation (see Foucault 1997a).

Biopolitics refers to 'a form of politics entailing the administration of the processes of life of populations' (Dean 1999, p. 98). It is 'the endeavour, begun in the eighteenth century, to rationalize problems presented to governmental practice by the phenomena characteristic of a group of living human beings constituted as a population: health, sanitation, birth rate, longevity, race' (Foucault 1997b, p. 73 in Dean 1999, p. 99).

Foucault famously used the metaphor of the Benthamite Panopticon to explain the workings of discipline as a mode of governance, or *diagram* of rule. The Benthamite prison involved a central tower from which a single guard could observe the prisoners, who could not tell when or if they were being observed. The result was that prisoners behaved *as if* they were being watched.

While this may sound a little too much like a 'big brother' scenario, it has some resonance with the ways in which modern societies operate. Think, for example, of seat-belt legislation, the requirement to wear bicycle helmets, and the injunction to eat healthy food. Once norms of desirable behaviour are set, people as political subjects become involved in *self*-surveillance and ***self*-regulation**. The government (in the narrow sense) 'enlists' other groups (doctors, psychologists, social scientists) in the task of setting those norms through the knowledges they produce. The argument here is that, due to self-regulation, the arm of the government can rest lightly. Theorists (Miller and Rose 1990, p. 9) working in this tradition – studies of governmentality – refer to government taking place 'at a distance'. According to Foucault, liberalism and **neoliberalism** are forms of rule (governmental rationalities) that display this character of 'government at a distance'.

'The norms used to judge normality are deployed everywhere so that health education and social work professionals are all part of what Foucault calls "carceral apparatuses"' (Shapiro 1981, p. 159).

Questions might well be raised about the relevance of a governmentality perspective today. In the post-9/11 period in the United States and elsewhere there are increasing displays of *sovereign* power in explicit curtailment of civil rights (see Chapter 10). The implication here is that self-regulation has become less important as a mode of governance while sovereignty and discipline have regained pre-eminence. In this vein, some argue that neoliberalism is in decline (e.g. Snyder 2001), lessening the relevance of governmentality, referring to government at a distance, as a way of thinking about forms of rule.

However, with Foucault's triangle in mind (see above), hybrid forms of rule are to be expected. For example, Dean (1999, p. 134–35) points out that, within liberal regimes, those deemed not to possess the characteristics necessary for 'bearing the freedoms and responsibilities of a citizen' are subjected to a broad range of disciplinary, sovereign and other interventions. At different times, groups marked in this way have included 'those furnished with the status of the indigent, the degenerate, the feeble-minded, the aboriginal, the homosexual, the delinquent, or even, and much more generally, the minor' (see Chapter 3). To avoid the forms of exclusion and punishment meted out to these groups, the 'free subject of liberalism' comes to regulate their own behaviours (*self*-regulation). Practices that set groups of people against each other in these ways are called 'dividing practices' because 'The subject is either divided inside himself (sic) or divided from others' (Foucault 1982, p. 208; see Chapter 1).

Identifying dividing practices and tracking their effects (Question 5) are key tasks within a WPR approach. Examples in this book include 'Work for the Dole' (Chapter 3), the quarantining of welfare payments (Chapter 3), drugs/alcohol and gambling policy (Chapter 4), and citizenship (chapter 7), among others.

It is important to stress that there is no suggestion here of intentional manipulation. For example, there is no suggestion of government plots to target drug 'addicts' for punishment as a way of making the rest of the population 'behave'. A governmentality approach does not work at the level of intentions. Rather, it is accepted that these forms of rule develop in order to maintain order within populations. However, just because forms of rule are unintentional does not mean that they should be endorsed uncritically. Rather, we need to be able to compare and assess various rationalities and techniques of rule. A WPR approach offers tools to perform these evaluations.

The way to recognise different forms of rule (or government rationalities) is through identifying and analysing *problematisations*. The term 'problematisation' appears in a good deal of contemporary social theory. It is usually introduced to indicate the need for critical interrogation. Freire (1972) encourages problematisation in this sense. Foucault uses the term in two ways: first, as in Freire, to signal the need to put taken-for-granted assumptions into question; and second, as a way into the thinking behind particular forms of rule. Indeed, late in his life (1984) Foucault describes the 'notion common to all the work I have done since *Histoire de la folie* [*History of Madness*, 2006/1961]', to be 'that of problematization', though, as he says, he never 'isolated the notion sufficiently' (Foucault 1988b, p. 257).

'In *Histoire de la folie* the question was how and why, at a given moment, madness was problematized through a certain institutional practice and a certain apparatus of knowledge. Similarly, in *Surveillier et punir* [*Discipline and Punish*, 1995/1975], I was trying to analyze the changes in the problematization of the relations between crime and punishment through penal practices and penitentiary institutions in the late eighteenth and early nineteenth centuries.' (Foucault 1988b, p. 257)

A WPR approach also uses 'problematisation' in two ways, but strives to make the different meanings clear. In propositions 1 and 2 (see beginning of this chapter) the term problematisation refers to the way/s in which particular issues are conceived as 'problems', identifying the thinking behind particular forms of rule. In proposition 3, the term means to interrogate, as is made clear in the statement: *It is important to problematise (interrogate) the problematisations on offer in current policies.* The more innovative understanding of the concept, used in propositions 1 and 2, is explored further here.

The fundamental insight generated by this use of the concept 'problematisation' is that, in order to understand the thinking behind forms of rule, we need to see how particular issues are thought about, or problematised. Osborne (1997, p. 174) makes the important observation that 'policy cannot get to work without first problematising its territory'. This idea links back to the assertion in the Introduction that the whole notion of 'policy' rests upon a presumption that policy 'fixes' things. There is an assumption therefore that 'problems' exist and can be identified, and indeed rectified. As Rose and Miller (1992, p. 181; emphasis in original) put it, government by its nature is a *'problematizing* activity'.

Dean and Hindess (1998, p. 9; emphasis added) make explicit the link between governmentality, as a study of different mentalities of rule, and problematisation when they describe a neoliberal 'mentality of rule' as 'a *style of problematisation*, a mode of reasoning that can best be identified by examining problematisations'. A WPR approach takes this basic insight – that problematisations provide an entry point into how rule is thought – but introduces a methodology that encourages a wider application of this argument. It makes the case that *every policy*, by its nature, constitutes a problematisation.

This deviation from the governmentality approach means that, instead of problematisations being 'relatively rare', appearing in the 'specific situations in which the activity of governing comes to be called into question, the moments and the situations in which government becomes a problem' (Dean 1999, p. 27), they are ubiquitous. Because *every policy* constitutes a problematisation, it is fair to say that, in effect, we are governed *through* problematisations rather than through policies. This shift in focus produces a broad field for analysing how rule takes place.

The use of problematisation in a WPR approach is also different from its usage in Foucault and in some other governmentality scholars (e.g. Garland 2001; see Chapter 5) in another respect. For Foucault, that which 'instigates' the process of problematisation has a more material existence than in a WPR approach (see discussion in Rabinow 2003, pp. 18–19), as seen in this quote:

> Actually, for a domain of action, a behavior, to enter the field of thought, it is necessary for a certain number of factors to have made it uncertain, to have made it lose its familiarity, or to have provoked a certain number of difficulties around it. These elements result from social, economic, or political processes. (Foucault 1984, pp. 4–5)

By contrast, in a WPR approach there is no assumption that some set of 'difficulties' sparks a 'response' from governments. Rather, the approach recommends a critical interrogation of *assumed* 'problems'. To repeat a point made elsewhere, this position does not deny that there are troubling conditions that require redress. However, the emphasis is *not* on the nature of those conditions but rather on the shape of the implied 'problems' in specific proposals.

This shift in emphasis from putative conditions that provoke 'responses' to assumed 'problems' creates room for greater contestation around the ways in which policies constitute 'problems'. At no level are policies seen as driven by social change. In addition, true to its poststructuralist premises, no concept or category is accepted as value-free and uncontested. For example, while in Garland (2001, p. 90; see Chapter 5) rising crime rates in the 1980s and 1990s are assumed to be at least part of the reason for increasingly punitive criminal justice practices, in a WPR approach the category 'crime' needs to be recognised as contested. Hence, any talk of 'rising crime rates' must consider what kinds of behaviours are constituted as 'crime' (e.g. street crime) and which are excluded (e.g. crime 'at the top'; Bauman 2000, pp. 40–42). In a WPR understanding, punitive criminal justice practices, therefore, create 'crime' as a specific form of 'problem' that needs to be interrogated, rather than accepted.

A WPR approach elaborates a methodology for interrogating and evaluating problematisations through extracting and scrutinising the problem representations they contain. What is seen as in need of fixing – the 'problem' – can be 'read off' from the plan of action that is proposed. This understanding of the 'problem', which I call a *problem representation*, is the place to start if you wish to understand how an issue is being understood.

This leads us to our second proposition.

PROPOSITION 2: STUDY PROBLEMATISATIONS (THROUGH ANALYSING THE PROBLEM REPRESENTATIONS THEY CONTAIN), RATHER THAN 'PROBLEMS'

The shift in focus from 'problems' to problematisations, and to the problem representations they contain, sharply distinguishes a WPR approach from more conventional forms of policy analysis. Several authors (Colebatch 1998, 2006; Parsons 1995) have usefully surveyed the full range of approaches to policy studies and policy analysis. Colebatch (2006, pp. 6–10) identifies three perspectives, which he calls 'authorized choice', 'structured interaction' and 'social construction':

- **'Authorized choice'**, described elsewhere as **'comprehensive rationalism'** (Bacchi 1999, pp. 22–24), conceives of policies as technical 'fixes' to readily identifiable problems. This approach sees policy as reactive in the sense described in the introduction to Chapter 1.
- **'Structured interaction'**, described elsewhere as **'political rationalism'** (Bacchi 1999, pp. 24–31), stresses the many and competing voices involved in defining policy 'problems' and deciding policy directions. The analyst, in this view, needs to offer advice about what is do-able, given political constraints, to move in what is described as a desirable direction.
- **Social construction**, according to Colebatch (2006, p. 9), directs attention to the ways in which participants in the policy process 'make sense of the world' and to 'the organisational forms and social practices through which governing is accomplished'. His position here appears to be closer to what is described as 'constructivism'. A distinction can be drawn

between *constructivism* that sees the person as 'actively engaged in the creation of their own phenomenal world' and social *constructionism*, which emphasises the extent to which our understandings of the world are the product of social forces (Burr 2003, p. 19–20). The latter position, favoured by a WPR approach, emphasises the role of socio-political processes on shaping forms of knowledge (Phillips 1995, p. 8).

Colebatch (2006, p. 16) makes the important point that what gets considered as policy work depends on one's conceptual framework. Paradigms matter in how policy is conceived. As Guba (1990, p.18) explains, a paradigm consists of one's ontology (what we believe about the nature of things), one's epistemology (what we think we can know about the nature of things), and one's methodology (how we think we can go about finding out about the nature of things). He distinguishes among four paradigms: positivist, post-positivist, critical theory and constructivist. Denzin and Lincoln (2004, p. 38) develop a more complex map of 'interpretive paradigms', including feminist/Afrocentric, Ethnic, Cultural Studies, Queer Theory and poststructuralist paradigms.

For our purposes some simple distinctions can be drawn (see 'Guide to paradigms in major policy approaches', Chapter 10, for more detail). 'Authorised choice' theorists generally accept that it is a relatively simple matter to diagnose the 'problems' of an age and to offer advice about how to solve them, and are clearly positivist. The values of those offering 'advice' are seen as outside of the process of analysis. While 'structured interactionists' argue that policy analysts need to acknowledge and take heed of their own values, they believe that value disagreements can be worked through rationally. In addition, while structured interactionists are sensitive to the importance of problem *definition*, there is still an assumption that it is clear what a *desirable* direction involves, locating them also within a positivist paradigm. Social constructionist (and constructivist) approaches are diverse (Phillips 1995), but generally accept that knowledge is a human construction. Hence, there is no outside or Archimedean point from which to offer policy recommendations. As post-positivists, constructionists put in question the nature of a policy 'problem'.

WPR draws upon constructionist premises. It challenges the presumption in both 'authorised choice' and 'structured interaction' approaches that governments react to 'problems' that somehow exist in the world separate from the ways in which 'problems' are conceived. Rather, a WPR approach sees governments as active in the creation or production of policy 'problems'.

However, WPR takes a particular turn within social construction theory. It makes the case that, among the many competing constructions of a 'problem' that are possible, governments play a privileged role because their understandings 'stick' – their versions of 'problems' are formed or constituted in the legislation, reports and technologies used to govern. Hence, these versions of 'problems' take on lives of their own. They exist *in the real*.

Recall, there is no suggestion of intentionality or manipulation here. Nor are we talking about 'wicked problems' (Colebatch 2006, pp. 125–6; Rittel & Webber 1973), those that are deemed to be 'intractable' and hence difficult to 'solve'. Rather, 'problems' are constituted (given a shape) in the simple act of making policy. This focus on the political dimension of 'problem' creation makes the approach **poststructuralist**. The primary focus is on 'the textually-unstable and always contestable nature of social reality' (Dumont 1998, p. 229).

According to Colebatch (2006, p. 16), social construction analyses are of academic interest only, with little to offer practitioners (possibly due to his particular understanding of social construction; see above). I beg to differ. While there is no declared interest in producing more *effective* policy, the conviction that how 'problems' are represented matters – that some people are harmed and that some benefit from particular problem representations – means that a WPR approach offers valuable insights into the processes of governing. In addition, the broader scope, incorporating the complex interrelationships between government administration and professionals, between government and the human sciences in the production of governing knowledges, creates a new framework for thinking through the implications of any policy advice offered to government. Indeed, given that policy analysts are themselves often social scientists or kinds of professionals, a WPR approach demands a form of self-scrutiny, or reflexivity (see below), about one's role in governing that should lead to more thoughtful contributions. This reflexivity involves scrutiny of one's own problematisations and the problem representations they contain.

If one's focus is to shift from 'problems' to problematisations and, more specifically, to the problem representations they contain, how is one to proceed? First, we need to be able to identify problem representations. To achieve this goal, a WPR approach picks up and systematises Foucault's suggestion that we focus attention on 'prescriptive texts' or 'practical texts', 'the supposedly minor texts of those who actually made policy and wielded power' (Rabinow 2003, p. 49). In a WPR approach, policies are 'prescriptive' texts since they tell us what to do. As a result, policies and their accompanying methods of implementation provide points of entry to the problematisations and problem representations that require scrutiny.

> 'The domain I will be analyzing is made up of texts written for the purpose of offering rules, opinions, and advice on how to behave as one should: *"practical" texts*, which are themselves objects of a "practice" in that they were designed to be read, learned, reflected upon, and tested out, and they were intended to constitute the eventual framework of everyday conduct.' (Foucault 1986, pp. 12–13; emphasis added)

Importantly, Foucault had a dual focus, as does a WPR approach – the practices on the basis of which problematisations are formed (Question 3) and the thinking that 'guides or justifies' those practices (Question 2):

Problematization doesn't mean representation of a pre-existing object, nor the creation by discourse of an object that doesn't exist. It is the totality of discursive or non-discursive practices that introduces something into the play of true and false and constitutes it as an object for thought (whether in the form of moral reflection, scientific knowledge, political analysis, etc.). (Foucault 1988b, p. 257)

Since Foucault specifies that problematisation 'doesn't mean representation of a pre-existing object', the notion of problem *representation* needs clarification. Representation in a WPR approach is not opposed to the 'real'. As Shapiro (1988, p. xi) says, 'representations do not imitate reality but are the practices through which things take on meaning and value …'. A problem representation therefore is the way in which a particular policy 'problem' is constituted *in the real* (see discussion above).

Problem representations are elaborated in *discourse*. The concept of discourse is notoriously difficult, not least because it means different things in different analytic traditions. In a WPR approach the term 'discourse' does not refer merely to language nor to the tradition of discourse analysis that looks at language usage, including turn-taking (Bacchi 2005; see also Carabine 2001). Rather, discourses are socially produced forms of knowledge that set limits upon what it is possible to think, write or speak about a 'given social object or practice' (McHoul and Grace 1993, p. 31). For example, the ways in which globalisation, human capital and lifelong learning are 'spoken' about creates them as forms of social knowledge that make it difficult to speak outside of the terms of reference they establish for thinking about people and social relations. The point to remember is that these 'knowledges' do not exist apart from the statements that constitute them. In this sense, they are fictions. However, they are powerful fictions due to their commonly accepted status as truth. Calling something a 'discourse' means putting its truth status into question.

There is no suggestion here that everything dissolves into language. Rather, a WPR approach accepts Foucault's (1991c, p. 70) premise that discourses 'form a practice which is articulated upon the other practices'. Discourses accomplish things. They make things happen, most often through their truth status. As Dean (1999, p. 64) says, 'we should not underestimate the role of language in constructing worlds, problems and persons as governable entities'.

Foucault was particularly interested in the discourses (or truth claims), which he called 'discursive formations', associated with the human sciences and the professions (Sawyer 2002, pp. 436–7). These truth claims can be described as 'knowledges', rather than as 'knowledge', to assert their contested status. The role of these knowledges in governing (how rule happens) is a dominant theme in Foucault and in a WPR approach. Question 2 in a WPR approach aims to open up discourses and discursive formations to critical scrutiny by identifying their underlying conceptual logics. Examining binaries, concepts and categories within discourses assists in this task (see Chapter 1).

Youth suicide revisited

In Chapter 1 we had a first look at how the 1995/97 *National Youth Suicide Prevention Strategy* represented the 'problem' of 'youth suicide'. The strategy committed resources to four priority areas:

- ■ $12 million to enhance counselling services
- ■ $3 million to parenting programs
- ■ $2 million to the education and training of professionals
- ■ $1 million for research activities

(Parliament of the Commonwealth of Australia 1997, p. 2)

- • **By examining these expenditures, consider which other knowledges are involved in governing 'youth'.**

Some discourses have greater status than other discourses. These tend to be discourses that are institutionally sanctioned, the products of the institutional (non-discursive) practices that sustain them. For example, we live in a capitalist economy and we have institutions such as the law, education, marriage and family, and the church. Discourses that reinforce the existence and influence of these institutions tend to be discourses of status.

> 'Each society has its régime of truth, its "general politics" of truth: that is, the types of discourse which it accepts and makes function as true; the mechanisms and instances which enable one to distinguish true and false statements, the means by which each is sanctioned; the techniques and procedures accorded value in the acquisition of truth; the status of those who are charged with saying what counts as true' (Foucault 1980a, p. 131).

Foucault (1980b) also emphasised the importance of what he called 'subjugated knowledges', referring to those 'knowledges' less likely to be sanctioned. He identifies two classes of subjugated knowledges: erudite knowledges that have been silenced, and 'indigenous knowledges', that survive at the margins. Erudite knowledges encompass dissenting opinions and theories that are not widely recognised, while 'indigenous knowledges' consist of local beliefs and understandings, and 'unqualified, even directly disqualified knowledges', such as those of the psychiatric patient, the ill person or the delinquent. For Foucault, these knowledges provide points of rupture to challenge conventional 'knowledges'. The purpose of genealogy (see Chapter 1 and below) is to uncover subjugated knowledges and to unite them in order to rediscover the history of struggle and conflict – 'the memory of hostile encounters' (Foucault 1980b, p. 83).

'Let us give the term *genealogy* to the union of erudite knowledge and local memories which allows us to establish a historical knowledge of struggles and to make use of this knowledge tactically today.' (Foucault 1980b, p. 83; emphasis in original)

In order to be politically relevant, analysis of discourse/s in a Foucauldian-influenced approach such as WPR must address 'the conditions of exercise, functioning, of institutionalization of scientific discourses' (Foucault 1991c, p. 65). To this end Foucault directs attention to the set of rules, called the rules of formation, 'which at a given period and for a given society define':

> The limits and forms of *appropriation*. What individuals, what groups or classes have access to a particular kind of discourse? How is the relationship institutionalized between the discourse, speakers and its destined audience? How is the relationship of the discourse to its author indicated and defined? How is struggle for control of discourses conducted between classes, nations, linguistic, cultural or ethnic collectivities? (1991c, p. 60; emphasis in original)

The 'rules of formation' of discursive practices mark the meeting point of discourse 'with the nondiscursive domains of institutions, political events and economic processes' (Bernauer 1992, p. 92), and are explored through Questions 3 and 6 of a WPR approach. There we ask questions about how specific discourses legitimate certain speakers – those who meet certain qualifications (Bernauer 1992, p. 92), and about which statements have institutional force. To understand the emergence of medical discourse, for example, it is necessary to identify the 'political specification of who had the legal right to practice', 'which publications could properly disseminate medical knowledge', and 'which institutions should be created to manage medicine' (McHoul and Grace 1993, p. 54).

Importantly, discourses are not homogeneous but contain internal tensions and contradictions, which leave them susceptible to challenge and reshaping. For Foucault, as for a WPR approach, in the struggle for 'control of discourses' the 'perspective affirmed is that of those who resist' (Simons 1995, p. 91). However, before we can theorise resistance, a task undertaken later in the chapter, we need to examine how power is understood in this form of analysis.

The concept of power in a WPR approach again takes its direction from Foucault. Foucault rather famously talks about power as a positive force, in the sense of making things happen rather than in the sense of something good or laudable. Foucault's intention here is to challenge the conventional way in which power is thought about as preventing people from doing things they may wish to do, or compelling them to do things they may not wish to do. In this conventional understanding of power the individual is conceptualised as separate and independent from the power being exerted. Foucault challenges this conception of the **humanist** individual. He wants to show that, to a considerable extent, who we are, is an *effect* *of power*. Power shapes our conceptions of ourselves and of the world at the very deepest levels. In this sense, power is positive, or productive (of who we are), rather than negative or restrictive. Individuals are a product of power. As a result, it is inappropriate to think about power as a possession, as something that some people have and that others lack. In opposition to this view, Foucault (1980b, p. 98) describes power as something that *circulates*.

'The individual is not to be conceived as a sort of elementary nucleus, a primitive atom, a multiple and inert material on which power comes to fasten or against which it happens to strike, and in so doing subdues or crushes individuals. In fact, it is already one of the prime effects of power that certain bodies, certain gestures, certain discourses, certain desires, come to be identified and constituted as individuals.' (Foucault 1980b, p. 98)

Rose (2000) offers a useful example of this understanding of power. He explores the conception of freedom in democratic liberal regimes. In his interpretation, liberal governance takes place through *producing* political subjects who imagine themselves to be free and who act accordingly.

If power is *productive* rather than *possessed*, we need to study how it operates and what it produces rather than talking about who holds 'it'. Also, since power is not something that is *possessed*, it should be studied 'in its effects rather than its sources and at the margins rather than at the centre' (Gunn 2006, p. 709). Question 3 in a WPR approach focuses on the *operations* of power, on the practices, strategies and technologies by which rule takes place. Question 5 targets the *effects* of power.

To understand the relationship of a WPR approach to other forms of critical social theory, it is useful to locate its position on power in relation to Steven Lukes' well-known typology of three dimensions of power. In Lukes, a one-dimensional view of power is concerned with 'who prevails in cases of decision-making where there is observable conflict' (Lukes 1974, p. 10). For Lukes, battles between political parties or interest groups to determine what gets onto the political agenda reflect this one-dimensional understanding of power. A two-dimensional view directs attention to the way power 'may be, and often is, exercised by confining the scope of decision-making to relatively "safe issues"' (Lukes 1974, p. 18). Here Lukes draws upon the important work of Bachrach and Baratz (1963) who expand the understanding of policy-making processes to include not just what governments do (decisions), but also what they do not do (non-decisions). An example offered earlier noted that, if good public child care is not available (a non-decision), people's lives are significantly affected. Lukes' three-dimensional view of power extends this analysis to consider how power is exerted by influencing, shaping or determining people's wants and desires. This way of exercising power impedes people 'from having grievances by shaping their perceptions, cognitions and preferences in such a way that they accept their role in the existing order of things' (Lukes 1974, pp. 23–24).

This last, three-dimensional understanding of power sounds very much like what Foucault has in mind with his idea of power as productive of individuals, but important differences in perspective need to be identified. Reflecting his Marxist heritage, Lukes (1974, p. 34) talks about 'interests', generally meaning economic interests, as if they are readily identifiable. Lukes (1974, p. 45) also appears to accept the Marxian view of 'false consciousness', which implies that the 'masses', for whatever reason, fail to recognise the 'truth' perceived by (some) Marxist theorists. The conviction that some have 'false' consciousness suggests that some others have 'true' consciousness.

By contrast, in a WPR approach there is no pure outside from which to exercise these judgements; hence, the insistence on the need to subject one's own problem representations to reflexive scrutiny, explained in more detail in the next section. In addition, groups of people, such as classes, are not seen as having innate 'interests', though members of such groups can conduct themselves in ways that benefit themselves or others. Finally, the role of professionals and other experts, including doctors, psychiatrists and social workers, in producing governing knowledges and governable subjects moves a WPR analysis outside of a purely economic mode of analysis. Studying problematisations and problem representations, rather than 'problems', therefore, creates a new agenda for policy analysis. We become immersed in reflections on the complex range of forces that produce us as particular kinds of political and governable subjects. It is therefore imperative that we proceed to ask questions about how that rule takes place, a task pursued in the third and final proposition.

PROPOSITION 3: INTERROGATE EXISTING PROBLEMATISATIONS THROUGH SCRUTINISING THE PREMISES AND EFFECTS OF THE PROBLEM REPRESENTATIONS THEY CONTAIN

WPR is a critical, rather than a descriptive, form of analysis. It involves critical reflection on (i.e. problematisation of) the problem representations identified in public policies. Foucault specifies the nature of this critique: 'A critique does not consist in saying that things aren't good the way they are. It consists in seeing on what type of assumptions, of familiar notions, of established, unexamined ways of thinking the accepted practices are based' (Foucault, 1994, p. 456).

Question 2 of a WPR approach takes up this suggestion. It directs researchers to identify assumptions and presuppositions within identified problem representations in specific policies as a means of exploring the political rationalities that characterise our age. Harris (1999, p. 34) explains that:

> Programmes of government translate political rationalities into actual measures for governing populations: they involve theories, explanations and particular ways of both thinking and doing things … Thus, for example, social security programmes incorporate certain theories about the level of income needed to safeguard against unjustifiable hardship, suppositions about the relationships between equity, redistribution and competition, and notions about work incentive and benefit levels.

Given that this is the case, it follows that it is possible to work backwards, as a WPR methodology suggests, 'reading off' political rationalities from the presuppositions within programmes or policies. As mentioned in Chapter 1, this task lines up with Foucault's archaeological project. Scheurich (1994) usefully explores archaeology as a form of critical policy analysis.

In a WPR approach it is deemed to be inadequate simply to *identify* assumptions and presuppositions (political rationalities) in identified problem representations, however. Rather, they are to be *assessed*. Question 5 invites students and other researchers to 'evaluate' problem representations in policies by their effects. In a WPR approach, as with Foucault, assessing 'effects' involves identifying the implications of problem representations for complex and interconnected power relations, remembering the focus on power as productive. McHoul and Grace (1993, p. 35) usefully explain the connection between discourses, power and effects:

> [I]f discourses don't merely represent 'the real', and if in fact they are part of its production, then which discourse is 'best' can't be decided by comparing it with any real object … Instead discourses (forms of representation) might be tested in terms of how they can actually intervene in real struggles.

As we saw in Chapter 1, a WPR approach offers three ways to 'test' the operation of problem representations in 'real struggles' by examining:

■ discursive effects: the limits imposed on what can be said or thought;
■ subjectification effects: how subjects are constituted within problem representations; and
■ lived effects: the material impact of problem representations on bodies and lives.

The first of these effects — discursive effects — rests on the proposition that the assumptions and presuppositions identified in Question 2 close off particular ways of thinking, particular avenues for exploring social relations. Clearly, if a problem representation leaves the impression that it is possible to think of a situation in only one way, there could well be important dimensions of an issue that are excluded or unexplored. A WPR approach invites students and other researchers to speculate about other possible ways of representing 'problems' as a means to exploring the silences in identified problem representations (Question 4). Close attention to the role of discourses in constraining ways of thinking is crucial here.

Mungullah 'Community Revitalisation' Shared Responsibility Agreement

'Date: 1 January 2005

Shared Responsibility Agreements are agreements between governments and Indigenous communities to provide discretionary funding in return for community obligations. The new arrangements developed from an initiative of the Council of Australian Governments and replace the previous ATSIC [Aboriginal and Torres Strait Islander Commission] system of funding ...

The Commonwealth Government has committed between $657, 300 (Factsheet 2005) and $727, 310 (Indigenous Portal, 2007) towards the planning and construction of the new facilities [community hall, recreational facilities] ...

The Mungullah community will be involved in the construction of the Community Hall, where local Community Development Employment Projects (CDEP) will provide labour. A "no school, no play" policy will be enforced by the community to encourage school attendance. The community will conduct monthly events to promote healthy lifestyles, and agree to support the events held at the facilities.' (Australian Government 2005)

- **What is the 'problem' of low school attendance of Aboriginal children represented to be in Shared Responsibility Agreements?**

- **Do you see any silences?**

For this Activity see de Plevitz 2006.

The second kind of effects – subjectification effects – involves how subjects are constituted in problem representations. It builds upon Foucault's insights into 'discoursing subjects', subjectification and subject-positions. As noted above, a key element of Foucault's conception of social relations is his challenge to conventional Western understandings of the humanist individual as self-contained and autonomous.

'[T]here are not on the one hand inert discourses, which are already more than half-dead, and on the other hand, an all-powerful subject which manipulates them, overturns them, renews them; but [that] discoursing subjects form a part of the discursive field ... Discourse is not a place into which subjectivity irrupts; it is a space of differentiated subject-positions and subject-functions.' (Foucault 1991c, p. 58)

Poststructuralist discourse psychologists develop the concepts of subjectification and subject-positions in useful ways (Burr 2003). Criticising conventional social psychology for its focus on internal psychic structures and processes, as if these inhere within individuals, these scholars direct attention to the shaping or constitutive impact of discourses. In this vein Davies (1994) elaborates the political situation of subjects operating within a society suffused by discourses that define their very being.

Along similar lines a WPR approach works from the premise that the discursive elaboration of problem representations constitutes political subjects of particular types, and that how this occurs has political ramifications – stigmatising some, exonerating others, and keeping change within limits. For example, the stigmatising of 'problem gamblers' in much public policy detracts attention from widespread cultural endorsement of gambling and the tax benefits that accrue to governments (see Chapter 4).

Examining subjectification effects is challenging. It requires close attention to how the 'problem' is represented in particular policies, how those represented to be 'troublesome' are described, and how those so targeted might absorb, or challenge, that message.

Here it is important to remember that regimes of governance do not *determine* forms of subjectivity; they *elicit* them (Dean 1999, p. 32). In addition, strategies and practices initiated from 'below', for example, by Indigenous peoples, are themselves constitutive 'rather than merely resistant or adaptive to governmental programmes in state or professional agencies' (Petersen 2003, p. 198). Hence, it is possible to accept that we as political subjects are constituted within discourses while retaining a space for political 'agency', an issue pursued later in this chapter.

> '[A] governmental analytics invites readers to think about individual subjects as being produced in specific social policy practices, for example, as worker-citizens in workfare programs, as parent-citizens in child and family services or consumer-citizens in a managerial and marketised mixed economy of welfare' (Marston and McDonald 2006, p. 3).

Social Responsibility Agreements revisited

In the above Activity the task was to identify silences in the problem representation in the Mungullah Shared Responsibility Agreement of 2005. The Mungullah agreement specified 'no school, no play', tying the provision of funds for sports facilities to school attendance. A number of similar Agreements specify similar sorts of conditional arrangements, e.g. 'no school, no pool'; 'no school, no scouts' (de Plevitz 2006).

- **Consider how Social Responsibility Agreements constitute the subjectivity of participating Aboriginal people.**

- **Consider forms of strategy 'from below' that would constitute different subjectivities or subject positions.**

Discourse analytic approaches tend to neglect the impact of discourses on how people live their lives on a day-to-day basis, and on how non-discursive factors interact with discourses. The notion of 'lived effects' – our third kind of effects – provides a corrective here, directing attention to the material impact of problem representations. Drawing upon feminist body theory (Beasley and Bacchi 2007; Pillow 2003), there is a particular focus on the 'lived materiality' of subjectivity (Pullen and Tyler 2007, p. 9).

While Foucault identified the 'body' as 'an object-effect of discursive practices' (Shapiro 1992, p. 16) and biopolitics as a dominant mode of governing, in his earlier work there is at times an over-reliance on discourse as an analytic lens. For example, his suggestion in 1977 that women come to think about rape as like shoving 'a fist in someone's mouth' (Foucault 1988a in Plaza 1980, p. 31) pays insufficient attention to the shaping influence of non-discursive factors, such as the differential social location of women and men, on one's embodied experience. On this issue, the differential social value and significance accorded female and male bodies cannot help but have marked effects on women's and men's 'consciousness' (Gatens 1995, p. 104).

On the other side, the discursive elaboration of problem representations produces real consequences in living arrangements. For example, if welfare is constituted a 'hand-out' rather than a right, the amounts distributed as welfare will be affected, posing real life and death consequences for recipients (Dean 2006).

The kind of assessment of effects offered in a WPR approach is clearly contentious and gives a whole new meaning to policy 'evaluation'. There is no calculus offered, no cost-benefit analysis, no balance sheet. Rather, students and other researchers are invited to engage in political conversation about where particular problem representations have led and are likely to lead. Those problem representations that are held to produce deleterious consequences (rewarding some at the expense of others) are to be rethought. In order for rethinking to occur, their current status as the 'truth' must be questioned. That is, we need to know that an identified problem representation is not the only way to think about an issue. Here, *genealogy* offers a way forward. By tracing the practices and processes that have produced a problem representation (Question 3) it becomes possible to see that things could have been different. The objective is to recover 'countless lost **events**' (Foucault 1977, p. 155 in Dumont 1998, p. 222) in order to destabilise current taken-for-granted ways of conceiving 'problems'. The way in which abortion *became* a legal and moral 'problem' in nineteenth-century Britain provides an example (see Chapter 1).

In genealogy, attention is directed to the power relations that allowed and allow particular problem representations to emerge and gain status. Whereas archaeology (Question 2) fleshes out the forms of problematisation through which an issue is thought, genealogy (Question 3) 'studies the wider system of practices out of which such problematizations emerge' (Bernauer 1992, p. 158). By de-inevitablising problem representations, genealogy provides a crucial counterbalance to the possible tendency in some governmentality studies to see political rationalities as determinative (see O'Malley 2001, p. 19).

Alongside genealogy, it is possible to employ cross-cultural comparisons to destabilise identified problem representations. That is, it is useful to see if 'problems' are represented differently in different cultural contexts. RSI is offered in Chapter 1 as an example where it is useful to ask – how has Australia come to recognise a form of injury that has proved to be invisible in the United States?

This kind of question is uncommon in conventional comparative public policy studies where there tends to be a focus on measurement (e.g. unemployment rates, female employment rates, rates of defence spending, and so on), and speculation about why differences occur – for example, why one country rather than another engages more women in waged labour. By contrast a WPR approach would subject such selected indicators of 'success' to scrutiny, asking how they represent specific 'problems'. Asking this kind of question opens up a different kind of inquiry into how governing takes place, a form of inquiry that makes it possible to identify similarities in modes of governance across borders ('travelling ideas'), while paying attention to contextual factors that make a difference. As Popkewitz and Brennan (1998, p. 12) describe, this re-conception 'shifts attention from notions of geographically bound contexts that develop in chronological sequences to notions of regions bound by a discursive "field" and uneven time dimensions'.

A note on methodology needs to be made here. Both genealogical and cross-cultural studies of the kind recommended here require long detailed records of decision-making, together with the identification of specific institutional developments that support particular ways of seeing (problematisations). In a book of this sort, it is possible only to suggest the forms of questions and kinds of areas that require closer scrutiny should you decide that such a study is necessary to your analytic project. This point will be repeated at places in the text where genealogical and cross-cultural studies are recommended. For now, we need to address directly the kind of political vision that inspires a WPR approach to policy analysis.

Politics and explanation

A WPR approach has an explicitly normative agenda. It presumes that some problem representations benefit the members of some groups at the expense of others. It also takes the side of those who are harmed. The goal is to intervene to challenge problem representations that have these deleterious effects, and to suggest that issues could be thought about in ways that might avoid at least some of these effects. However, there is no presumption that patterns of harm and benefit are predictable and even in their distribution. The idea that capitalism or patriarchy explains everything we need to know about exploitation and oppression is rejected. Social relations are more complex than this. Hence, we need a close analysis of how problems are represented to identify places where it may be possible to intervene in order to reduce deleterious effects.

We discussed above Foucault's notion of the 'discoursing subject' and how this idea poses challenges for thinking about political 'agency'. The question that arises is – if we are constituted *within* discourse, if 'governing is concerned with the fabrication of certain kinds of subjectivity and identity' (Dean 1999, p. 67), where is the space for critical judgement? Poststructuralist psychologists offer some assistance here. Centrally, political subjects are directed to scrutinise their own discursive positioning. As Davies (1994, p. 45–6) puts it, 'The viewer must catch themselves in the act of seeing in particular ways'. Detailed introspection, a 'consciousness turned upon itself', becomes required political practice. This is what is meant by reflexivity. A WPR approach builds reflexivity into the analysis by directing students and other researchers to apply the set of questions in the approach to their own problematisations and the problem representations they contain. Engaging closely with a wide variety of diverse perspectives and experiences increases the likelihood of identifying limitations within one's own problem representations (see Bacchi 2009).

Going further, a WPR approach creates the opportunity to consider how resistance and challenge occur. The whole analysis is geared to distance us from the authority of problem representations judged to have harmful effects, opening them up to critical interrogation, to questioning. The goal is not to identify some extra-discursive reality but to develop strategic interventions 'in humanly-created narrations that try to justify the miseries of the poor' (Dumont 1998, p. 233) and of other outgroups. Question 6 invites reflections on these strategies. It directs attention to the ways in which identified problem representations secure their authority, and to opportunities for disruption. One option is to highlight tensions and contradictions within problem representations that are judged to have harmful consequences. Another is to consider discourses as resources for re-problematisation. Foucault describes discourse as an 'asset', one that 'from the moment of its existence . . . poses the question of power; an asset that is, by nature, the object of a struggle, a political struggle' (Foucault 1972, p. 120).

This idea of discursive resources (or 'assets') builds upon the view of discourses, introduced earlier, as plural, complex and, at times, inconsistent. In this vein, for example, while 'rights' as a concept is part of a Western *epistême,* based on the idea of the autonomous individual, appeals to 'rights' can be raised in response to a specific practice and thus can be directed at suspending or even at altering relations of power. Think, for example, of demands for human rights, including the *right* to housing and the *right* to adequate food (United Nations 1948).

There are resonances here with the idea of strategic framing, an important idea within sociological framework theory (Verloo 2001). However, strategic framing refers to the *intentional* shaping of an argument in order to gain adherents to a particular political position or cause. By contrast, invoking rights as a strategy for change within a WPR approach is *not* seen as a deliberate attempt to sway people to a particular point of view. Rather, it is one position that the discourse of rights makes available. That is, 'strategies of rule create new avenues for action' (Petersen 2003, p. 198) and 'new governmental spaces' (Larner and Craig 2005, p. 421).

> 'But to analyze a discursive formation ... is to weigh the "value" of statements. A value that is not defined by their truth, that is not gauged by the presence of a secret content; but which characterizes their place, their capacity for circulation and exchange, their possibility of transformation, not only in the economy of discourse, but, more generally, in the administration of scarce resources.' (Foucault 1972, p. 120)

Through combining a range of techniques (archaeology, genealogy, cross-cultural comparisons) which destabilise problem representations identified within policies, a WPR approach encourages students and other researchers to question conventional ways of thinking about policy 'problems' and the nature of policy itself. Given the overall intent to reflect on how we are governed, it opens up the possibility to think about how we could be governed differently (see Pavlich 2001). Moreover, because how we are governed shapes who and what we are in certain ways, the approach enables us to think about whether or not this is the way we wish to be. It encourages us to:

> ... question over and over again what is postulated as self-evident, to disturb people's mental habits, the way they do and think things, to dissipate what is familiar and accepted, to reexamine rules and institutions and on the basis of this re-problematization ... to participate in the formation of a political will. (Foucault 1988b, p. 265)

Hence, it is no coincidence that a WPR approach takes the form of a set of questions, rather than endorsing a particular agenda for change. As mentioned in the Introduction, the underlying objective is to offer a new paradigm – 'problem' *questioning* – to challenge the authority currently bestowed on 'problem' *solving*. The overall goal is to create a 'right to the problems' (Deleuze 1994, p. 158), meaning a right to question how 'problems' are thought about rather than simply accepting the shape they are given. This form of intervention is crucial because, as we have seen, a great deal depends on the shape of 'problems', on what they are represented to be.

> 'My position is that it is not up to us to propose. As soon as one "proposes" – one proposes a vocabulary, an ideology, which can only have effects of domination. What we have to present are instruments or tools that people might find useful.' (Foucault 1988a, p. 197)

Summary

The chapter begins with three propositions central to a WPR approach:

1. We are governed through problematisations.

2. We need to study problematisations (through analysing the problem representations they contain), rather than 'problems'.

3. We need to problematise (interrogate) the problematisations on offer through scrutinising the premises and effects of the problem representations they contain.

Each proposition identifies an element of the innovation involved in a WPR approach to policy analysis. The idea that we are governed through problematisations signals an interest in forms of rule including but beyond the state, and involves a study of the thinking behind different forms of rule (governmental rationalities). The insistence that we study problematisations through the problem representations they contain rather than 'problems' puts in question the declared objective of most studies of public policy – to assist governments to solve 'problems'. The call to interrogate the problematisations on offer in current policies indicates a critical intent, a desire to rethink the ways in which we are governed due to concerns and hesitations about the effects of particular forms of rule. We have here a whole new agenda for policy studies. The following chapters explore this agenda through an application of the approach in a range of selected sites.

Questions

1. What is meant by governmentality?

2. What does it mean to say that a WPR approach is interested in how rule takes place including but beyond the state?

3. How did the growth of population influence forms of governance?

4. How is the concept of discourse understood in a WPR approach to policy analysis?

5. What does it mean to say that we are governed through 'knowledges'?

6. What does it mean to challenge the idea of a humanist subject?

7. How can you assess the value of competing problem representations?

8. What strategies are available to 'de-inevitablise' particular problem representations? Why is this considered to be a worthwhile thing to do?

9. Is objective research possible? What does it mean to suggest that researchers need to become reflexive about their research and their research practices?

What's the problem represented to be?
An approach to policy analysis

1. What's the problem (e.g. of 'problem gamblers', 'drug use/abuse', domestic violence, global warming, health inequalities, terrorism, etc.) represented to be in a specific policy? See what the policy proposes and 'read off' the implied 'problem' from this proposal.

2. What presuppositions or assumptions underlie this representation of the 'problem'? This question involves a form of Foucauldian *archaeology*, identifying underlying conceptual logics and political rationalities in specific policies. Identify key concepts, binaries, and categories. Think beyond national and/or cultural boundaries to address this question.

3. How has this representation of the 'problem' come about? This question involves a form of Foucauldian *genealogy*, focusing on the practices and processes that led to the dominance of this problem representation (or of these problem representations).

4. What is left unproblematic in this problem representation? Where are the silences? Can the 'problem' be thought about differently? Cross-cultural comparisons and comparisons of problem representations over time (see Question 3) will be useful here, alongside the discourse analysis conducted in Question 2..

5. What effects are produced by this representation of the problem? Consider three kinds of effects: discursive effects; subjectification effects; lived effects. Include effects due to dividing practices. The following sub-questions will assist here: What is likely to change with this representation of the 'problem'? What is likely to stay the same? Who is likely to benefit from this representation of the 'problem? Who is likely to be harmed? How does the attribution of responsibility for the 'problem' affect those so targeted and the perceptions of the rest of the community about who is to 'blame'?

6. How/where is this representation of the 'problem' produced, disseminated and defended? How could it be questioned, disrupted and replaced? Consider past and current challenges to this representation of the 'problem'. Consider the discursive resources available for re-problematisation.

Apply this list of questions to your own problem representations. This stage of the analysis requires a form of reflexivity, which involves subjecting the grounding assumptions in one's own problem representations to critical scrutiny.

REFERENCES

ABS (Australian Bureau of Statistics) 2007, *3301.0 Births 2006*.

AUSTRALIAN GOVERNMENT 2005, Mungullah 'Community Revitalisation' Shared Responsibility Agreement, Indigenous Portal, <www.atns.net.au>, accessed 8 July 2008.

BACCHI, C. 1999, *Women, Policy and Politics: The Construction of Policy Problems*, Sage, London.

BACCHI, C. 2005, 'Discourse, Discourse Everywhere: Subject "Agency" in Feminist Discourse Methodology', *Nordic Journal of Women's Studies*, vol. 13, no. 3, pp. 198–209.

BACCHI, C. 2009, 'The Issue of Intentionality in Frame Theory: The Need for Reflexive Framing', in *The Discursive Politics of Gender Equality: Stretching, Bending and Policymaking*, eds E. Lombardo, P. Meier & M. Verloo, Routledge, London.

BACHRACH, P. & BARATZ, M. S. 1963, 'Decisions and Nondecisions: An Analytical Framework', *American Political Science Review*, vol. 57, no. 3, pp. 632–42.

BAUMAN, Z. 2000, 'Social Uses of Law and Order', in *Criminology and Social Theory*, eds D. Garland & R. Sparks, Oxford University Press, Oxford.

BEASLEY, C. & BACCHI, C. 2007, 'Envisaging a New Politics for an Ethical Future: Beyond Trust, Care and Generosity – Towards an Ethic of "Social Flesh"', *Feminist Theory*, vol. 8, no. 3, pp. 279–98.

BERNAUER, J. W. 1992, *Michel Foucault's Force of Flight: Toward an Ethics for Thought*, Humanities Press, New Jersey.

BURR, V. 2003, *Social Constructionism*, 2nd edition, Routledge, London.

CARABINE, J. 2001, 'Unmarried Motherhood 1930–1990: A Genealogical Analysis', in *Discourse as Data: A Guide for Analysis*, eds M. Wetherell, S. Taylor & S. J. Yates, Sage, in Association with The Open University Press, London.

COLEBATCH, H.K. 1998, *Policy*, Open University Press, Buckingham.

COLEBATCH, H.K. 2006, *Beyond the Policy Cycle: The Policy Process in Australia*, Allen & Unwin, Crows Nest.

DAVIES, B. 1994, *Poststructuralist Theory and Classroom Practice*, Deakin University, Geelong.

DEAN, M. 1999, *Governmentality: Power and Rule in Modern Society*, Sage, London.

DEAN, M. 2006, 'Governmentality and Powers of Life and Death', in *Analysing Social Policy: A Governmental Approach*, eds G. Marston & C. McDonald, Edward Elgar, Cheltenham, UK.

DEAN, M. & HINDESS, B. 1998, *Governing Australia: Studies in Contemporary Rationalities of Government*, Cambridge University Press, Cambridge.

DELEUZE, G. 1994, *Difference and Repetition*, Trans. P. Patton, Columbia University Press, New York.

DENZIN, N. K. & LINCOLN, Y. S. 2004, 'Methodological Issues in the Study of Social Problems', in *Handbook of Social Problems: A Comparative International Perspective*, ed. G. Ritzer, Sage, London.

DE PLEVITZ, L. 2006, 'No School, No Funds: Shared Responsibility Agreements and Indigenous Education', *Indigenous Law Bulletin*, vol. 55, <www.austlii.edu.au>, accessed 7 July 2008

DUMONT, C. 1998, 'The Analytical and Political Utility of Poststructuralism: Considering Affirmative Action', *Canadian Journal of Sociology/Cahiers canadiens de sociologie*, vol. 23, no. 2/3, pp. 217–37.

FOUCAULT, M. 1972, *The Archaeology of Knowledge*, Trans. A. M. Sheridan Smith, Pantheon, New York.

FOUCAULT, M. 1977, 'Nietzsche, genealogy, history', in *Language, Counter-Memory, Practice: Selected Essays and Interviews*, ed. D. F. Bouchard, Cornell University Press, Ithaca.

FOUCAULT, M. 1979, *The History of Sexuality, Volume I, An Introduction*, Trans. R. Hurley, Allen Lane, London.

FOUCAULT, M. 1980a [1977], 'Truth and Power', in *Power/Knowledge: Selected Interviews and Other Writings 1972–1977/Michel Foucault*, ed. C. Gordon, Trans. C. Gordon & others, Harvester Press, Sussex.

FOUCAULT, M. 1980b [1976], 'Two Lectures', in *Power/Knowledge: Selected Interviews and Other Writings 1972–77/Michel Foucault*, ed. C. Gordon, Trans. C. Gordon & others, Harvester Press, Sussex.

FOUCAULT, M. 1982, 'The Subject and Power', in *Michel Foucault: Beyond Structuralism and Hermeneutics*, 2nd edition, eds H. Dreyfus & P. Rabinow, University of Chicago Press, Chicago.

FOUCAULT, M. 1984, 'Polemics, Politics and Problematizations', based on an interview conducted by P. Rabinow, Trans. L. Davis, in *Essential Works of Foucault, Vol. 1: Ethics*, New Press, New York, <www.foucault.info/foucault/interview.html>, accessed 9 August 2008.

FOUCAULT, M. 1986 [1984], *The Use of Pleasure. The History of Sexuality*, Volume 2, Trans. R. Hurley, Viking Press, London.

FOUCAULT, M. 1988a [1977] 'Confinement, Psychiatry, Prison', in *Michel Foucault: Politics, Philosophy, Culture: Interviews and Other Writings, 1977–1984*, ed. L. D. Kritzman, Trans. A. Sheridan & others, Routledge, New York.

FOUCAULT, M. 1988b [1984], 'The Concern for Truth', in *Michel Foucault: Politics, Philosophy, Culture. Interviews and Other Writings, 1977–1984*, ed. L. D. Kritzman, Trans. A. Sheridan, Routledge, London.

FOUCAULT, M. 1991a [1980], 'Questions of Method', in *The Foucault Effect: Studies in Governmentality*, eds G. Burchell, C. Gordon & P. Miller, University of Chicago Press, Chicago.

FOUCAULT, M. 1991b [1978], 'Governmentality', in *The Foucault Effect: Studies in Governmentality*, eds G. Burchell, C. Gordon & P. Miller, University of Chicago Press, Chicago.

FOUCAULT, M. 1991c [1968], 'Politics and the Study of Discourse' in *The Foucault Effect: Studies in Governmentality*, eds G. Burchell, C. Gordon & P. Miller, University of Chicago Press, Chicago.

FOUCAULT, M. 1994 [1981], 'So is it Important to Think?', in *Power: Essential Works of Foucault 1954–1984*, vol. 3, ed. J. D. Faubion, Trans. R. Hurley & others, Penguin, London.

FOUCAULT, M. 1995 [1975], *Discipline and Punish: The Birth of the Prison*, Vintage, New York.

FOUCAULT, M. 1997a [1979], 'The Birth of Biopolitics', in *Michel Foucault: Ethics, Subjectivity and Truth*, ed. P. Rabinow, The Free Press, New York.

FOUCAULT, M. 1997b, *The Essential Works 1954–1984, vol.1, Ethics, Subjectivity and Truth*, ed. P. Rabinow, The New Press, New York.

FOUCAULT, M. 2006 [1961], *History of Madness*, Routledge, New York.

FREIRE, P. 1972, *Pedagogy of the Oppressed*, Penguin Books, New York.

GARLAND, D. 2001, *The Culture of Control: Crime and Social Order in Contemporary Society*, University of Chicago Press, Chicago.

GATENS, M. 1995, *Imaginary Bodies: Ethics, Power and Corporeality*, Routledge, London.

GUBA, E. C. 1990, 'The Alternative Paradigm Dialog', in *The Paradigm Dialog*, ed. E. Guba, Sage, London.

GUNN, S. 2006, 'From Hegemony to Governmentality: Changing Perceptions of Power in Social History', *Journal of Social History*, vol. 39, no. 3, pp. 705–721.

HACKING, I. 1986, 'Making up People', in *Reconstructing Individualism: Autonomy, Individuality and the Self in Western Thought*, eds T. Heller & C. Brooke-Rose, Stanford University Press, Stanford, California.

HARRIS, P. 1999, 'Public Welfare and Liberal Governance' in *Poststructuralism, Citizenship and Social Policy*, eds A. Petersen, I. Barns, J. Dudley & P. Harris, Routledge, London.

KRITZMAN, L. D. ed. 1990, *Michel Foucault: Politics, Philosophy, Culture: Interviews and Other Writings, 1977–1984*, Trans. A. Sheridan & others, Routledge, New York.

LARNER, W.& CRAIG, D. 2005, 'After Neoliberalism? Community Activism and Local Partnerships in Aotearoa New Zealand', *Antipode*, vol. 37, no. 3, pp. 402–424.

LUKES, S. 1974, *Power: A Radical View*, Macmillan, London.

MARCUSSEN, M. & TORFING, J. 2006, *Democratic Network Governance in Europe*, Palgrave Macmillan, Houndmills.

MARSTON, G. & MCDONALD, C. 2006, 'Introduction: Reframing Social Policy Analysis' in *Analysing Social Policy: A Governmental Approach*, eds G. Marston & C. McDonald, Edward Elgar, Cheltenham, UK.

MCHOUL, A. & GRACE, W. 1993, *A Foucault Primer: Discourse, Power and the Subject*, Melbourne University Press, Melbourne.

MILLER, P. & ROSE, N. 1990, 'Governing Economic Life', *Economy and Society*, vol.19, no. 1, pp. 1–31.

O'MALLEY, P. 2001, 'Genealogy, Systematisation and Resistance in "Advanced Liberalism"', in *Rethinking Law, Society and Governance: Foucault's Bequest*, eds G. Wickham & G. Pavlich, Hart Publishing, Portland, Oregon.

OSBORNE, T. 1997, 'On Health and Statecraft' in *Foucault, Health and Medicine*, eds A. Petersen & R. Bunton, Routledge, London.

PARLIAMENT OF THE COMMONWEALTH OF AUSTRALIA 1997, House of Representatives Standing Committee on Family and Community Affairs, *Aspects of Youth Suicide: Summary Report of a Seminar*, May, <www.aph.gov.au>, accessed 14 August 2007.

PARSONS, W. 1995, *Public Policy: An Introduction to the Theory and Practice of Policy Analysis*, Edward Elgar, Aldershot, UK.

PAVLICH, G. 2001 'The Art of Critique or How Not to be Governed Thus', in *Rethinking Law, Society and Governance: Foucault's Bequest*, eds G. Wickham & G. Pavlich, Hart Publishing, Oregon.

PETERSEN, A. 2003, 'Governmentality, Critical Scholarship, and the Medical Humanities', *Journal of Medical Humanities*, vol. 24, no. 3/4, pp. 187–201.

PHILLIPS, D. C. 1995, 'The Good, the Bad, and the Ugly: The Many Faces of Constructivism', *Educational Researcher*, vol. 24, no. 7, pp. 5–12.

PILLOW, W. S. 2003, 'Bodies are Dangerous: Using Feminist Genealogy as Policy Studies Methodology', *Journal of Educational Policy*, vol. 18, no. 2, pp. 145–60.

PLAZA, M. 1980, 'Our Costs and their Benefits', *m/f: a feminist journal*, vol. 4, pp. 28–39.

POPKEWITZ, T. S. & BRENNAN, M. 1998, 'Restructuring of Social and Political Theory in Education: Foucault and a Social Epistemology of School Practices', in *Foucault's Challenge: Discourse, Knowledge, and Power in Education*, eds T. S. Popkewitz & M. Brennan, Teachers College, Columbia University, New York.

PULLEN, A. & TYLER, M. 2007, 'Crafting/Grafting the Gendered Self: Labouring Selves as Situated, Multiple and Corporeal', paper presented at the 5th international interdisciplinary Gender, Work and Organization Conference, 27–29 June 2007, Keele University, Staffordshire, <www.genderportal.unisg.ch>, accessed 8 July 2008.

RABINOW, P. 2003, *Anthropos Today: Reflections on Modern Equipment*, Princeton University Press, Princeton.

RITTEL, H. & WEBBER, M. 1973, 'Dilemmas in a General Theory of Planning', *Policy Sciences*, vol. 4, pp. 155–69, Elsevier Scientific Publishing Company, Amsterdam.

ROSE, N. S. 2000, *Powers of Freedom: Reframing Political Thought*, 1st edition 1999, Cambridge University Press, Cambridge, UK.

ROSE, N. & MILLER, P. 1992, 'Political Power Beyond the State: Problematics of Government', *The British Journal of Sociology*, vol. 43, no. 2, pp. 173–205.

SAWYER, R. KEITH 2002, 'A Discourse on Discourse: An Archaeological History of an Intellectual Concept', *Cultural Studies*, vol. 16, no. 3, pp. 433–56.

SCHEURICH, J. J. 1994, 'Policy Archaeology: A New Policy Studies Methodology', *Journal of Education Policy*, vol. 9, no. 4, pp. 297–316.

SHAPIRO, M. J. 1981, *Language and Political Understanding: The Politics of Discursive Practices*, Yale University Press, New Haven & London.

SHAPIRO, M. J. 1988, *The Politics of Representation: Writing Practices in Biography, Photography and Policy Analysis*, University of Wisconsin Press, Madison.

SHAPIRO, M. J. 1992, *Reading the Postmodern Polity: Political Theory as Textual Practice*, University of Minnesota Press, Minneapolis.

SIMONS, J. 1995, *Foucault and the Political*, Routledge, New York.

SNYDER, R. 2001, *Politics after Neoliberalism: Reregulation in Mexico*, Cambridge University Press, Cambridge, UK.

UNITED NATIONS 1948, *Charter for Human Rights*, General Assembly Resolution, 217A (III), <www.un.org/Overview/rights.html>, accessed 17 August 2008.

VERLOO, M. 2001, 'Another Velvet Revolution? Gender Mainstreaming and the Politics of Implementation', *IWM Working Paper No. 5*, IWM, Vienna.

WALTERS, M. & HAAHR, J. H. 2005, *Governing Europe: Discourse, Governmentality and European Integration*, Routledge, New York.

Welfare, 'youth' and unemployment

Chapter 3

GETTING STARTED

To apply a WPR approach to policy analysis, start by identifying a policy, program or policy proposal that you wish to study. The raw material for the analysis can consist of policy statements, public addresses, parliamentary debates, government reports, pieces of legislation, court decisions and the like. These become our 'practical texts' (see Chapter 2; Foucault 1986, pp. 11–12), the entry-points for analysis.

The issue of text selection is discussed in Chapter 1. There it is mentioned that the task of text selection is itself an interpretive exercise. You will probably select a policy or program that interests you because it is relevant to your life at this point in time, or because it is attracting public debate. Either reason contains interpretive implications. If a policy interests you, reflect on why that is the case and how your reasons influence your views about the subject. If you select a policy because it is attracting public debate, reflect on the sorts of related issues that are relevant and on how the issue is represented in the media. The goal in both cases is to flesh out the context for your interpretive starting point.

A policy tends to be associated with a policy area, for example, with 'welfare policy' or 'education policy'. More broadly, policies tend to be thought about as social policies or as economic policies. The goal of a WPR approach is to challenge boundaries where they exist, and to question the way policy 'problems' are often made to appear as discrete and self-evident. Hence, in your analysis, think of links (connections) between your selected policy and other policy areas. If you have chosen a policy commonly described as within the realm of 'social' policy, think also of the important and necessary links with economic decision-making. Finally, keep in mind related economic and political developments within the state, country or municipality upon which you are focusing, as well as relevant international developments.

Once you have selected a policy, identify and collect other documents associated with the policy and with the techniques, or mechanisms, developed to implement it. Politicians' statements can also be included as part of the relevant information, though they need to be treated with care. Remember that we are not interested in such comments as attempts to *persuade* (as rhetoric). Rather, the objective is to identify the deep-seated conceptual premises that make such comments possible.

The task is then to apply the full set of questions in a WPR approach (see Chapter 1 and the expanded version of the questions at the end of Chapter 2), including the injunction to apply the questions to your own problem representations. At the end, supported by the analysis you have performed, you can offer your assessment of the policy, including possible suggestions for change.

QUESTION 1: WHAT'S THE PROBLEM REPRESENTED TO BE?

Work for the Dole Legislation (1997)

As a way into the broad topic of welfare, 'youth' and unemployment, our 'practical text' is the 1997 Work for the Dole legislation. On 19 March 1997 the then Minister for Schools, Vocational Education and Training in the Howard-led Coalition government, Dr David Kemp, introduced the legislative framework for the Work for the Dole initiative. He introduced a *Social Security Legislation Amendment (Work for the Dole) Bill 1997 (Cth)* that amended the *Social Security Act 1991 (Cth)* (Parliament of Australia 1991) to:

- remove provisions preventing a person from being required to Work for the Dole;
- establish a maximum number of hours of work for the dole per fortnight;
- allow participants to receive an extra $10 a week to cover extra costs (Kemp 1997).

Recall that a WPR approach begins by examining what is proposed as a change and working backwards to see how that constitutes the problem. In this case provisions are removed that prevent a person from being required to work for the dole (unemployment benefit). Hence, the problem is constituted to be the ability to access unemployment benefits *without* being required to work. Remember that asking Question 1 is a clarification exercise. You can expect the answer to Question 1 to be fairly straightforward.

Importantly, the Bill stipulated that eligible participants will be those aged between 18 and 24 who have been unemployed for at least six months and who are not in case management or an employment training program. The scheme initially included scope for older participants. Some places were made available for older unemployed people in 1998. From 1 July 2002 the scheme included people aged 35 to 39, and involvement was optional for 'job seekers' aged 40 to 49 (Yeend 2004).

Related statements and policy documents provide pointers to the rationales (governmental rationalities) for the policy, preparing us for Question 2.

When launching the Work for the Dole (WFTD) initiative, Minister Kemp (1997) declared:

> It will help break the *cycle of despair* experienced by thousands of young Australians who have been unemployed for many months or years. They will now be able to make a *valuable* contribution to their community through a *worthwhile* work experience. It will build up their *self esteem* and help establish a *work ethic*. (emphasis added)

The targeted age group in the initial WFTD Bill creates the 'problem' of unemployment among young people (aged 18 to 24) as a specific 'problem'. Recall that problem representations tend to nest one within the other, making it necessary to ask 'what's the problem represented to be?' over and over again (on 'nesting', see Chapter 1). So, it becomes necessary to ask – what's the 'problem' of *youth* unemployment represented to be? We explore this question in due course.

A 1999 Request for Public Submissions by the Government's Reference Group on Welfare Reform makes it possible to delve more deeply into the broader problem representation produced in the *Work for the Dole Bill*. The preamble reads:

> The Federal Government has announced a review of the welfare system to find ways of assisting *people who are disadvantaged* that strike a better balance between its ongoing commitment to maintain a strong safety net and its responsibility to develop policies and strategies allowing all Australians to participate fully in the workforce where they are able. The Government *is concerned that there is an increasing reliance by Australians on welfare*, with around one in five people of workforce age on income support payments. (Department of Family and Community Services 1999; emphasis added)

Six principles are identified to guide reform in the area:

- Maintaining equity, simplicity, transparency, and sustainability;
- Establishing better *incentives* for people receiving social security payments, so that work, education and training are rewarded;
- Creating greater *opportunities* for people to increase *self-reliance* and *capacity-building*, rather than merely providing a *passive* safety net;
- Expecting people on income support to *help themselves* and contribute to society through increased social and economic participation in a framework of *mutual obligation*;
- Providing choices and support for individuals and families with more tailored assistance that focuses on *prevention and early intervention*; and

■ Maintaining the Government's *disciplined approach* to fiscal policy. (Department of Family and Community Services, 1999; emphasis added)

Those making public submissions were asked to frame their advice against terms of reference that stipulated the government's desire to reduce 'welfare dependency'. The Minister for Employment Services at the time, Tony Abbott, announced there would be a 'further tightening of "mutual obligation" requirements on unemployed people'. He continued:

It is the end of unemployment as it has been known over the past two decades ... For people on unemployment benefits, the Government's aim is to replace *long-term idleness at taxpayers' expense* with a *real job* if possible, but *useful activity* in the community if not. (Colebatch and Saltau 1999, p. 3; emphasis added)

In the 1999 Request for Public Submissions (above) the 'problem' is expressly identified as a concern 'that there is an increasing reliance by Australians on welfare'. The Bill itself and supporting ministerial media statements assist us in 'fleshing out' the rationales for, or the thought behind, this concern (many other sources could have assisted in this task). Put briefly, 'welfare dependency' is considered to produce inadequate and dysfunctional adults, and is attributed to the way in which obligation-free welfare acts as a disincentive to undertake work and training.

QUESTION 2: WHAT PRESUPPOSITIONS OR ASSUMPTIONS UNDERLIE THIS REPRESENTATION OF THE 'PROBLEM'?

A specific understanding of social relations underpins WFTD. People are to be encouraged to 'help themselves' and to become 'self-reliant', or independent. The binary independence/dependence structures the discussion, with 'welfare *dependency*' as the negative pole.

Labour of some form is considered a necessary and valuable part of character development. For Kemp (1997; emphasis added) 'young Australians' need to be able to make a 'valuable contribution' to the community through 'a worthwhile *work* experience'. The result will be higher self-esteem and a 'work ethic'. Abbott (Colebatch and Saltau 1999, p. 3) sets 'idleness' against 'useful activity'. Ideally, people are to be given 'real jobs'. The performance of some kind of work commitment remains the focus and the goal.

The conception of the individual revealed here is a familiar one in Western Christian societies where the value of 'hard work' is well entrenched. The reference to 'the Government's *disciplined* approach to fiscal policy' sits comfortably within this framework, also suggesting that welfare policy must fit 'given' fiscal imperatives. More can be learnt about the presuppositions underpinning the problem representation by examining some key words and categories, putting into practice the form of discourse analysis introduced in Chapter 1.

'Youth' and their 'problems'

WFTD initially targeted a specific age category, young people between the ages of 18 and 24. It is not unusual for policies to be age-related. Think, for example, of 'old age pensions'. However, it is necessary to reflect on the meaning and purposes of these categories. Recalling Hacking (1986; see Chapter 1), Rose and Miller (1992, p. 174) reflect on the power to 'make up people': 'Power is not so much a matter of imposing constraints upon citizens as of "making up" citizens capable of bearing a kind of regulated freedom'.

Chapter 2 notes that a WPR approach draws upon social constructionist premises. In this vein, 'youth' needs to be considered a socially constructed category. There is no universal meaning of 'youth'. Rather, the *content* of the category is determined by social, cultural and historical context.

Over forty years ago Philippe Ariès (1962) showed that notions of childhood are historical. That is, our conception of childhood today is very different from previous eras. In the 'Middle Ages', for example, children were thought of as miniature adults. This thinking was reflected in the justice system of the period. Before 1847, in England, the only criminal law that related to a child's age was that a child below the age of seven was deemed to be incapable of committing an offence. Anyone above that age was tried and sentenced as an adult. In 1814 five children under the age of ten were condemned to the death sentence (Jones 1998, p. 14).

The term 'juvenile delinquent' first appeared in a *Report of the Committee Investigating the Causes of the Alarming Increase of Juvenile Delinquency in the Metropolis*, written in London in 1816. A Society for the Reformation of Juvenile Delinquents was established in New York in 1819 (Jones 1998, p. 22).

By the start of the twentieth century psychiatrists had coined the term 'adolescence' to signal a stage of development, a transition between child and adult. Here we can observe the role of 'experts' in category construction, reflecting the broad focus on modes of governing in a WPR approach – including but also moving beyond the state. As Cohen (1988, p. 21) points out, the power to classify is the 'purest of all deposits of professionalism'.

'Adolescence' is constituted to be a 'breathing space' between 'innocent' childhood and the 'realities' of adulthood. Adolescents are seen as *partially* rational beings (Jones 1998), less reliable and less responsible than adults (Wyn and White 1997, p. 13). They are described as risk-takers and rebels, with a sense of crisis around their activities. This characterisation allows 'youth' to be marked out for forms of illiberal treatment that would not be tolerated for adults, an instance of *dividing practices* (see Chapters 1 and 2). Think, for example, of youth wages, curfews, and restrictions on all sorts of activities, including drinking, smoking, and access to X-rated games and DVDs. In these ways the category 'youth' functions to facilitate a wide range of governmental objectives, around policing, education, population and economic concerns.

The category 'youth' operates in public policy as if it referred to a distinct minority group, rather than to a phase of life we all live through. At the same time, there are all sorts of inconsistencies in the way the category is deployed. In Australia in the early twenty-first century, a sixteen-year-old can drive a car but cannot appear in the family court in a case over their residency, and cannot make their wishes known except through an advocate to act in their 'best interests'. An eighteen-year-old can vote, get married and stand for political office. However, under the Commonwealth Government's Youth Allowance program (see Activity below), that same eighteen-year-old is considered to be living at home and dependent upon their parents until age twenty-five.

WFTD was able to target eighteen- to twenty-four-year-olds initially, therefore, because of deep-seated assumptions about the nature and development of the individual. 'Youth unemployment' is constituted a distinct kind of 'problem' because of the conviction that 'character' is formed in these years. Recall Kemp's (1997) concern about developing a 'work ethic', which supports the broader conviction that 'hard work' is good for you. Young people need to work, it is argued, to acquire 'skills', which are portrayed as something individuals can develop to improve their human 'capital'. Some of these underlying presuppositions and assumptions appear again in crime (Chapter 5) and education (Chapter 9) policy. Presuppositions such as the ones identified above can be seen to constitute forms of governmental rationality, the thought behind government (see Chapter 2).

Youth wages

On 16 March 2006 the Full Bench of the Industrial Relations Commission set a minimum wage for South Australia for the first time. The figure was set at $484.40 a week for workers aged over 21. Employees under 17 were given 50 per cent, or $242.20 a week, rising by 10 per cent for each year over 17 (Bildstien 2006).

- **How do 'youth wages' fit into dominant conceptualisations of the individual in Western capitalist societies?**

- **Are youth wages fair?**

For a different perspective on this topic see the Fact Sheet (2004) produced by the Australian Democrats, <www.democrats.org.au/docs/2004/Youth_Wages.pdf>, accessed 10 May 2008.

Youth Allowance

In 2008 young people in Australia can get a Youth Allowance if they meet the following criteria:

- aged 16–24 and studying full-time (or aged 15 if considered independent); or
- aged 16–24 and a full-time Australian Apprentice (or aged 15 if considered independent); or
- aged 16–20 (or aged 15 if considered independent) and 'actively looking for suitable work , or undertaking a combination of approved activities such as part-time work and training, or have a temporary exemption from the activity test (for example, due to illness)'; or
- are under 21 and are 'the principal carer of a dependent child between 6 and 15 years of age if partnered or between 8 and 15 if single, are actively looking for suitable work or working more than 15 hours a week, undertaking an approved activity such as Work for the Dole or have a long- or short-term exemption from the activity test', and
- meet residence requirements. (Australian Government 2008)

- **Consider how 'youth' is represented in the Youth Allowance Guidelines. What presuppositions underlie the criteria?**
- **How does the Youth Allowance fulfil governance objectives?**

Keywords: 'welfare dependency' and 'mutual obligation'

As noted in Chapter 2, particular words and expressions become focal points in political struggles. In Williams' (1983, p. 15) terms, 'keywords' operate in two ways: 'they are significant, binding words in certain activities and their interpretation; they are significant, indicative words in certain forms of thought'. Williams (1983, p. 24) also draws attention to the role played by members of a 'dominant class' and of 'particular professions' in shaping the meanings of key concepts. A WPR approach acknowledges both these dynamics – the embedding of concepts in governmental practices and programs, *and* the uneven power relations involved in shaping the meaning of concepts.

In this vein, 'welfare dependency' and 'mutual obligation' (or 'mutual responsibility') function as keywords in Australian welfare policy. Importantly, these terms echo developments elsewhere. 'Mutual obligation' has its origins in Tony Blair's Third Way politics (Macintyre 2001). 'Welfare dependency' is a topic of concern in many liberal democracies, including the United States (Peck 1998). These terms can be considered to be 'travelling ideas', in the sense introduced in Chapter 2. That is, it is important to identify similarities in modes of governance across borders, while paying attention to contextual factors that make a difference.

The keywords of 'welfare dependency' and 'mutual obligation/responsibility' need to be understood within contemporary debates about the nature of citizenship. As Macintyre (2001, p. 83) explains, the idea of mutual obligation reflects a 'new social contract', 'based on the belief that there can be "no rights without responsibilities"'. Citizens are constituted as needing to *earn* entitlements, rather than as having them 'bestowed' upon them. Contrast is drawn between deserving *active* citizens, and undeserving *passive* citizens, who become overly reliant (dependent) on welfare and who are presumed to become dysfunctional as a result. The reference to a '*passive* safety net' in the 1999 Welfare Group's call for public submissions (see above) needs to be read in this context. At times, in this version of citizenship, rights, as a topic of concern, disappears altogether. The emphasis on citizen responsibilities is an important theme in contemporary welfare governance, pursued under Question 3.

The meaning of citizenship

In the lead-up to the 2007 Federal election, the Howard-led Coalition government introduced a citizenship test, requiring those wanting to become Australian citizens to answer correctly 60% of twenty multiple-choice questions. An accompanying TV advertisement stressed the *responsibilities* and *privileges* accompanying citizenship. Rights were not mentioned. (Stilgherrian 2007)

- **What are the implications of the emphasis on responsibilities and the declining attention to rights in contemporary discussions of citizenship?**

- **Should immigrants sit tests to become citizens?** *(see Chapter 7)*

QUESTION 3: HOW HAS THIS REPRESENTATION OF THE 'PROBLEM' COME ABOUT?

The purpose of Question 3 is to identify key points in the development of contemporary welfare regimes that have led to the identified problem representation of 'welfare dependency'. The point of the exercise is to establish that problem representations have a history (genealogy) and that hence they could be otherwise. The objective is to see particular developments as singular *events*, rather than as part of an evolution towards an inevitable end-point. As discussed in Chapter 2, detailed archival work is required to produce genealogies. Here it is possible only to highlight themes that need pursuing.

Walters (2001) alerts us to the need to think historically about the concept of 'unemployment'. This term, which has a commonsense status in contemporary political debate, he argues, was 'discovered' in the late nineteenth century. Prior to that time, 'the condition of the unemployed was understood either as an issue of overpopulation (Malthus), or ascribed to factors exogenous to the market system (for example, a severe winter, sun spots (Jevons) [i.e. a theory developed in 1875 by the economist Stanley Jevons], Napoleonic wars)' (Walters 2001, p. 63). Several developments were necessary to produce 'unemployment' as a 'systemic and impersonal phenomenon', in other words, to 'create' unemployment as we 'know' it today:

■ the rise of social-survey based research;
■ the development of a more holistic conception of society;
■ the political demands of the labour movement.

Recalling the central importance of population in new ways of thinking about political relationships (Chapter 2), by the beginning of the twentieth century, unemployment – along with other phenomena including suicide, crime and poverty – was being conceptualised at a *social* or group level.

Over the course of the twentieth century in Europe and other Anglo-Saxon countries a regime of *social* governance emerged. A consensus (called the 'Keynesian settlement') – based on the ideas of the economist John Maynard Keynes (1883–1946) and on T. H. Marshall's (1893–1981) defence of *social* rights, alongside civil and political rights – defended the view that the state has a duty to provide citizens with a 'modicum of economic welfare and security' (Marshall 1950, pp. 10–11). Security against risk was socialised (Rose 2000, p. 158). Through national schemes such as compulsory social insurance (unemployment benefit, accident insurance, health and safety legislation), the state assumed responsibility for the management of a whole variety of 'risks'. Within these technologies of government, the individual was constituted a 'social citizen' (Rose 2000, p. 159).

This history needs to be supplemented with recognition that the commitment to 'social rights' has always been hedged with qualifications and with critics. Rose and Miller (1992, p. 196; emphasis added), for example, point out that 'welfarism is a "*responsibilizing*" mode of government'. They use the example of social insurance which, they argue, constituted the insured citizen 'in a definite *moral* form': 'payment would qualify an individual to receive benefits, would draw the distinction between earned and unearned benefits, and teach the lessons of contractual *obligation, thrift and responsibility*.' On these grounds Walters (2004, p. 249) describes social insurance as a 'new kind of dividing practice': 'Only those whose stamped insurance booklets could prove they were "regular" workers would be eligible for insurance benefits when sick or unemployed. The irregular would be weeded out and redistributed to less dignified forms of support.' In this vein, Australia's 1945 Social Security legislation contained a work test – unemployed people were required to be actively looking for work if they were to receive benefits. From this history we can see that WFTD has its antecedents, even within the period considered to be the heyday of social governance in Australia, an example of hybrid governmental forms of rule.

Other kinds of dividing practices were at work. Australia's *Unemployment and Sickness Benefits Act 1944,* for example, excluded 'aboriginal natives of Australia' unless the Department was satisfied that, by reason of their 'character, standard of intelligence and development' – qualities implicitly put in question by their formulation as points of exception to the standard rule – it was reasonable that they receive the benefit (Standing Committee on Legal and Constitutional Affairs 2006, paragraph 3.38). In 1977 the Fraser government in Australia introduced an early version of WFTD in Aboriginal communities. Called equivalent employment grants, benefits were tied to work for local councils (Peterson and Sanders 1998, p. 20).

Keeping this colonial backdrop in mind, in the governing of welfare since the 1980s there have been definite shifts away from the socialising of risk Rose describes above, towards an *individualisation* of risk and a focus on targeted groups of individuals, e.g. families, communities. The same trend is observable in the governing of crime (see Chapter 5). As Rose (2000, p. 247) describes:

> … the collectivization of risk in the social state is being displaced: individuals, families, firms, organizations, communities are, once again, being urged by politicians and others to *take upon themselves* the responsibility for the security of their property and their persons, and that of their own families. This individualization of risk is intensified by the multiplication of perceptions of risk through media reporting, in which crime risks are posed as an inexcusable intrusion on the right of each individual to a life of untroubled lifestyle maximization. (emphasis in original)

The 'problem' of 'welfare dependency' needs to be understood within the context of these developments. Tying welfare benefits to work obligations forms part of a wider trend Lewis describes as the 'social policy of conditionality', in which citizenship rights come to depend upon performance of particular duties. The 'active citizen', who is held to be 'responsible', replaces the older welfare 'notion of universalism and need' (Lewis 2004, p. 25). Within such a politics, says Rose (2000, p. 265), the aim of welfare interventions is 'to encourage and reconstruct self-reliance in both providers and recipients of services'. Rose maintains that this ambition 'is shared by neo-liberals, communitarians, third-sector enthusiasts, and moralistic market democrats such as Clinton and Blair'.

From the 1980s, in Australia, the two major parties have concurred that the 'problem' of unemployment has something to do with the unemployed themselves – that it is due to a 'problem' of (poor) character and/or a lack of 'skills'. This representation of the 'problem' can be 'read off' from the full range of mechanisms introduced to 'manage' unemployment, such as self-help facilities, case management, job-search training, job clubs and training programs. According to Dean, however, there remain important differences in the ways in which these services are to be *delivered*:

> Under the Labor incumbency of 1983–96, the national state introduced case-management approaches to unemployment, and coordinated access to job-search assistance, employment exchange services, training, job-creation schemes and even subsidized jobs. The unemployed person entered into a contract with a national state

that promised access to benefits and services, including the guarantee of a job for the long-term unemployed in return for compliance with the demand that the unemployed practice their 'freedom' in a certain way, that is, as active job seekers . . . In August 1996, the new conservative (Liberal-National) Australian government . . . rescinded the notion of a job guarantee, and 'cashed out' most publicly funded job-creation and job-subsidy schemes. In doing so, the conservative government hoped to establish a fully competitive market in what it calls 'employment placement enterprises'. (Dean 1999, p. 160)

While in both these cases governing is to take place through instilling norms and values (**normalisation**), including those of 'responsibility, initiative, competitiveness and risk-taking, and industrious effort' (Young of Graffam 1992, p. 33 in Dean 1999, p. 162), the specific mode of delivery constitutes target groups quite differently. In effect, in the later Liberal-National focus on *private* placement services, the unemployed are reconstituted as *consumers* (see Question 5 below) — lacking, however, the clout and value normally associated with consumerism.

The genealogy of 'dependency'

The concept of 'welfare dependency' has become ubiquitous in recent years in several Western industrialised democracies. It can be identified as a 'travelling idea' (or more precisely a travelling problem representation), whose journey needs to be tracked. Hence, we can usefully draw upon the insights generated by scholars in other sites.

For example, Fraser and Gordon (1994, p. 310–11) want to understand why debates about poverty and inequality in the United States are being framed in terms of welfare dependency: 'How did the receipt of public assistance become associated with dependency, and why are the connotations of that word in this context so negative?'. To this end they offer what they describe as a *genealogy* of the concept of dependency within the United States, with the declared aim of de-familiarising 'taken-for-granted beliefs in order to render them susceptible to critique and to illuminate present-day conflicts'. Further, they pursue the gender and racial subtexts of this discourse, and the tacit assumptions that underlie it.

A few key points from their analysis include:

- in the dependence/independence binary that underpins the notion of welfare dependency, independence is associated with paid labour, denying the importance of all the other kinds of caring work that people do and need;
- dependency is 'racialised' through associations with slavery;
- medical and psychological discourses play a significant role in constituting dependency as pathology;
- links drawn between welfare dependency and other forms of 'dependency' imply a form

of addiction, as seen in Vice-President Dan Quayle's reference to the 'narcotic of welfare' (Fraser and Gordon 1994, p. 327; see Chapter 4).

Dean (1999), an important governmentality scholar, raises qualms about the sort of genealogy Fraser and Gordon produce. He argues that there are important differences between the kind of 'ideology critique' offered by Fraser and Gordon, and a Foucauldian 'analytics of government' (governmentality). According to Dean (1999, p. 65), in *governmentality* studies, the emphasis is on the ways in which specific terms such as 'dependency' become embedded in government practices – how they 'actually allow practices and programmes of reform to operate' – rather than seeing them as 'components of ideology', whose function is to conceal the reality of class power. Therefore, in Dean's view, it is 'somewhat absurd to imagine that we can do without such categories'. Language, in this interpretation, is not 'a second-order phenomenon shaped by more fundamental forces and conditions', but 'an integral component within ways of doing things' (Dean 1999, p. 64). This kind of understanding, says Dean (1999, p. 65), 'makes it possible to grasp the reason for the longevity and difficulty of abandoning such notions within public policy'.

As mentioned earlier, a WPR approach acknowledges *both* the ways in which concepts are embedded in governmental practices and programs (highlighted by Dean), *and* the uneven power relations involved in shaping the meaning of concepts (recognised by Fraser and Gordon). Genealogy in this understanding is recognised as accomplishing two things:

- it offers a detailed story of how dependence and independence became governmental categories, and the governmental functions they continue to serve; and
- it provides insights into the power relations that affect the success of some problem representations and the defeat of others.

There is recognition, therefore, that some groups have more influence than others in ensuring that particular problem representations 'stick', much in the way that Fraser and Gordon suggest – though, as Dean says, there is no necessary implication that deep structures of class or gender *determine* these outcomes. In subsequent chapters we draw upon this poststructural premise to explore the contested meanings of 'crime' (Chapter 5), 'health' (Chapter 6) and 'knowledge' (Chapter 10).

QUESTION 4: WHAT IS LEFT UNPROBLEMATIC IN THIS REPRESENTATION OF THE 'PROBLEM'? WHERE ARE THE SILENCES? CAN THE 'PROBLEM' BE THOUGHT ABOUT DIFFERENTLY?

As established in Questions 2 and 3, the 'problem' of unemployment is represented to be due to the character and behaviour of the unemployed, who are described as 'passive', as 'despairing' and dependent, lacking self-reliance and self-esteem (see above). Borrowing economic language, the 'problem' here is represented to be a *supply-side* 'problem'. Something is held to be amiss with the nature (character) of the supply of labour (the workers themselves). This is why the unemployed are said to need training and assistance in getting themselves 'job ready'.

What is missing from this analysis? Where are the silences? Directly challenging the emphasis on deficiencies in the (character of) supply, some accounts constitute the 'problem' of unemployment to be a matter of lack of *demand*. According to Mitchell (2003), for example, 'There are simply not enough jobs':

> While governments of all persuasions have spent billions on labour market programs and training schemes to encourage more assiduous and effective search behaviour by the unemployed, the employment outcomes from these programs have been poor. Simply put – you can't search for jobs that aren't there.

Along similar lines, Judith Bessant (1997) offers a close analysis of a range of policy proposals addressed to 'youth unemployment' in the 1990s. She notes the focus on training schemes, which represent the 'problem' to be a lack of skills within young people. According to Bessant, this focus fails to recognise the disintegration of the full-time labour market resulting from decreasing investment in jobs and increasing investment in automation, and the export of 'semi-skilled' and 'unskilled' work to developing economies as part of economic globalisation.

The more recent identification of 'skills shortages' as a pressing 'problem' in Australia, while appearing to make unemployment a 'non-problem', continues to constitute those who have difficulty finding work as the ones lacking 'skill'. On these grounds, employers use 457 visas to bring migrants to Australia, workers who in some accounts can be paid less (see Chapter 7). It is possible, however, to challenge the idea that 'skills' are something sitting outside subjects, waiting to be acquired – that human beings are 'skill-*acquiring*' and 'skill-*possessing*' creatures (Bastalich 2001). For example, Armstrong and Armstrong (1990, p. 124) make the case that the meaning of skill is 'primarily determined by *power*, not by job content' (Armstrong and Armstrong 1990, p. 124; emphasis added). This suggestion puts the whole discourse of skills, a concept foundational to human capital theory and much education theory (Chapters 9 and 10), into question.

The character of unemployment

A 2002 Report prepared for the Federal Employment Minister, Mal Brough, identified 'eight kinds of unemployed': Drivers (16 per cent), Strugglers (8 per cent), Drifters (13 per cent), the Disempowered (15 per cent), the Selective (7 per cent), the Dependent (12 per cent), Cruisers (16 per cent) and the Withdrawn (13 per cent). Brough is reported to have described 'cruisers' as 'the quintessential dole bludgers' and expressed his determination to 'flush out people "holidaying" on benefits' (Crabb 2002).

- **Considering this report as an example of category construction, what is accomplished by dividing up the unemployed into these categories?**
- **Are there silences in this representation of the 'problem'?**

Poverty is barely mentioned (i.e. is a silence) in welfare policy discussions, though one could expect quite reasonably that people without paid work would lack adequate material resources. The 1999 Request for Public Submissions by the government's Reference Group on Welfare Reform, referred to earlier, announced that its review of the welfare system was intended to 'find ways of assisting people who are disadvantaged' (Department of Family and Community Services 1999). This *discourse of disadvantage* requires its own analysis (recall the need to ask 'what's the problem represented to be?' repeatedly), and other scholars (Eveline 1994; Bletsas 2007) can assist with this task.

Eveline (1994), for example, emphasises how a 'disadvantage discourse', by focusing attention on targeted recipients, makes it difficult to recognise and confront the social advantages accrued by other groups. Hence, she is concerned at the dominance of the language of disadvantage in discussions about women's position in society. In her view, the language of women's *disadvantage* makes men's *advantages* invisible.

In the case of welfare, the focus on disadvantage is often matched up with an emphasis on opportunities and choices. In the Public Submission one guiding principle is 'Providing choices and support for individuals and families with more tailored assistance that focuses on prevention and early intervention' (Department of Family and Community Services, 1999). There are important links here with the dominant understanding of equality in Australia as a matter of access to opportunities, i.e. 'equal opportunity' (see Chapter 8). The emphasis on choices and opportunities produces life chances as more or less within an individual's control. The promise of 'assistance' meanwhile positions welfare recipients as needing some form of help or 'uplift', ignoring the range of structural factors that impact on people's lives. The reference to 'prevention' and 'early intervention' likewise targets recipients as requiring 'fixing up' in some way. It should not be assumed, however, that the use of the term 'poverty', rather than 'disadvantage', in and of itself necessarily shifts the focus to structural factors since in many cases poverty is itself deemed to be an outcome determined by poor choices (Bletsas 2007, p. 69; Rose 2000, p. 265).

McDonald (1991, p. 28) is disturbed at the lack of reference to poverty in setting youth wages. He points out that in ABS data collections, 'the young are either dependents or separate income units', and that, in reality, 'the situation is not as clear cut as this since many young people, both students and workers, receive income of their own but are part of the economy of their parents'. He points to the large numbers of young people living in poverty because of assumptions about parental support. There could also be links here with the numbers of young homeless people, though this is not usually how the 'problem' of homelessness is represented (a WPR approach could usefully be applied here as well).

Can the 'problem' be thought about differently?

The kind of analysis performed above opens up new ways to think about the 'problem' of unemployment. Clearly, by identifying what is not problematised in a problem representation – here the problem representation of 'welfare dependency' – you are already beginning to reflect upon conditions and situations that, in your view, ought to be considered part of the discussion but which are excluded. At this stage in the analysis, it is appropriate to direct attention to the deep-seated conceptual presuppositions that structure dominant representations of the 'problem', uncovered in Question 2. Cross-cultural and/or historical accounts can also assist in the task of opening up alternative representations of the 'problem'.

The dependent/independent binary appears in several places in the discussion of unemployment. The concept of 'welfare dependency' with its opposite as 'self-reliance' rests upon this binary (see Department of Community and Family Services 1999). This understanding (or conceptual logic) of 'man' as autonomous and independent is well-entrenched in Western political philosophy (Lloyd 1984). However, in some cultures, more emphasis is placed on interdependence (Turner 1986). Certainly, if we include bodies as part of our analysis, it is clear that at times, for example, at birth, when we are ill, and when we get old, we are *all* dependent on someone else (Beasley and Bacchi 2000). Characterisations of dependency as a negative state, therefore, need to be closely interrogated.

In discussions of unemployment in Australia the concept of 'work' almost invariably refers to 'participation in the workforce' (see Department of Community and Family Services 1999). Abbott (Colebatch and Saltau 1999) referred to 'real jobs' in this context. The idea behind WFTD is that, if 'real jobs' are unavailable, some 'useful activity in the community' will be substituted. The *form* of community contribution commonly mimics 'real jobs', with the goal of 'capacity-building' through the acquisition of 'skills' (see discussion of 'skills' above).

Many kinds of useful social activity remain invisible in this way of conceptualising work. Most obviously the caring activities performed in the main by women are unacknowledged. Important questions about the power to produce certain activities as 'work' and as 'skilful', and other activities as 'not work' or 'unskilled', need to be raised here. Bringing unpaid domestic labour into the analysis also opens up recent discussions about work-life or work-family balance, though again it would be desirable to subject specific proposals made in relation to this issue to a WPR analysis.

QUESTION 5: WHAT EFFECTS ARE PRODUCED BY THIS REPRESENTATION OF THE 'PROBLEM'?

The purpose of Question 5 is to provide a means for assessing policies. As noted elsewhere, the kind of assessment offered in a WPR approach works at a level completely different from evaluations that attempt to measure 'outcomes'. It examines three, overlapping kinds of effects: discursive effects, subjectification effects and lived effects.

Discursive effects

Discursive effects are those created by the limits imposed on what can be thought or said within particular problem representations. Above we saw how the discourse of welfare dependency makes it difficult to think about human *interdependence*. The discourses of 'mutual obligation' and 'mutual responsibility' also close off the opportunity to talk about people's 'rights'. The discursive construction of WFTD leaves the unemployed as the 'problem' due to their presumed lack of abilities ('skills') and/or their assumed character flaws (implied laziness). The dominance of this problem representation makes it difficult to draw attention to living and working conditions that harm some and benefit others.

Subjectification effects

Subjectification effects are those that accompany the ways in which subjects are constituted within particular problem representations. They relate to the subject positions available in relevant discourses. In WFTD welfare recipients are constituted as in deficit, lacking 'skills' that need to be acquired, lacking self-esteem and 'in despair' (see Kemp 1997). They are deemed to need 'incentives ... so that work, education and training are rewarded' (Department of Family and Community Services 1999). In effect, they are seen to be the 'problem'.

In WFTD welfare recipients are located outside the community of tax-payers (Colebatch and Saltau 1999, p. 3), with an implied status of second-class citizens. Those within the community of tax-payers are encouraged to think of welfare recipients as 'other' and as lesser. Dividing practices are at work here.

Subjectification, as noted in Chapter 1, also refers to the ways in which people take up particular understandings as their own. The argument here is that policies do not stand outside us but produce us as particular kinds of subjects through rewarding certain forms of behaviour. Rose (2000, p. 214), for example, describes how current modes of governance produce calculating selves, 'endowed with a range of ways of thinking about, calculating about, predicting and judging their own activities and those of others'. Unsurprisingly, in this climate, a study of young people's attitudes to welfare (Edwards 1995) finds 'a remarkable persistence of the traditional opposition to "welfare" both for themselves and for others, and belief that it might be undeserved'.

While this kind of analysis may appear to create a bleak prognosis for those who wish to see change, it is important to remember that government rationalities *elicit* forms of subjectivity; they do not *determine* them (Dean 1999, p. 32). In addition, strategies and practices initiated from 'below' are themselves constitutive (Petersen 2003, p. 198). This issue is pursued under Question 6.

Lived effects

Lived effects refer to the impact of problem representations on people's embodied existence. In a WPR approach, problem representations are understood as forms of intervention that affect people's day-to-day lives. The initial targeting of young people for WFTD relied upon conceptions of 'youth' as unreliable, dependent and as needing to develop 'skills'. The accompanying requirement to engage in an Activity Test in order to receive a Youth Allowance (see Activity on 'Youth Allowance') shapes the lives of many young people in ways that limit what they are able to do. The failure to perform 'approved activities' can result in financial hardship and poverty.

The constitution of work as participation in the labour force impacts severely on many women. For example, in countries such as the United States and Canada, unemployment benefits are funded from contributions made while in 'productive' labour. Those who make no contributions are given a lower level of benefits, called 'social assistance'. Women who work part-time or who spend most of their lives in the unpaid activity of caring for their families automatically receive the lower benefit, with clear repercussions for their living standards – another example of dividing practices among those in receipt of welfare. In this way problem representations can have life and death effects (Dean 2006).

Once you have examined the three categories of effects identified in a WPR approach, it is important to reflect on the sub-questions associated with this part of the analysis (see expanded list of questions at the end of Chapter 2): What is likely to change with this representation of the 'problem'? What is likely to stay the same? Who is likely to benefit from this representation of the 'problem? Who is likely to be harmed? How does the attribution of responsibility for the 'problem' affect those so targeted and the perceptions of the rest of the community about who is to 'blame'? The objective here is to consider the impact of problem representations on fundamental social relations.

Single parents' pensions

In 2005 the Federal Howard-led Coalition introduced legislation which put in place Parenting Payment Activity Agreements. Under these Agreements, sole parents must look for at least 15 hours of work a week once their child turns six (see Australian Government 2005, Schedule 4, for details).

- **What is the problem of single parents'/mothers' pensions represented to be in this legislation?**
- **How is work understood in this policy?**
- **Are there silences?**
- **What effects (discursive, subjectification, lived) accompany this representation of the 'problem'?**

For this Activity see Gray and Collins 2007, and Carabine 2001.

The identified problem representation of 'welfare dependency' marks the unemployed as responsible for their situation. A result is the stigmatising of this group. The power relations that produce these effects – and often also the economic policies that might otherwise be argued to create the conditions generating unemployment in particular labour fields – remain invisible. Substantive changes in the social relations of employment are unlikely.

QUESTION 6: HOW/WHERE IS THIS REPRESENTATION OF THE 'PROBLEM' PRODUCED, DISSEMINATED AND DEFENDED? HOW CAN IT BE QUESTIONED, DISRUPTED AND REPLACED?

The problem representation of 'welfare dependency' is almost hegemonic in contemporary Australia. It is important to reflect on how this has occurred. The role of the media in co-constituting this problem representation needs to be considered (see Chapter 10), all the while recognising that contesting representations occasionally get an airing.

In addition, remembering that 'problematization' is 'the totality of discursive and non-discursive practices that introduces something into the play of true and false' (Foucault 1988, p. 257), specific institutions, including the multitude of individuals and agencies involved in 'servicing' the jobless, play a role in sustaining 'welfare dependency' as a problem representation. Think, for example, of the thousands of job placement services offered through Centrelink (2008).

The role of the media

A 2007 article in *The Advertiser* ran the headline *'Labor will restrict welfare to deadbeats'*. The article reported on the proposal by the Rudd Labor Party in the lead-up to the 2007 election to quarantine welfare payments to parents of 'at-risk' children 'in an attempt to stem the alarming rate of child abuse and neglect'. As part of what became known as 'the intervention', the Howard-led Liberal Coalition government instituted quarantining of half of the welfare payments made to all Aboriginal people in outback communities (Kenny 2007; see Chapter 5).

- **How does the quarantining of welfare payments represent the 'problem' of welfare?**

- **How are welfare recipients constituted within this problem representation?**

- **What difference does it make that payments to *all* Aboriginal parents in some communities (rather than to the parents of 'at-risk' children) were quarantined?**

Recognising that the categories of dependence and independence are embedded within governmental practices and services in this way means that we 'cannot simply wish away such forms of knowledge or the programmes of reform they make possible' (Dean 1999, p. 65). In order to contest such ways of thinking, says Dean, we need to rely on other forms of social science knowledge and other forms of expertise.

Referring back to our earlier discussion in this chapter about the divergent views of Dean, and Fraser and Gordon, on whether 'welfare dependency' is a governmental category or a reflection of ideology, it is possible to make the case that the analysis offered by Fraser and Gordon (1994) provides exactly the kind of social science knowledge Dean seeks. While it could be argued that deconstruction of the form they produce is unlikely to have much impact on government practices, their successful mobilisation of competing understandings of key terms could well provide useful conceptual resources to those who have the opportunity to reshape those practices. McDonald (1991), Bessant (1997), and Mitchell (2003), who appear earlier in the chapter, also produce social science contributions that pose challenges to a 'welfare dependency' problem representation. There are doubtless many others.

The large numbers of the population who refuse to take up the techniques established to govern them indicates another form of resistance. In 2003, for example, it was reported that 200 000 of a scheduled 500 000 people failed to attend their compulsory Job Network interviews (Crabb, Szego and Milburn 2003). Since these activities 'from below' are themselves constitutive of subjectivity (Petersen 2003), the picture is hardly a seamless web of docile subjects shaped by governmental discourses.

The idea that discourses can be considered 'assets' to be used in ways that destabilise dominant understandings (Shapiro 1988, p. 12; see Chapter 2) opens up additional space for contestation and change, though this task is challenging and must be undertaken with care. For example, to destabilise the way in which 'work' is equated with participation in the labour force (as in the WFTD discourse), some feminists talk about the value of 'caring work'. One objective of this intervention is to revalue upwards women's social contribution through caring activities. A danger here is that this move might encourage the placing of a monetary value on care and consideration, and might mark caring work as explicitly 'women's work' (see Beasley and Bacchi 2007).

More usefully it is possible to problematise the way in which some people are currently rewarded for exercising authority *over* other people, but are *not* rewarded for encouraging cooperation. This careful reframing of the 'problem' problematises *hierarchy*, rather than the *devaluing of care*, and hence appears to promise more in the way of transformative job relations (Bacchi 1999, p. 86).

SUBMIT YOUR OWN PROBLEMATISATIONS TO A WPR ANALYSIS

As the example of 'caring work' illustrates, it is important to test or assess one's proffered re-problematisations. The best way to do this, consistent with a WPR approach, is to postulate the sorts of policy changes you would wish to enact and then to work backwards to see how they represent the 'problem'. Your subsequent task is to apply the full list of questions to the identified problem representation/s. Given that, as political subjects, we are constituted *within* the problem representations we have identified (see Question 5; subjectification effects), particular attention needs to be paid to unexamined assumptions and presuppositions. The objective here is, while recognising contextual constraints, to identify proposals that constitute the 'problem' in ways that minimise losses and maximise gains in terms of one's overall social vision.

SUMMARY

The goal of identifying how rule takes place involves a close examination of policies and their accompanying techniques of application. In this chapter, WFTD, its accompanying mechanisms, such as Centrelink and Job Network, and the social services that support them, create categories of citizens that are 'manageable'. A wide range of experts, including social workers and psychologists, participate in this governance regime. Specific groups – the jobless, young people, many women, and Aboriginal peoples – suffer most from the creation of the 'problem' of unemployment as 'welfare dependency'.

QUESTIONS

1. What does it mean to look for 'conceptual logics' in problem representations (see Chapters 1 and 2)? Can you identify any conceptual logics operating in the Work for the Dole scheme?

2. Category construction is an important part of policy making (see Chapter 1). Can you identify where category construction plays a part in discussions of unemployment policy?

3. Identify some key words or key terms related to the Work for the Dole legislation. What can we learn from reflecting on the history (genealogy) of these concepts?

4. What is meant by subjectification (see Chapter 1)? What kinds of subjects are constituted in Work for the Dole legislation?

5. What is meant by 'dividing practices' (see Chapters 1 and 2)? Is this a relevant concept to employ in reflecting on unemployment legislation?

6. When you apply the WPR approach to your own suggestions for dealing with the unemployment 'problem', what do you discover?

REFERENCES

ARIÈS, P. 1962 *Centuries of Childhood: a Social History of Family Life,* Trans. R. Baldick, Random House, New York.

ARMSTRONG, P. & ARMSTRONG, H. 1990, *Theorizing Women's Work*, Network Basics Series, Garamond Press, Toronto.

AUSTRALIAN GOVERNMENT 2005, *Employment & Workplace Relations Legislation Amendment (Welfare to Work and Other Measures) Act*, No. 154, <www.comlaw.gov.au>, accessed 22 July 2008.

AUSTRALIAN GOVERNMENT 2008, 'Youth Allowance' Centrelink, <www.centrelink.gov.au>, accessed 21 December 2008.

BACCHI, C. 1999, *Women, Policy and Politics: The Construction of Policy Problems*, Sage, London.

BASTALICH, W. 2001, *Politicising the Productive: Subjectivity, Feminist Labour Thought and Foucault*, PhD thesis, Departments of Politics and Social Inquiry, University of Adelaide.

BEASLEY, C. & BACCHI, C. 2000, 'Citizen Bodies: Embodying Citizens – a Feminist Analysis', *International Feminist Journal of Politics*, vol. 2, no. 3, pp. 337–58.

BEASLEY, C. & BACCHI, C. 2007, 'Envisaging a New Politics for an Ethical Future: Beyond Trust, Care and Generosity – Towards an Ethic of "Social Flesh"', *Feminist Theory*, vol. 8, no. 3, pp. 279–98.

BESSANT, J. 1997, 'The Liberal-National Government and Youth: "Training for Real Jobs"', *Australian Journal of Public Administration*, vol. 56, no. 2, pp. 18–31.

BILDSTIEN, C. 2006, 'Workers Guaranteed Minimum Wage', *The Advertiser*, 16 March.

BLETSAS, A. 2007, 'Contesting Representations of Poverty: Ethics and Evaluation', *Policy and Society*, vol. 26, no. 3, pp. 63–81.

CARABINE, J. 2001, 'Unmarried Motherhood 1830–1990: A Genealogical Analysis', in *Discourse as Data: A Guide for Analysis*, eds M. Wetherell, S. Taylor & S. J. Yates, Open University Press, Milton Keynes.

CENTRELINK 2008, 'Finding a job?', <www.centrelink.gov.au>, accessed 23 July 2008; last modified 6 April 2008.

COHEN, S. 1988, *Visions of Social Control: Crime, Punishment and Classifications*, Polity Press, Cambridge.

COLEBATCH, T. & SALTAU, C. 1999, 'Push to Make More Jobless Work for the Dole', *The Age*, 18 December, p. 3.

CRABB, A. 2002, 'Minister Pursues Dole "Cruisers"', *The Age*, 21 May.

CRABB, A., Szego, J. & Milburn, C. 2003, 'Jobless Lost in Matrix as Job Search System Splutters Along', *The Age*, 19 July.

DEAN, M. 1999, *Governmentality: Power and Rule in Modern Society*, Sage, London.

DEAN, M. 2006, 'Governmentality and Powers of Life and Death', in *Analysing Social Policy: A Governmental Approach*, eds G. Marston & C. McDonald, Edward Elgar, Cheltenham, United Kingdom.

DEPARTMENT OF FAMILY AND COMMUNITY SERVICES 1999, 'Request for Public Submissions', Reference Group on Welfare Reform, appeared in *Weekend Australian*, 23–24 October, 1999, p. 19, copyright Commonwealth of Australia, reproduced by permission.

EDWARDS, A. 1995, *Youth: a Problem for Whom?* Brotherhood of St Laurence, Melbourne.

EVELINE, J. 1994, 'The Politics of Advantage', *Australian Feminist Studies*, Special Issue: *Women and Citizenship*, vol. 19, pp. 129–54.

FOUCAULT, M. 1986 [1984], *The Use of Pleasure. The History of Sexuality*, Volume 2, Trans. R. Hurley, Viking Press, London.

FOUCAULT, M. 1988 [1984], 'The Concern for Truth', in *Michel Foucault: Politics, Philosophy, Culture: Interviews and Other Writings, 1977–1984*, ed. L. D. Kritzman, Trans. A. Sheridan & others, Routledge, New York.

FRASER, N. & GORDON, L. 1994, 'A Genealogy of *Dependency*: Tracing a Keyword of the US Welfare State', *Signs*, vol. 19, no. 2, pp. 309–36.

GRAY, S. & COLLINS, P. 2007, 'The Interplay of Welfare-to-Work and WorkChoices', *Hecate*, vol. 33, no. 1, pp. 126–40.

HACKING, I. 1986, 'Making up People', in *Reconstructing Individualism: Autonomy, Individuality and the Self in Western Thought*, eds T. Heller & C. Brooke-Rose, Stanford University Press, Stanford, California.

JONES, T. 1998, *Producing the Juvenile Offender*, Honours Thesis produced for the Politics Department, University of Adelaide.

KEMP, D. 1997, *Media Release*: Work for the Dole Legislation, <www.dest.gov.au>, accessed 12 July 2007.

KENNY, M. 2007, 'Labor Will Restrict Welfare to Deadbeats', *The Advertiser*, 14 July.

LEWIS, G. 2004, '"Do not go gently ..."; Terrains of Citizenship and Landscapes of the Personal', in *Citizenship: Personal Lives and Social Policy*, ed. G. Lewis, The Policy Press in association with The Open University, Bristol.

LLOYD, G. 1984, *The Man of Reason: 'Male' and 'Female' in Western Philosophy*, University of Minnesota Press, Minneapolis.

MACINTYRE, C. 2001, 'Welfare, Citizenship and the Third Way', in *Left Directions: Is There a Third Way?*, eds P. Nursey-Bray & C. Bacchi, University of Western Australia Press, Perth.

MARSHALL, T. H. 1950, *Citizenship and Social Class*, Cambridge University Press, Cambridge.

McDONALD, P. 1991, 'Youth Wages and Poverty', *Family Matters*, vol. 28, pp. 28–31.

MITCHELL, B. 2003, 'There are Simply Not Enough Jobs', *The Age*, 14 April.

PARLIAMENT OF AUSTRALIA 1991, *Social Security Act*, Commonwealth Consolidated Acts, <www.austlii.edu.au>, accessed 29 October 2008

PARLIAMENT OF AUSTRALIA 1997, *Social Security Legislation Amendment (Work for the Dole) Bill*, Commonwealth of Australia Bills, <www.austlii.edu.au>, accessed 29 October 2008.

PECK, J. 1998, '*Workfare*: A Geopolitical Etymology', *Environment and Planning D: Society and Space*, vol. 16, no. 2, pp. 133–61.

PETERSEN, A. 2003, 'Governmentality, Critical Scholarship, and the Medical Humanities', *Journal of Medical Humanities*, vol. 24, no. 3/4, pp. 187–201.

PETERSON, N. & SANDERS, W. 1998, *Citizenship and Indigenous Australians: Changing Conceptions and Possibilities*, Cambridge University Press, New York.

ROSE, N. S. 2000, *Powers of Freedom: Reframing Political Thought*, 1st edition 1999, Cambridge University Press, Cambridge, UK.

ROSE, N. & MILLER, P. 1992, 'Political Power Beyond the State: Problematics of Government', *The British Journal of Sociology*, vol. 43, no. 2, pp. 173–205.

SHAPIRO, M. 1988, *The Politics of Representation: Writing Practices in Biography, Photography and Policy Analysis*, University of Wisconsin Press, Madison.

STANDING COMMITTEE ON LEGAL AND CONSTITUTIONAL AFFAIRS, Senate Inquiry Report 2006, *Unfinished Business: Indigenous Stolen Wages*, Commonwealth of Australia, <www.aph.gov.au>, accessed 22 July 2008.

STILGHERRIAN, 2007, *The Citizenship Dog-Whistle*, 2 October, <http://stilgherrian.com/politics/citizenship-dog-whistle>, accessed 6 February, 2009.

TURNER, D. H. 1986, *Transformation and Tradition: A Report on Aboriginal Development in/on the Northern Territory of Australia*, Department of Community Development, Darwin.

WALTERS, W. 2001, 'Governing Unemployment: Transforming "the Social"?', in *Rethinking Law, Society and Governance: Foucault's Bequest*, eds G. Wickham & G. Pavlich, Hart Publishing, Oregon.

WALTERS, W. 2004, 'Secure Borders, Safe Haven, Domopolitics', *Citizenship Studies*, vol. 8, no. 3, pp. 237–60.

WILLIAMS, R. 1983 [1976], *Keywords: A Vocabulary of Culture and Society*, Fontana Press, London.

WYN, J. & WHITE, R. 1997, *Rethinking Youth*, Sage, London.

YEEND, P. 2004 'Mutual Obligation/Work for the Dole', E-Brief Online Only issued 27 November 2000, updated 15 June 2004, Parliamentary Library, Parliament of Australia, <www.aph. gov.au>, accessed 14 July 2008.

YOUNG OF GRAFFAM, LORD 1992, 'Enterprise Regained', in *The Values of the Enterprise Culture: the Moral Debate*, eds P. Heelas and P. Morris, Routledge, London.

FURTHER READING

BEASLEY, C. & BACCHI, C. 2005, 'The Political Limits of "Care" in Re-imagining Interconnection/ Community and an Ethical Future', *Australian Feminist Studies*, vol. 20, no. 46, pp. 49–64.

BURGESS, J., MITCHELL, W. F., O'BRIEN, D. J. & WATTS, M. J. 2000, 'The Developing Workfare Policy in Australia: A Critical Assessment', *Journal of Socio-Economics*, vol. 29, pp. 173–88.

GOODMAN, J. 1997, 'New Deals and Privatising Employment in Australia', *Journal of Australian Political Economy*, vol. 40, pp. 27–43.

HAGE, G. 2003, *Against Paranoid Nationalism: Searching For Hope in a Shrinking Society*, Pluto Press, Annadale, Victoria.

KELLIE, D. 1998, 'Unemployed? Board the Enterprise for a Brave New World and a "Real" Job: A Critique of the New Strategy for Reducing Unemployment', *Australian Journal of Social Issues*, vol. 33, no. 3, pp. 285–302.

MACINTYRE, C. 1999, 'From Entitlement to Obligation in the Australian Welfare State', *Australian Journal of Social Issues*, vol. 34, no. 2, pp. 108–12.

PIXLEY, J. 1997, 'The Meanings of Dole and Dolework: The Crimes of Unemployment', *Arena Magazine*, vol. 30, pp. 27–29.

WELFARE RIGHTS CENTRE 2002, 'Kicking Them While They're Down ... Youth Allowance and Youth Poverty', National Welfare Rights Centre, Sydney, <www.welfarerights.org.au/pages/ policypapers.aspx>, accessed 11 August 2008.

'Dangerous' consumptions: Drugs/alcohol and gambling policy

Chapter 4

GETTING STARTED (A SECOND TRY)

This chapter examines policy developments in areas that share some commonalities, despite the fact that it is unusual to treat them together. The topics under study – drugs/alcohol and gambling – are regulated by the government, albeit to different extents. They are also spoken about in very similar terms, as things ('commodities') we all partake of, but that are 'dangerous' when 'consumed' in 'excess' or without proper supervision. The language of addiction appears in relation to both drugs/alcohol and gambling, as does the language of 'harm minimisation'. How are these 'problems' represented in existing policy? And what can a 'what's the problem represented to be?' approach contribute to clarifying what is at stake in these contentious policy areas? Finally, reflecting the guiding concern of the book, what can we learn about how we are governed by looking at drugs/alcohol and gambling policy?

As in Chapter 3, a specific policy ('practical text'; see Chapter 2) in each of the topic areas will be subjected to the battery of questions in a WPR approach. As part of the analysis, related texts will be drawn upon to supply contextual details and to 'flesh out' identified problem representations. The underlying objective is to reflect on the relationship between 'dangerous consumptions' and governance, understood in the broad sense of general societal administration.

QUESTION 1: WHAT'S THE PROBLEM REPRESENTED TO BE?

Tough on Drugs: the *National Illicit Drug Strategy*

The Howard-led Coalition (Liberal-National Party) government introduced the *Tough on Drugs* strategy in 1997. Funding commitments for the next five years included the following key initiatives:

■ the Australian Federal Police was allocated $159.6 million;

■ the National Crime Authority was allocated $22.5 million;

■ the Australian Customs Service was allocated $88.4 million, plus $58 million for eight new Australian Customs Service Bay class vessels to 'strengthen the Australian Customs Service's capacity to intercept illicit drugs' (Australian Government 2006).

Funds were also committed to education and rehabilitation. The first instalment allocated:

■ $43.8 million '*attacking the drug barons* . . . to prevent illegal drugs entering Australia by more effective interception techniques';

■ $14 million 'to educate our children and the wider community about the extreme danger of drugs'; and

■ $29.8 million on rehabilitation and research spending 'to re-integrate drug users into the community and support *frontline* professions such as GPs and hospital staff to adequately counsel users' (Bureau of International Narcotics and Law Enforcement Affairs 1998; emphasis added).

Recalling that a WPR approach starts with a policy or policy proposal, examines the recommended interventions and works backwards to see what the 'problem' is represented to be, drugs in *Tough on Drugs* is represented to be predominantly a law and order problem, with clear links to the issues covered in Chapter 5. Most funding is committed to policing and in particular to policing Australia's borders. In this instance, the 'problem' is represented to be traffickers – in Manderson's (1993) terms, 'Mr Big' – and therefore largely a supply-side 'problem', specifically the supply of *illicit* drugs. To deal with 'demand', young people are to be warned of 'extreme danger'. The strategy looked to 'moral leadership' in '*combating* the *menace* of illicit drugs' (Bureau of International Narcotics and Law Enforcement Affairs 1998; emphasis added). In addition, a raft of state and federal statutes impose penalties, either prison or fines, on those who 'possess' (Manderson 2005), manufacture, distribute and/or 'use' illicit drugs.

Tough on Drugs, as is indicated in the term 'tough', was meant to mark a departure from earlier, 'softer' approaches (Bessant 2008, p. 210). The target here was the *National Campaign Against Drug Abuse* (NCADA), which ran between 1985 and 1997. NCADA, a program endorsed by state premiers and the Commonwealth, introduced the concept of 'harm minimisation' (discussed below) to Australian drug policy as a counter to prohibitionist approaches to illicit drugs, which aimed at the reduction of drug use through criminal sanctions. NCADA, influenced in part by the HIV/AIDS epidemic, challenged the effectiveness of prohibition, emphasising instead *harm* reduction through needle exchange programs, methadone treatment, safe sex and other education programs, and rehabilitation programs. Alongside these initiatives, NCADA endorsed sophisticated intelligence-gathering on illicit drugs and more effective law enforcement measures (Makkai *et al*. 1991).

Though there are important differences in emphasis between *Tough on Drugs* and NCADA, which should not be underestimated, there are also overlaps – the focus on law enforcement, education and rehabilitation – reminding us that modes, or styles, of governing are plural, diverse and often hybrid in character. Moreover, some of the ambiguity around the meaning of harm minimisation, discussed below, indicates that, even in 'softer' accounts, the drug user – who is portrayed as needing help and healing – becomes the 'problem'. There are resonances here with current approaches to 'problem gambling' and, more specifically, to 'problem *gamblers*'.

National Framework on Problem Gambling 2004–2008

In 2003 the Ministerial Council on Gambling, including representatives from the federal, state and territory governments, produced a *National Framework on Problem Gambling*. The Key Focus Areas, Objectives and Strategies include:

■ Public Awareness, Education and Training – 'to promote a greater understanding of the nature of the gambling product, the potential for *harm* and the availability of help and support.'
■ Responsible Gambling Environments – 'to minimise the likelihood of *recreational* gamblers developing *problem* gambling behaviours.'
■ Intervention, Counselling and Support Services – 'to enhance problem gambling support and treatment services that are effective, accessible and culturally appropriate.'
■ National Research and Data Collection – 'to inform the implementation and further development of the national framework and its strategies' (Ministerial Council on Gambling 2004; emphasis added).

A WPR approach can usefully be applied to each area:

■ The Public Awareness strategy produces the 'problem' as a lack of information about 'problem gambling issues' and 'the nature of gambling products'.
■ The Responsible Gambling Environments strategy specifies the need for Codes of Practice to 'promote responsible practices by operators', covering advertising and promotions, and

strategies to promote 'informed decision-making by consumers' and to 'enable gamblers to limit their expenditure or time spent gambling, for example, through pre-commitment measures and appropriate controls over financial transactions'. Here the 'problem' is represented to be irresponsible conduct of gambling by some operators and lack of accessibility by 'consumers' to means to self-impose limits on their gambling.

■ The call for 'Intervention, Counselling and Support Services' produces the 'problem gambler' as the 'problem' needing help and support.

■ The National Gambling Research Program includes a proposal for a major study of 'problem gamblers', 'including their profile, attitudes, gambling behaviour and the impact of proposed policy measures on them'. It solicits research on the 'feasibility and consequences of changes to gaming machine operation, such as pre-commitment of loss limits, phasing out note-acceptors, imposition of mandatory breaks in play and the impact of linked jackpots'. These proposals imply an inability on the part of 'problem gamblers' to deal with the enticement of gambling. Research will also be conducted on patterns of gambling with a focus on strategies for 'harm reduction' in specific communities and populations, 'such as Indigenous, rural, remote or culturally and linguistically diverse communities, young people or older people'. More will be said about 'harm reduction' or 'harm minimisation' approaches, and about the targeting of specific communities, in due course.

In contrast to *Tough on Drugs*, where the focus is primarily on *supply*, in the *National Framework* problem gambling is produced mainly as a *demand* 'problem'. Although there is reference to the possibility of 'irresponsible' operators, most of the recommendations address presumed character or personality weaknesses among some 'consumers' who need assistance dealing with *their* 'problem'. The preamble to the *Framework* draws a clear distinction between 'problem gamblers' and those for whom 'gambling is a legitimate part of their leisure and *recreation*', people 'who gamble . . . in a *responsible* manner and enjoy gambling as entertainment'. Proposals like the pre-commitment of loss limits make self-regulation part of the strategy. The declared objective is to 'achieve a balance between maximising the benefits and *minimising the potential harm* of gambling to the community' (Ministerial Council on Gambling 2004; emphasis added).

QUESTION 2: WHAT PRESUPPOSITIONS OR ASSUMPTIONS UNDERLIE THIS REPRESENTATION OF THE PROBLEM?

Through examining how the selected policies are discursively elaborated, we can probe more deeply into the conceptual logics underpinning the identified problem representations in *Tough on Drugs* and the *National Framework*. Specifically, under Question 2, we identify implied or explicit binaries, and other keywords or concepts, and consider how they shape the meaning of the 'problem'.

Licit/illicit drugs

Tough on Drugs, as already noted, specifies concern with *illicit* drugs. This alerts us to the need to reflect on the nature of so-called *licit* drugs, and to speculate on why they are treated differently. The most common 'licit' drugs are tobacco and alcohol, though we could also include caffeine and prescription drugs (pharmaceuticals). The ill-effects of usage, measured, for example, in terms of deaths and DALYs (Disability-Adjusted Life Years: one DALY represents one lost year of 'healthy life'), are either just as high or higher for 'licit' drugs as for 'illicit' drugs (AIHW 2007, pp. 34–37), but 'licit' drugs are not proscribed. Alcohol, for example, is not a prohibited drug, although its use is restricted by age. In the period 2004–05 the Howard-led government spent ten times as much on illicit and other 'drugs of dependence' programs ($10.7 million) as on national initiatives to reduce 'alcohol-related harm' ($1.2 million) (AIHW 2008, p. 34).

Here it is useful to reflect on the criteria (categories) that are used to measure the effects of specific drugs. That is, while it is possible to draw inferences from the kinds of information that compare health effects (deaths and DALYs) for different drugs, the technique of data collection also needs to be seen as part of a problem representation and indeed as part of governance. What is measured reveals what is problematised (see Activity on ' "Risky" drug use').

'Risky' drug use

In the most recent of twelve volumes collecting statistics on drug use in Australia, Table 7.11 reports on the 'proportion of employed recent drinkers who missed work because of alcohol use or illness/injury, who went to work under the influence of alcohol, and who usually drank at work, by risk category, Australia, 2001'. The risk categories are divided into short-term risk and long-term risk, and into gradations of risk (low to high) within each of these divisions (AIHW 2007, p. 63).

- **What is the 'problem' of drug use represented to be in these statistics?**

- **How do these statistics relate to governmental objectives?**

The most common explanation for prohibiting some drugs rather than others is that those that are prohibited are associated with a range of serious 'problems', including addiction. For example, links are commonly drawn between heroin use on the one side and, on the other side, crime, the spread of AIDS through needle use, and death due to overdose. However, it could be argued that criminalisation of heroin use is a major *cause* of these concerns. For example, the prohibition of substances such as heroin is largely responsible for its inflated price, which in turn may act to encourage theft. Similarly, prohibition means that the available supply of heroin is often adulterated with other substances, requiring injection and hence needle use to get the desired effect. Also, the most common cause of overdose is an encounter with pure heroin by someone used to an adulterated product. So, it is possible to argue that criminalisation of heroin use actually *exacerbates* the concerns it is meant to *reduce*. Hence, we are left to wonder what the purposes of prohibitionist approaches could be. Perhaps the answer lies in addiction.

Addiction

Addiction is a keyword in drug policy. Increasingly it is also being used in relation to gambling. Usefully, Melissa Bull (1996) provides a 'genealogical analysis of the "discovery" of the modern phenomenon of addiction'. She locates it as part of the apparatus of governance developed in the nineteenth century to regulate 'social' and 'anti-social' behaviour (see Chapter 5). Bull notes that early attempts at regulation of drugs such as heroin/opium (laudanum) were linked to public health concerns — deaths from poisonings and the 'dosing' of children. In this period the medical and pharmaceutical professions became self-regulating bodies. Part of the carving out of their domain involved gaining a monopoly on the sale of opium and other 'poisons'. The concept of 'addiction' created the 'problem' of drug use as a *medical specialism*.

By making this point Bull is not denying the biological reality of neuroadaption to opiates. It is the category of 'the addict' that troubles her. Drug addiction is produced primarily as a character flaw, in much the same way that obesity is seen today (see Guthman and DuPuis 2006). Health is equated with *self*-discipline (see Chapter 6). The cultivation of self-control though education (see Chapter 9) becomes part of the treatment regime, as seen also in the NCADA (above). Paradoxically, as Bull (1996) notes, 'cure' becomes the *responsibility* of the individual patient. Ultimately, then, this representation of the 'problem' ends up working *against* recognising the neuroadaption to opiates.

In Australia today medicine continues to function as a gate-keeper on the legitimate uses of drugs. The 'non-medical' use of drugs is illegal. The distinction between 'licit' and 'illicit' drugs also depends on medical authority. For example, currently, a distinction is drawn between 'licit' prescription medications and 'illicit' use of pain killers and tranquillisers for 'non-medical purposes' (AIHW 2007, p. 24).

Responsible/irresponsible use

'Licit' drugs, such as alcohol, and gambling practices are governed through another binary — responsible *versus* irresponsible use. The term 'responsible' has become a keyword in contemporary liberal and neoliberal modes of governance. In Chapter 3 we identified a shift in the understanding of citizenship from an emphasis on *rights* to an emphasis on *responsibilities*, and a shift from *socialised* management of risk to *individualised* risk-management — holding individuals or groups of individuals (e.g. families, communities) increasingly responsible for more and more aspects of their lives. The operation of a responsible/irresponsible dichotomy in drug and gambling policy ought to be considered in the light of these observations.

The term 'responsible' features largely in the *National Framework on Problem Gambling 2004-2008*. Operators are to become *responsible* and to produce '*Responsible* Gambling Environments'. A distinction is drawn between 'problem gamblers' and 'recreational gamblers', people 'who gamble . . . in a *responsible* manner and enjoy gambling as entertainment' (Ministerial Council on Gambling 2004; emphasis added).

Responsible drinking is also widely promoted, both by the government and by the industry-funded body, DrinkWise. Foster's — a large brewing company and one of the founding sponsors of DrinkWise — endorses responsible drinking messages on labelling, a responsible drinking promotion strategy and 'compulsory responsible service of alcohol agreements with sponsored organizations' (Foster's 2006).

A particular kind of political subject is presumed in representations of 'responsible' gamblers and 'responsible' drinkers, one who ought, normally, to display rationality and self-control. Gambling and drinking 'in moderation' is considered to be a 'legitimate part of their leisure' (Ministerial Council on Gambling 2004). The 'problem' is represented to be displays of 'excess' by specific individuals who are considered to lack this rationality and self-control.

Harm minimisation

As we saw above, *Tough on Drugs* was developed, at least in part, to counter the NCADA focus on harm minimisation, which was seen as a 'soft' option. Those who want to draw attention to what they perceive to be limits in the kind of law and order agenda defended in *Tough on Drugs* continue to argue that the goal of drug policy should be 'harm minimisation'. The principle of harm minimisation forms the basis of Australia's *National Drug Strategy 2004–2009* (Ministerial Council on Drug Strategy 2004), the mission of which is 'to improve health, social and economic outcomes by preventing the uptake of harmful drug use and reducing the harmful effects of illicit drugs in Australian society' (Australian Government 2007).

A 'harm minimisation' discourse, popular in both national and international forums, is generally meant to sit in opposition to prohibitionist approaches, and to shift the focus away from the kind of moralising that underpins prohibitionist rhetoric. However, the phrase is open to interpretation and seems often to sit comfortably alongside approaches with a strong commitment to deterrence. As Wellbourne-Wood (1999, p. 411) says, the imperative often becomes *use* minimisation rather than *harm* minimisation.

Going further, countering the claim that harm minimisation approaches *bypass* moralism, the term 'harm' itself invites moral reflection. What is harm? Harm to whom? To users or to society? There is often an undercurrent of concern with social 'breakdown' in harm minimisation rhetoric, which is closer to prohibitionist concerns than is comfortable. Hence, we should not be surprised to find that many prohibitionists are happy to endorse harm minimisation proposals. As Valverde (1998, p. 179) notes, 'switching to the language of harm does not necessarily help to produce consensus about treatment'.

To gain credibility, those who subscribe to harm minimisation draw heavily on scientific 'evidence'. For example, the articles of the month selected by the International Harm Reduction Association frequently offer details of scientific interventions, installing science and medicine as regulators of 'truth' (<www.ihra.net>; see Chapter 10).

'Risk', 'high risk', 'at risk'

Though the keyword 'risk' does not appear in our selected 'practical texts', it is a dominant part of current problem representations in the drugs/alcohol and gambling policy domains. For example, the AIHW (2007, p. xii) publication, *Statistics on Drug Use in Australia*, refers to 'risky and high-risk alcohol consumption' (see Activity on 'Risky' drug use). 'Risky' behaviours are represented to be 'irresponsible' behaviours, with the (ill) effects sheeted home to those who so behave. As a contemporary governance category, 'risk' is prolific. We will see it again in Chapter 6 on health policy.

'Tackling Drugs: Government and Communities Working Together'

'**Objective**: to reduce drug related harm within the community by building individual, family and community resilience.

Policy:

1. An integrated whole of government approach to preventing anticipated harm and reducing actual drug related harm.

2. This approach will be based on "positive pathways", with a focus on developing resilience in the early years of life as a key strategy to reduce drug-related harm.

3. The approach will also incorporate recognised "transition points" and identified "recovery points" in people's lives to introduce, reinforce or restore resilience.

Resilient individuals, families and communities with a positive outlook on life are better able to overcome and recover from the tough times in their lives' (Government of South Australia 2002, p. 1, 4).

- **What is the 'problem' represented to be in the concept of 'resilience'?**

- **Are there any silences in this representation of the 'problem' of drug use?**

National Binge Drinking Strategy

'The Rudd Government has announced a new national strategy to address the binge drinking epidemic among young Australians.

This national strategy will begin with three practical measures to help reduce alcohol misuse and binge drinking among young Australians:

- ■ $14.4 million to invest in community level initiatives to confront the culture of binge drinking, particularly in sporting organizations; and
- ■ $19.1 million to intervene earlier to assist young people and ensure that they assume personal responsibility for their binge drinking;
- ■ $20 million to fund advertising that confronts young people with the costs and consequences of binge drinking' (Australian Labor Party 2008).
- **What is the 'problem' of binge drinking represented to be in this strategy?**
- **Are there any silences in this representation of the 'problem'?**

QUESTION 3: HOW HAS THIS REPRESENTATION OF THE 'PROBLEM' COME ABOUT?

Question 3 invites us to conduct genealogies of problem representations. As noted in Chapter 2, the kind of close attention to detail required in genealogy lies beyond the scope of this volume. Here only broad strokes are possible, such as the brief summary above of Bull's (1996) genealogy of 'addiction'.

On drug policy Race (2005) usefully notes that in the 1920s and 1930s the 'problem' of drug use was seen to lodge in the substances themselves, which were described as 'dangerous' (*Dangerous Drugs Act 1920 (UK)*; *Dangerous Drugs Act 1959 (Tas)*). In the 1950s, 1960s and 1970s, says Race, governing strategies shifted to a focus on 'use' and 'misuse' of drugs (*Misuse of Drugs Act 1971 (UK)*; South Australia, 1979 *Royal Commission into the Non-Medical Use of Drugs*), and hence to a focus on 'users' – reflecting expressed concerns about 'rebellious youth', 'moral decay' and potentially declining productivity. Increasing references to 'non-medical' use indicate the expanding role of medicine as overseer of legitimate 'use'.

International influences on Australia's drug laws should also be noted. *Tough on Drugs* had a clear resonance with the US 'war on drugs', begun under President Richard Nixon in the early 1970s. In addition, the US played a leading role in the drafting of the *United Nations Single Convention on Narcotic Drugs* (1961), which codified all existing multilateral treaties on drug control. The principal objectives were:

... to limit the possession, use, trade in, distribution, import, export, manufacture and production of drugs exclusively to medical and scientific purposes and to address drug trafficking through international cooperation to deter and discourage drug traffickers. (International Narcotics Control Board 2008)

Australia ratified the Convention in 1967 and passed a *Narcotics Drug Act*, which set up a system of licensing and permits for manufacture and distribution of drugs covered by the *Single Convention*. In 1999 the International Narcotics Board, set up to administer the Convention, warned Australia that some state-planned heroin trials might be in contravention of the *Single Convention* if they were not conducted under medical supervision. If Australia ignored the advice of the UN body, there were concerns that Australia's $150 million legal opiates trade might be put at risk. The expressed concern of the UN agency was that the argument of harm reduction might lead to legalisation of heroin (Mann 1999).

Diagnosing drug 'abuse'

The medical professions play an important role in establishing the character of drug 'abuse'. For example, the fourth edition of the *Diagnostic and Statistical Manual of Mental Disorder* (DSM), issued by the American Psychiatric Association, offers the following definition of 'substance abuse':

■ A maladaptive pattern of substance use leading to clinically significant impairment or distress, as manifested by one (or more) of the following, occurring within a 12-month period.

■ Recurrent substance use resulting in a failure to fulfil major role obligations at work, school, or home (e.g. repeated absence and poor work performance related to substance use);

■ Recurrent substance use in situations in which it is physically hazardous (e.g. driving an automobile or operating a machine when impaired by substance use);

■ Recurrent substance-related legal problems (e.g. arrests for substance-related disorderly conduct);

■ Continued substance use despite having persistent or recurrent social or interpersonal problems caused or exacerbated by the effects of the substance (e.g. arguments with spouse about consequences of intoxication, physical fights).

(MedicineNet.com 2003)

• **What is the 'problem' of 'substance abuse' represented to be in this definition?**

• **How does this way of defining 'substance abuse' contribute to governance goals?**

Strategies in governing gambling have evolved in almost the opposite direction to drugs, with a shift from gambling as *deviance*, at least in Britain and some European states, prior to World War II, to gambling as *leisure* (McMillen 1996). Following a period of selective legalisation from 1900 to the 1940s, and a period of government endorsement and market growth from

World War II to the 1970s, Australia has been experiencing a period of commercialisation, competition and market expansion. Currently each state government has introduced its own distinctive regulatory regime to guide the administration and control of machine gaming, including poker machines.

As indicated in the *National Framework on Problem Gambling* (Ministerial Council on Gambling 2004), if there is a 'problem' in gambling, it is associated with those who seem unable to exercise appropriate control over their gambling. In this vein, the Victorian state government funds *Gambler's Help*, a free counselling and referral service for 'problem gamblers' and their families (State Government of Victoria 2008).

Diagnosing 'pathological' gambling

In a 2000 issue of the *Electronic Journal of Gambling Issues*, Alex Blaszczynski offers a typology of 'pathways to pathological gambling'.

1. 'Normal' pathological gambling subgroup:

    These gamblers 'lose transient control over their behaviour because of irrational cognitions, which lead to a series of poor judgments and they become temporarily over-involved in gambling'. They 'require minimal interventions, counselling and support strategies and may resume controlled gambling post intervention. Self-help groups such as Gamblers Anonymous are effective, as are self-control self-help educational materials'.

2. Emotionally vulnerable pathological gamblers:

    'These are gamblers who participate for emotional reasons: to dissociate as a means of escaping painful life stresses, to reduce boredom, or to deal with unresolved intrapsychic conflicts or childhood traumas.' 'They require more extensive therapeutic interventions including stress management and problem-solving skills.'

3. Biologically based impulsive pathological gamblers:

    'This subgroup is defined by the presence of neurological or neurochemical dysfunction.' 'These gamblers may require intensive cognitive behavioural interventions aimed at impulse control over longer terms. Medications aimed at reducing impulsivity through its calming effects may be considered' (Blaszczynski 2000).

*   **What is the 'problem' of 'pathological gambling' represented to be in this typology?**

*   **How does this way of representing the 'problem' of 'pathological gambling' contribute to governance objectives?**

QUESTION 4: WHAT IS LEFT UNPROBLEMATIC IN THIS REPRESENTATION OF THE 'PROBLEM'? WHERE ARE THE SILENCES? CAN THE 'PROBLEM' BE THOUGHT ABOUT DIFFERENTLY?

There are both differences and similarities in the ways in which our selected examples of drugs/alcohol and gambling policy represent the respective 'problems' of drug abuse and 'excessive' gambling. Examining the differences first, *Tough on Drugs* produces the 'problem' as mainly a *supply-side* problem, while the *National Framework on Problem Gambling* constitutes the 'problem' as predominantly a *demand* problem. Hence, for *Tough on Drugs*, the issue of demand is underplayed, while for the *National Framework*, the character and source of supply is under-examined.

The 'war against drugs', as is clear in *Tough on Drugs*, is primarily a war against 'evil' traffickers and only secondarily against users, who are portrayed to be weak and easily-led. The focus on trafficking, as mentioned above, produces the 'problem' of 'illicit' drug use as a supply-side 'problem'. The implication is that, if the supply can be reduced, the 'problem' will go away. This emphasis tends to discount the reasons people use drugs, including alcohol. Moreover, the fact that we live in a drug-using and drug-promoting culture remains under-analysed. In addition, the focus on traffickers and criminalisation diverts attention from the role of law in producing some of the effects, including crime, needle use and overdose, commonly attributed to 'illicit' drugs (see discussion above).

In relation to the *National Framework on Problem Gambling*, the 'problem' is seen to reside in the character of 'problem gamblers', the identified source of the demand for gambling products. The complex reasons people gamble – financial need, cultural pressures – are unexamined in this representation of the problem. Moreover, the focus on demand makes it difficult to problematise the nature of the supply, the way in which gambling is produced, packaged and promoted.

In the *National Framework* some attention is paid to the topic of supply under the key focus area of 'Responsible Gambling Environments'. Specifically, there is reference to the need to 'further develop and implement Codes of Practice and/or regulatory frameworks to promote responsible practices by operators, and informed decision making by consumers' (Ministerial Council on Gambling 2004). In this proposal the 'consumer' is produced as a rational decision-maker who requires only good information (see discussion below under 'subjectification effects'). Also, Codes of Practice tend to produce the 'problem' as 'the absence of a clear body of ethical standards defining appropriate and inappropriate conduct in worker-client [or 'consumer'/industry] relationships' (White 1993, p. 83). There is no way within this representation of the 'problem' to probe more deeply into inequitable power relations that lie at the heart of the transaction.

Turning now to similarities, silences common to the ways in which drug use and gambling are problematised in our selected policies/programs include: silence around government revenue, silence around social inequalities, and silence around modes of governance. Each of these will be discussed in turn.

Recalling that a WPR approach challenges the common separation between 'social' and 'economic' policy, it recognises that social policies often assume a particular shape due to decisions regarding government finance. 'Adequate' revenue is commonly represented to be a legitimate and necessary part of effective governance, diverting attention from decisions about how revenue is acquired, divided up and spent. This representation of the 'problem' has important repercussions in the policy areas under scrutiny.

For example, federal government revenue associated with tobacco products increased from $4.3 billion in 1995–96 to nearly $6.7 billion in 2004–05. Net federal government revenue associated with alcohol increased from $3.6 billion in 1995–96 to an estimated $5.1 billion in 2004–05. In both these cases, excise taxes were the major source of revenue (AIHW 2007, pp. 7, 16). Both tobacco and alcohol remain 'licit' drugs, despite the abundant evidence of associated health 'problems'.

Similarly, gambling taxes provide a significant share of state tax revenue – 13.8 per cent in South Australia in 1997–98 and 15.2 per cent in Victoria in the same period. Revenue concerns have played a significant role in states' decisions regarding introduction and numbers of poker machines (Australian Institute for Gambling Research 1999). Federal-state financial relations set the backdrop here since 'the states' distorted incentives to use gambling as a revenue raiser . . . have been compounded by the distribution methodology of the Commonwealth Grants Commission, which penalises below average tax raising efforts' (Productivity Commission 1999, p. 52). The problem representations in drugs and gambling policy, identified in our selected policies/programs – e.g. the 'problem' of 'drug barons' in drug policy and of 'problem gamblers' in gambling policy – make it difficult to reflect on these connections between government policy and revenue issues.

These identified problem representations produce other silences. For example, the emphasis on 'drug barons' in drug policy and on 'problem gamblers' in gambling policy diverts attention from the fact that in both areas there are correlations between the activities (of drug use and 'excessive' gambling) and socio-economic status. In many countries there is clear inverse association between socio-economic position and smoking, while the prevalence of non-drinking shows an inverse relationship with occupational status (Marmot 1997; Broom 2008, p. 135). Concerning gambling, the Victorian Independent Gambling Research Panel found a 'very high correlation between disadvantaged households and communities and gambling' (National Interest 2004).

The *National Framework* (Ministerial Council on Gambling 2004) appears to direct some attention to this concern. It indicates as a priority research area, to 'research patterns of gambling and consider strategies for harm reduction in specific communities and populations, such as Indigenous, rural, remote or culturally and linguistically diverse communities, young people or older people'. However, the proposal, framed as it is within a 'problem gambler' paradigm, tends to produce members of these communities, primarily, as simply *more susceptible* than others to the 'lures' of excessive gambling – rather than reflecting on social and environmental explanations for correlations between particular sub-groups of the population and 'excessive' gambling. Hence, such targeting tends to reinforce the common characterisation of those sub-groups as deficient in terms of moral responsibility (Race 2005, p. 3). Meanwhile, those who can, quite literally, afford to be 'excessive' gamblers go unnoticed.[1]

Other research (Dickerson 2003) suggests that loss of control over expenditure of time and money during a session of betting is a common and 'natural' experience for regular betters, not just for targeted minorities. Moreover, according to Volberg (2007), the disproportionate labelling of certain minorities as 'problem gamblers' has a serious, deleterious effect. She makes the case that such targeting facilitates the transfer of wealth from poor to rich by reducing the job prospects of the former, for example. Such targeting can therefore serve to reinforce the inequities that produce the 'problem' in the first place. Nor is it clear to what extent a 'harm minimisation' problematisation, expressed in the reference to 'harm reduction' (in the quote from the *National Framework* above), addresses structural inequalities (Miller 2001, p. 176).

In terms of modes of governance 'illicit drugs' and 'irresponsible' drinking and gambling operate to facilitate social order, a primary governance objective, by characterising the activities of targeted groups as examples of 'bad conduct'. 'Users' (abusers, addicts) are marked as 'other', which encourages 'appropriate' behaviour among the majority. Following Race's (2005, p. 2) argument, 'illicit' drug use and 'excessive' gambling serve to set the boundaries on 'legitimate' consumer behaviour. Put simply, identifying 'addicts' as the 'other', allows the rest of the population to continue consuming, 'wisely' no doubt. Dividing practices are at work here. To the extent that harm minimisation approaches produce drug users as problematic, they share this governmental logic.

Valverde (1998, p. 26) extends this analysis to indicate the ways in which 'illicit' drug use (and, I would suggest, 'problem gambling') marks the boundaries of the realm of freedom. She makes the case that we are encouraged to believe we are free on the grounds that we can demonstrate the self-control that 'others' (the 'drug addicts', the 'problem gamblers', the 'obese') appear to lack. All the while, however, we are (self)regulating our behaviour to avoid the punishment and stigma meted out to those who, we are told, behave 'badly'. Keeping the focus on drug traffickers, drug 'abusers' and 'problem gamblers' as problematic individuals, diverts attention from this broader governance objective of societal management. In this understanding, drug and gambling laws are seen primarily, therefore, to serve a symbolic and normalising function.

There is no suggestion of conspiracy in this kind of analysis. Rather, a form of social unconscious operating at the level of management of population (see Chapter 2) provides the backdrop to understanding how we are governed through the categories of 'risk', of 'excess' and of 'responsible use'. The pervasiveness of this tendency to individualise 'social problems', seen also in the previous chapter, impacts upon the ways in which we think about ourselves and others. Hence, it helps to explain the success of neoliberal regimes that discount social structural factors in shaping people's lives. These subjectification effects are addressed under the next question.

QUESTION 5: WHAT EFFECTS ARE PRODUCED BY THIS REPRESENTATION OF THE 'PROBLEM'?

A number of the points pertinent to Question 5 have already been discussed in the analysis offered above. Indeed, I hope it is becoming clear that separation of the questions in a WPR approach is not always necessary or even advisable. Nor is it necessary to conduct and write up one's research as if to a formula. The layout of Chapters 3 and 4 separates the questions in the approach schematically for two reasons: first, to ensure that every question gets raised; and second, to show how the same basic material can look slightly different through a different lens (question). Subsequent chapters offer a more integrated form of analysis, with notation (e.g. **Q1, Q2**) signalling when specific questions have been applied.

Question 5, identifying the effects produced by particular problem representations, is important because it asks students and other researchers to identify the dimensions or aspects of a problem representation that either impress or concern them. In other words, it encourages assessment and judgement. This is a necessary part of the WPR approach; otherwise, we would be left with nothing but *competing* representations of 'problems'.

Discursive effects

Discourses produce 'truths'. Under discursive effects the goal is to identify the 'truths' that are generated. The question becomes – how are the 'problems' of drug use and gambling discursively constructed or elaborated? While it is the case that some people take a variety of drugs and some participate in gambling, policies governing drug-taking and gambling practices characterise those involved in these activities in ways that function as 'truths'.

The 'law and order' discourse of *Tough on Drugs* makes drug use a matter of illegal behaviour. The dominant 'problem gambler' discourse in the *National Framework* produces gambling as a legitimate leisure activity, abused by some. The binaries licit/illicit, responsible/ irresponsible, and the concept 'addiction', cut across these problem representations. 'Illicit' drug-users and 'problem gamblers' are marked as addicts. Some drugs, such as alcohol, and gambling are constituted as legitimate activities when engaged in 'responsibly'. 'Addiction' and 'irresponsible' behaviours are created as 'truths'. To question these 'truths' it is possible to draw upon the analyses within Questions 2, 3 and 4 above, which illustrate that other 'truths' are available.

As an example of the power of dominant discourses, a 1995 study conducted by the National Drug Strategy found that the people surveyed identified alcohol and tobacco as the drugs causing most death in Australia. However, when asked to name the drugs they thought of when people talked about a 'drug problem', almost two-thirds mentioned cannabis and other 'illicit' drugs (National Drug Strategy 1996, p. 7).

Subjectification effects

Centrally important to the task of assessment is judgement concerning the ways in which specific problem representations produce subjects. Recall that in a WPR approach policy is a creative exercise. It creates 'problems' and it creates political subjects by eliciting certain behaviours, feelings and views.

Two different groups of political subjects are produced by the dominant problem representations we have traced: the minority 'marked' group – the drug 'abusers' and the 'problem gamblers' – and the majority 'unmarked' group – those who are characterised as 'responsible'. The dominant problem representations in both drugs/alcohol and gambling policy create the 'marked' groups as problematic, as troublesome. They are stigmatised and hence marginalised. The 'unmarked' group consists of rational 'consumers', who need only to be 'informed' in order to be 'in control'. Feminist body theory (Bacchi and Beasley 2002) challenges this distinction between political subjects who 'control' their bodies and those 'controlled by' their bodies, showing how this dichotomy can serve to reduce the civic entitlements of members of 'marked' groups.

Lived effects

Directing attention to lived effects means thinking about the material consequences of identified problem representations for individuals' day-to-day lives. Living with stigma is clearly one such effect for both 'illicit' drug users and those labelled 'problem gamblers'. Volberg (2007), as we saw above, suggests that this stigmatisation – which can affect how people are treated, and hence their job prospects and other life chances – can facilitate the transfer of wealth from poor to rich, reinforcing social inequalities.

QUESTION 6: HOW/WHERE IS THIS REPRESENTATION OF THE 'PROBLEM' PRODUCED, DISSEMINATED AND DEFENDED? HOW COULD IT BE QUESTIONED, DISRUPTED AND REPLACED?

As in the case of welfare (Chapter 3), the media plays a major role in 'co-constituting' the identified dominant problem representations (see Chapter 10). Consider the following headlines:

- 'Bag snatcher, 60, fed pokie addiction' (*The Advertiser*, 15 March 2003)
- 'Banned, but addict still played pokies for 17 hours' (*The Advertiser*, 1 March 2006)

- ■ 'We should lock up addicts [referring to drug use], says key adviser' (*The Age*, 1 March 2003)
- ■ 'Alarm as report shows one in 10 teens abuse drugs' (*The Advertiser*, 25 February 2008)
- ■ 'This is Melbourne at night: "alcohol-fuelled anarchy"' (*The Age*, 23 February 2008)
- ■ 'Alcohol abuse "biggest social problem"' (*The Advertiser*, 7 March 2007)

We are bombarded with simple slogans about the state of social relations and about who is to blame for 'problems'. The language of addiction is ubiquitous. In addition, we have seen how the public policies selected for examination in this chapter *produce* and hence reinforce these representations of the 'problem'. More confronting still, important professional groups, including many social scientists, have investments in these problem representations. Indeed they are often hired to research the very categories this chapter suggests need to be problematised, e.g. 'addiction', 'responsible use', 'problem gamblers'.

Resistance continues to occur, however. For example, a household survey on attitudes to drugs conducted in 1996 found that fully a third supported the legalisation of the personal use of cannabis (National Drug Strategy 1996). The pervasiveness of a particular problem representation does not guarantee its acceptance.

In addition there have been a number of attempts to construct counter-discourses to contest prohibitionist approaches to drug use. Harm minimisation is one such discourse. While still resting in the main on a conception of drug users as problematic, the discourse shifts analysis from punishment to treatment, a less physically coercive option.

Some analysts have suggested that framing drug use as a health problem serves to shift the focus from the dominant moralistic framing to a more neutral framing. Brook and Stringer (2005, p. 323) caution against this move, pointing out that some prohibitionists are quite happy to describe drug 'addicts' as 'diseased'. The recent 'discovery' of links between cannabis and psychosis, and the political use of this 'evidence' to increase surveillance and penalties, bears out their argument.

Cannabis and psychosis fact sheet

'Are There Any Dangers in Using Cannabis?
Most people who use cannabis don't experience any obvious harmful effects, but regular use may produce a number of short term effects including paranoia, confusion, increased anxiety, and even hallucination, which can last up to several hours. Longer term risks may include asthma and bronchitis, cancer of the mouth, throat, and lungs, poor concentration and memory, learning difficulties and occasionally, psychosis.

> *Who is Most At Risk From Cannabis Use?*
> People most at risk are those with a family history of psychotic illness or those who have already experienced a psychotic episode. So, people with a family history of psychotic illness should avoid drugs like cannabis, completely, and *try other, healthier ways of relaxing*'
> (State Government of Victoria, 2002; extracts; emphasis added).
>
> • **What is the 'problem' of cannabis use represented to be in this *Fact Sheet*?**
>
> • **How does the category of 'risk' operate in the advice given?**

In the area of gambling, some reformers defend a consumer protection public health model, based around the social determinants of health, discussed in Chapter 6 (National Interest 2004). The Productivity Commission (1999) adopts a consumer protection approach, arguing that gambling 'consumers' do not have enough information to make 'informed consent', mimicking a medical paradigm. Usefully, this way of representing the 'problem' draws attention to the practices of gaming industries. It also identifies governments as co-producers through their taxation practices. However, the primary focus remains on community impact and on reducing 'harm for players and for the broader community', leaving little space to challenge the stigma attached to 'excessive' gambling associated with those characterised as lacking in self-control. In addition, the problem is represented to be lack of information, with the 'informed consumer' constituted as a rational decision-maker.

Some analysts, intent on challenging prohibitionist problem representations in drug policy, shift the focus from 'problematic' sub-cultures to broader trends in mainstream culture, described as overly materialist/consumerist and excessively individualist (Eckersley 2005). There remain tendencies in these analyses, however, to accept the labelling of some drug use (and perhaps 'excessive' gambling) as 'disease' or 'psychosocial disorders' (Eckersley 2001, p. 66). No explanation is offered for why these behaviours are considered problematic *only in some instances*. To address this issue requires reflection on the *symbolic* uses of 'excess' in modes of governance, discussed under Question 4. Hence, challenging the constructed dichotomy between responsible/irresponsible behaviours becomes an important intervention in contemporary debates about how we are governed.

SUBMIT YOUR OWN PROBLEM REPRESENTATIONS TO A WPR ANALYSIS

Always challenging, the prospect of subjecting your own problem representations to a WPR analysis is particularly difficult in these areas, given the media bombardment regarding drug 'abuse' and 'problem gambling'. It has become commonplace to refer to a whole range of activities, including eating and shopping, as *addictions*. Asking questions about foundational presuppositions in these ways of thinking and the uneven effects they produce for different sectors of the population (see analysis above) may act to destabilise these ubiquitous problem representations.

The suggestion that harm minimisation approaches to drug use require scrutiny may arouse opposition or even hostility among those convinced that harm minimisation represents a significant step forward from punitive prohibitionist approaches. Indeed, some might wonder about the feasibility of problematising harm minimisation at a time when harm minimisation approaches have been under attack. On this point a WPR approach is sensibly pragmatic. It acknowledges that it may not always be possible or even useful to dispense with particular problem representations in specific situations. Context affects the feasibility of challenging particular problem representations However, a sharp eye to problematic assumptions and effects within our own problem representations can provide a basis for reflecting on how best to develop proposals that come as close as possible to desired objectives. Elsewhere I have characterised this kind of self-scrutiny as 'reflexive framing' (Bacchi 2008).

SUMMARY

In this chapter we subjected selected documents in drugs/alcohol and gambling policy to the questions in a WPR approach. We found that in *Tough on Drugs* (1997) the dominant problem representation is a law and order framing. In the *National Framework on Problem Gambling* the 'problem', in the main, is represented to be 'problem gamblers'. While 'harm minimisation' presents a challenge to punitive 'responses', to an extent it continues to produce the behaviours of drug users and 'problem gamblers' as problematic. In each case political subjects are constituted as rational and in control, with minority groups who are deemed to lack these characteristics requiring surveillance and guidance. The dividing practices at work here punish and stigmatise select minorities and in so doing produce largely quiescent majorities.

QUESTIONS

1. How does *Tough on Drugs* represent the 'problem' of drug use?
2. How does the *National Framework on Problem Gambling* represent the 'problem' of gambling practices?
3. How are subjects constituted within both policies/programs? With what effects?
4. Who is likely to gain from these problem representations? Who is likely to be harmed?
5. What is likely to change with these representations of the 'problem'? What is likely to stay the same?
6. How could these dominant problem representations be disrupted?

---

1 I would like to thank Anne Wilson for this point.

REFERENCES

AUSTRALIAN GOVERNMENT 2006, *Tough on Drugs—Fact Sheet*, Attorney-General's Department, Canberra.

AUSTRALIAN GOVERNMENT 2007, *Crime Prevention: Illicit Drugs*, Attorney-General's Department, Canberra, <www.ag.gov.au>, accessed 14 April 2008.

AUSTRALIAN INSTITUTE FOR GAMBLING RESEARCH 1999, *Australian Gambling Comparative History and Analysis*, Victorian Commission for Gambling Regulation, published by the Victorian Casino and Gaming Authority, Melbourne, <www.vcgr.vic.gov.au>, accessed 20 April 2008.

AIHW (AUSTRALIAN INSTITUTE OF HEALTH AND WELFARE) 2007, *Statistics on Drug Use in Australia*, Drug Statistics Series, no. 18, AIHW, Canberra.

AIHW (AUSTRALIAN INSTITUTE OF HEALTH AND WELFARE) 2008, *National Public Health Expenditure Report 2005–06*, no. 32, Cat. No. HWE 39, AIHW, Canberra.

AUSTRALIAN LABOR PARTY 2008, *Media Statement*: National Binge Drinking Strategy, 10 March, <www.alp.org.au>, accessed 20 June 2008.

BACCHI, C. 2009, 'The Issue of Intentionality in Frame Theory: The Need for Reflexive Framing', in *The Discursive Politics of Gender Equality: Stretching, Bending and Policymaking*, eds E. Lombardo, P. Meier & M. Verloo, Routledge, London.

BACCHI, C. & BEASLEY, C. 2002, 'Citizen Bodies: Is Embodied Citizenship a Contradiction in Terms?' *Critical Social Policy*, vol. 22, no. 2, pp. 324–52.

BESSANT, J. 2008, 'From "Harm Minimization" to "Zero Tolerance" Drugs Policy in Australia: How the Howard Government Changed its Mind', *Policy Studies*, vol. 29, no. 2, pp. 197–214.

BLASZCZYNSKI, A. 2000, 'Pathways to Pathological Gambling: Identifying Typologies', *The Electronic Journal of Gambling Issues*, vol.1, <www.camh.net/egambling/issue1/feature/index.html>, accessed 20 June 2008.

BROOK, H. & STRINGER, R. 2005, 'Users, Using, Used: a Beginner's Guide to Deconstructing Drugs Discourse', *International Journal of Drug Policy*, vol. 16, no. 5, pp. 316–25.

BROOM, D. 2008, 'Hazardous Good Intentions? Unintended Consequences of the Project of Prevention', *Health Sociology Review*, vol. 17, no. 2, pp. 129–40.

BULL, M. 1996, 'Power and Addiction: the Making of the Modern Addict', *Australian Journal of Social Issues*, vol. 31, no. 2, pp. 191–208.

BUREAU OF INTERNATIONAL NARCOTICS AND LAW ENFORCEMENT AFFAIRS 1998, *International Narcotics Control Strategy Report*, US Department of State, Washington, DC, <www.uplink.com.au/lawlibrary/Documents/Docs/Doc69.html>, accessed 13 August 2008.

DICKERSON, M. 2003, 'Exploring the Limits of "Responsible Gambling": Harm Minimisation or Consumer Protection?' Proceedings of the 12th Annual Conference of the National Association for Gambling Studies, Melbourne, <www.ncalg.org>, accessed 19 June 2008.

ECKERSLEY, R. 2001, 'Culture, Health and Well-being', in *The Social Origins of Health and Well-being*, eds R. Eckersley, J. Dixon & B. Douglas, Cambridge University Press, Melbourne.

ECKERSLEY, R. 2005, '"Cultural Fraud": The Role of Culture in Drug Abuse', *Drug and Alcohol Review*, vol. 24, no. 2, pp. 157–63.

FOSTER'S 2006, *Foster's Alcohol in the Community: Policy Incorporating Responsible Marketing Guidelines*, Foster's Group Ltd, <www.fosters.com.au>, accessed 28 July 2008.

GOVERNMENT OF SOUTH AUSTRALIA 2002, *Tackling Drugs: Government and Communities Working Together*, Social Inclusion Initiative, Government of South Australia, Adelaide.

GUTHMAN, J. & DUPUIS, M. 2006, 'Embodying Neoliberalism: Economy, Culture, and the Politics of Fat', *Environment and Planning D: Society and Space*, vol. 24, no. 3, pp. 427–48.

INTERNATIONAL NARCOTICS CONTROL BOARD 2008, 'Single Convention on Narcotic Drugs, 1961', <www.incb.org/incb/convention_1961.html>, accessed 28 July 2008.

MAKKAI, T., MOORE, R. & MCALLISTER, I. 1991, 'Health Education Campaigns and Drug Use: the "Drug Offensive" in Australia', *Health Education Review*, vol. 6, no. 1, pp. 65–76.

MANDERSON, D. 1993, *From Mr Sin to Mr Big: A History of Australian Drug Laws*, Oxford University Press, Melbourne.

MANDERSON, D. 2005, 'Possessed: Drug Policy, Witchcraft and Belief', *Cultural Studies*, vol. 19, no. 1, pp. 35–62.

MANN, S. 1999, '$150m opiates trade at risk', *The Age*, 18 December.

MARMOT, M. 1997, 'Inequality, Deprivation and Alcohol', *Addiction*, vol. 92, no. 1, pp. 13–20.

McMillen, J. 1996, 'Understanding Gambling: History, Concepts and Theories', in *Gambling Cultures: Studies in History and Interpretation*, ed. J. McMillen, Routledge, London.

MEDICINENET.COM 2003, 'Definition of Substance Abuse', <www.medterms.com>, accessed 13 January 2009.

MILLER, P. 2001, 'A Critical Review of the Harm Minimization Ideology in Australia', *Critical Public Health*, vol. 11, no. 2, pp. 167–78.

MINISTERIAL COUNCIL ON DRUG STRATEGY 2004, *The National Drug Strategy: Australia's Integrated Framework 2004–2009*, Australian Government Department of Health and Ageing, Canberra.

MINISTERIAL COUNCIL ON GAMBLING 2004, *National Framework on Problem Gambling, 2004–2008*, Australian Government Department of Families, Housing, Community Services and Indigenous Affairs, Canberra, <www.gamblingresearch.org.au>, accessed 28 July 2008

NATIONAL DRUG STRATEGY 1996, *Household Survey*, Survey Report, AGPS, Canberra.

NATIONAL INTEREST 2004, 'Demise of the Gambling Research Panel', Radio National, 24 October, <www.abc.net.au>, accessed 11 March 2006.

PRODUCTIVITY COMMISSION 1999, *Australia's Gambling Industries*, Report no. 10, Asinfor, Canberra.

RACE, K. 2005, 'Recreational States: Drugs and the Sovereignty of Consumption', *Culture Machine*, vol. 7, <www.culturemachine.net>, accessed 17 December 2008.

STATE GOVERNMENT OF VICTORIA 2002, *Cannabis and Psychosis Fact Sheet*, Victorian Government Health Information, Department of Human Services, Melbourne.

STATE GOVERNMENT OF VICTORIA 2008, 'Gambler's Help',<www.gspot.org.au/>, accessed 28 July 2008.

UNITED NATIONS 1961, *Single Convention on Narcotic Drugs*, Economic & Social Council, United Nations, New York.

VALVERDE, M. 1998, *Diseases of the Will: Alcohol and the Dilemmas of Freedom*, Cambridge University Press, Cambridge.

VOLBERG, R. A. 2007, 'Legal Gambling and Problem Gambling as Mechanisms of Social Domination? Some Considerations for Future Research', *American Behavioral Scientist*, vol. 51, no. 1, pp. 56–85.

WELLBOURNE-WOOD, D. 1999, 'Harm Reduction in Australia: Some Problems With Putting Policy into Practice', *International Journal of Drug Policy*, vol. 10, no. 5, pp. 403–13.

WHITE, W. 1993, 'A Systems Perspective on Sexual Exploitation of Clients by Professional Helpers', *Dulwich Centre Newsletter*, nos. 3 & 4, pp. 77–87.

FURTHER READING

DUFF, C. 2004, 'Drug Use as a "Practice of the Self": Is There Any Place For an "Ethics of Moderation" in Contemporary Drug Policy?', *The International Journal of Drug Policy*, vol. 15, no. 5, pp. 385–93.

KEENE, H. 2003, 'Critiques of Harm Reduction, Morality and the Promise of Human Rights', *International Journal of Drug Policy*, vol. 14, no. 3, pp. 227–32.

KORN, D., GIBBONS, R. & AZMIER, J. 2003, 'Framing Public Policy Towards a Public Health Paradigm for Gambling', *Journal of Gambling Studies*, vol. 19, no. 2, pp. 235–56.

O'MALLEY, P. 1999, 'Consuming Risks: Harm Minimization and the Government of "Drug Users"', in *Governable Places: Readings in Governmentality and Crime Control*, ed. R. Smandych, Aldershot, Dartmouth.

ROOM, R. 2005, 'Stigma, Social Inequality and Alcohol and Drug Use', *Drug and Alcohol Review*, vol. 24, no. 2, pp. 143–55.

WALKER, M. 1996, 'The Medicalisation of Gambling as an "Addiction"', in *Gambling Cultures: Studies in History and Interpretation*, ed. J. McMillen, London, Routledge.

Crime and justice

Chapter 5

SHIFTING GEAR

In this chapter we take the insights generated in previous chapters and apply them in slightly different ways. First, due to the wide-ranging character of the topic 'crime and justice', we show how a WPR approach is useful in reflecting upon the various frameworks (theories) used to analyse criminal justice and policing policy. As noted in the Introduction, since all theories posit forms of explanation, they necessarily contain problem representations. Sorting through criminal justice theories in this way is necessary because these theories are marshalled to defend particular policies. They form some of the 'knowledges' through which we are governed.

Next, we reflect on recent contributions by governmentality scholars to the study of developments in criminal justice. Our purpose here is to draw attention to the usefulness of reflecting on governmental rationalities (or regimes of governance) that display particular styles of problematisation (see Chapter 1), while highlighting two themes:

- the importance of recognising the multifarious and overlapping nature of governmental rationalities;
- the need to incorporate poststructural insights into the contestability of key referents such as 'crime'.

Our 'practical texts' for this chapter – Anti-Social Behaviour Orders and the National Emergency Response in Australian Aboriginal remote communities – illustrate these themes.

Instead of systematically applying each question in a WPR approach to these texts, as we did in Chapters 3 and 4, this chapter produces a more integrated analysis. Notations, e.g. **Q1**, **Q2**, etc., are inserted to signal when a particular question is being applied. This method is used in subsequent chapters. The reasons for this change in style of analysis are several. First, separate application of the questions, as noted earlier, can result in some repetition. Also, the point of the analysis determines which questions are foregrounded. That is, a researcher may be particularly interested in the subjectification effects **(Q5)** of a selected policy or policy proposal. They may not be immediately interested in its genealogy **(Q3)**. Or, the reverse may be the case. As a consequence, every question need not always be addressed in every analysis, although it is useful to keep the full set of questions in mind. Students are advised to return to the lists of questions provided in Chapters 1 and 2 when a notation appears in the chapter.

CRIMINAL JUSTICE THEORY

Criminal justice and policing policy have already appeared as important markers of policy approaches in Chapter 4 on drugs/alcohol and gambling policy. There we noted that in *Tough on Drugs* drug use was constituted a 'law and order' problem. It is now time to consider just what this means — what is the 'problem' of 'law and order' represented to be? As mentioned above, this question leads to consideration of criminal justice theories.

In a sense, all problematisations are theories, since they include speculation on the causes of specific social developments. For the same reason it is possible and useful to approach all theories as problematisations, inviting the application of a WPR approach to the ways in which different theories represent the 'problem'. It is fairly common to describe theories in terms of paradigms, drawing attention to the ontological and epistemological premises they support. A WPR approach assists in this task **(Q2)** but also raises questions about the genealogical development of specific theories, and hence about the power aspects of this development **(Q3)**. Here it accepts McClure's (1992, p. 365) insight that theorising is 'a political practice always and inescapably implicated with power'. The power dimensions of theorising form a major focus in this book and a central theme in Chapter 10.

According to Henry and Milovanovic (1996, pp. 1–3) criminological theory 'comprises several competing theoretical frameworks, each rooted in a different discipline'. They identify:

■ theories influenced by economics, such as classical criminology, situational or rational choice theory, and 'routine activities or opportunity theory';

■ theories with connections to different branches of psychology, including bio-psychological theories, personality theories, psychoanalytic approaches, and social psychology;

■ theories influenced by sociology and human geography that 'shift the causal force from the individual or social interaction at a group level to the human organizational level'; and

■ crime theories influenced by political theory, philosophy or history 'that give major
   emphasis to power and interests as the active forces in generating crime'.

Henry and Milovanovic (1996, p. xi) proceed to examine the foundational assumptions of
these different theoretical positions, focusing in particular on competing conceptions of
human nature, society and social order, the role of law, definitions of crime, crime causation,
and justice policy and practice. These foundational assumptions form the conceptual logics
of a WPR approach (Q2). For example, theories based in economics presume a self-interested
rational criminal who will stop offending only when, for example, the costs of criminal activity
are too high or crime targets prove too difficult to access. By contrast, theories influenced by
sociology and human geography emphasise the ways in which the 'social environment places
some people in disorganized or structurally strained settings', while criminology influenced
by (some) political theory emphasises the 'inequitable construction of laws'. Despite these
differences, these various theoretical positions share a common starting point – a concern to
explain the 'crime event' (Henry and Milovanovic 1996, p. 3).

   As Henry and Milovanovic (1996, p. 2) point out, each of these theories generates quite
different policy recommendations:

■ economically-based theories favour 'punishment, deterrence and situational manipulation';
■ sociological theories tend to encourage the 'expansion of legitimate opportunities';
■ theories targeting the inequitable construction of laws underpin demands for forms of
   societal reorganisation, including the 'redistribution of wealth and development of a
   justice system aimed at limiting harm rather than being responsive to class power' (Henry
   and Milovanovic 1996, p. 2).

Because different criminal justice theories underpin specific policies, it is possible to uncover
theoretical premises in crime policy by starting with the policy and working backwards to
uncover epistemological and ontological assumptions, as a WPR approach recommends. The
other questions in the approach draw attention to the genealogy (Q3) of specific theories, what
is unanalysed in specific theories (Q4), which effects can be associated with different theoretical
stances (Q5), and how specific theories have gained influence (Q6), always acknowledging
resistance and the possibility of re-problematisation. The injunction (at the end of the list
of questions in a WPR approach) to apply the full set of WPR questions to our own problem
representations, in this instance, means interrogating our own theoretical presumptions. The
goal of the analysis is to identify and confront the power involved in producing particular
meanings of crime.

Approaches to criminal justice and policing policy

A good deal of the contention around crime and justice issues concerns whether or not prisons reduce crime. While one newspaper article claims that 'Tough crime laws proved to fail' (Goode 2003), a second heralds that 'Figures show prison stops crime' (Saunders 2003). Whereas the first article expresses concern about prison as the 'university of crime', increasing the numbers of 'repeat offenders', and supports 'community-based sentencing programs' as alternatives to imprisonment, the latter describes prison as a deterrent: 'Crime, such as any other money-making activity, entails some degree of rational calculation, and the greater the risk of getting caught and punished, the less inclined we are to do the deed' (Saunders 2003).

These adversarial positions capture the difference between two underlying paradigms in approaches to criminal justice policy: one aimed at punishment and deterrence, and the second aimed at rehabilitation and reintegration through social interventions, e.g. parenting courses, drug education classes, assisted housing. Both sides in this debate accept that 'crime' is a readily identifiable occurrence.

A deterrence approach

Situational policies, which include strategies such as enhanced street lighting, drinking age laws and speed cameras, fit within the deterrence paradigm, and reflect economics-based theoretical premises (see above). The underlying assumption (Q2) in these sorts of policies is that people commit crime because they can and, hence, that the best way to reduce crime is to reduce the *opportunities* for crime to occur. The underlying logic is that altered perceptions of risk, effort and reward will affect the decisions of those who might otherwise offend. Clarke (1997) developed a typology of situational crime interventions based on four main opportunity-reducing mechanisms: increase in perceived effort, increase in perceived risk, reduction in anticipated reward, and removal of excuses. Criminals, in this view, are rational actors who make judgements about the feasibility and rewards of their criminal activities. The nature of crime is taken for granted.

Minimum Drinking Age Laws (MDAL)

The current Rudd government's concern about binge drinking, particularly among young people, has led to speculation about the possibility of raising the MDAL from 18 to 21 years old. The Health Minister, Nicola Roxon, announced that 'The Federal Government would consider raising the legal drinking age and increasing alcohol taxes if there was a community push for such measures' (Gartrell, Best and Park 2008).

- **How do these proposals represent the 'problem' of binge drinking?**

- **What theoretical position on criminal justice underpins these proposals?**

- **What assumptions about human nature are reflected in these proposals?**

Social interventionist strategies

Social interventionist strategies, theoretically grounded in sociology, political theory and at times psychology (see above), start from the presumption that people are driven to crime by their circumstances, that is, by difficult or pathological environments. Hence, to reduce crime it is deemed to be necessary to modify those circumstances. There is often an expressed commitment to tackle and reduce inequalities (Muncie 2000, p. 219), with 'inclusive citizenship' a frequently endorsed goal (Q2).

The Commonwealth Government's National Crime Prevention Report *Pathways to Prevention* (Developmental Crime Prevention Consortium 1999) provides a useful example of social interventionist crime policy. The Report rejects a conservative 'law and order' diagnosis based on 'single-cause explanations such as bad genes or dysfunctional parenting' (Marston and Watts 2003, p. 153). It also rejects simple punitive responses such as increased policing powers. Rather it argues that:

> The roots of criminal offending are complex and cumulative . . . embedded in social as well as personal histories. To uncover significant risk factors that are the facilitating conditions for entry into a criminal career requires a life course perspective that views each young offender as someone who is developing over the life course and in specific social settings. (Developmental Crime Prevention Consortium 1999, p. 4)

Despite the rejection of simple punitive 'responses', the researchers who drafted this report share an important basic premise with deterrence approaches – they take the categories of 'crime' and 'criminality' for granted (Marston and Watts 2003, p. 154). The 'problem' of crime is linked to 'risk factors', including 'genetic and biological characteristics of the child, family characteristics, stressful life events and community or cultural factors' (Developmental Crime Prevention Consortium 1999, p. 11). The researchers also rely 'heavily – yet – silently' on 'longstanding views about the essential nature of adolescence' (Marston and Watts 2003, p. 156; see Chapter 3 for discussion).

Significantly, 'structural factors' such as socio-economic disadvantage and neighbourhood violence and crime are considered 'risk factors'. But, as Marston and Watts (2003, p. 156) note, the lists of 'at risk' factors are 'conceived in narrow developmental terms' and are 'so wide ranging as to render any attempt at prediction extremely difficult'.

There are more 'radical' versions of a social interventionist agenda, focusing, for example, on the inequitable impact of criminal law on 'disadvantaged' groups. In these accounts the way in which law functions to privilege some and harm others is addressed. However, the predominant focus in social interventionist strategies remains on 'fixing up' the poor and other groups called 'disadvantaged' (see Chapter 3 on the 'disadvantage' discourse). Predominantly, the goal is integrative, ensuring a smooth-functioning society, rather than transformative, altering systemic inequalities.

Social Inclusion Policy

In the lead-up to the 2007 election, the Labor Party announced its support for a 'social inclusion policy'. Labor's social inclusion initiatives rest on the assumption 'that a purely income based approach does little to address the causes of disadvantage. They [their social inclusion initiatives] all heavily focus on re-engagement and social and economic participation as a means of overcoming social disadvantage' (Gillard and Wong 2007). In a speech to the ACOSS National Annual Conference in 2007, the then Shadow Minister for Employment and Industrial Relations, and Shadow Minister for Social Inclusion, Julia Gillard, explained:

> This won't be a memorial to good intentions – it will be about action and hard-headed economics ... Such an agenda must have two guiding principles:
>
> ■ it must tackle the social exclusion of individuals and communities; and
>
> ■ it must invest in the human capital of all our people, especially the most disadvantaged. (Gillard 2007)

'Social exclusion', explained Gillard (2007; emphasis added), '*can happen* as a result of problems that *emerge* during life, or *it can start* from birth'.

- **Which premises underpin a social inclusion approach to poverty?**
- **What are the links between social inclusion and social interventionist approaches to crime control?**
- **Do you see any silences?**

For this Activity see Bletsas 2007.

Evidence-based crime policy

'Evidence-based' approaches to crime policy deserve separate comment because of the ways in which they cut across the deterrence and social interventionist paradigms. The wide endorsement of this policy approach across a range of policy areas is a major theme in the book. Evidence-based policy, as we shall see in Chapter 6, has its origins in medicine and has subsequently become popular in a wide array of policy fields, including education, social welfare, road safety and crime policy (Hutchinson and Meier 2007). The grounding premise in evidence-based studies is that it is possible to measure and assess interventions in the real world against specified outcomes. In crime policy, specific strategies – be they proposals such as enhanced street lighting (i.e. situational) or parenting classes (i.e. social interventionist) – are evaluated in terms of their ability to reduce 'crime'. The question becomes 'what works' in crime reduction.

Evidence-based policy has broad international support. For example, in January 2003 in the United States, the Coalition for Evidence-Based Policy and the Justice Department launched an official collaboration to advance 'evidence-based crime and substance-abuse policy' (Council for Excellence in Government 2003). The grounding premise (Q2) is that 'Crime prevention should be rational and should be based on the best possible evidence' (Welsh and Farrington 2005, p. 338). The goal is to produce a *science* of crime control (Grabosky 2003). As in medicine (see Chapter 6), systematic reviews of RCTs (randomised controlled trials) report on the success, or otherwise, of targeted crime-reduction strategies.

The science of crime control

In an ABC Radio National interview on evidence-based crime control, Peter Grabosky, from the Research School of Social Sciences, Australian National University, declared:

'Australian governments spend billions of our tax dollars each on criminal justice and crime prevention. With what effect? What return are we getting on this investment? Applying scientific method and a bit of economics, can answer these questions.

Some social programs simply don't work. Others may even have harmful effects. But there are those programs that not only do work, they even pay for themselves, by *helping people to become healthy, productive taxpaying citizens rather than a drain on our social welfare and criminal justice systems.* I challenge our governments, Commonwealth, State and Territory, to identify what does work, what is cost effective, and to invest our tax dollars there.' (Grabosky 2003; emphasis added)

- **What presumptions underpin Grabosky's analysis?**

- **Can 'crime control' be scientific?**

There are clear and obvious links between situational modification crime policies, economics-based theory, and evidence-based methods in the emphasis, for example, on empirical measurement. However, as already noted, social interventionist policy proposals often endorse the *same* evidence-based methodology. For example, the National Crime Prevention Report (Developmental Crime Prevention Consortium 1999, p. 5), described above, made the case that there is 'scientifically persuasive evidence' that 'interventions early in life can have long term impacts on crime and other social problems such as substance abuse'. Similarly, Labor's social inclusion agenda (see Activity on 'Social Inclusion Policy') endorses 'an evidence-based approach, including the setting of targets and the development of the detailed plans to meet them' (Gillard and Wong 2007, p. 4).

While some social interventionists mount challenges to evidence-based evaluations on the grounds that these evaluations cannot capture and deal with the 'complexity of multi-*problem* individuals, families and organizations' (Trinder and Reynolds 2000; emphasis added), it is becoming increasingly difficult to bypass the imperative to fit one's research to an evidence-based framework. Importantly, for our purposes, such a framework, of necessity, takes the meaning of what constitutes 'crime' for granted (Q2). That is, the 'problem' against which 'evidence' is to be 'applied' is presumed to exist separately from deliberations about how to 'solve' it. This premise is roundly challenged by a WPR approach. It should also be noted that analyses that talk about the complexity of 'multi-*problem* families' (and hence the inadequacy of 'simple' evidence-based interventions) also produce the 'problem' in ways that require interrogation. To this end we turn to poststructuralist criminal justice theory.

Poststructuralist criminal justice theory

Poststructuralist criminal justice theory puts the key referent 'crime' in question and hence perceives serious limitations in both deterrence and social interventionist approaches to 'crime' control (although there are some links with social intervention theories that identify the inequitable impact of criminal law on 'disadvantaged' groups as a 'problem'). In poststructuralist criminal justice theory, crime is identified as a social construction. Its status as an independent entity is denied (Q2).

For example, constitutive criminology, named and developed by Henry and Milovanovic (1996, p. 103), redefines crime as *harm*. Two kinds of harm are identified:

- 'harms of reduction', which occur 'when an offended party experiences a loss of some quality relative to their present standing'; and
- 'harms of repression', which occur 'when an offended party experiences a limit or restriction preventing them from achieving a desired position or standing'.

With this definition of crime, constitutive criminology draws the conclusion that current laws *exclude* many behaviours that *should be* called crime, including 'much of what currently stands for business practices, government policies, hierarchical social relations' and 'a lot of what occurs in family life, since these arenas of power are premised upon the inequality that liberates the expression of agency to the creation of pain' (Henry and Milovanovic 1996, p. 116).

In this view, conventional approaches to crime, be they deterrence-based or social interventionist in character, miss a good deal of crime. For example, conventional approaches tend to focus on 'street crime', whereas poststructural approaches, like constitutive criminology, draw attention to 'suite' or white collar crime (Henry and Milovanovic 1996, p. 203; see Sutherland 1940). Centrally important, therefore, is recognising that what is considered to be 'crime' rests 'on the power to define [what 'crime' is], and the power to police certain transgressions whilst ignoring or giving little attention to others' (Muncie 2000, p. 217). Power, in this view, produces meaning in ways that divert attention from the 'law breaking of the powerful', and that produce 'common' criminals as 'pathologized' subjects (Henry and Milovanovic 1996, p. 201). In the main, both deterrence and social interventionist approaches to criminal justice – significant governing 'knowledges' – neglect this operation of power.

Trade Practices Amendment (Cartel Conduct and Other Measures) Bill 2008

'The Bill creates two criminal offences in Part IV of the TPA [Trade Practices Amendment] and equivalent offences in the Competition Code enacted in each state and territory.

    First, a person commits an offence if:

- the person <u>makes</u> a contract or arrangement, or arrives at an understanding (CAU), with the intention of dishonestly obtaining a benefit; and
- the CAU [contract, arrangement or understanding] contains a cartel provision.
    Second, a person commits an offence if:
- a CAU contains a cartel provision; and
- the person <u>gives effect to</u> the cartel provision with the intention of dishonestly obtaining a benefit.

The Bill provides that a cartel provision is a provision of a CAU that relates to price-fixing; restricting outputs in the production and supply chain; allocating customers, suppliers or territories; or bid-rigging, by parties that are, or would otherwise be, in competition with each other.

    The maximum penalties for the offences are:

- for an individual – a term of imprisonment of five years and a fine of $220,000; and
- for a corporation – a fine that is the greater of $10 million or three times the value of the benefit from the cartel, or where the value cannot be determined, 10% of annual turnover.' (Australian Government 2008)

- **How does the government's draft Bill on criminalising cartel behaviours constitute the category of crime?**

- **How are subjects constituted within the draft Bill?**

- **Are there any silences?**

For this Activity see Fisse 2006.

Poststructuralist criminology is also keenly interested in the subjectification effects (**Q5**) of legal and non-legal instruments that cause harm – the ways in which people are produced either as 'choosing subjects', who deserve to be punished (deterrence approaches), or as 'passive subjects shaped by the world', who need to be rehabilitated (social interventionist approaches) (Henry and Milovanovic 1996, p. 16). Attention is drawn, for example, to the ways in which specific social interventions, including those that focus on early childhood development and social inclusion, produce 'self-controlled citizens' and 'normalization of the total social body' (Henry and Milovanovic 1996, p. 1, 111).

In this context the scope of analysis is broadened beyond specific laws to include the full range of instruments and discourses that discipline political subjects. On this point Henry and Milovanovic (1996, p. 202) note that 'it is not human subjects that are constituted but that gendered subjects are constituted'.

Feminist poststructuralists, like Adrian Howe (1994), map the differential impact of disciplinary power on lived female bodies. Offering a more fully *social* understanding of punishment, Howe emphasises the range of non-legal, implicit disciplinary controls that harm women. By targeting the mothers of 'misbehaving' (mainly) male young people, Anti-Social Behaviour Orders, discussed later in the chapter, demonstrate clearly one way in which laws reflect gendered discourses, affecting how women experience themselves and others in and out of the legal system.

As ways forward, Henry and Milovanovic (1996, p. 111) offer a number of strategies, some short- to medium-term, others longer term. To begin, they acknowledge that strategies have to be put in place to deal with those they describe as 'excessive investors' in harm, 'whose past actions render them a present physical danger to others'. For the short-term, they endorse a strategy they call 'social judo' – a form of 'radical refraction' that channels others' exercise of power over us into their 'exercise of power over themselves or toward constructive outcomes' (Henry and Milovanovic 1996, pp. 220–221).

For the longer term they recommend 'peacemaking criminology' (see Pepinsky and Quinney 1991) – criminology which explicitly rejects 'the idea that violence can be overcome by the use of state violence'. They also develop the concept of *replacement* discourse, which, they argue, is different from oppositional discourse because it offers genuine, *new* alternative frameworks of meaning rather than buying into *existing* terms of reference. The idea of 'newsmaking criminology' (see Barak 1988), which they put forward as a form of replacement discourse, is discussed in Chapter 10. For each proposed intervention, Henry and Milovanovic (1996, p. 214) emphasise the need for reflexivity, in tune with the call in a WPR approach to subject *our own* problematisations to critical scrutiny.

CRIMINAL JUSTICE POLICY AND GOVERNMENTALITY

As noted in Chapter 1 a WPR approach shares the premise in governmentality studies that it is useful and important to track *styles of problematisation* in regimes of governance (i.e. governmental rationalities; Q2). In relation to regimes of governing justice, Garland (2001) describes a shift from *penal welfarism*, as a governmental rationality, that, in his view, dominated the 1960s and 1970s in the UK and the USA, to a more recent *'culture of control'*. Penal welfarism – which rested on the belief that humans may be coerced into unlawful behaviour by deprivation – focused predominantly on rehabilitation (see social interventionist theory above), with links to the social welfare governance regime associated with Marshall and Keynes (see Chapter 3). In the new social control paradigm, by contrast, crime is perceived to be a rational act of greedy or unscrupulous individuals. Rather than the 'subjects of need' of penal welfarism, convicted offenders are treated as 'entrepreneurial actors' (Garland 1997, p. 191), whose behaviours can be modified through situational controls (see economics-based criminology theory above).

According to Garland (2001, p. 75), the transition from 'penal welfarism' to a control regime reflects two developments:

- a range of changes in citizens' personal lives in the workplace and in the community, including dramatic economic and technological upheavals, and changes in family structure due, for example, to women's increasing labour force participation (2001, p. 82) – all of which 'can be traced back to the process of capital accumulation and the unceasing drive for new markets, enhanced profits, and competitive advantage' (2001, p. 78);
- the reaction of free-market, socially conservative politics to these changes.

Rising crime rates, hedonistic consumerism and low levels of family cohesion combined, says Garland (2001, pp. 194–5), to create a 'wave of anxiety' that reactionary politics was able to exploit.

According to Garland (2001, Chapter 5) rising crime rates create a predicament for the sovereign state. Incapable of controlling crime but unable to acknowledge publicly that this is the case, states draw a distinction between the *punishment* of crime, which 'remains the business of the state (and becomes once again a significant symbol of state power)', and the *control* of crime, which increasingly is deemed to exist beyond the remit of the state in significant respects (Garland 2001, p. 120). In terms of *punishment*, the prison is rediscovered, not as a mechanism of reform or rehabilitation, but as a means of incapacitation and punishment that satisfies public demands for retribution and public safety. For the latter task of *control* (of crime), the state enlists the help of private (non-state) actors and forges alliances with civil society. More and more responsibility for *crime control* is devolved to individuals, families, organisations and communities. This trend is identifiable in schemes such as 'Crime Stoppers' and 'Neighbourhood Watch'. According to Garland (1997, p. 190), it produces 'responsibilised, security-conscious crime preventing' subjects (Garland 1997, p. 190), *homo prudens*, to use O'Malley's (1992) term.

We have here a schizophrenic state (Owen 2007; see also O'Malley 1999). On the one hand it invokes the old myth of sovereign power while on the other hand it adapts a range of 'technical' strategies that focus more on procedures than on outcomes. The myth of sovereign power is displayed through expressive rhetoric (e.g. *'Tough on Drugs'*; Chapter 4), presumptive minimum sentences (e.g. mandatory sentencing; see the Introduction) and, as Campbell (2008) identifies, reductions in due process rights. The technical strategies include procedural initiatives such as crime mapping, which consists of 'the actuarial description or even prediction of the distribution of crime risks in a given territory' (Cauchie and Chantraine 2006, p. 9). In addition to being used by the police, this technique has been introduced in North America to inform people about trends in crime in their neighbourhood:

> Internet users can now access their personal map of crime distribution based on their own specific, previously defined criteria. Acting as good *homo prudens*, they may then, theoretically, identify those neighbourhoods, or even streets, to be avoided. (Cauchie and Chantraine 2006, p. 9)

As Cauchie and Chantraine (2006, p. 3) point out, while the more technocratic character of developments such as 'crime mapping' appears to be less judgemental than the forms of punishment meted out in punitive regimes, in effect political subjects are '(re)moralized' within and through the new technologies (**Q5**). That is, individuals are held to be at fault if they fail to take appropriate measures to ensure their own and their family's security, or if they put themselves in the path of criminal behaviour. For example, women in particular have increased responsibility to avoid places identified as 'risky'.

This example illustrates how the concept of risk provides a useful entry point for identifying specific *regimes of governance* (**Q2**). In Chapter 3, we noted that the socialisation of risk in schemes such as social insurance has given way in Western industrialised states since the 1980s to more individualised methods for limiting 'risk'. The same trend is observable in current crime policy and again in health policy (Chapter 6). Therefore, to help specify the nature of a particular regime of governance, instead of treating the term 'risk' as descriptive of some assumed reality, the task becomes understanding the different ways in which 'risk' is conceptualised (the kind of 'problem' 'risk' is represented to be) – i.e. as either a social risk to be managed by the state (welfarist regimes) or as an individual risk (neoliberal regimes).

At the same time it is important not to oversimplify regime 'types'. As Garland (2001) makes clear, crime policy shows a *blending* of managerial (neoliberal) techniques and disciplinary (neoconservative) methods of rule. In the context of Foucault's triangle of rule, *including* sovereignty, discipline and government (governmentality) (Foucault 1991, p. 102; see Chapter 2), it therefore illustrates that governance regimes are overlapping and multifarious (**Q2**).

For this reason it is perhaps unwise to differentiate penal welfarism from more sovereign and disciplinary approaches to crime *too sharply*. According to Zedner (2002) it is questionable whether penal welfarism ever fully dominated practice in the USA and the UK in the 1960s and 1970s. Similar caveats about the presumably social nature of mid-twentieth century social security in Britain and Australia were raised in The Introduction. On this point of recognising the complexity of governance regimes, it is also advisable to remember that *competing* criminal justice theoretical traditions, including social interventionist and poststructuralist approaches, *continue* to demand attention and to exert influence, even within a 'culture of control'.

By focusing in each instance (in studying each 'practical text') on how the 'problem' is represented, a WPR approach facilitates identification of the multifarious dynamics operating in specific situations. One such dynamic is *dividing practices* (see Chapters 1 and 2). It is important, for example, to recognise that the 'rediscovery' of the prison in the current era (as a means of incapacitation and punishment) is an uneven event. Criminal justice both punishes the poor excessively (Garland 2001, p. 102) and is 'racialised'. That is, in the USA and in Australia, Afro-Americans and Aboriginal people respectively are significantly over-represented in prisons (Davis 1998; Loff and Cordner 2001). We need to ask, therefore – what in the representation of the 'problem' of 'crime' produces this effect?

True to its poststructural principles, a WPR approach insists that, in order to answer this question, the key referent 'crime' needs to be put in question. While it is clearly the case that such referents cannot be wished away due to their integration in government practices (Dean 1999, p. 65), accepting them as givens can mean neglecting important levels of dispute and contestation, and the ways in which power shapes the meanings of key terms. Leaving key referents unchallenged can, therefore, produce the impression that 'problems' are real and compelling, *driving* lawmakers to 'respond'. For example, although Garland (2001, p. 76, 77, 201; emphasis added) insists that the control 'response' he identifies is 'by no means inevitable' – that 'structurally related' is not the same as 'structurally determined' – his 'practical *problem-solving*' theory accepts, at a basic level, that crime is a social fact rather than a cultural product. To see how a WPR approach addresses these questions we turn to our 'practical texts'.

ANTI-SOCIAL BEHAVIOUR ORDERS

The Rann Labor government in South Australia is considering introducing anti-social behaviour orders (ASBOs), based on a UK model. The idea of 'naming and shaming' 'troublemakers', as part of an ASBO, was touted in 2006. Under this proposal police would be able to post notices displaying a person's photo, specifying their actions and why they are being named. 'Youth' are a particular target. The then Attorney-General Michael Atkinson stated that the '"name and shame" proposal was all about creating a circuit-breaker for youths headed toward a life of crime' (Kelton 2006).

In the UK, ASBOs were first introduced under the *Crime and Disorder Act 1998 (UK)* and have been amended and expanded by the *Police Reform Act 2002 (UK)* and the *Anti-Social Behaviour Act 2003 (UK)*. Anti-social behaviour is defined as behaviour that causes or is likely to cause harassment, alarm or distress. ASBOs may be made against an individual deemed to have behaved in this manner if the court finds that the order is 'necessary to protect persons from further anti-social acts' (UK 1998, Section 1). While an ASBO is a civil order, *breaching* an ASBO constitutes a criminal offence, and can result in a prison sentence of up to five years or, for those under seventeen years of age, a detention and training order of up to two years. ASBOs can ban any individual over ten years of age both from carrying out specific acts and from entering certain geographical areas. They last a minimum of two years, but can be imposed for longer periods of time. Contrary to criminal law, hearsay evidence is admissible (Youth Affairs Council of South Australia 2007). The sorts of behaviours targeted include graffiti, vandalism and loitering.

In the UK, ASBOs may be applied for by police forces, local councils, housing trusts and 'registered social landlords' (RSLs) – independent housing organisations registered with the Housing Corporation. The making of an ASBO may constitute grounds for eviction (Winford 2006). While, if introduced by the Rann government, ASBOs would mark a new departure in Australian legal governance, South Australians have had the right to apply for the eviction of 'anti-social' tenants since 1995 under the *Residential Tenancy Act* (Hunter, Nixon and Slatter 2005).

In the UK, ASBOs form part of a broader agenda to deal with 'anti-social behaviour'. Associated laws include:

- Individual Support Orders (ISOs), introduced in 2003, which require offending juveniles to attend sessions with specialists such as drug counsellors and psychologists. Breach of an ISO can lead to the parent being fined.
- Acceptable Behaviour Contracts (ABCs), which are voluntary agreements aimed at getting offending juveniles to alter 'undesirable' behaviours.
- Parenting contracts and orders which target the parents of 'unruly children'. Contracts typically involve good parenting classes. Orders can place court-mandated obligations on parents.
- Curfew and dispersal powers which 'effectively ban children from public places and allow police to deal with them if they do not comply' (Casciani 2006).

ASBOs illustrate the argument above that governance regimes are complex and multi-faceted. In the main, ASBOs involve discipline and deterrence (**Q2**), supporting Garland's (2001; see above) argument about a shift from penal welfarism to punishment and deterrence. However, some associated policies, such as ABCs, encourage *self-regulation*, a form of governance associated with liberal and neo-liberal modes of rule. In addition, orders to see psychologists and other professionals indicate support for rehabilitation, a social interventionist strategy illustrating alliances between government, and medical and other 'experts' in governance projects.

ASBOs have attracted a good deal of criticism from civil libertarians. In the main, these critics agree that 'anti-social behaviours' are 'problems' that need to be 'addressed'. The main objection to deterrence approaches is that they neglect the 'underlying causes' of such behaviours. Supporting social interventionist premises, critics of ASBOs tend to recommend 'remedial interventions' (Hunter 2001). In this vein the Youth Affairs Council (2007; emphasis in original) makes the case that ASBOs work 'only when applied in conjunction with early intervention orders, support for behavioural change, education, programs that respond to the *causes* of the behaviour, and diversion programs for young people'. Supporting this approach Welsh and Farrington (2005, p. 344) produce a systematic review (see evidence-based policy above) evaluating the effects of 'child social skills or social competence training' on 'anti-social behaviour'.

Other critics of ASBOs probe more deeply into 'underlying causes'. For example, according to Jennifer Duncan of the Youth Affairs Council (Heywire 2007), to 'remedy anti-social behaviour, we need to remedy poverty, disadvantage and exclusion'. In her view the 'key problem with the anti-social behaviour system is that it serves to further exclude individuals whom we actually want to bring back into our communities'. This form of social inclusion agenda (see Activity on 'Social Inclusion Policy') focuses on (re)integration and continues to accept the existence of something called 'anti-social behaviour', a category put into question in a WPR analysis.

The 'problem' for ASBOs involves a range of property offences (Q1). A particular notion of 'public' space is created – space belonging to some, often shop owners, but not to 'others', often young people (Q2). The discourse of 'troubled youth' frames ASBOs. Atkinson's (Kelton 2006; see above) description of the 'naming and shaming' proposal as a 'circuit-breaker for youths headed toward a life of crime' reflects this construction of 'youth' as a period of dangerous instability (Q2; see Chapter 3).

The factors that make only certain forms of property 'infringements' problematic tend to escape analysis. For example, reflecting on a 1996 proposal in the South Australian Parliament for curfews on young people, Simpson (1997, p. 15) draws attention to the 'privatising' of many public spaces, which is 'subtle and incremental but lies behind much of the alienation young people experience in society' (Q3, Q4). In a similar vein, Middendorp (2002) observes that Melbourne's public space is 'increasingly unfriendly to its disadvantaged citizens', particularly the homeless.

Hunter (2001) shows the way in which presumptions about the value of nuclear families affect the implementation of ASBOs in Britain (Q2). Women-headed households, it seems, are far more likely to lose their homes than other tenants. A broader gender discourse is at work (Q2) in the way in which women are held responsible for male behaviours, often the behaviours of their male children, illustrating the point made earlier that we are constituted as *gendered* subjects (Q5).

In terms of other effects (Q5) tying social housing to behaviour makes citizenship conditional on behaviour, part of a wider trend described as the 'social policy of conditionality' (see Lewis

2004, p. 25 and Chapter 3). Going further ASBOs create a form of non-criminal behaviour as potentially criminal – those who breach an ASBO face possible prison sentences. In this way the web of surveillance incorporates what a person *might do*, rather than what they *have done*. Attorney-General Atkinson endorsed new control orders in exactly these terms: 'We know that if certain people congregate in a certain place and do certain things that crime will follow. The crime may be hard to prove, the precursor is easy to prove because it is in everyone's face' (Kerrison 2007).

Dividing practices are at work in the ways in which ASBOs are applied. In the UK some social groups are more likely to be targeted than others (Q5). For example, a 2005 study by the British Institute for Brain Injured Children reported that approximately 35 per cent of ASBOs have been applied to young people with a diagnosed mental illness or learning disability (Youth Affairs Council 2007).

Stigmatising some subjects as 'troublesome' facilitates governing of the majority who see themselves as *unlike* the targeted group. This dynamic helps explain the broad support for ASBOs (Q5). In a 2005 British poll, some 82 per cent supported ASBOs (MORI Social Research Institute Survey 2005 in Winford 2006, p. 3, fn 2). At the same time there are signs of resistance (Q6) in the identified tendency of some to sport ASBOs as 'badges of honour' (Youth Affairs Council 2007). Hunter (2001, p. 409) also found that many of the mothers held responsible for the (mis)behaviours of their (mainly) sons described themselves as 'good parents'.

The *lived effects* of the orders can be devastating (Q5). In many cases the orders are breached (i.e. the 'offending' behaviour is repeated). Currently one in four recipients of an order is imprisoned (Youth Affairs Council 2007). Many more end up with no place to live (Hunter 2001).

To re-conceptualise the 'problem', the category 'anti-social behaviour' needs to be put in question (Q4, Q6). A few provocative questions assist in this task: Why is advertising that sexualises young children not considered anti-social behaviour? Why is it not considered anti-social behaviour for large pharmaceutical companies to test drugs in 'third world' countries? Why is the killing of thousands of Iraqi people not considered anti-social behaviour?

To apply a WPR analysis to one's own problem representations requires a firm commitment to put taken-for-granted categories and assumptions under scrutiny. Above, we saw that it is necessary:

■ to consider that the key referent 'crime' is often interpreted narrowly;
■ to reflect on those institutions and people who play central roles in designating what is meant by 'crime'; and
■ to put in question definitional assumptions in both punitive approaches to crime and in meliorative approaches, such as rehabilitation.

School enrolment and attendance initiatives

On 1 April 2008 the then New South Wales Premier, Morris Iemma, announced his intention to introduce gaol sentences for parents who failed to send their children to school. The introduction of anti-truancy laws formed part of the government's commitment to keep children in school. The school-leaving age has been raised to 16 in New South Wales and to 17 in South Australia.

According to Iemma, 'Good education is the best possible start that kids can have in their life' (Ralston 2008). In a press conference he declared that 'it was time that the issue of school enrolments and truancy became one of parental responsibility' (Benson 2008).

- **What is the 'problem' of truancy represented to be in this proposal?**
- **Who is held responsible for the 'problem'?**
- **Are there any silences?**
- **How could the 'problem' be re-conceptualised?**

NATIONAL EMERGENCY RESPONSE: 'STABILISE', 'NORMALISE' AND 'EXIT'

Our second 'practical text' is the National Emergency Response in Australian Aboriginal remote communities. On 21 June 2007 the Howard-led Coalition government in Australia announced a swathe of measures to 'tackle child abuse in Northern Territory Indigenous communities' under the heading of National Emergency Response legislation, sometimes described as 'the intervention'. The measures included:

- Take control of Aboriginal townships through five-year leases to improve property and public housing.
- Six-month ban on alcohol on Aboriginal land.
- Ban on X-rated pornography and audits of computers to identify illegal material.
- Welfare reform to quarantine 50 per cent of payments, to ensure they are spent on necessities such as food. This action will follow the parent wherever that parent may go, so the obligation cannot be avoided simply by moving to another part of Australia.
- Enforcing school attendance by linking income support and family assistance payments to school attendance for all people living on Aboriginal land. The Government will also ensure that meals are provided to children at school, with parents paying for the meals.
- Increasing police numbers …
- Clean-up and repair of communities by work-for-the-dole participants.
- Scrapping the permit system for common areas, road corridors, and airstrips on Aboriginal land. ('Iron Fist' 2007)

In addition, the Federal Government directed the Northern Territory Government to remove customary law as a mitigating factor for sentencing and bail conditions (Brough 2007a).

John Howard, Prime Minister at the time, declared that it was time for intervention to combat the 'national emergency' of child sex abuse in Indigenous communities, identified in the *Little Children are Sacred Report*, prepared by the Northern Territory Board of Inquiry into the Protection of Aboriginal Children from Sexual Abuse (Anderson and Wild 2007). The then Minister for Families, Community Services and Indigenous Affairs, Mal Brough, announced that the intervention would involve a three-phase strategy of 'stabilisation', 'normalisation' and 'exit' (Colebatch 2007a).

'The intervention' positively *invites* a WPR analysis, not least because presumed connections between land acquisition, the quarantining of welfare payments and child sexual abuse are certainly not obvious. Other connections, for example, between access to alcohol and pornography, and child abuse, may appear to be clearer, though the assumed links are never explicitly laid out. Also, the overt description of the strategy as an exercise in *normalisation*, a key analytic concept in Foucault's work (see Chapter 2), invites comment.

A little background is needed to understand the context for 'the intervention'. First, there had been numerous earlier reports identifying sexual abuse in remote Aboriginal communities as a 'problem', extending as far back as 1993 (Coorey 2001). Second, in the lead-up to 'the intervention' the Howard government had failed in its attempts to reclaim some leaseholds that had been granted to some Aboriginal communities. Finally, under the permit system – scrapped in 'the intervention' – non-Aboriginal people required permission to enter selected outback communities.

More generally it is important to have a longer view of the policy context for 'the intervention' (Q3). Conventionally, approaches to Aboriginal/non-Aboriginal affairs in Australia are divided chronologically: segregation and 'protection' (from settlement to early-twentieth century); assimilation (from 1937); integration and self-determination associated with the 1972 Whitlam Labor government; and self-management, a term introduced by the Fraser Liberal government in 1976. The Hawke and Keating Labor governments (1983–1996) used both self-determination and self-management as governing concepts, with Keating initiating a reconciliation agenda in 1991. Self-determination involved the creation of an elected representative Aboriginal council, ATSIC (Aboriginal and Torres Strait Islander Commission), and some recognition of native title land claims (*Native Title Act 1993 (Cth)* (Parliament of Australia 1993)).

The Howard-led Coalition government (1996–2007) had as a goal the reversal of self-determination which, in its view, had failed to provide a 'fix' for the poverty and 'problems' afflicting remote Aboriginal communities. In 2004 it disbanded ATSIC. The take-over of Aboriginal leaseholds and the ending of the permit system in 'the intervention' create the 'problem' of child sexual abuse as part of outback Aboriginal culture (Q1, Q2), signalling that the Howard government had given up on remote Aboriginal communities (Rowse 2007a). The land acquisition initiatives constitute communal land ownership and Indigenous collective decision making as 'responsible for the social collapse of Indigenous society' (Dodson 2007a, p. 24). When criticised for lack of consultation with leaders of the Aboriginal community, Howard declared that they were 'part of the problem' (Schubert and Murdoch 2007, p. 6).

Several presuppositions underpin this representation of the 'problem' (Q2). Howard's 'intervention' rests upon a belief in free market economics and 'a moral paradigm of property' (Rowse 2007b, p. 54). There is a presumption that 'only private ownership of land can generate wealth and provide the basis of community cohesion and functionality' (Dodson 2007b). A Western, Protestant and indeed Christian self is established as the norm for 'good behaviour'. In Howard's words:

> Most nations experience some level of cultural diversity while also having a dominant cultural pattern running through them. In Australia's case, that dominant pattern comprises Judeo-Christian ethics, the progressive spirit of the Enlightenment and the institutions and values of British political culture. (Mansell 2007, p. 75)

In Howard's view, 'Their [remote Aboriginal peoples'] future can only be as part of the mainstream of the Australian community' (Ravens 2007).

The 'stabilising' stage of the intervention involved sending Australian troops and additional police into the 'prescribed communities'. The language of 'emergency' served to justify this 'response'. Howard drew an analogy between the 'discovery' of child sexual abuse and hurricane Katrina (Boulden and Morton 2007, p. 163). Here the 'problem' is created as a short-term and temporary phenomenon that can be 'fixed' with 'militarised surveillance' (Hinkson 2007, p. 294), denying the history of Aboriginal dispossession and exploitation (Q2, Q4). Child abuse is produced as a 'crime' that can be 'fixed' through a stricter law and order regime, ignoring the well-identified complexities of the phenomenon (Q4). To say this is not to deny that many Aboriginal people welcomed an increase in the police presence, something they had been demanding for many years (Boulden and Morton 2007, p. 167).

The policing dimension of the intervention places it within a coercive model of criminal justice and a disciplinary mode of governance (Q2). So too do the banning of alcohol and pornography, the quarantining of welfare payments and the introduction of Work for the Dole labour initiatives (see Chapter 3). However, by labelling the second stage of the intervention 'normalisation', Brough hints at the more complex governmental objective signalled by land acquisition and abolition of CDEP initiatives (see Activity below) – to produce Aboriginal people as entrepreneurs who act 'responsibly'. Unsurprisingly, given the pervasiveness of a responsibilisation discourse in current governance regimes (Q2; see Chapters 3 and 4) – a discourse targeting *individual* behaviours – and the accompanying subjectification effects (Q5), this goal is embraced by many Aboriginal people, notably Noel Pearson (2007). Importantly, this particular vision of Aboriginal people as investors in themselves is also *contested* by many outspoken Aboriginal citizens and activists (**Q6**).

Some critics of 'the intervention' put the case that Howard had misidentified the 'problem', which was much too complex to be addressed with such a blunt instrument as the National Emergency Response. The laws were described as 'knee-jerk' (Rintoul and Lunn 2007, p. 4), with 'gaping holes', neglecting, for example, the need for counselling and rehabilitation services (Colebatch 2007b). As part of a social interventionist agenda, a wide array of 'therapeutic' professionals became involved in addressing the 'problem' of 'intergenerational trauma' (Phillips 2007; **Q3**).

While targeting a specific racial group is proscribed by the *Racial Discrimination Act* (1975) the government invoked the 'special measures' provision of the Act to legitimise 'the intervention', declaring its sole purpose to be '*securing the advancement* of Indigenous Australians' (Brough 2007b; emphasis added). This proposal constitutes the 'problem' to be a state of degeneracy among Aboriginal people (**Q1**; see Chapter 8). This dividing practice has stigmatising effects, reflected and encouraged in the media (**Q5**, **Q6**). On the day after the 'emergency' measures were announced, the front page of *The Australian* (Karvelas 2007) headlined in large bold print, 'Crusade to save Aboriginal kids'. A feature article (McKenna 2007) in the same edition proclaimed 'Damaged generation', beneath a striking, surreal picture of a gargantuan black hand with demon-like fingernails about to engulf a small Aboriginal figure.

Casting Aboriginal peoples as 'lesser' and 'damaged' provides the rationale for illiberal treatment, much in the way that 'youth' are singled out for increased surveillance on the grounds that they are only 'partially rational' (see Chapter 3 and discussion of ASBOs above). The Health Minister at the time, Tony Abbott (2006), justified a 'new paternalism' in precisely these terms: 'It seems the fundamental problem is not lack of spending (although it could always be higher) but the culture of directionlessness in which so many Aboriginal people live.' Silenced in this representation of the 'problem' are the comparatively low levels of alcohol consumption among Aboriginal people, and the high levels of child sexual abuse in non-Aboriginal communities, most recently identified as a 'problem' in Catholic communities (Perry 2008; **Q4**).

Contestation and disruption take a number of forms (**Q6**). Some examples, which deserve more attention than space allows, include:

- Altman (2007a, p. 308) counters appeals to the 'real economy' of Noel Pearson with a 'hybrid economic model';
- Dodson (2007a, p. 24) highlights the need for the 'dominant society' to respect and resource 'Indigenous authority';
- Wright (2007) turns the disadvantage discourse (see Chapter 3) on its head by referring to 'dysfunctional governments';

■ Arabena (2006) highlights the need for 'positive infrastructure', such as libraries, playgrounds and picture theatres, instead of more 'imposed violence';

■ Tumarkin (2007) draws on the work of Eisenbruch (1991) to offer 'cultural bereavement' as a replacement discourse for PTSD (Post-Traumatic Stress Disorder): 'Let's stop thinking of trauma as the domain of experts, and, instead, begin reclaiming it as something that belongs first and foremost within the shared public sphere'.

Jobs and training for Indigenous people

Joe Hockey, Minister for Employment and Workplace Relations, and Mal Brough, Minister for Families, Community Services and Indigenous Affairs, in the Howard-led Coalition government, announced the termination of the Community Development Employment Projects (CDEP) as a further key step in the Emergency Response being implemented in the Northern Territory.

'Under the changes', said Brough, 'it is expected that some 2000 people will be assisted off CDEP into real work. Others will be given better opportunities for training and participation by being transitioned onto income support, with the normal participation requirements including access to Job Network services, Structured Training and Employment Projects (STEP) or Work for the Dole.

These changes will mean a renewed focus on helping Indigenous people to become work ready, assisting them find jobs both within and outside their communities and improving their work related skills through education, training and work experience.

While acknowledging the role that CDEP has played in many communities, it has become a destination for too many. We need to do much better to improve the long-term prospects for economic independence for those living in the remote areas of the Northern Territory' (Hockey and Brough 2007).

• In the proposal to end CDEP programs, what is the 'problem' of Aboriginal unemployment represented to be?

• Which assumptions and presuppositions underpin this representation of the 'problem'?

• Do you see any silences?

For this Activity see Altman 2007b.

SUMMARY

In this chapter we examined the ways in which criminal justice theory and policy represent the 'problem' of 'crime'. We compared deterrence-based approaches and social interventionist initiatives, showing how both see 'crime' as a clear-cut and readily observable phenomenon. The increasing reliance of both paradigms on evidence-based methodologies is noted. The examples of ASBOs (Anti-Social Behaviour Orders) and 'the intervention' into remote Aboriginal communities, which combine punitive, disciplinary and governmental ('government at a distance'; see Chapter 2) logics, illustrate the hybrid character of governance regimes. They also highlight the need to question assumptions that the meaning of 'crime' is obvious and uncontroversial.

QUESTIONS

1. How do ASBOs represent the 'problem' of 'crime'?
2. How does the National Emergency Response represent the 'problem' of child sexual abuse in remote Aboriginal communities?
3. Who is likely to gain from these problem representations? Who is likely to be harmed?
4. What is likely to change with these representations of the 'problems'? What is likely to stay the same?
5. How are subjects constituted within both policies/programs? With what effects?
6. How could these problem representations be disrupted?

REFERENCES

ABBOTT, T. 2006, 'The "New Paternalism"', On Line Opinion, 28 June, <www.onlineopinion. com.au>, accessed 24 April 2008.

ALTMAN, J. 2007a, 'In the Name of the Market?' in *Coercive Reconciliation: Stabilise, Normalise, Exit Aboriginal Australia*, eds J. Altman & M. Hinkson, Arena Publications, North Carlton, Melbourne.

ALTMAN, J. 2007b, 'Neo-Paternalism and the Destruction of CDEP', *Arena Magazine*, vol. 90, 1st August, pp. 33–35.

ANDERSON, P. & WILD, R. 2007, *Ampe Akelyernemane Meke Mekarle Report* (*Little Children are Sacred*), Northern Territory Board of Inquiry into the Protection of Aboriginal Children from Sexual Abuse, <www.nt.gov.au>, accessed 23 April 2008.

ARABENA, K. 2006, 'Quick-fix Solutions to Violence Don't Work', *The Age*, 20 May.

AUSTRALIAN GOVERNMENT 2008, 'Criminal Penalties for Serious Cartel Conduct – Draft Legislation', Discussion Paper, 11 January, <www.treasury.gov.au>, accessed 23 July 2008.

BARAK, G. 1988, 'Newsmaking Criminology: Reflections on the Media, Intellectuals, and Crime', *Justice Quarterly*, vol. 5, no. 4, pp. 565–87.

BENSON, S. 2008, 'Parents Face Jail for Truant Kids Under New Laws', *Daily Telegraph*, <www. news.com.au>, accessed 28 July 2008.

BLETSAS, A. 2007, 'Contesting Representations of Poverty: Ethics and Evaluation', *Policy and Society*, vol. 26, no. 3, pp. 63–82.

BOULDEN, K. & MORTON, J. 2007, 'Don't Crash the Ambulance', in *Coercive Reconciliation: Stabilise, Normalise, Exit Aboriginal Australia*, eds J. Altman & M. Hinkson, Arena Publications, North Carlton, Melbourne.

BROUGH, M. 2007a, *Media release*: National Emergency Response to Protect Aboriginal Children in the Northern Territory, 21 June, <www.facsia.gov.au>, accessed 28 July 2008.

BROUGH, M. 2007b, *Families, Community Services and Indigenous Affairs and other Legislation Amendment (Northern Territory National Emergency Response and other Measures) Bill 2007*, Second Reading Speech, *Hansard*, 7 August, 2007, <www.facsia.gov.au>, accessed 28 July 2008.

CAMPBELL, L. 2008, 'The Culture of Control in Ireland: Theorising Recent Developments in Criminal Justice', *Web Journal of Current Legal Issues*, vol. 1, <http://webjcli.ncl.ac.uk>, accessed 23 July 2008.

CASCIANI, D. 2006, 'ASBOs and Orders: A glossary', *BBC News community affairs*, <http://newsvote.bbc.co.uk>, accessed 12 July 2007.

CAUCHIE, J-F. & CHANTRAINE, G. 2006, 'Use of Risk in the Government of Crime: New Prudentialism and New Penology', *Champ Pénal*, Vol. II, <http://champpenal.revues.org/document467.html>, accessed 23 July 2008.

CLARKE, R. 1997, *Situational Crime Prevention: Successful Case Studies*, 2nd edition, Harrow and Heston, New York.

COLEBATCH, T. 2007a, 'Learning a Purpose in Life', *The Age*, 26 June.

COLEBATCH, T. 2007b, 'Much Goodwill But Gaping Holes Need Filling', *The Age*, 23 June.

COOREY, L. 2001, *Child Sexual Abuse in Rural and Remote Australian Indigenous Communities: A Preliminary Investigation*, Senate Select Committee on the Administration of Indigenous Affairs, Canberra, <www.aph.gov.au>, accessed 28 July 2008.

COUNCIL FOR EXCELLENCE IN GOVERNMENT (2003) *Coalition for Evidence-Based Policy*, <www.excelgov.org>, accessed 16 April 2008.

DAVIS, A. 1998, 'Masked Racism: Reflections on the Prison Industrial Complex', *Colorlines: the national newspaper on race and politics*, Fall, pp. 1–4.

DEAN, M. 1999, *Governmentality: Power and Rule in Modern Society*, Sage, London.

DEVELOPMENTAL CRIME PREVENTION CONSORTIUM 1999, *Pathways to Prevention: Developmental and Early Intervention Approaches to Crime in Australia*, Commonwealth Attorney-General's Department, Australian Government Publishing Service, Canberra, <www.crimeprevention.gov.au>, accessed 20 June 2008.

DODSON, P. 2007a, 'Whatever Happened to Reconciliation?' in *Coercive Reconciliation: Stabilise, Normalise, Exit Aboriginal Australia*, eds J. Altman & M. Hinkson, Arena Publications, North Carlton, Melbourne.

DODSON, P. 2007b, 'An Entire Culture is at Stake', *The Age*, 14 July.

EISENBRUCH, M. 1991, 'From PTSD [Post-Traumatic Stress Disorder] to Cultural Bereavement: Diagnosis of Southeast Asian Refugees', *Social Science & Medicine*, vol. 33, no. 6, pp. 673–80.

FISSE, B. 2006, 'The Proposed Australian Cartel Offence: The Problematic and Unnecessary Element of Dishonesty', Sydney Law School Research Paper no. 06/44, <http://papers.ssrn.com>, accessed 21 April 2008.

FOUCAULT, M. 1991 [1978], 'Governmentality', in *The Foucault Effect: Studies in Governmentality*, eds G. Burchell, C. Gordon & P. Miller, University of Chicago Press, Chicago.

GARLAND, D. 1997, '"Governmentality" and the Problem of Crime: Foucault, Criminology, Sociology', *Theoretical Criminology*, vol. 1, no. 2. pp. 173–214.

GARLAND, D. 2001, *The Culture of Control: Crime and Social Order in Contemporary Society*, University of Chicago Press, Chicago.

GARTRELL, A., BEST, C. & PARK, N. 2008 'Government to Consider Raising the Legal Drinking Age', *Courier Mail*, 24 March, <www.news.com.au>, accessed 15 October 2008.

GILLARD, J. 2007, 'An Australian Social Inclusion Agenda', Speech to ACOSS National Annual Conference, <www.alp.org.au>, accessed 23 July 2008

GILLARD, J. & WONG, P. 2007, 'An Australian Social Inclusion Agenda', Australian Labor, <www.alp.org.au>, accessed 23 July 2008.

GOODE, A. 2003, 'Tough Crime Laws Proved to Fail', *The Advertiser*, 15 March.

GRABOSKY, P. 2003, 'The Science of Crime Control', *Ockham's Razor*, ABC Radio National, 15 June.

HENRY, S. & MILOVANOVIC, D. 1996, *Constitutive Criminology: Beyond Postmodernism*. London: Sage.

HEYWIRE 2007, 'Youth Council Warns Against Behavioural Orders', 24 August, <www.abc.net.au/news>, accessed 15 April 2008.

HINKSON, J. 2007, 'The "Innocence" of the Settler Imagination', in *Coercive Reconciliation: Stabilise, Normalise, Exit Aboriginal Australia*, eds J. Altman and M. Hinkson, Arena Publications, North Carlton, Melbourne.

HOCKEY, J. & BROUGH, M. 2007, *Joint Media Release*: Jobs and Training for Indigenous People in the Northern Territory, 13 July, <www.facsia.gov.au>, accessed 28 July 2008.

HOWE, A. 1994, *Punish and Critique: Towards a Feminist Analysis of Penalty*, Routledge, London.

HUNTER, C. 2001, 'Taking the Blame and Losing the Home: Women and Anti-social Behaviour', *Journal of Social Welfare and Family Law*, vol. 23, no. 4, pp. 395–410.

HUNTER, C., NIXON, J. & SLATTER, M. 2005, 'Neighbours Behaving Badly: Anti-Social Behaviour, Property Rights and Exclusion in England and Australia', *Macquarie Law Journal*, vol. 5, pp. 149–76.

HUTCHINSON, T. P. & MEIER, A. J. 2007, 'Evidence-Based Anything: Priorities for Librarians', *Electronic Journal of Academic and Special Librarianship*, vol. 8, no. 2, pp. 1–9, <http://southernlibrarianship.icaap.org/content/v08n02/hutchinson_t01.html>, accessed 16 April 2008.

'IRON FIST' 2007, 'Measures Announced by the Federal Government to Tackle Child Abuse in Northern Territory Indigenous Communities', *The Australian*, 22 June, p. 4.

KARVELAS, P. 2007, 'Crusade to Save Aboriginal Kids', *The Australian*, 22 June.

KELTON, G. 2006, 'Name and Shame Laws "on Agenda for a Year"', *The Advertiser*, 13 February.

KERRISON, J. 2007, 'Anti-Social Behaviour Orders', *Stateline South Australia*, 24 August. <www.abc.net.au/stateline>, accessed 15 April 2008.

LEWIS, G. 2004, '"Do Not Go Gently ..."; Terrains of Citizenship and Landscapes of the Personal' in *Citizenship: Personal Lives and Social Policy*, ed. G. Lewis, The Policy Press in association with The Open University, Bristol.

LOFF, B. & CORDNER, S. 2001, 'Death Rate of Aborigines in Prisons is Increasing', *The Lancet*, vol. 357, no. 9265, p. 1348.

MANSELL, M. 2007, 'The Political Vulnerability of the Unrepresented', in *Coercive Reconciliation: Stabilise, Normalise, Exit Aboriginal Australia*, eds J. Altman & M. Hinkson, Arena Publications, North Carlton, Melbourne.

MARSTON, G. & WATTS, R. 2003, 'Tampering With the Evidence: A Critical Appraisal of Evidence-Based Policy Making', *The Drawing Board: An Australian Review of Public Affairs*, vol. 3, no. 3, pp. 143–63.

MCCLURE, K. 1992, 'The Issue of Foundations: Scientized Politics, Politicized Science and Feminist Critical Practice', in *Feminists Theorize the Political*, eds. J. Butler & J. Scott, Routledge, New York.

MCKENNA, M. 2007, 'Damaged Generation', *The Australian*, 22 June 2007, p. 13.

MIDDENDORP, C. 2002, 'Homelessness and Public Space: Unwelcome Visitors', *Parity*, vol. 15, no. 1, p. 18.

MUNCIE, J. 2000, 'Decriminalizing Criminology', in *Rethinking Social Policy*, eds. G. Lewis, S. Gewirtz & J. Clarke, Sage, London.

O'MALLEY, P. 1992, 'Risk, Power and Crime Prevention', *Economy and Society*, vol. 21, no. 3, pp. 252–75.

O'MALLEY, P. 1999, 'Volatile and Contradictory Punishment', *Theoretical Criminology*, vol. 3, no. 2, pp. 175–96.

OWEN, T. 2007, 'Culture of Crime Control: Through a Post-Foucauldian Lens', *Internet Journal of Criminology*, <www.internetjournalofcriminology.com>, accessed 28 July 2008.

PARLIAMENT OF AUSTRALIA 1993, *Native Title Act*, <www.austlii.edu.au>, accessed 28 May 2008.

PEARSON, N. 2007, 'Aborigines Have to Save Themselves', *The Age*, 19 May.

PEPINSKY, H. & QUINNEY, R. 1991, *Criminology as Peacemaking*, Indiana University Press, Bloomington, Indiana.

PERRY, M. 2008, 'Pope Apologises for Church Sexual Abuse in Australia', Reuters, <www.alertnet.org/thenews/newsdesk/SYD41034.htm>, accessed 28 July 2008.

PHILLIPS, G. 2007, 'Healing and Public Policy', in *Coercive Reconciliation: Stabilise, Normalise, Exit Aboriginal Australia*, eds J. Altman & M. Hinkson, Arena Publications, North Carlton, Melbourne.

RALSTON, N. 2008, 'Truancy Parents Face Jail', *The Advertiser*, 2 April.

RAVENS, T. 2007, 'PM's Warning to Indigenous Communities', *The Advertiser*, 29 August.

RINTOUL, S. & LUNN, S. 2007, '"Knee-jerk" Laws Break the Law', *The Australian*, 22 June, p. 4.

ROWSE, T. 2007a, 'A New Dawn for Indigenous Australia?' *The Age*, 23 June.

ROWSE, T. 2007b, 'The National Economy and Indigenous Jurisdictions', in *Coercive Reconciliation: Stabilise, Normalise, Exit Aboriginal Australia*, eds J. Altman & M. Hinkson, Arena Publications, North Carlton, Melbourne.

SAUNDERS, P. 2003, 'Figures Show Prison Stops Crime', *The Advertiser*, 24 January.

SCHUBERT, M. & MURDOCH, L. 2007, 'Forces Set for [Northern Territory] Sex Abuse Strike', *The Age*, 23 June.

SIMPSON, B. 1997, 'Youth Crime, the Media and Moral Panic', in *Youth, Crime and the Media: Media Representation of and Reaction to Young People in Relation to Law and Order*, eds J. Bessant & R. Hill, National Clearinghouse for Youth Studies, Hobart, Tasmania.

SUTHERLAND, E. H. 1940, 'White Collar Criminality', *American Sociological Review*, vol. 5, pp. 1–12.

TRINDER, L. & REYNOLDS, S. eds 2000, *Evidence-Based Practice: A Critical Appraisal*, Blackwell, Oxford.

TUMARKIN, M. 2007, 'Beyond Pity', *The Age*, 21 July.

UK PUBLIC ACTS 1998, *Crime and Disorder Act*, <www.opsi.gov.uk>, accessed 15 October 2008.

UK PUBLIC ACTS 2002, *Police Reform Act*, <www.opsi.gov.uk>, accessed 23 October 2008.

UK PUBLIC ACTS 2003, *Anti-Social Behaviour Act*, <www.opsi.gov.uk>, accessed 23 October 2008.

WELSH, B. C. & FARRINGTON, D. P. 2005, 'Evidence-Based Crime Prevention: Conclusions and Directions for a Safer Society', *Canadian Journal of Criminology and Criminal Justice*, vol. 47, no. 2, pp. 337–54.

WINFORD, S. 2006, 'A New (Legal) Threat to Public Space: The Rise and Rise of the ASBO', Fitzroy Legal Service, <www.fitzroy-legal.org.au>, accessed 16 April 2008.

WRIGHT, A. 2007, 'We Have a Vision. What We Need is Authority', *The Advertiser Review*, 30 June.

YOUTH AFFAIRS COUNCIL OF SOUTH AUSTRALIA 2007, 'Anti-Social Behaviour Orders', *Issues Paper* 1, <www.yacsa.com.au>, accessed 19 June 2008

ZEDNER, L. 2002, 'Dangers of Dystopias in Penal Theory', *Oxford Journal of Legal Studies*, vol. 22, no. 2, pp. 341–68.

16 ANALYSING POLICY: WHAT'S THE PROBLEM REPRESENTED TO BE?

FURTHER READING

CUNEEN, C. 2001, *Conflict, Politics and Crime: Aboriginal Communities and the Police*, Allen & Unwin, Sydney.

FLINT, J. 2002, 'Social Housing Agencies and the Governance of Anti-Social Behaviour', *Housing Studies*, vol. 17, no. 4, pp. 619–37.

HODGKINSON, S. & TILLEY, N. 2007, 'Policing Anti-Social Behaviour: Constraints, Dilemmas and Opportunities', *Howard Journal of Criminal Justice*, vol. 46, no. 4, pp. 385–400.

LEA, T., KOWAL, E. & COWLISHAW, G. eds 2006, *Moving Anthropology: Critical Indigenous Studies*, Charles Darwin University, Darwin.

MATTHEWS, R., EASTON, H., BRIGGS, D. & PEASE, K. 2007, *Assessing the Use and Impact of Anti-Social Behaviour Orders*, Researching Criminal Justice Series, Policy Press, Bristol.

PEARSON, N. 2000, *Our Right to Take Responsibility*, Noel Pearson & Associates, Cairns.

STENSON, K. 2000, 'Crime Control, Social Policy and Liberalism', in *Rethinking Social Policy*, eds G. Lewis, S. Gewirtz & J. Clarke, Sage, London.

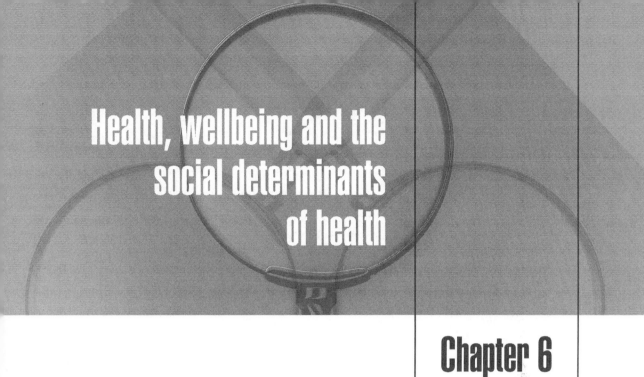

Health, wellbeing and the social determinants of health

Chapter 6

CROSSING BORDERS

Our overriding question in a WPR approach to policy analysis is – how are we governed? How does rule take place? In tune with a governmentality perspective the answer to this question involves more than the institutions of government, understood conventionally, and more than networks of social groups which have something to do with governments in this narrow, institutional sense. Rather, we are reflecting broadly on how order is maintained. There is no assumption in this analysis that order should *not* be maintained. The impulse is inquisitive and probing, not libertarian. The goal is to provide insights into how we have come to be governed in particular ways and at what costs for whom.

In this perspective it is important to think of policy areas (e.g. health, education, finance, foreign policy) as *interconnected* at a basic conceptual level, rather than as separate and distinct policy fields. As an example, in Chapter 4 we observed that drug use and gambling are sometimes represented to be *health* 'problems'. So, drug use and gambling are governed, in part, through invoking the idea of health. Going further, how 'health' is conceptualised (the kind of 'problem' 'ill-health' is represented to be) has important implications for the particulars of the policy recommended or adopted. For example, concerning 'illicit' drugs, abolitionists are happy to talk about drug users as 'sick people', who therefore need monitoring and 'rehabilitation'. By contrast, those intent on questioning the representation of 'problem gamblers' as 'addicts' suggest conceptualising gambling as a *public health* issue in an attempt to shift the focus from individual users to harm minimisation.

Health, it appears, is a slippery concept rather than a fixed idea or a measurable quantum. As with 'crime' (Chapter 5), its meaning is contested, and this contestation influences and is reflected in the health policy field. That is, competing theories about the nature of 'health' and the causes of 'ill-health' play significant roles in the debates surrounding health policy. These theories form some of the 'knowledges' through which we are governed.

To further our understanding of health policy, therefore, we require some background on the theories — the competing understandings of health and of 'disease' prevention — that inform health policy. This background is provided in the first section below. We then proceed to examine a selection of *practical texts* in the health policy field in order to better understand the role that these competing perspectives play in shaping health policy. Our practical texts include:

- three reports produced under the auspices of the **World Health Organization** on the social determinants of health;
- a discussion paper from the South Australian Health Department on 'research transfer'.

The underlying objective is to draw attention to the ways in which different and competing understandings of 'health' and, indeed, of 'health policy' play important roles in how we are governed.

Reminder

The six questions in a WPR approach can be followed systematically — addressing each question separately and in order — as in Chapters 3 and 4. More commonly, the questions form part of an integrated analysis, with specific questions applied where the analysis occasions their use. This chapter follows the second, integrated form of analysis, employing the notation **Q1, Q2**, etc. where a specific question has been applied. Until students are completely familiar with the questions in the approach, it is advisable to look back to the original list (either the abbreviated form in the Introduction and Chapter 1, or the expanded version at the end of Chapter 2) when such notation appears.

THEORETICAL APPROACHES TO HEALTH POLICY

Broadly, it is possible to identify two competing theoretical paradigms within health policy: a *biomedical* paradigm that focuses on technology-based medical care and biomedical public health interventions such as immunisation and health screening; and a *social* paradigm that understands health as a *social* phenomenon, a product of complex environmental and social factors.

In the *biomedical* paradigm health is understood as the absence of disease, and the focus is primarily on *physical* disease. Bodies are considered to be like machines that break down and that can be fixed (Lewis 2005, p. 95). The target can be either the individual patient in the doctor's surgery, or the wider health of the population, as part of *public* health policy.

In the *social* paradigm, by contrast, 'health' is understood as more than just the absence of disease. The term 'wellbeing' is often used to signal a more holistic understanding. For example, in the *Preamble to the Constitution* of the World Health Organization (WHO 1946) health is described as a 'state of complete physical, mental and social wellbeing'.

The *social* paradigm of health emphasises the importance of societal factors (as opposed to biological factors) in determining health and illness. For example, the First International Conference on Health Promotion, held in Ottawa in 1986, listed the 'fundamental conditions and resources for health' as 'peace, shelter, education, food, income, a stable ecosystem, sustainable resources, social justice and equity' (Ottawa Charter for Health Promotion 1986). In this wide-ranging agenda health policy clearly moves beyond a disease model and involves many government agencies, not just health departments. Adherents of this view tend to talk about a *new* public health agenda to indicate the shift in focus from biomedical to social factors.

Both biomedical and social approaches comfortably fit Foucault's observation that modern industrialised states attend to the health of populations (biopolitics) to maintain order and economic security (see Chapter 2). Turner (1997) makes the case that this concern with population produces a *functional* understanding of health – that is, health becomes what is required to make governing possible and successful. In Turner's (1997, p. xv) words, 'health is a form of policing which is specifically concerned with the quality of the labour force'. Significantly but unsurprisingly, given this governance objective, a functional emphasis can be found both in states strongly influenced by a social democratic tradition, like Sweden, and in those characterised as 'liberal welfare states', like the United States (Esping-Andersen 1990). This broad governance objective is signalled in the widespread collection and study of population-based health statistics (epidemiology).

'At the end of the eighteenth century, it was not epidemics that were the issue, but something else – what might broadly be called endemics, or in other words, the form, nature, extension, duration, and intensity of the illnesses prevalent in a population. These were illnesses that were difficult to eradicate and that were not regarded as epidemics that caused more frequent deaths, but as permanent factors which – and that is how they were dealt with – sapped the population's strength, shortened the working week, wasted energy, and cost money, both because they led to a fall in production and because treating them was expensive. In a word, illness as phenomena affecting a population.' (Foucault 2003, pp. 243–44)

Sweden's *Public Health Policy Report* 2005

'Health is not just crucial to the individual but also to the public economy. Studies indicate that health impacts the public economy more than the economy impacts health. Health leads to greater growth as a result of a more productive workforce, more productive years, better learning capacity, greater creativity and better potential for coping with change. Reduced ill-heath means that more of society's resources can be used productively.' (Swedish National Institute of Public Health 2005)

- **What kind of a 'problem' is health represented to be in this report?**

- **What effects follow from this representation of the 'problem'?**

- **Are there any limitations in this understanding of health? Could it be conceived differently? With what effects?**

Preventive approaches to health

Preventive approaches to health cross-cut the biomedical and social paradigms (Broom 2008). Hence, when there are references to 'prevention' within specific health policy initiatives, it is important to ask – what kind of a 'problem' is 'prevention' represented to be? And, what follows from particular understandings of 'prevention'? A key point of dispute has been the extent to which individuals should be held responsible for their (poor) health, due to (poor) lifestyle 'choices'.

The biomedical paradigm, while primarily *curative* in orientation, has, in addition, a *preventive* dimension. 'Preventive medicine' is designated a 'specialty practice'. Immunisation and screening programs are examples of biomedical *preventive* programs, as is 'preventive surgery' (see Activity on 'Preventive Medicine' below). Recently there is a trend within preventive medicine to direct attention to behaviours that are believed to be the underlying causes of disease, such as 'smoking, unsafe sexual practices, dietary habits, and lack of exercise' (Alexander and Lawrence 2002, p. 977). This shift in focus to individual behaviours as the cause of disease, as we shall see, has adherents in the social paradigm as well.

In the social paradigm's more holistic understanding of health as 'wellbeing' the scope of preventive interventions extends far beyond screening and immunisation programs. As we saw in the quote from the Ottawa Charter (1986) above, within this paradigm, things such as peace, social justice and a stable ecosystem can be considered contributors to the prevention of ill-health. In this tradition, the *Alma-Ata Declaration* (1978), produced by an International Conference on Primary Health Care, declared health to be a fundamental human right whose realisation requires the action of many other social and economic sectors in addition to the health sector. The Conference identified 'Health for All' as a basic human right and 'primary health care' as the means of achieving this goal.

Preventive Medicine

Example 1: *'Fighting disease before it strikes'*

'New Zealand-born Professor Brennan is head of the Memorial Sloan-Kettering Cancer Centre in New York. He said diagnostic technology, a spin-off from the Human Genome Project, was being used increasingly to identify high-risk groups to specific forms of cancer.

"For some cancers the accuracy ranges from a 100 per cent certainty through to people who just have an increased risk", he said.

"This puts us in a position to target treatment and prevention. Given a patient carries an hereditary form of cancer which he or she is certain to get, then the patient can have surgery to remove an organ before the cancer develops".' (Hailstone 2002)

Example 2: *'Melbourne study yields first pointers on anti-cancer diet'*

'More than 10 years into what may be Australia's biggest medical experiment, the first results are emerging on the link between cancer and diet among more than 40,000 Australians ...

The project was born in the late 1980s when Cancer Council Victoria epidemiologist Graham Giles sat down and divided cancer causes into a pie chart.

More than a third was put down to smoking (this has since fallen sharply), followed by a lot of tiny slices, such as radiation, chemical exposure and reproductive habits (breast cancer from having children late).

But by far the biggest piece – more than half the pie – was a mystery best described by the words diet and lifestyle.' (Noble 2003)

- **Does 'preventive surgery' fit within a biomedical or a social paradigm of health? Where does a focus on diet fit?**

- **How does the understanding of preventive health in the above examples limit what can be discussed? (Q4)**

It is important to note the dominance of *curative* medical approaches over *preventive* medical approaches to health locally and internationally, both within the medical profession and within government priorities. In the United States preventive medicine is currently in a state of decline from 2.3 per cent of all United States physicians in 1970 to 0.9 per cent in 1997 (Lane 2000). In the health budgets of developed countries, 30 to 50 per cent of funding goes to hospital and nursing-home care, 10 to 20 per cent is spent on pharmaceuticals, and just 2.8 per cent is committed to prevention and public health (OECD 2004 in Lewis 2005, p. 19 fn 2). In South Australia in 2002–03 less than 2 per cent of all health spending went towards public health initiatives, with breast and cervical cancer screening, prevention of harmful drug and alcohol use, and food standards and hygiene, among the top spending areas (Hurrell 2006). Because they attract so little public funding, Lewis (2005, p. 171) describes disease prevention, health promotion, and public health measures as the '"Cinderella" areas of the health sector'.

Alma-Ata Declaration 1978
Chapter VII

'Primary health care:

1   reflects and evolves from the economic conditions and sociocultural and political characteristics of the country and its communities and is based on the application of the relevant results of social, biomedical and health services research and public health experience;

2   addresses the main health problems in the community, providing promotive, preventive, curative and rehabilitative services accordingly;

3   includes at least: education concerning prevailing health problems and the methods of preventing and controlling them; promotion of food supply and proper nutrition; an adequate supply of safe water and basic sanitation; maternal and child health care, including family planning; immunization against the major infectious diseases; prevention and control of locally endemic diseases; appropriate treatment of common diseases and injuries; and provision of essential drugs;

4   involves, in addition to the health sector, all related sectors and aspects of national and community development, in particular agriculture, animal husbandry, food, industry, education, housing, public works, communications and other sectors; and demands the coordinated efforts of all those sectors;

5   requires and promotes maximum community and individual self-reliance and participation in the planning, organization, operation and control of primary health care, making fullest use of local, national and other available resources; and to this end develops through appropriate education the ability of communities to participate;

6   should be sustained by integrated, functional and mutually supportive referral systems, leading to the progressive improvement of comprehensive health care for all, and giving priority to those most in need;

7   relies, at local and referral levels, on health workers, including physicians, nurses, midwives, auxiliaries and community workers as applicable, as well as traditional practitioners as needed, suitably trained socially and technically to work as a health team and to respond to the expressed health needs of the community.' (WHO 2006)

However, attempts continue to be made to draw attention to the *social* influences on health. For example, *social* epidemiology (Kreiger 2001) and a social determinants of health (SDH) perspective emphasise the broad social and economic conditions that influence health. A particular focus within SDH is the marked disparities in the health of sub-groups within populations ('health inequalities' or 'health inequities'). A cultural economy perspective complements SDH by emphasising the role of *culture* in shaping behaviours that have health consequences. For example, Hinde and Dixon (2005) stress the impact of the automobile culture in Western industrialised states on weight gain. In this tradition, Eckersley (2005, p. 159) identifies materialism, consumerism and (excessive) individualism as 'more distal social causes of disease'.

The social determinants of health inequalities

Example 1: *'Wealth a sign of far better health'*
'Residents of Adelaide's lower-income suburbs are more likely to die from cancer, heart disease, accidents and poisonings than those from more affluent areas.

    The data is revealed in the *Social Health Atlas of Australia* [Glover *et al.*, 1999] released yesterday . . .

    The report's joint author, John Glover, of the University of Adelaide's public health information development unit, said the report showed health inequities were "entrenched". "This issue really needs to be addressed at the highest level of governments", he said yesterday.' (Lloyd and Hannon 2000)

Example 2: *'Doctors prescribe end to racism as a cure for Aboriginal health'*
An article in *The Age* (Gray 1999) on a major report into Aboriginal and Torres Strait Islander health described the contrast between Aboriginal and non-Aboriginal people's health in Australia as 'startling'. The report showed that more than one in two Aboriginal men died before the age of 50 in contrast to most non-Aboriginal men who could expect to reach age 75. The age expectancy for Aboriginal women was reported as 61.7 years compared to non-Aboriginal women who could expect to live to age 81.

    The article quoted Dr. Rob Moodie, head of the State Government-funded health promotion agency VicHealth, who had worked in Alice Springs for six years at one of the oldest and largest Aboriginal community health services in Australia. In his view, more doctors, medicine and check ups mark only the beginning steps towards improving Aboriginal health. He said that he had learned that the reason people got sick is due to more than germs:

    'It's really the social and economic determinants of health . . . It's whether someone has got a job, it's their educational levels and really, it's the amount of control they have over their own destiny . . . Discrimination causes ill-health, there's no doubt about it.' (Gray 1999)

- **Does a focus on health inequalities fit within a biomedical or a social/holistic understanding of health?**

- **What is the 'problem' of ill-health represented to be in a social inequalities analysis?**

- **Are there any silences?**

Health and prevention: contestation

As has already been signalled, there is considerable contestation about both the meaning of *health* and the meaning of *prevention* in the public health literature. This contestation spills over into disagreements about the meaning of:

- population health;
- primary health;
- social epidemiology; and
- SDH.

We shall look briefly at each area.

With reference to population health, Canada's Public Health Agency (2008) has mounted a challenge to a holistic understanding of health. The argument is that making health synonymous with wellbeing 'confused health with its determinants'. According to the Agency:

> The population health approach recognizes that health is a capacity or resource rather than a state, a definition which corresponds more to the notion of *being able to pursue one's goals*, to acquire skills and education, and to grow. This broader notion of health recognizes the range of social, economic and physical environmental factors that contribute to health. The best articulation of this concept of health is 'the capacity of people to adapt to, respond to, or control life's challenges and changes'. (Frankish *et al.* 1996 in Public Health Agency of Canada 2008; emphasis added)

The focus in this definition of population health is on people *taking charge* of their health, which can be seen as consonant with an emphasis on *lifestyle as a key determinant of health*. Insofar as this focus moves from the broad social influences on wellbeing to the *ability to respond* to 'life's challenges', as in the above quote, attention to the nature of those challenges, their causes and their differential impacts on sectors within the population, is cancelled out of the analysis (**Q4**).

There are connections here with the 'equality of capability' idea endorsed in the WHO Commission on the Social Determinants of Health (CSDH 2005), discussed below. In both cases the individual is produced as responsible for their health, evoking the themes of individual responsibilisation and self-regulation (**Q5**) that have been identified in earlier chapters as part of a dominant way of thinking in current governmental regimes. So, to declare oneself a proponent of population health, commonly associated with a social and preventive paradigm, does not end the dispute about what the 'problem' is.

Similarly, a tension exists within PHC (Primary Health Care) between primary *medical* care (referred to as 'selective primary care') – which is located within the biomedical paradigm and which focuses on disease prevention at an individual level – and *comprehensive* primary health care, which embraces the broader, holistic understanding of health and a social model of health promotion. The latter endorses a social justice agenda and emphasises the importance of lay (as opposed to expert) knowledge and community 'empowerment' (Keleher 2001).

So too there are important distinctions between *social* epidemiology and epidemiology as simply the collection of population-level health statistics, with the former committed to identifying broad social causes of population-level health patterns. Krieger (2001) identifies three main theories within social epidemiology. A psychosocial strand tends to focus on stressed people, while a more materialist (Marxist) tradition emphasises the conditions causing stress. A third multi-level stream in social epidemiology, called 'ecosocial theory', identifies the pathways by which broad structural influences impact on the lives and bodies of affected individuals **(Q5)**.

There are similar kinds of dispute within SDH. For example, some who promote SDH put more emphasis on individual behaviours while others support a more critical SDH approach that emphasises the role governments play in creating specific social, economic and environmental contexts that help to make people either 'ill' or 'well'. The language of 'up-stream', 'mid-stream' and 'down-stream' is used to situate both SDH researchers and SDH health interventions. The greater the emphasis on structural/environmental factors, the further 'up-stream' they travel in their identification of social determinants **(Q1, Q2)**.

Some studies within SDH identify *social* factors that work *through* individual behaviours, commonly referred to as 'risk factors'. There is a tendency in this position to hold individuals responsible for putting themselves at risk of ill-health because of what they eat or drink, or due to lack of exercise or engaging in 'risky' sexual practices (see Nettleton 1997). Risk in this instance — individualised rather than socialised (see Chapter 3) — can lead to stigma and discrimination, *dividing people* into 'active citizens', who are portrayed as able to manage their own health, and 'targeted populations, who require intervention in management of risks' (Guthman and Dupuis 2006, p. 443) **(Q5)**. For those 'risks' over which the individual has no control, such as age, the implication is still that the person needs to take charge of their behaviours *given their location in a high risk group*. Factors such as growing up in slums, by contrast, are unlikely to be identified as health 'risks' **(Q4)**.

The Tick Test

'Risk factors of type 2 diabetes

☐ I am over 45 years of age and have high blood pressure

☐ I am over 45 years of age and am overweight

☐ I am over 45 and one or more members of my family has diabetes

☐ I am over 60 years of age

☐ I have heart disease or have had a heart attack

☐ I had high blood sugar levels while I was pregnant (gestational diabetes)

☐ I have polycystic ovary syndrome and am overweight

☐ I am over 35 and am an Aboriginal or Torres Strait Islander

☐ I am over 35 and am a Pacific Islander, from a Chinese cultural background or from the Indian sub-continent

If you have ticked one or more of the above then you are at risk of diabetes.' (Diabetes Australia 2006)

- **What are you supposed to do with this information?**

- **How is subjectivity constituted in information about risks? (Q5)**

Preventive Health

Example 1: *'Prevention of Obesity in Children and Young People: New South Wales Government Action Plan 2003–2007'*

'The Action Plan aims to:

- ■ increase healthy nutrition, increase physical activity and decrease sedentary living to prevent childhood overweight and obesity;

- ■ provide quality programs, services and infrastructure to increase physical activity, decrease sedentary living and increase healthy nutrition;

- ■ achieve social, health, economic and environmental benefits arising from the priorities of childhood overweight and obesity.' (NSW Department of Health 2003, p. 2)

Example 2: *'Children urged to get active'*

'TV commercials will be used to encourage kids to get off the couch and exercise for an hour a day in a new campaign against childhood obesity.

The ads, showing a red couch bouncing children into a swimming pool, will air from tomorrow.

An Australian Institute of Health and Welfare study released last year found more than a fifth of Australian children were overweight or obese.

Launching the $6 million campaign yesterday, federal Health Minister Tony Abbott urged parents to be better role models for their children but rejected calls to regulate junk food advertising.

"For every image of someone wolfing down some KFC, there will now be an image of someone getting off the couch and being active", he said.' (*The Age*, News, 4 February 2006)

Example 3: *The Sydney Principles*

'Guiding principles for achieving a substantial level of protection for children against the commercial promotion of foods and beverages.

   Actions to reduce commercial promotions to children should:

1. Support the rights of children
2. Afford substantial protection to children
3. Be statutory in nature
4. Take a wide definition of commercial promotions
5. Guarantee commercial-free childhood settings
6. Include cross border media
7. Be evaluated, monitored and enforced.'

(International Obesity Taskforce 2006; see the website in References for the expanded version)

- **What is the 'problem' of obesity represented to be in each of the above examples?**

- **What presuppositions underpin the different problem representations? (Q2)**

- **How are subjects constituted in the three representations? (Q5)**

- **Are there any silences? (Q4)**

For this Activity see Coveney 2008.

Evidence-based medicine

Like 'prevention', 'evidence-based' medicine (EBM) and 'evidence-based' health sciences (EBHS) cut across the biomedical and social paradigms. Indeed, as we shall see, few researchers currently are able to position themselves *outside* an evidence-based paradigm. The grounding premise of evidence-based medicine is that, when 'healthcare professionals perform an action, there should be evidence that the action will produce the desired outcome' (Holmes *et al*. 2006, p. 181). Clinicians are to find and appraise research systematically in order to discover 'what works'. The assumption is that the outcome will benefit patients.

Because evidence-based *medicine* is the precursor to evidence-based *policy*, which is a topic of particular interest in this book, it is relevant to say something about its development (**Q3**). Evidence-based medical practice originated in the work of Archie Cochrane (1972) who argued that Randomised Controlled Trials (RCTs) offer the most effective means to judge health interventions. As a beneficial side-effect, Cochrane explained, *systematic reviews* (syntheses) of RCTs promise to save health dollars. In 1993 the UK established the Cochrane Collaboration as an international venture to pursue this agenda, followed in 1999 by the Campbell Collaboration, which extended the medical paradigm to social science research, including educational research (see Chapter 9) and criminology (see Chapter 5).

Initially, the evidence-based approach was *researcher-led*, with the expressed objectives of improving health policy outcomes and strengthening the accountability mechanisms by which policy decisions were made. According to Donald (2001, p. 279), 'People were fed up with the extent to which politicians' whims could change their lives — not obviously for the better', based as they were on 'ideological opinion'. The argument here is that *evidence* can be useful in challenging ideologically-driven policy. The focus on efficiency and effectiveness, however, means that the evidence-based approach finds a happy home among governments influenced by 'the instrumentalist mood of managerial reforms' that 'infiltrated public administration practices in western democracies over the past three decades' (Marston and Watts 2003, p. 146; **Q3**).

A number of concerns about an evidence-based health agenda have since been voiced. Questions are raised about the narrowness of the forms of evidence deemed to be acceptable. With RCTs adopted as the 'gold standard' of evidence-based knowledge, the clinician, who is 'presumed to know the truth of disease', is privileged over other ways of knowing, delegitimising embodied lay knowledges (Holmes *et al.*, 2006, p. 183; **Q4**). There are also concerns that governments can select 'evidence' that suits specific political agendas and as a 'resource-rationing tool' (Marston and Watts 2003, p. 148; **Q4**). More fundamentally, single-minded concentration on evidence diverts attention from the designated 'problem' about which 'evidence' is solicited and, hence, from what the 'problem' is represented to be (**Q4**).

This issue will be revisited towards the end of the chapter when we consider the so-called 'know-do' gap in SDH policy.

Poststructural approaches to health policy

Amidst all the identified contestation around meanings of 'health', 'prevention' and 'evidence', how are we to understand and assess health policy? Health, it should be noted, is an indeterminate goal (Osborne 1997, p. 179). That is, what it means to be healthy depends on time and place, and on cultural norms. Also, inevitably, health policy is doomed to fail, since we are all bound to die at some stage (Osborne 1997, p. 186).

Hence, to make sense of health policy, our focus needs to shift from some notion of an 'ideal' health policy to styles of problematisation and underlying rationalities of rule (**Q2**), and the effects (**Q5**) that accompany particular modes of governance. This means studying how specific policies create their object 'health' (as, for example, the absence of disease or as a broader sense of wellbeing), and how they constitute relationships among states, citizens and experts. It is this form of analysis that a WPR approach facilitates.

As suggested elsewhere in the text, a WPR approach to policy analysis poses a fundamental challenge to *reactive* accounts of policy that describe governments as *addressing* 'problems', as if these exist outside of (exogenous to) the realm of government (see introduction to Chapter 1). Hence, in terms of health policy, the focus shifts from consideration of policy 'responses' to health 'problems' to how 'health' is imagined and created, and with what repercussions for the political subjects involved. The objective becomes identifying and teasing out the various implications (effects) that accompany different modes of rule (**Q5**), and identifying places to contest those aspects of policies that in our judgement produce deleterious consequences (**Q6**).

One particular area of interest for poststructuralists is subjectification effects. The idea that policy is productive, in the Foucauldian sense of *making things happen* (see Chapter 2), alerts us to the ways in which policies affect the subjectivities of the people they target. Here the key idea is that individuals do not stand outside policies. To an extent, who and what (we think) we are (i.e. our subjectivity) reflects the policy context (**Q5**). For example, the production of citizens as 'consumers of health' (Petersen 2003, p. 193), with the accompanying emphasis on individual behaviours and on individual responsibility for health, produces citizens who, to an extent, accept and live this narrative. Hence, they can come to judge both their own behaviours and those of others against expectations set by policy makers and allied professionals. We saw this same dynamic illustrated in Chapter 4 on drugs/alcohol and gambling policy, where the labelling and stigmatising of 'addicts' elicits 'responsible' consumption.

An analysis of this type includes reflection on the role of the state in producing these effects but also looks beyond the state to consider the complex relationships and dependencies formed among states, political subjects, doctors and other professionals, including health professionals and health researchers. For example, alongside the creation of patients as consumers we see the production of doctors as service providers. Potentially then doctors become subject to the kinds of surveillance that accompany other forms of 'client-provider' relationships, regardless of the possible unsuitability of such surveillance in a health context.

'Shedding light on medical care'

'Should doctors and hospitals be forced to provide more detail to patients?

The *Health Services Policy Review discussion paper*, released last week, said privatisation of public services and other moves to increase competition in health had been allowed to surge while better consumer information was neglected ...

Referring to health report cards, the report said: "Australian health consumers also want ... to know, for example, whether as a private patient their hip replacement operation is likely to be more successful at the Epworth or the Melbourne Private Hospital or one of the public hospitals. Consumers want to know not only the waiting time, but also where they are likely to have the best outcome."

The Australian Medical Association and various specialists' colleges, including surgeons, oppose report cards and call centres.

The federal president of the AMA, Dr David Brand, said "score cards" would encourage hospitals and doctors to "fudge the figures".' (Toy 1999)

- **How are the subjectivities of health services users and of doctors constituted in the idea of health 'report cards'? (Q5)**

- **Are there any silences? (Q4)**

Importantly, there is no presumption in poststructural analysis that modes of governing *determine* outcomes and subjectivities. As Question 6 in a WPR approach makes clear, there is always room for resistance and re-problematisation. The option of refusal (opting out) is always there and many people select this course of action, sometimes with deleterious consequences for their wellbeing, e.g. losing access to important health services.

In addition, as seen elsewhere, dominant discourses can provide resources for making particular kinds of demands. Petersen (2003, p. 199), for example, identifies how the women's health movement and the health consumer movement have drawn upon narratives of empowerment and choice to challenge the 'authority of professional power' and to make important political claims for recognition. Popkewitz (1998, pp. 14, 19) cautions on possible dangers in this reframing. He draws attention to the way in which the 'insertion of voice into postmodern discourses rhetorically positions marginalized social and economic groups as agents of their own emancipation and liberation' (see also Cruikshank 1994 and Chapter 10). This kind of critical reflection on all problem representations, including those in attempts at re-problematisation, marks a clear distinction between a WPR approach and much sociological framework theory (Bacchi 2009).

'Health checks miss target'

'South Australians at the greatest risk of chronic disease are shunning a health service designed to help them look after their health.

Medicare figures show fewer than 10 000 South Australians have undergone a health check since the preventive health check program was introduced in November 2006.

The program is designed for people aged 45 to 49 who are at risk of chronic disease, such as the obese, heavy smokers or drinkers, people who do not exercise or those who have poor nutrition. GPs receive a Medicare rebate if they provide the health check.' (Anderson 2008)

- **What model of health (biomedical or social) underpins preventive health checks of the kind endorsed in this example? What model of prevention (individual or environmental/social) is implied?**

- **Does the minimal success of the health checks suggest a form of resistance to this mode of governance?**

- **How are doctors implicated in this mode of governance?**

Given the complexity of the health field, it is useful to include in one's analysis a fairly systematic set of questions, considering whether an identified program, piece of legislation or report:

- represents the 'problem' of 'ill-health' to be either a *biomedical* or a *social* 'problem';
- represents the 'problem' of 'ill-health' to be either a *curative* or a *preventive* 'problem';
- represents 'prevention' to be a *biomedical* or *social* 'problem';
- represents 'prevention' to be an *individual* or *social/environmental* 'problem'.

Consider also how subjects are constituted within the selected policy – for example, as passive *or* active 'clients', as embodied *or* as purely rational decision-makers, and with what effects in each case.

The objective is to make visible the multiple and overlapping forms of rule (political rationalities) enshrined in selected programs, projects or legislation (**Q2, Q3**), to identify silences and ambiguities where they exist (**Q4**), to assess the implications that flow from specific ways of representing the 'problem' (**Q5**), and to identify forms of resistance (**Q6**), always keeping in mind the need to subject one's own problem representations to critical scrutiny.

In the next sections we pursue these themes through a closer look, first, at the complex area of the social determinants of health and, second, at the related topic of 'research transfer'.

THE SOCIAL DETERMINANTS OF HEALTH: A CONTESTED FIELD

As mentioned above, there is more than one incarnation of the idea of SDH. We saw, for example, that it is possible to examine *social* causes of ill-health, such as poor nutrition, and still sheet home responsibility to *individuals*, by focusing on individual behaviours that become characterised as 'risk factors'. A challenge to this representation of the 'problem' has been mounted through the call to address the social determinants of health *inequalities* (or health *inequities*) – the ways in which social and environmental influences harm some groups more than other groups.

To address this issue, in 2005 the World Health Organization established the Commission on Social Determinants of Health (CSDH). The Commission directed its attention to the 'specific social determinants that deepen health inequities'. Moreover, there was a commitment from the outset to 'give greatest emphasis to policies that address major *structural* determinants of health, such as *labor market policies* and the *education system*, rather than "downstream" actions more focused on *individual risk factors*' (Irwin *et al.* 2006, p. 6; emphasis added). In tune with the United Nations Millennium Development Goals (United Nations 2008), set in 2000, the Commission recognised the need for 'multisectoral action to reach health objectives' (Irwin *et al.* 2006, p. 5), referring to the need to involve many government agencies, not just health departments.

Since its creation the Commission has produced two drafts of a conceptual framework for action on the social determinants of health (CSDH 2005, 2007) and a final report (CSDH 2008). In this section the two drafts will be compared with each other and against another WHO report on the social determinants of health, produced by the Measurement and Evidence Knowledge Network (MEKN 2007). These three documents will serve as 'practical texts'. Our goal is to identify competing problem representations within these texts and to subject these problem representations to the questions in a WPR analysis. Such a comparison alerts us to the complex influences shaping policy documents and to intense contestation over the kind of 'problem' 'ill-health' is represented to be.

As might be expected, since WHO produced all three documents, they share a number of key parameters and perspectives. All three, for example, are located firmly within a *social* rather than a *biomedical* paradigm. That is, all three are committed to identifying *socially preventive* ways to address the issue of health inequities, as opposed to *preventive medicine* approaches (see above). The three documents also share an explicit normative commitment to equity as a desirable policy goal. To this end the three documents clarify that, with Graham (2004), they believe it is important to draw a distinction between SDH approaches, pure and simple, and the social determinants of health *inequities*. The authors of all three documents are clearly concerned when SDH is reduced to examining the social influences on health at an *individual* level. In addition, the three documents emphasise the usefulness of a 'gradient' approach to health inequities that examines the 'association of SEP [socio-economic position] and health . . . at every level of the social hierarchy', in preference to approaches that target initiatives at groups 'below the threshold of poverty':

> A gradients model locates the cause of health inequalities not only in the disadvantaged circumstances and health-damaging behaviors of the poorest groups, but in the systemic differences in life chances, living standards and lifestyles associated with people's unequal position in the socio-economic hierarchy. (CSDH 2007, pp. 42, 51)

Finally, all three documents acknowledge health inequities *between* countries as well as *within* countries, and the importance of intersectoral cooperation, given that 'Many of the solutions to addressing the social determinants lie outside the health sector' (MEKN 2007, p. 62; **Q1, Q2**).

It is less clear if the authors of the two discussion papers on a conceptual framework for action (CSDH 2005, 2007) and the authors of the MEKN Report (2007) agree on the basic *causes* of health inequities (**Q1**). The two conceptual framework documents, in particular the 2007 version, are much more explicitly political than the MEKN Report. The 2007 version, for example, includes a section on theories of power (CSDH 2007, pp. 15–16) and emphasises that 'the quality of SDH is [in turn] shaped by the policies that guide how societies (re)distribute material resources among their members' (CSDH 2007, p. 21). In its historical overview the 2007 draft identifies 'neoliberal economic models' and 'mandated market-oriented reforms that emphasized efficiency over equity as a system goal' as responsible for the failure of early initiatives such as *Health for All* (see above; **Q1, Q3**). Looking to developing countries the authors criticise the structural adjustment programs (SAPs) imposed on many developing countries by international financial institutions [i.e. the **World Bank** and the **International Monetary Fund**] for mandating 'sharp reductions in governments' social sector spending, constraining policymakers' capacity to address key SDH' (**Q1, Q3**). By contrast the MEKN Report (2007) has *nothing to say* about neoliberalism or about the role of international financial institutions (**Q4**).

While all three documents describe social stratification as a key 'problem' in addressing the social determinants of health inequalities (**Q1**), with socioeconomic position (SEP), gender, ethnicity and sexuality identified as key 'social stratifiers', the CSDH discussion papers are much more explicit about their alternative political vision. There are clear endorsements, for example, of a strong welfare state (CSDH 2007, pp. 7, 22–23). More specifically there are strong statements about the need for significant structural change (**Q1**):

> A rigorous analysis of social determinants may lead to the conclusion that significantly reducing health gradients would require profound structural changes in many

contemporary societies, e.g. in the functioning of markets and the redistributive role of the state. (CSDH 2005, p. 7)

By contrast, the MEKN Report (2007, p. 93) declares that a 'pragmatic approach' to change is desirable and that 'It is all too easy to blame global capitalism or distant shadowy forces as responsible for the general state of inequity'.

There are interesting differences between the 2005 and 2007 versions of the conceptual framework, which are not surprising given that the former is clearly described as 'a basis for discussion' (CSDH 2005, p. 4). For example, in 2005 there is no mention of neoliberalism or of the need for an explicitly political analysis, and only a passing mention of power. Rather, Sen's (1992) capability approach and the concept of 'health opportunity' feature significantly in 2005 but rate only a passing mention in 2007:

> A just government does not promote one particular conception of the good life. It leaves the choice of plans open to individuals. However, a just government *is* obligated to provide the enabling conditions that make it possible for each individual to freely choose her life-plan…Importantly, the factor to be equalized is not health status but *health opportunity*, since individuals may employ their positive freedom to choose a way of life that compromises health in the pursuit of other goals. (CSDH 2005, p. 6; emphasis in original)

The commitment to structural change in 2007 may explain the almost complete disappearance in that later document of this emphasis on *choosing* healthy lives, though assumptions about individual agency and 'freedom' are still prominent. Despite the references to the (possible) need for 'profound structural change' (see above) the model for change remains a liberal one, 'ensuring *fair access* to basic goods and opportunities that condition *people's freedom to choose* among life-plans they have reason to value' (CSDH 2007, p. 8; emphasis added; **Q2**).

All three documents raise the subject of **social capital** as an important dimension of a social determinants approach to health inequities (**Q2**). However, the 2007 discussion paper, by contrast with the 2005 version and with the MEKN Report, is much more guarded in its appraisal, describing the concepts of social cohesion and social capital as occupying 'an unusual (and contested) place in understanding of SDH':

> We share with Muntaner (2004) the concern that the current interest in 'social capital' may further encourage depoliticized approaches to population health and SDH. Indeed, it is clear that the concept of social capital has not infrequently been deployed as part of a broader discourse promoting reduced state responsibility for health, linked to an emphasis on individual and community characteristics, values and lifestyles as primary shapers of health outcomes. (CSDH 2007, p. 41)

All three documents accept the usefulness of evidence-based approaches to proposed health policy interventions (or at least the 2005 and 2007 discussion papers do not raise political questions about the methodology[1]), confirming that the evidence-based discourse cuts across biomedical and social paradigms, and is becoming near hegemonic in social and medical research (**Q2, Q3**). The MEKN Report offers a strong and sophisticated defence of evidence-based policy. It makes clear that, in the view of the authors, an evidence-based methodology does not necessarily presume an objectivist epistemology (MEKN 2007, p. 95): 'There is no such thing as value neutral science' (MEKN 2007, p. 99). A commitment to equity is placed up front, as is a commitment to reducing *socially* determined health inequities. This latter goal is to be encouraged through 'equity proofing' (p. 21) and Health Impact Assessments (p. 58). In addition, the MEKN Report challenges the idea of a 'hierarchy of evidence', with RCTs as the 'gold standard' (p. 20). Rather, space is created for all forms of 'knowledge' – quantitative, qualitative and 'tacit'. 'Tacit' knowledge is described as 'taken-for-granted assumptions about the world, which all human beings have in their minds' (p. 91). There is even recognition that 'Scientific argument will be marshaled in support of the anti-health equity position' (p. 16), revealing some awareness of the political stakes involved in evidence-based medicine.

Nonetheless, the MEKN Report continues to assume that an evidence-based methodology can '*inform* policy- and management decision-making' (MEKN 2007, p. 47; **Q2**; emphasis added). Hence, what is *not* put in question are the arrangements by which governments seek or solicit research 'evidence' (**Q4**). The issue of *who gets to set research questions* (the 'problems' to address) is treated as a practical rather than as a political issue:

> For example, policy makers and strategic planners are more interested in higher level questions of what works (questions of effectiveness) and what are the best buys (questions of cost effectiveness) in order to be able to make decisions about the most efficient and effective deployment of resources. (MEKN 2007, p. 40)

The MEKN authors are clearly aware that the nature of the questions asked in health research is critical to the kinds of 'discoveries' that will be made (p. 39), but still there is no suggestion that researchers should do other than *address* the questions (i.e. the 'problems') that decision-makers pose (MEKN 2007, p. 47). This issue becomes particularly significant if one is willing to accept the kind of political analysis produced by the CSDH in 2007, which suggests that the priorities of some governments, described as neoliberal, may *not* lie with redressing health inequities. In this case getting researchers to shape their research to the priorities of those governments – providing 'evidence' to 'solve' pre-set 'problems' – could well mean that the SDH agenda is undercut (**Q5**). We pursue this possibility in the last section.

'RESEARCH TRANSFER': A MISSING PART OF THE PUZZLE

One of the most significant discussions currently taking place with regard to the social determinants of health inequities is why more is *not* happening despite the increased awareness (the 'knowledge') of causal connections between *social* conditions and *poor health*. To put it bluntly, there is lots of *evidence* that poverty correlates with forms of ill-health but there are few serious attempts to reduce or eradicate poverty. This so-called 'know-do gap' has become the focus of international conferences (WHO 2005) and of a whole sub-discipline within health research, called health services research (CHSRF 2006). Towards the end of the MEKN Report (2007, p. 100) the refrain is repeated: 'In spite of all this knowledge it sometimes seems that we are powerless in the face of the problem'.

The 'know-do gap' in health equities research is seen as part of a more general 'problem' of inadequate 'uptake' of research 'evidence', described as a 'problem' of ineffective 'research transfer' (Q1). It sits alongside another 'gap' 'problem', the so-called '10/90 gap', identified by the Commission on Health Research for Development in 1990, which notes that only 10 per cent of global health research is devoted to conditions, mainly in developing countries, that account for 90 per cent of the 'global disease burden' (Baguley 2008).

A discussion paper from the South Australian Health Department on 'Research Transfer' will serve as our 'practical text', our way into understanding how the 'problem' of ('ineffective') 'research transfer' is being represented. The following proposals, among others, are put forward to improve 'research transfer':

- The tendency for researchers and decision makers to work in isolation needs to be broken down. More opportunities for partnership and collaboration are needed, and current *linkages* between researchers and decision makers need to be developed and strengthened. Decision makers should be involved in all stages of research, from the *development of the research question*, to the dissemination and implementation of the results.
- The unit of research transfer should be the *synthesis* and summary of knowledge, rather than the single study.
- Decision makers need to be more transparent about their aims and objectives. They need to make clear what *information* they want, why they want it, and how they intend to use it. Research funders can facilitate the communication of decision maker priorities to the research community and *use the incentive of their funding* to encourage the production of research evidence that is *relevant* to decision making.
- The Department needs to clarify its expectations of researchers in regard to dissemination. For example, the Canadian Health Services Research Foundation requires every research report to apply a 1:3:25 format: 1 page of main messages, followed by a 3 page executive summary, followed by a complete report of the research, which may be a maximum of 25 pages. (South Australian Health Department 2008; emphasis added)

In these proposals the 'problem' of ('ineffective') 'research transfer', in the main, is represented to be failure of a particular kind of communication between researchers and policy-makers (Q1). This is clear in the emphasis on making information more accessible and user-friendly, through syntheses (emphasised by the Cochrane Collaboration; see above) and a 1:3:25 format for research reports.

There is also an emphasis on the need to involve 'decision makers' more closely in setting research agendas, a proposal more clearly enunciated in the Department's endorsement of 'user-*driven* research', with users identified as policy-makers and administrators (Government of South Australia 2007a; see Bacchi 2008). User-driven research means that researchers 'are required to address the specific questions provided under the [government's] research themes' (Government of South Australia 2007b). A chart depicting 'Evidence-Based Decision Making' in the *Research Transfer Discussion Paper* repeats this message: an arrow labelled 'Issues & priorities' connects 'decision makers' to 'research funders', with a second arrow labeled 'priority issues & questions' connecting 'research funders' to 'researchers'. In this model research priorities are set by governments and directed to researchers *via* funding bodies. Working backwards from these proposals – as per a WPR analysis – the 'problem' of ('ineffective') 'research transfer' is seen to be due to researchers having *too much discretion* in what they research (Q1). The assumption is that it is appropriate and necessary for governments to set research priorities, the 'problems' to be researched (Q2).

There are important silences in this representation of the 'problem' (Q4). First, the way in which research questions direct and limit research agendas is not considered. And, second, the idea that governments should be the ones to set research priorities and hence research agendas fails to raise for consideration the particular goals and objectives of those governments. As mentioned earlier, given that some governments may not rate redressing health inequities a priority, it is highly unlikely that research with this objective in mind will be funded and, hence, conducted if those governments set research priorities.

While this point might appear to be obvious, it is not raised by those committed to 'evidence-based research' (see MEKN 2007). Perhaps this is unsurprising given the increasing reliance of researchers on government funding (Q3). The ways in which this reliance affects the subjectivities of researchers is certainly a factor that needs to be considered. According to Ball (2001, p. 266), funding-driven research makes researchers 'think about ourselves as individuals who calculate about ourselves, "add value" to ourselves, improve our productivity, live an existence of calculation, make ourselves relevant' (Q5). Meanwhile, the highly political nature of research is hidden in the innocuous language of 'information' (see above; Q2, Q4; also see Chapter 10).

The main message that emerges from this application of the WPR approach is that, in order to understand how rule takes place, there is a need to take into account modes of governance and their organisational practices, in particular in this instance funding regimes, and institutional arrangements among states, funding bodies, intermediary research institutions and individual researchers (**Q3, Q6**). However, it remains important to remember that challenges to regimes of governance with effects we find disturbing are possible. Indeed, some of the concepts and language associated with 'evidence-based policy' can be used as 'assets' (see Chapter 1) to question the 'effectiveness' of 'user-*driven* research'. It could be argued, for example, that, because research questions shape understandings of 'problems' in important ways, the 'wrong' questions may well produce poor 'outcomes'. On these grounds it becomes possible to make the case that a wide range of participants, including the lay public (Popay *et al.* 2003; Bolam 2005) and civil society groups (Sanders *et al.* 2004), ought to be involved in framing research questions (**Q6**).

What's in a question?

'Two priests who, being unsure if it was permissible to smoke and pray at the same time, wrote to the Pope for a definitive answer. One priest phrased the question "Is it permissible to smoke while praying?" and was told it was not, since prayer should be the focus of one's whole attention: the other priest asked if it is permissible to pray while smoking and was told that it is, since it is always appropriate to pray' (Postman 1993, p. 126).

- **What is the point of this anecdote?**
- **What does it suggest about the role of questions (priorities, 'problems') in the research process?**

Thinking across the insights generated through examining our practical texts, it may well be necessary to put the whole idea of 'health policy' under scrutiny. Both the CSDH (2007, p. 58) and the MEKN Report (2007, p. 62) note that every government department needs to be involved in a committed effort to reduce health inequities. This recognition that every aspect of our existence has health consequences leads to questions about the usefulness of a 'health department' and a 'health policy'. To what extent, we may well ask, does 'health policy' function as a residual category for issues deemed to be either 'too hard' or simply 'impracticable'? For example, to what extent is the approximate 17-year gap in life expectancy between Aboriginal people and non-Aboriginal Australians a 'health problem'? Or, to what extent is the gap due to factors that are contentious and potentially expensive to deal with, such as racism and dispossession? In this sense, as Osborne (1997, p. 197) says, 'a focus on health as such might be seen as something of a diversion' when 'The point might be – still – to change society'.

SUMMARY

In this chapter we have seen the importance of reflecting on the meanings imputed to the key referent 'health' in health policy. We have also considered the various ways in which the idea of prevention is understood. In particular, preventive approaches that target individual behaviours have been distinguished from approaches that emphasise the impact of wide-ranging social and environmental factors on health, wellbeing and inequities in health (SDH). The latter approach draws to our attention the ways in which *all policies* are implicated in health and wellbeing, suggesting that the very idea of 'health policy' is a mechanism of governance. With this insight the increasingly common view that governments, rather than representatives from the broader community, should set priorities for health research takes on added significance.

QUESTIONS

1. What does it mean to say that health is a residual category in government policy? Give an example.

2. How are subjects constituted in screening programs, for example, mammography and pap smears?

3. To what extent are citizens currently held responsible for their own health and the health of 'significant others'? Is there a gender subtext in this message?

4. Identify possible silences in the current emphasis on individual responsibility for health monitoring and fitness.

5. Is it appropriate for governments to set or 'drive' the priorities for health research (i.e. 'user-driven research')? Why or why not? What does a WPR approach contribute to consideration of this issue?

6. What forms of social change would be needed to advance a social determinants of health inequities agenda?

---

1 The Final Report of the CSDH (2008) questions the appropriateness of RCTs (Randomized Controlled Trials) for assessing SDH interventions and offers a 'broader view' of evidence as including observational studies, case studies and field visits. However, the Report does *not* address the political implications of the evidence-based paradigm, attesting to its current authority

REFERENCES

ALEXANDER, M. & LAWRENCE, R. S. 2002, 'Preventive Medicine', *Encyclopedia of Public Health*, ed. L. Breslow, Macmillan Reference, vol. 4, pp. 977–78.

ANDERSON, L. 2008, 'Health Checks Miss Target', *The Advertiser*, 5 March.

BACCHI, C. 2008, 'The Politics of Research Management: Reflections on the Gap Between What We "Know" [About SDH] and What We Do', *Health Sociology Review*, vol. 17, no. 2, pp. 165–76.

BACCHI, C. 2009, 'The Issue of Intentionality in Frame Theory: The Need for Reflexive Framing', in *The Discursive Politics of Gender Equality: Stretching, Bending and Policymaking*, eds E. Lombardo, P. Meier & M. Verloo, Routledge, London.

BAGULEY, D. 2008, 'Introducing the 10/90 Gap', *Alma Mata Global Health Network*, <www.almamata.net>, accessed 23 July 2008.

BALL, S. J. 2001, '"You've Been NERFed!" Dumbing Down the Academy: National Educational Research Forum: "a national strategy – consultation paper": a brief and bilious response', *Journal of Education Policy*, vol. 16, no. 3, pp. 265–8.

BOLAM, B. L. 2005, 'Public Participation in Tackling Health Inequalities: Implications From Recent Qualitative Research', *The European Journal of Public Health*, vol. 15, no. 5, pp. 447–62.

BROOM, D. 2008, 'Hazardous Good Intentions? Unintended Consequences of the Project of Prevention', *Health Sociology Review*, vol. 17, no. 2, pp. 129–40.

CHSRF (Canadian Health Services Research Foundation) 2006, *Innovation Through Collaboration: Working Together for an Evidence-Informed Health System*, Report of the 8th Annual Invitational Workshop, 21–22 March, Vancouver, British Columbia, <www.chsrf.ca>, accessed 16 September 2006.

COCHRANE, A. 1972, *Effectiveness and Efficiency: Random Reflections on Health Services*, Nuffield Provincial Hospital, London.

COVENEY, J. 2008, 'The Government of Girth', *Health Sociology Review*, vol. 17, no. 2, pp. 129–40.

CRUIKSHANK, B. 1994, 'The Will to Empower: Technologies of Citizenship and the War on Poverty', *Socialist Review*, vol. 23, no. 4, pp. 29–55.

CSDH (Commission on Social Determinants of Health) 2008, *Closing the Gap in a Generation: Health Equity Through Action*, Final Report, Commission Secretariat, Department of Equity, Poverty and Social Determinants of Health, World Health Organisation, Geneva, <www.who.int>, accessed 29 August 2008.

CSDH (Commission on Social Determinants of Health) 2005, *Towards a Conceptual Framework for Analysis and Action on the Social Determinants of Health*, Discussion Paper for the Commission on Social Determinants of Health, Geneva, <www.who.int>, accessed 16 July 2008.

CSDH (Commission on Social Determinants of Health) 2007, *A Conceptual Framework for Action on the Social Determinants of Health*, Discussion paper, Commission Secretariat, Department of Equity, Poverty and Social Determinants of Health, World Health Organization, Geneva, <www.who.int>, accessed 2 May 2008.

DIABETES AUSTRALIA 2006 'The Tick Test', copyright Diabetes South Australia. Reprinted with permission.

DONALD, A. 2001, 'Commentary: Research Must be Taken Seriously', *British Medical Journal*, vol. 323, pp. 278–9.

ECKERSLEY, R. 2005, '"Cultural Fraud": The Role of Culture in Drug Abuse', *Drug and Alcohol Review*, vol. 24, no. 2, pp. 157–63.

ESPING-ANDERSEN, G. 1990, *The Three Worlds of Welfare Capitalism*, Princeton University Press, New Jersey.

FOUCAULT, M. 2003 [1976], 'Chapter 11: 17 March 1976' in *'Society Must Be Defended': Lectures at the Collège de France, 1975–76*, eds F. Ewald & A. Fontana, Trans. D. Macey, Penguin Books, London.

FRANKISH, C. J., GREEN, L. W., RATNER, P. A., CHOMIK, T. & LARSEN, C. 1996, *Health Impact Assessment as a Tool for Population Health Promotion and Public Policy*, Institute of Health Promotion Research, University of British Columbia, Vancouver, <www.phac-aspc.gc.ca>, accessed 16 July 2008.

GLOVER, J., HARRIS, K., TENNANT, S. & WATTS, V. 1999, *A Social Health Atlas of Australia*, Series of nine atlases covering each State and Territory, and Australia, Public Health Information Development Unit, University of Adelaide, Adelaide.

GOVERNMENT OF SOUTH AUSTRALIA 2007a, *Strategic Health Research Program: Guidelines 2006–2007*, Government of South Australia, Adelaide.

GOVERNMENT OF SOUTH AUSTRALIA 2007b, *Strategic Health Research Program: Research Priorities 2006–2007*, Government of South Australia, Adelaide.

GRAHAM, H. 2004, 'Social Determinants and Their Unequal Distributions: Clarifying Policy Understandings', *The Milbank Quarterly*, vol. 82, no, 1, pp. 101–24.

GRAY, D. 1999, 'Doctors Prescribe End to Racism as a Cure for Aboriginal Health', *The Age*, 14 August.

GUTHMAN, J. & DuPUIS, M. 2006, 'Embodying Neoliberalism: Economy, Culture, and the Politics of Fat', *Environment and Planning D: Society and Space*, vol. 24, no. 3, pp. 427–48.

HAILSTONE, B. 2002, 'Fighting Disease Before it Strikes', *The Advertiser*, 14 May.

HINDE, S. & DIXON, J. 2005, 'Changing the Obesogenic Environment: Insights From a Cultural Economy of Car Reliance', *Transportation Research Part D*, vol. 10, pp. 31–53, <www.sciencedirect.com>, accessed on 10 August 2006.

HOLMES, D., MURRAY, S. J., PERRON, A., & RAIL, G. 2006, 'Deconstructing the Evidence-Based Discourse in Health Sciences: Truth, Power and Fascism', *International Journal of Evidence Based Healthcare*, vol. 4, no. 3, pp. 180–6.

HURRELL, B. 2006, 'Your Health's Worth $68', *The Advertiser*, 16 March.

INTERNATIONAL OBESITY TASKFORCE 2006, *The Sydney Principles*, <www.iotf.org/sydneyprinciples>, accessed 29 April 2008.

IRWIN, A., VALENTINE, N., BROWN, C., LOEWENSON, R., SOLAR, O., BROWN, H., KOLLER, T. & VEGA, J. 2006, 'The Commission on Social Determinants of Health: Tackling the Social Roots of Health Inequities', *PLoS Med*, vol. 3, No. 6, e106, pp. 0749–0751, <http://medicine.plosjournals.org>, accessed 20 December 2008

KELEHER, H. 2001, 'Why Primary Health Care Offers a More Comprehensive Approach for Tackling Health Inequities Than Primary Care', *Australian Journal of Primary Health*, vol. 7, no. 2, pp. 57–61.

KRIEGER, N. 2001, 'Theories for Social Epidemiology in the 21st Century: an Ecosocial Perspective', *International Journal of Epidemiology*, vol. 30, no. 4, pp. 668–77.

LANE, D. 2000, 'A Threat to the Public Health Workforce: Evidence From Trends in Preventive Medicine Certification and Training', *American Journal of Preventive Medicine*, vol. 18, no. 1, pp. 87–96.

LEWIS, J. 2005, *Health Policy and Politics: Networks, Ideas and Power*, IP Communications, Melbourne.

LLOYD, K. & HANNON, K. 2000, 'Wealth a Sign of Far Better Health', *The Advertiser*, 15 April.

MARSTON, G. AND WATTS, R. 2003, 'Tampering With the Evidence: A Critical Appraisal of Evidence-Based Policy-Making', *The Drawing Board: An Australian Review of Public Affairs*, vol. 3, no. 3, pp. 143–63.

MEASUREMENT AND EVIDENCE KNOWLEDGE NETWORK (MEKN) 2007, *The social determinants of health: developing an evidence base for political action*, Final Report to the World Health Organization, Geneva, <www.who.int>, accessed 2 May 2008.

MUNTANER, C. 2004, 'Commentary: Social Capital, Social Class and the Slow Progress of Psychosocial Epidemiology', *International Journal of Epidemiology*, vol 33, no. 4, pp. 1–7.

NETTLETON, S. 1997, 'Governing the Risky Self: How to Become Healthy, Wealthy and Wise', in *Foucault, Health and Medicine*, eds A. Petersen & R. Bunton, Routledge, London.

NSW DEPARTMENT OF HEALTH 2003, *Prevention of Obesity in Children and Young People: Government Action Plan 2003–2007*, North Sydney, NSW Department of Health, <www.health.nsw.gov/obesity>, accessed 30 April 2008.

NOBLE, T. 2003, 'Melbourne Study Yields First Pointers on Anti-Cancer Diet', *The Age*, 6 September.

OECD (Organisation for Economic Co-operation and Development) 2004, *OECD Health Data*, OECD, Paris.

OSBORNE, T. 1997, 'Of Health and Statecraft', in *Foucault, Health and Medicine*, eds A. Petersen & R. Burton, Routledge, New York.

OTTAWA CHARTER FOR HEALTH PROMOTION 1986, First International Conference on Health Promotion, 21 November, WHO/HPR/HEP/95.1, <www.who.int>, accessed 26 April 2008.

PETERSEN, A. 2003, 'Governmentality, Critical Scholarship, and the Medical Humanities', *Journal of Medical Humanities*, vol. 24, nos. 3/4, pp. 187–201.

POPAY, J., BENNETT, S., THOMAS, C., WILLIAMS, G., GATRELL, A. & BOSTOCK, L. 2003, 'Beyond "Beer, Fags, Egg and Chips"? Exploring Lay Understandings of Social Inequalities in Health', *Sociology of Health & Illness*, vol. 25, no. 1, pp. 1–23.

POPKEWITZ, T. S. 1998, 'The Culture of Redemption and the Administration of Freedom as Research', *Review of Educational Research*, vol. 68, no. 1, pp. 1–34.

POSTMAN, N. 1993, *Technopoly: The Surrender of Culture to Technology*, 1st edition 1992, Vintage Books, New York.

PUBLIC HEALTH AGENCY OF CANADA 2008, 'What is the Population Health Approach?', Public Health Agency of Canada, <www.phac-aspc.gc.ca>, accessed 29 August 2008.

SANDERS, D., LABONTE, R., BAUM, F. & CHOPRA, M. 2004, 'Making Research Matter: a Civil Society Perspective on Health Research', *Bulletin of the World Health Organization*, vol. 82, no. 10, pp. 757–63.

SEN, A. K.1992, *Inequality Re-examined*, Clarendon Press, Oxford, England.

SOUTH AUSTRALIAN HEALTH DEPARTMENT 2008, 'Research Transfer Discussion Paper', <www.health.sa.gov.au>, accessed 30 April 2008.

SWEDISH NATIONAL INSTITUTE OF PUBLIC HEALTH 2005, *The 2005 Public Health Policy Report*, <www.fhi.se>, accessed 16 July 2008.

THE AGE 2006, 'Children Urged to Get Active', News, 4 February.

TOY, M. 1999, 'Shedding Light on Medical Care', *The Age*, 10 April.

TURNER, B. 1997, 'Foreword. From Governmentality to Risk: Some Reflections on Foucault's Contributions to Medical Sociology', in *Foucault, Health and Medicine*, eds A. Petersen & R. Bunton, Routledge, New York.

UNITED NATIONS 2008, *Millennium Goals*, <www.un.org>, accessed 23 July 2008.

WHO 2005 'Bridging the know-do gap in global health', WHO Knowledge Management Strategy, 10–12 October, Geneva, <www.who.int>, accessed 21 July 2008.

WHO (World Health Organization) 2006, *Alma-Ata Declaration*, Regional Office for Europe, <www.euro.who.int>, accessed 21 July 2008.

WHO 1946, *Preamble to the Constitution*, as adopted by the International Health Conference, 22 July, <www.who.int/hpr/NPH/docs/declaration_almaata.pdf >, accessed 26 April 2008. Reprinted with permission.

FURTHER READING

BROOM, D. & DIXON, J. eds 2007, *The 7 Deadly Sins of Obesity*, UNSW Press, Sydney.

ECKERSLEY, R., DIXON, J. & DOUGLAS, B. eds 2001, *The Social Origins of Health and Wellbeing*, Cambridge University Press, Melbourne.

LIN, V. & GIBSON, B. eds 2003, *Evidence-Based Health Policy: Problems & Possibilities*, Oxford University Press, Oxford.

O'MALLEY, P. 1996, 'Risk and responsibility', in *Foucault and Political Reason: Liberalism, Neo-liberalism and Rationalities of Government*, eds A. Barry, T. Osborne & N. Rose, UCL Press, London.

POPAY, J., WILLIAMS, G., THOMAS, C. & GATRELL, T., 1998, 'Theorising Inequalities in Health: The Place of Lay Knowledge', *Sociology of Health and Illness*, vol. 20, no. 5, pp. 619–44.

WASS, A. 2000, *Promoting Health: The Primary Health Care Approach*, 2nd edition, Harcourt Sanders, Sydney.

Population, immigration, citizenship:'Securing' a place in the world

Chapter 7

CHECKING OUR BEARINGS

The interconnected policy areas – population, immigration and citizenship – provide an ideal opportunity to revisit some of the theoretical precepts underpinning a WPR approach to policy analysis. Given the explicit focus on methods of governing *population*, we have a chance to look again at the rather difficult concept of governmentality. In addition, the chapter provides an opportunity to illustrate the ways in which a WPR approach broadens the scope of policy analysis beyond national borders, beyond policy 'specialisms', and beyond the state (see the Introduction).

Before we begin, it is useful to note that the kinds of theoretical debates around these three policy 'areas' are quite different from those traced in relation to 'crime' (Chapter 5) and to 'health' (Chapter 6). Compared to crime, which is clearly considered to be undesirable and hence reduced, and to health, which is clearly considered to be desirable and hence increased, key debates around population and immigration are precisely about whether they should be increased or lowered, and what these shifts mean for 'citizens'. The key referents, if you will, are not as fixed. As we shall see, the current globalisation discourse destabilises objectives further.

To explore these issues, we use the following 'practical texts': the Maternity Payment (dubbed the 'baby bonus') introduced in Australia in 2004; 457 Visas for 'temporary, long stay immigrants' (introduced in 1996); and Australia's new *Citizenship Act 2007 (Cth)* (Australian Government 2007a).

Reminder

The six questions in a WPR approach can be followed systematically – addressing each question separately and in order – as in Chapters 3 and 4. More commonly, the questions form part of an integrated analysis, with specific questions applied where the analysis occasions their use. This chapter follows the second, integrated form of analysis, employing the notation Q1, Q2, etc. where a specific question has been applied. Until students are completely familiar with the questions in the approach, it is advisable to look back to the original list (either the abbreviated form in the Introduction and Chapter 1, or the expanded version at the end of Chapter 2) when such notation appears.

THINKING ABOUT 'POPULATION'

As we saw in Chapter 2, Foucault used the term 'governmentality' in two ways: first, to refer to a particular way of thinking about and exercising governmental power, traced to late eighteenth-century Europe, that focused on the health and welfare of the population; and, second, as a more general way of referring to modes of rule. In this second meaning govern-*mentalities* are the ways in which rule is imagined and hence rationalised; they are 'diagrams' of rule (Deleuze 1988, p. 44) or 'rationalities' (rationales) of rule. You can think of the Panopticon (see Chapter 2), for example, as a *diagram* of rule.

As raised in Chapter 2, it is important *not* to think of these 'mentalities of rule' as planned and intentional. Rather, they emerge from a complex array of developments. To say that 'mentalities of rule' are unplanned, however, does not mean that some groups do not benefit more than others from their deployment. In fact, we have focused throughout on the ways in which dividing practices form a key element of current dominant forms of rule, with exactly these effects (Q5).

If there are diverse ways of governing a people, how are we to discern and assess the 'govern-mentalities' of our time? A WPR approach achieves this objective by directing attention to the ways in which 'problems' are conceptualised ('what's the problem represented to be?') within specific policies (Q1). By looking at the way 'problems' are represented – examining the 'problem-space' (Dean 1999, p. 123) – we can identify specific logics/rationalities of governance (styles of problematisation) at work and put them under critical scrutiny. Since we are governed through problematisations (see Chapter 2) – that is, since how an issue is problematised determines what does and does not get done, and how particular groups may be treated – it is crucial to scrutinise closely problematisations and the problem representations that they contain. Remembering that modes of rule are most often hybrids, we can observe and study them most effectively by examining the assumptions and presuppositions that lodge within identified problem representations (Q2).

To repeat a central premise, we are *not* looking for assumptions that exist in people's heads as belief systems or as attitudes, but rather we are looking for assumptions (the 'logics') that are necessary to specific problem representations. In the discussion on crime, for example, it was shown that different approaches to the area supported very different assumptions about what counts as 'crime'. The shift in focus then is from 'problems' that are *presumed* to provoke government 'responses' to the ways in which 'problems' are 'thought'.

Population, as we have identified, is a pivotal term in Foucault's work on governmentality. In his view, growth in population size posed particular challenges for modern governments. As a consequence, emphasis shifted from defence of territory to the disposition of people.

> 'We are dealing not with the defence of territory so much as "the imbrication of men and things", "men" in their myriad relations with climate, wealth, resources, the territory and so on' (Foucault 1991, p. 92 in Larner and Walters 2006b, p. 3).

Foucault directed attention to the way in which modern governments deal with 'population' as a kind of organic body, a 'species body' (Foucault 1979, p. 139). We come to talk about 'population' as if it is a single entity with a common destiny. We measure marriage *rates* and poverty *rates*, employment *rates* and suicide *rates*. The interest is not in a *particular* marriage or suicide, but in the number of marriages or suicides that take place in a particular place – most often in a country but sometimes in states or provinces within countries, or in regions – and how these marriages or suicides are patterned over time. For example, there is concern if the marriage *rate* declines or the suicide *rate* increases. Censuses serve as a kind of collective accounting on the size and 'health' of the population within specific bounded territories. Contemporary discussions about the Australian birth *rate* provide an ideal entry-point for reflecting further on this aspect of modern modes of governance (see below).

There are clear links between this focus on population and the historical emergence of nation-states (or sub-states, e.g. provinces). The concern is with the size and 'health' of *bordered* populations. However, a governmentality approach, concerned as it is with 'modes of rule' – with how governing is rationalised – has implications beyond nation-state borders. To put it simply, modes of rule adopted by certain nation-state governments tend to impact on the forms of international rule that operate. In addition, given the prevalence and significance of international state actors, such as the World Bank and the International Monetary Fund, questions need to be asked about the 'modes of governance' these bodies display. For these reasons, as Valverde and Mopas (2006, p. 235) attest, 'studies of policy and security that are influenced by Foucauldian work on governance are no longer tethered to the nation-state even when their particular form is a national police force or a national criminal justice programme'. In this vein, a WPR approach starts with 'practical texts', most often *national* policy texts, but endeavours to build from these starting points to gain insights into modes of governance that have international implications.

A governmentality approach encourages another kind of 'cross-border' study. In several places in the text I have emphasised that a WPR approach stresses interconnections across policy 'areas' that are conventionally treated as discrete. Thinking about 'govern-mentalities' helps to explain why this focus is considered necessary. The argument here is that, if we are looking to identify underlying assumptions that characterise particular modes of rule, keeping in mind that these modes of rule may well be hybrid in form, we should *expect* to find commonalities in 'ways of thinking rule' across policy 'fields'.

To this point the book has identified several commonalities in 'ways of thinking rule' in contemporary Australia and more widely in the Western industrialised world. For example, the theme of increasing individual 'responsibilisation' has emerged as a mode of rule in criminal justice policy (Chapter 5), in drugs/alcohol and gambling policy (Chapter 4), and in much health policy (Chapter 6). The idea of evidence-based policy is also emerging as a mode of rule (see Chapters 5, 6 and 10).

Walters (2004), following Foucault, usefully identifies *security* as another important modern govern-mentality. As he describes, security is a dominant motif in national and international governance, but it also appears in forms of social insurance (social *security*; see Chapter 3). Today we hear about 'energy *security*', 'food *security*' and 'water *security*'. In these discourses, 'security' operates as the flip-side of risk, discussed in Chapters 5 and 6. We gain important insights into how rule takes place by reflecting on the kinds of thought that shape the role that security plays in modern governance. To this end, we need to ask – what kind of a 'problem' is 'security' represented to be? what does it mean to make people secure? Secure from what? Which people? – questions we pursue later in our examination of selected 'practical texts'.

The third 'cross-border' movement encouraged by a WPR approach de-centres state (national; sub-national) government in another way. While keeping the state as an important player, governance is understood in a broad sense to capture the multitudes of agencies and groups involved in establishing order. Foucault was centrally interested in the role played by medicine, particularly psychiatry, and by the social sciences. The government (in the narrow sense) 'enlists' other groups (medicos, psychologists, social scientists) in the task of governing. It does this through the knowledges they produce. As we have seen in earlier chapters, a wide range of social actors, including some health professionals (Chapters 4 and 6) and some criminologists (Chapter 5) support and promote a 'responsibilisation' govern-mentality. Bigo (2002) directs attention to the role played by security professionals in reinforcing a 'securitization' discourse. The ways in which researchers reinforce dominant modes of governance *simply through the execution of their research* is a topic we discuss in more detail in Chapter 10.

A WPR approach offers ways both to identify govern-mentalities (governmental rationalities) and to subject them to critical scrutiny. By tracing how particular modes of rule have become established ways of governing – tracing their genealogy (Q3) – it is possible to 'lay bare the relations of power that produce sites of governance' (Lui 2006, p. 131). Power, it should be remembered, is thought about, not as 'something possessed by given actors (individual, capital, state)', but as something that is exercised though heterogeneous discourses and practices. It operates through 'multifarious practical, technical manifestations' (Larner and Walters 2006b, pp. 3–4) that need to be carefully examined (**Q2, Q3**). A key objective is to 'de-inevitablise' existing accounts of the global present, to see that things could be otherwise and to show that, in order for existing social relations to appear 'natural', society has to be organised in the precise manner that it is.[1] As Lui (2006, p. 131) puts it, 'A world of territorial sovereign states and a humanity of national citizens have come about due to specific historical conditions; there is nothing necessary about either institution'.

By asking what fails to be problematised (**Q4**) and reflecting on the range of effects – discursive, subjectivising, and lived (**Q5**) – that accompany specific modes of rule (**Q2**), it becomes possible to consider what needs to change and how to go about it (**Q6**). A central issue that deserves the utmost attention is the extent to which governmental rationalities influence who we are – what we imagine ourselves to be. The need to subject our own problem representations to critical scrutiny follows from this insight.

The 'practical texts' in this chapter have been selected to allow us to explore the three 'cross-border movements' in governance discussed in this opening section:

- flows across national boundaries, with international implications;
- flows across policy 'areas';
- flows between state and other governing 'parties', including professionals and social scientists.

The chapter develops the argument that policy areas that appear to be looking inwards toward nation-state building (the 'baby bonus') and policy areas targeting 'outsiders' (457 visas) converge in a singular image of state security and citizenship – 'securing' a place in the world.

THE MATERNITY PAYMENT

In the 2004–05 Budget Overview, titled *More Help For Families*, the Howard-led Coalition government introduced a Maternity Payment:

> To provide further help for families at the crucial period around the birth of a child, a new Maternity Payment of $3,000 for each new born child will be introduced from July 2004. This will increase to $4,000 in July 2006 and $5,000 in July 2008. (Australian Government 2004)

At a fairly obvious level, the 'problem' in this policy is represented to be an insufficient number of births in Australia (**Q1**). In other words, the policy is pro-natalist, encouraging more births. The issue becomes more complex when we probe further (**Q2** and following).

Some context is needed. To find out more about the space being governed (the 'problem-space') through this policy, identify the web of policies within which it sits. In addition, probe the debates surrounding the topic. Remember that in a WPR analysis our objective is not to expose the declared commitment to 'more help for families' as empty rhetoric, though it may well be the case that it is, but to uncover the assumptions and presuppositions (Q2) that allow such a declaration to be made.

The Maternity Payment is part of a package of measures, including the Family Tax Benefit Schemes A and B, and the Childcare Benefit, addressed to providing support for Australian families and 'help for those balancing work and family responsibilities'. A particular focus in the 2004–05 Budget is to 'improve rewards from work for families where a second earner is in part-time or casual work, providing additional assistance for women returning to work after having children', 'particularly those on low or middle incomes', by 'reducing effective marginal tax rates' (Australian Government 2004). The package of proposals therefore aims to make it easier, or at least more attractive, for women to return to paid work once they have had babies. The expanded 'problem-space' therefore includes a concern that there are inadequate numbers of women working in paid labour (Q1).

The Maternity Payment replaced an earlier 'baby bonus' policy, a complicated scheme that operated as a refundable tax offset for up to five years if women stayed home to care for their new-born babies instead of returning to paid work. In this scheme, the amount of baby bonus a 'primary care giver' (mostly women) received depended upon her taxable income prior to the birth. To receive the maximum tax rebate of $2 500, a woman would have had to be earning upwards of $60 000. A minimum payment of $500 per year was available for 'mothers on low incomes' (Costello 2002). Critics pointed out that, clearly, under the scheme those better off in terms of their salary stood to gain the most. Hence, the new 'baby bonus' was not tied to income previously earned; nor was it means-tested: 'This new benefit will be available to all families, regardless of the family's income' (Australian Government 2004).

The conjoining of a concern about the declining number of babies born and a desire to facilitate women's return to paid work after birth, along with an expressed commitment to 'balancing work and family' (Australian Government 2004), is certainly not restricted to Australia. Indeed, these three issues – declining birth rates, women's labour force participation, and the work/life balance – attract significant attention among governments and researchers in most industrialised countries (Duncan 2002; Gornick and Myers 2004). On these issues, the leading European social scientist, Esping-Andersen (2002), has proposed a new 'child-centred' approach to social policy and a new 'gender contract' that involves men assuming a larger proportion of domestic responsibilities as possible 'solutions' (creating the 'problem' as a particular sort of 'problem', which could be explored further through applying a WPR analysis).

If we dig a little deeper, it is possible to see what is driving this agenda. Most often, the desire for more babies and to get more women into the labour force is connected to an 'ageing population' problematic. With fewer babies and an 'ageing demographic', it is argued, insufficient taxpayers will exist to fund the anticipated welfare costs of the elderly (Q1).

This issue would be less of a 'problem', it is argued, if there were more babies and if more women engaged in paid labour. The 'trick', it seems, is to get women to do *both* — have the babies *and* engage in paid labour. Measures to address the 'work/life' balance are put forward to encourage this outcome. There are also links between the drive to increase women's labour force participation and expressed concerns about 'skills shortages', discussed below, but these are muted in the women-to-work discourse.

In the history of the Australian nation-state, concern for the numbers and composition (class, colour, ethnicity) of the population has been expressed on numerous occasions (Q3). In 1901 the new Commonwealth introduced an *Immigration Restriction Act* (Wilson, Thomson and McMahon 1996), otherwise referred to as the White Australia Policy, which prohibited a number of groups from immigration, including prostitutes, criminals, those considered to be insane, and anyone likely to become a cost to the public purse. The Act also gave immigration officers the prerogative to impose a dictation test on aspiring immigrants. The test was used primarily to exclude individuals on the basis of 'race'.

In 1903 a Birth Rate Royal Commission addressed concerns about Australia's declining and differential birth rate, captured in the slogan 'populate or perish'. The differential birth rate referred to the fact that fewer middle-class than 'lower-class' women were having babies. This 'unpatriotic' behaviour was sheeted home to middle-class women's interest in 'other' things, such as political causes and work outside the home, which prevented them from paying sufficient attention to their 'primary calling', motherhood (Bacchi 1980, p. 201). An assumption about heterosexual marital roles underpins this representation of the 'problem' (Q2).

To increase the birth-rate, in 1912 the government brought in a 'baby bonus' of 5 pounds for each viable birth (*Maternity Allowance Act 2006 (Cth)* (Australian Government 2006)). The link with the White Australia Policy was made clear in the declaration that 'the baby is the best immigrant' and in the administrative detail that denied the bonus to Aboriginal mothers (Q3). Officials in other 'Anglo-Saxon' countries with declining birth-rates (e.g. the USA, the UK, Canada) expressed fears about a 'race suicide scare' (Q3, Q6), indicating the way in which geopolitical space was conceptualised and problematised at the time (Q2).

Foucault (2003, p. 255) provides some insights here. He identifies a tension between a state's commitment to improve life and security for citizens (biopower) and the potential loss of citizen life in war. In his view this tension is reconciled through racism or racialism as a 'biological-type relationship' — approaching the world in terms of categories of people marked by their desirability or undesirability for the sake of a 'race':

The fact that the other dies does not mean simply that I live in the sense that his death guarantees my safety; the death of the other, the death of the bad race, of the inferior race (or the degenerate, or the abnormal) is something that will make life in general healthier: healthier and purer. (Foucault 2003, p. 255)

In terms of the 'degenerate' and the 'abnormal', recall the exclusion from immigration of prostitutes, criminals, the insane and paupers in the White Australia Policy. Usefully for our later consideration of migration policies, Foucault (2003, p. 256) explains that this kind of 'racial' (biopolitical) imperative includes 'every form of indirect murder: the fact of exposing someone to death, increasing the risk of death for some people, or, quite simply, political death, expulsion, rejection and so on.'

Whereas Foucault details the shift from concern for territory to concern for population in late eighteenth century European states, the two domains of governance were conjoined in Australia in the late nineteenth, early twentieth centuries. A vast land with settlers scattered around the coast seemed 'insecure' given what were described as the multitudinous 'yellow hordes' to the north. Aboriginal people were not considered part of the population, excluded as they were from the census until 1967 (Q2, Q3).

Pursuing the topic of the relationship between sovereignty and biopower Dean (1999, p. 203) suggests that biopolitics poses a particular challenge for liberal modes of rule that rely upon an espoused democratised form of sovereignty. He suggests that there is a tension between the need to be seen to respect the sovereignty of the people (democracy) and the need to balance population and resources (biopolitics). As Dean (1999, p. 113) says, 'at one level liberalism is a version of bio-politics; at another it exists in a kind of permanent tension with bio-political imperatives'. To reconcile these elements, liberal and neoliberal governments often achieve population goals though *indirect means* – government 'at a distance' (Miller and Rose 1990, p. 9; see Chapter 2) – for example, by *eliciting* desired behaviours from citizens rather than through legislating upon them directly.

As a result Western liberal democracies are governed through a mix (an 'assemblage') of means, which include:

- explicit regulation or disciplinary techniques;
- environmental or social liberal techniques – that is, shaping the environment to produce results deemed desirable;
- versions of neoliberalism – that is, finding ways to instil in the population responsibility for the development of characteristics deemed to be desirable.

Illiberal forms of regulatory or disciplinary rule become justified if it can be argued that sub-populations do not exhibit the characteristics necessary for self-sovereignty (Q2). We have already observed this rationale operating in specific, illiberal policies based on dividing practices around 'youth' (Chapter 3), so-called 'dole bludgers' (Chapter 3), 'drug users' (Chapter 4), and above, in the exclusion of Aboriginal people from the 1912 baby bonus and from national citizenship until 1967.

The 1903 Birth Rate Royal Commission employed an assemblage of governing techniques (Q3). It withheld from circulation the volume of evidence that contained contraceptive information, displaying a form of censorial regulation. The 5 pound 'baby bonus', by contrast, can be seen as a form of social liberal intervention, rewarding desired behaviours. The Commissioners also enjoined white, middle-class women to abandon their selfishness and to put motherhood first, encouraging self-regulation (Q5).

In current discussions about population levels, there is reliance on incentives (the 'baby bonus') and on persuasion to boost the birth rate, rather than on censorship and discipline. The target audience for persuasion continues primarily to be white, middle- or upper-middle class women. While visiting the academically elite MacRobertson Girls High School in Melbourne in 1999, the then Victorian Premier, Jeff Kennett, called upon the young women students to make a career out of motherhood. Comparing Australia to its more populous northern neighbours, he stated: 'We have an ageing population. Our women are not producing enough offspring to simply maintain our population level' (Dever 2005, p. 45). Reflecting similar sentiments, in a post-2004 budget interview, Federal Treasurer Peter Costello enjoined families: 'If you can have children, you have one for the father and one for the mother and one for the country' (Comment 2004).

Numerous newspaper reports ensure that women know the message to have more babies is directed at them (Q6). Beside a graph showing the increase in numbers of childless women by age between 1981 and 1996, *The Age* proclaims a 'Childless future for many women' (Colebatch 2000). Alongside a picture of babies scattered across an Australian flag, *The Advertiser* asks: 'Where have all the mothers gone?', and declares: 'Australian women of child-bearing age are on strike, unwilling or unable to contribute to population growth' (Kemp and Williams 2002). The symbolic positioning of the babies on the flag nicely captures the 'racial' imperative underlying the issue (see discussion above).

Despite the fact that women and their *birthing* decisions figure so prominently in the discussion, the dominant discourse around population growth or decline refers to *fertility* rates (Q2). Charts comparing Australia's 'fertility rate' with other countries, particularly with those in the region, feature regularly in the Australian press (Dalton 2003; also see Activity on '*Fertility*: How We Compare'). The view that some parts of the globe, primarily Asian and African countries, are 'out of control' in terms of population is assumed, echoing 1960s anxiety about the 'population explosion'. In that period Foundations from wealthy Western countries sponsored 'demographic missions' to 'third world' countries, to enjoin them to curtail their population growth (Rojas 2006, p. 100).

The term 'fertility' refers to a physiological capacity to bear offspring (see *The Children of Men* in the Activity opposite). The frequent use of the term in current discussions about Australia's birth rate, therefore, leaves the impression that the declining number of births is due to some form of physiological impairment, rather than the outcome of collective birth-controlling decisions and practices. In this way, 'Australia's' future is cast in terms of a spatial and cultural/'racial' struggle for security – usefully illustrating that sense of 'racism', conceived broadly, as a 'biological-type relationship' (**Q2**; see discussion above).

The 2004 package of family benefits, including the Maternity Payment, continue to support conventional heterosexual families with the woman/wife assuming responsibility for family nurture, despite careful references to 'second earners' (**Q2**). The modern family, according to Howard, will have 'one-and-a-half earners'. He fails to mention that women will most likely be the 'half earners', in unprotected part-time or casual jobs (see Pocock 2005; **Q4**; **Q5**). At the same time there have been attempts to use the 'fertility' 'crisis' as an 'asset' (see Chapters 1 and 2), to bolster demands for basic paid, publicly-funded maternity leave, still nonexistent in Australia (Dever 2005, p. 46), and for 'free child care' (Williams 2000; **Q6**).

The Children of Men

By P. D. James

'We should have been warned in the early 1990s. As early as 1991 a European Community Report showed a slump in the number of children born in Europe – 8.2 million in 1990, with particular drops in the Roman Catholic countries. We thought that we knew the reasons, that the fall was deliberate, a result of more liberal attitudes to birth control and abortion, the postponement of pregnancy by professional women pursuing their careers, the wish of families for a higher standard of living. And the fall in population was complicated by the spread of AIDS, particularly in Africa. Some European countries began to pursue a vigorous campaign to encourage the birth of children, but most of us thought the fall was desirable, even necessary. We were polluting the planet with our numbers; if we were breeding less it was to be welcomed. Most of the concern was less about a falling population than about the wish of nations to maintain their own people, their own culture, their own race, to breed sufficient young to maintain their economic structures. But as I remember it, no one suggested that the fertility of the human race was dramatically changing. When Omega came it came with dramatic suddenness and was received with incredulity. Overnight, it seemed, the human race had lost its power to breed' (James 1992, p. 9).

- **What is the difference between talking about a decline in the fertility rate and a decline in the birth rate?**

- **What effects follow from casting contemporary discussions about declining numbers of births in the language of fertility?**

'*Fertility*: How We Compare'

Births per woman per selected countries between 2000 and 2005

'Country	Rate
Hong Kong	1.0
Italy	1.2
Japan	1.3
Canada	1.5
United Kingdom	1.6
AUSTRALIA	**1.7**
France	1.9
New Zealand	2.0
Viet Nam	2.3
Indonesia	2.4'

(ABS 2005, p. 6; reported in *The Age*, 1 October 2005; emphasis added to 'fertility' in heading)

- **How does this chart represent Australia's 2005 birth rate?**

- **What is the significance of calling it a 'fertility rate'?**

- **What is the significance of positioning Australia as it does in a list of countries with comparative rates?**

- **Are there any silences?**

At times there has been ambivalence about the desirability of a 'population policy' within Australia, reflecting the tension identified by Dean (1999, p. 203) between reliance on an espoused democratised form of sovereignty and biopolitical imperatives (see discussion above). That is, advocating a government role in setting population goals appears, at one level, to infringe upon the apparent self-sovereignty of liberal individuals in making their birthing decisions. In this vein, in 1994 Richard Woolcott put the official position of the then Labor government at a United Nations conference on population:

> Australia does not have an explicit or formal population policy aimed at influencing the level of population . . . the Government decided that a formal population policy . . . would not be appropriate for Australia, given its low level of fertility and objectives of such a policy. (Jupp 1998, p. 172)

Significantly, at the time of Woolcott's comment, the great concern was *over*-population (on a world-wide scale) rather than *under*-population (on a national scale) – hence, the claim that Australia's 'low level of fertility' meant there was no need for government intervention in this area. Pressures for population control came from a number of sources, including groups such as Australians for an Ecologically Sustainable Population (AESP) and Australians Against Further Immigration (AAFI). Two inquiries were organised, one conducted by the National Population Council and a second parliamentary committee chaired by Barry Jones, ALP heavy-weight. Following these deliberations Labor signalled a change of mind on the need for a population policy. Its Draft Platform for the 1998 National Conference declared that a population policy 'would allow Australia to decide as a community the long term sustainable population we want rather than allowing population issues to be an incidental by-product of ad-hoc year-by-year decisions about annual immigration levels' (Jupp 1998, p. 173). By contrast, as late as January 2002, the Liberal Coalition refused to commit to a 'formal population policy' (Gillard 2002), with the introduction of the first 'baby bonus' policy later that year signalling a change of direction (Q3).

The growing concern about an 'ageing demographic', expressed alongside a need to make Australia economically competitive at the global level (a theme pursued in Chapter 9 on education policy), removed any reluctance to commit officially to population targets. Business interests were key drivers in this shift in direction. At the state (provincial) level, Business SA endorsed a range of policies, including paid maternity leave and 'family-friendly practices', to 'stem the loss of skilled young adults to other states' (Keane 2002; Q3).

As mentioned above, to date there has been a failure to deliver effective 'work/life' balance policies within Australia, with a wide range of deleterious effects for most women and for some men (Pocock 2005; Q5). Nor has the discussion moved on to the more substantive issue of finding ways to revalue upwards non-market activities, including the nurture of the young and the elderly (Manne 2002; Q4). The focus on the 'ageing population' also silences consideration of the approximate seventeen-year gap in life expectancy between Aboriginal and non-Aboriginal people (Adams 2003; Q4). In addition, the current concern to boost population numbers has effectively drowned out earlier warnings about the possible deleterious environmental consequences of an increased population (Krockenberger 2002; Q4).

The 2004–05 Maternity Payment signalled endorsement of the old nostrum, 'the baby is the best immigrant'. As we shall see in the next section, this explicit commitment to increasing 'home-grown' population sits somewhat uncomfortably alongside the Howard-led government's vigorous pursuit of more migrants. This tension is managed through portraying some migrants as 'problems' and others as desirable (dividing practices) for the sake of a 'race' (see discussion above). As with the Maternity Payment, the rationale is expressed in terms of 'securing' Australia's global competitiveness.

457 VISAS

In August 1996 the Howard-led federal government introduced a new temporary entry business visa which allowed employers to sponsor 'skilled' workers on a temporary basis – between three months and four years. Called the *Temporary (long stay) Business Visa (Subclass 457)*, they followed a Keating Labor government (1995) initiative to increase business migration. 457 visas require applicants to:

- be sponsored by an employer to fill a nominated position;
- have skills, qualifications, experience and an employment background which match those required for the position;
- have designated English language skills;
- demonstrate that they are to be paid at least the minimum salary level that applies at the time a decision is made on the visa;
- meet health and character requirements;
- make an Australian values statement.
  (Australian Government 2008)

To understand the 'problem-space' produced by this policy it is necessary to reflect on immigration policy more generally. As mentioned above, the Howard-led government vigorously pursued high levels of immigration at the same time as it campaigned against 'illegal' migrants, asylum seekers and 'boat people'. There was a shift in the pattern of immigration over Howard's early years in power (1996–2002), from 'family reunion' (60 per cent in 1995–96; 36 per cent in 2000–2001) to 'skilled migration' (25 per cent in 1995–96; 49 per cent in 2000–01). The percentage of migrants accepted for 'humanitarian reasons' remained frozen at 15 per cent (Colebatch and Taylor 2002).

The 457 visa, designed to facilitate the entry of 'skilled' 'foreign' workers on a part-time basis, represents the 'problem' as a shortage of 'skilled' Australian workers (Q1). Talk about a 'skills shortage' in Australia is ubiquitous at the time of writing – although the recent (September, October 2008) financial 'crisis' appears to be altering some of this discussion (Malkin 2008). The presumption that employers require access to a 'vast talent pool of international Candidates' (Live In Australia 2008) can be traced back to the 1995 Roach Report, which put the case that 'the old policies and procedures were unresponsive to business needs, impeded Australia's integration into the global economy and undermined the ability of individual businesses to compete effectively both domestically and abroad' (Kinnaird 1996; Q2, Q3).

Hence, 457 visas are underpinned by a globalisation discourse (Q2). To describe globalisation as a discourse takes the discussion away from competing attempts to measure it to examining ways in which assumptions about its existence and importance as a phenomenon have a range of effects – the ways in which 'globalisation' puts certain presumptions 'in the true' (Q5). In addition, examining the practices 'in time and space' that produce global connections undermines the tendency to create 'globalisation' as some inevitable and irresistible force (Larner and Walters 2004, p. 501). 457 visas are one such practice.

457 visas mark a radical deregulation from preceding temporary entry procedures. They eliminate the need for employers to 'labour market test' the job in question, and they install considerable self regulation by businesses (Birrell 1996; Q5). The rationale of 'skills shortages' ignores the possibility of increasing workforce participation among the under-employed, the unemployed, and those who are retired (Colebatch 2003; Q4). It also reduces the possibility of wage hikes that might have eventuated had the 'invisible hand' of the market, much in favour in business circles, been allowed to run its course (Q4, Q5).

National Skills Shortages Strategy 2005

'Skills shortages occur for a variety of reasons:

- ■ strong economy with low rates of unemployment;
- ■ growth of new industries with few ready-skilled tradespeople available;
- ■ relocation of new industries into different regions with a different skills base;
- ■ reduced interest in particular industries among potential job seekers;
- ■ location of industry, or project-based work, in rural or regional areas with a small skills base;
- ■ technology changes within an industry, especially production, resulting in new methods and therefore skills needs; and
- ■ changes in underpinning skills needs to successfully undertake trade training for example, Year 12 mathematics for some trades.'

(Australian Government 2005a)

- • **What kind of a 'problem' is the 'skills shortage' represented to be?**

- • **Are there any silences?**

For this Activity see Mitchell and Quirk 2005.

Since their introduction, 457 visas have increased in number and in the proportion of overseas migrants they admit to the country. Around 40 000 primary applicant visas were granted in 2005–06, with a total intake including family members of 71 000, a significant proportion of Australia's Net Overseas Migration of 134 600 in those years (ABS 2008). This figure of 71 000 represents a dramatic increase of 43 per cent over the 2004–05 period (Kinnaird 2006).

457 visa holders are Australia's version of the USA's and Europe's 'guest workers'. This phenomenon of 'temporary migration' is an effect of the increased people movement that has characterised the period from 1990 to the present, a movement driven by huge cross-national

inequalities in wages and standards of living, and differences in labour demand across countries (Pritchett 2003). Among industrialised countries there is now competition – conceptualised as a kind of race (see Chapter 8) – to 'hand-pick' migrants deemed to be desirable because of what they can contribute to the economy. According to Mark Peterson, Secretary of the Industry Department, in 2002, 'We [Australia] are currently in third place behind the United States and Canada' (Colebatch and Taylor 2002).

457 visas mark off some flows of people – 'skilled' migrants – who are deemed to be desirable, from other flows deemed to be undesirable, 'illegal migrants' or migrants judged not to possess 'skills' currently in demand. Hence, they act as a dividing practice at the international level. As Walters (2004, p. 249) states, the 'will to divide immiserated populations is alive and well', both in response to mass migration and within modern welfare policy (see Chapter 3). While on the one side some migrants are constituted a positive boon to economic market competition, on the other side 'others' are represented to be a threat to security and to the Australian 'way of life' (Q5). In this way 457 visas provide the means to reconcile territorial 'security' with economic liberalism (Walters 2004, p. 252).

To meet character requirements, 457 visa applicants can be required to provide police certificates for each country they have lived in for twelve months or more over the past ten years since turning sixteen. The requirement to make an Australian 'values' statement reinforces the impression that the applicants constitute a potential 'problem' or threat that needs to be managed (see below) (Q2, Q3). In these ways the visas fit what Bigo (2002) describes as a 'governmentality of unease'.

Walters (2004, p. 241) characterises this contemporary diagram of rule as 'domopolitics', which 'rationalises a series of security measures in the name of a particular conception of home': 'We may invite guests into our home, but they come at our invitation; they don't stay indefinitely'. One is reminded here of John Howard's campaign slogan in 2001: 'We will decide who comes to this country and the circumstances in which they come' (Forbes 2007).

Instead of seeing these developments as necessary and inevitable, a WPR approach invites us to observe and track the decisions and practices that lead to a particular way of governing (Q3). It also encourages critical reflection on identified modes of governance (Q2) to highlight inconsistencies and downsides (Q4, Q5). In the chapter so far we have observed an ignominious flexibility in the willingness to tap certain flows of population, all the while creating fear of the 'other', a fear implicated in the injunction directed at women to reproduce 'for the nation' (see Maternity Payment above). McPhee (2002) offers a poignant description of this dual-pronged diagram of rule:

There are two great waves of people moving around the world at present. We compete with other countries to take advantage of one of them – the tourists and backpackers, the individuals with the skills we need right now, and the corporations seeking to invest in secure economies and pleasant lifestyles. At the same time we endlessly justify turning our backs on the other great mass of people who have not benefited by economic growth or democratic government ...

The question of this country's sustainable population size goes much further than our economic and cultural ambitions or our real environmental constraints. It cannot be done in isolation. We cannot construct a picture of the country we want independently of the world.

In the next section we consider the extent to which Australia's New *Citizenship Act 2007 (Cth)* acknowledges, or fails to acknowledge, McPhee's insightful analysis.

AUSTRALIA'S NEW *CITIZENSHIP ACT 2007*

On 9 November 2005 the Minister for Citizenship and Multicultural Affairs, the Hon John Cobb, introduced new legislation to Parliament to update the *Australian Citizenship Act* (Australian Government 1948). Specific amendments include:

- removing the restrictive criteria on resumption of Australian citizenship and Australian citizenship by descent; and
- allowing grant of citizenship to adult children of former Australian citizens;
- allowing grant of Australian citizenship to people born overseas before 26 January 1949 with an Australian parent;
- streamlining the criteria for temporary residence in Australia to be allowed as a credit against the residence requirement for grant of Australian citizenship;
- increasing the residence requirement for grant of Australian citizenship from two years to three (Australian Government 2005b).

In September 2006 a further announcement was made to increase the residence requirement for migrants to four years, significantly delaying access to social and welfare benefits. These provisions became the *Australian Citizenship Act* (Australian Government 2007a), which was passed by the Australian Parliament on 1 March 2007 and received Royal Assent on 15 March 2007.

On 30 May 2007 an *Australian Citizenship Amendment (Citizenship Testing) Bill* (Australian Government 2007b) was introduced to Parliament. Implemented on 1 October 2007 it requires intending migrants to sit a Citizenship Test to assess English language skills and knowledge of 'Australian values'.

The new citizenship legislation is located within a wide and diverse web of policies, *including* the Maternity Payment and 457 visas discussed above. It captures in a single Act the tension identified between these other policies, with 457 visas soliciting (specific kinds of) *migrants* and the Maternity Payment encouraging *'home-grown'* population. While some provisions in the new legislation ease requirements for acquiring citizenship and hence represent the 'problem' to be *difficulty of access* to citizenship, the provisions on testing and increased residency before 'naturalisation' tighten access provisions, producing the 'problem' as *ease of access* to citizenship (Q1). As with the targeting of *skilled* migrants in 457 visas, this tension is resolved through a dividing practice: some migrants – those who can pass the test – are deemed to be more acceptable than others (Q2). As Hindess (2000a) argues, while citizenship is conventionally described in terms of positive national benefits for certain groups of people, the way in which it sorts people into desirable and undesirable camps needs to be perceived as a form of 'global governmentality' (see Larner and Walters 2006a).

Streamlining the criteria which allow temporary residence in Australia to be counted as a credit against the residence requirement for grant of Australian citizenship (see above) creates a pathway from 457 visas to full citizenship. However, given their role as sponsors, employers maintain an unequal power relationship vis-à-vis employed migrants in this arrangement (Q5). The increase in residency requirements from two to four years, meanwhile, means that some migrants are denied eligibility to a range of income support payments for this extended period of time (Q5), putting in mind Walters' characterisation of 'domopolitics' as including a domestic (welfare) as well as an international (migration) dimension (see above).

Supporters of international free trade often endorse the free movement of labour across borders as an alternative to the division of migrants into desirable and undesirable camps, as happens in 457 visas and the new *Citizenship Act*. Some supporters of the free movement of labour (see Bernstein and Weiner 1999) argue that letting down barriers to migrants gives nation-states access to cheap labour while minimising the costs of state services during the extended period of residence qualification. Other supporters of free movement (Legrain 2007) object strongly to discriminatory practices such as excessive residence requirements but accept that workers from 'under-developed' countries would be happy to assume jobs 'natives' refuse to perform. In neither case is the role of market liberalism in creating inter-state wage inequality, poor working conditions in some countries, and hence much people movement acknowledged (Q4).

The new Citizenship Test, based on a British model, formulates the question of how you 'integrate' newcomers as a particular sort of 'problem' (Walters 2004, p. 254). The emphasis on English-language skills reflects the expressed needs of employers, reinforcing the dominant neoliberal narrative of migrants as an economic resource. It also fits a particular communitarian conception of citizenship that emphasises participation, cultural identification, and citizenship as a type of social glue (Q2). In this vein, Leigh (2006) suggests that citizens are less likely to trust non-English speakers and hence are less likely to support a welfare regime that depends on willingness to pool social resources. In this paradigm of 'active citizenship', rights become conditional on fulfilment of responsibilities (see discussion in Chapters 3 and 6).

A second citizenship paradigm, based on the idea of a shared *political* culture rather than on *ethnic* cultural ties, privileges rights and democratic 'principles'. While not as homogenising as the communitarian model described above, 'political' liberalism of this kind reinforces the assumption that migrants need to conform to specific norms of *political* behaviour, such as voting and obeying existing laws, to gain acceptance (Davidson 1997; Q2). The distance between this paradigm and that which emphasises Australian 'values' is not then as great as is often imagined.

'Why has this test been introduced?'

'The objective of the test is to help migrants integrate and maximise the opportunities available to them in Australia, and enable their full participation in the Australian community as citizens. It provides a strong incentive for new arrivals to learn English and to understand the Australian way of life. From a broader perspective, it supports social cohesion and successful integration into the community.

Becoming a citizen involves a commitment to a shared future in Australia and core values. It means understanding the privileges that come with citizenship and also being able to fulfil the responsibilities that citizenship brings.

While migrants are not expected to leave their traditions behind, it is expected that they embrace Australian values and integrate into the Australian society. In becoming an Australian citizen, migrants are required to formally pledge their loyalty to Australia and its people.'

(Australian Government 2007c)

- **What kind of 'problem' is citizenship represented to be in the Citizenship Test?**

- **Are there any silences? Where, for example, are citizenship rights acknowledged?**

The notion of 'Australian values' in the Citizenship Test rests upon a political imaginary in which political subjects subscribe to certain principles. 'Values', however, are an open category, ambivalent and difficult to pin down. They invariably involve deep-seated assumptions about desired forms of governing that need to be identified. For Costello, Treasurer at the time the test was introduced, 'the values of Australia' include 'economic opportunity, security, democracy, personal freedom, the physical environment and "strong physical and social infrastructure"' (Garnaut 2006). In the emphasis on economic opportunity and personal freedom, 'individuals are constituted as the new footsoldiers of a laissez-faire form of capitalism' (Mitchell 2004, p. 645; Q2, Q5). On the other side, the ability to mark certain behaviours as 'un-Australian' is a powerful disciplinary mechanism (Q3, Q5; see discussion above of Foucault and 'indirect murder').

What are 'Australian values'?

The following two questions from the Citizenship Test purport to identify Australian values.

   'Which of the following are Australian values?

a. Men and women are equal

b. "A fair go"

c. Mateship

d. All of the above'

   'Australia's values are based on the ...

a. Teachings of the Koran

b. The Judeo-Christian tradition

c. Catholicism

d. Secularism'

The 'correct' answers are d. 'all of the above', and b. 'The Judeo-Christian tradition' (Packham and Malinauskas 2007).

- **What presuppositions underpin the 'values' identified as 'Australian'?**

- **Are there any silences?**

The presumption that 'Australian values' determine access to citizenship needs to be considered within recent debates about multiculturalism, branded by Costello as 'confused, mushy and misguided' (Garnaut 2006). A genealogy of multiculturalism (Q3; see below) reveals that the concept has played a significant role in the management of population within Australia for the past thirty years. Specific policies from within this period produce the 'problem', alternatively and sometimes simultaneously, as a matter of encouraging quiescence ('social cohesion'), of addressing social need (targeted welfare policies), or of economic integration. A tension can be identified between representing multiculturalism as a 'problem' of ethnic diversity on the one hand and as one of structural disadvantage on the other.

   The point of a genealogy is to show that the present (an 'event') is the outcome of many decisions, not the result of a smooth and uninterrupted evolution. It was shown above, for example, that the categories which distinguish asylum seekers from 'skilled migrants', though appearing 'normal' and 'natural', are in fact neither natural nor inevitable – they are interventions *at a specific time and place*. The effect of producing such an analysis is to bring to the fore the contestation surrounding political developments, destabilising what appears to be self-evident and hence unchangeable.

A genealogy of multiculturalism: A beginning

The following points, among others, would be pursued to produce an understanding of the 'multiple determinations and logics' (Walters 2004, p. 250) associated with multiculturalism in Australia:

- the genesis of the term in Canada and its role in diffusing the sharp division between French and English Canada;
- the first promulgation of the term by the incoming Whitlam Labor government and its association with the official ending of the White Australia policy;
- the development of multiculturalism as a formal policy under the Fraser Liberal Coalition government between 1975–1983;
- the Galbally Report of 1978, which listed social cohesion, cultural identity and equality of opportunity and access as the key principles essential for a multicultural society;
- the establishment of targeted social services for migrants;
- the establishment of ethnic radio and television (SBS);
- the disallowance of tax rebates for remittances to overseas dependents;
- the Hawke Labor government's 1989 *National Agenda for a Multicultural Australia*, which called upon the three tiers of Government – Commonwealth, State and local – to 'intervene where necessary to manage our diversity in the interests of cultural tolerance, social justice and economic efficiency' (Australian Government 1989);
- the abolition of the Office for Multicultural Affairs in 1996 and the location of multicultural policy in the Department of Immigration and Multicultural Affairs;
- the NMAC (National Multicultural Advisory Council) Report, *Australian Multiculturalism for a New Century: Towards Inclusiveness* (1999), which recommended adoption of the term 'Australian multiculturalism' to recognise and celebrate 'Australia's cultural diversity' and its contribution to 'Australia's strategic international interests' (NMAC 1999);
- the change in the name of the Department of Immigration and Multicultural Affairs to the Department of Immigration and Citizenship in 2006.

Concerning the issue of resistance (Q6) Walters (2004, p. 256) raises the provocative possibility that initiatives such as the *Citizenship Act* are, in fact, a *defensive* form of governance – that they signal the disquiet of those who find it increasingly difficult to 'protect' national regimes from 'flows of people that cannot be contained by the political boundaries of the state' (Larner and Walters 2006b, p. 7). In this understanding, political subjects who explore forms of 'flexible' citizenship (Ong 1999) become the drivers of potentially far-reaching change in ways of imagining national and international governance, illustrating that acts 'from below' are also constitutive (see Chapter 2).

Further, the current determination to defend borders and shape population by drawing upon certain flows of people and excluding (disciplining) others creates additional tension for liberal regimes wanting to reconcile an espoused democratised version of sovereignty and biopolitics (see discussion above). There are numerous signs that to achieve the objective of 'desirable' populations, legislators in many 'democratic' states are increasingly willing to compromise democratic accountability through censorship and other forms of surveillance (see Chapter 10). On this issue, Pécoud and de Guchteneire (2005, p. 6) make the following observation:

> To what extent can tough measures of border controls coexist with the harmonious functioning of democracies? The liberal values and human rights that guide societies cannot stop at their borders: they must guide countries' behaviour toward outsiders arriving at their gates ... In other words the evolution of migration controls towards greater harshness might eventually back-fire and threaten the liberal principles and freedoms that lie at the core of democratic societies.

SUMMARY

In this chapter we have explored forms of rule (govern-mentalities) that cut across policy areas affecting levels and character (composition) of population, and the criteria of citizenship. Two cross-cutting 'diagrams of rule' have been identified: 'securitisation', premised on bordered nations, and 'domopolitics' (Walters 2004), through which the declared 'interests' of particular nations are given priority over those of other nations/peoples (Q2). The marking of particular groups, including some women, most Aboriginal people, and many migrants, as 'other' is an important effect of these modes of rule (Q5). The predominance of these discourses drowns out the voices of those wishing to imagine a different kind of world where people are valued by more than their workplace 'skills' and where world-wide environmental concerns get treated seriously (Q4, Q6).

So long as governance is equated with improving the health and welfare of 'population', we need to direct attention to the following:

■ how a 'desirable' population is characterised and who gets to play a leading role in that characterisation;

■ the methods used to achieve the ends of 'population' 'shaping';

■ the effects on targeted populations;

■ how less harmful effects might be achieved.

QUESTIONS

Drawing upon the policies and policy proposals introduced in this chapter, consider the following questions:

1. What kind of a 'problem' is Australia's population size represented to be? Are there silences in dominant representations of the 'problem'?

2. What kind of a 'problem' is Australia's ageing demographic represented to be? Are there silences in dominant representations of the 'problem'?

3. What kind of a 'problem' is the 'skills shortage' represented to be? Are there silences in dominant representations of the 'problem'?

4. What kind of a 'problem' is migrant 'integration' represented to be? Are there silences in dominant representations of the 'problem'?

---

1 I would like to thank Angelique Bletsas for this point.

REFERENCES

ABS 2005, *Australian Social Trends*, 4102.0, <www.abs.gov.au>, accessed 21 July 2008.

ABS (Australian Bureau of Statistics) 2008, *3412.0 – Migration, Australia, 2005–06*, <www.abs.gov.au>, accessed 14 May 2008.

ADAMS, P. 2003, 'Greying, in Black and White', *Weekend Australian Magazine*, 24–25 May, p. 13.

AUSTRALIAN GOVERNMENT 1948, *Australian Citizenship Act*, Attorney-General's Department, Commonwealth of Australian Law, <www.comlaw.gov.au>, accessed 30 October 2008.

AUSTRALIAN GOVERNMENT 1989, *National Agenda for a Multicultural Australia*, Department of Immigration and Citizenship, Canberra, <www.immi.gov.au>, accessed 15 May 2008.

AUSTRALIAN GOVERNMENT 2004, *More Help for Families*, 2004–05 Budget – Overview, Canberra. <www.budget.gov.au/2004-05>, accessed 2 August 2008.

AUSTRALIAN GOVERNMENT 2005a, *National Skills Shortages Strategy*, Department of Education, Science and Training, Canberra, <www.getatrade.gov.au/skills_needs.htm>, accessed 14 May 2008

AUSTRALIAN GOVERNMENT 2005b, *Australian Citizenship Bill 2005*, Bills Digest no. 72 2005–06, <www.aph.gov.au>, accessed 1 August 2008.

AUSTRALIAN GOVERNMENT 2006, *Occasional Paper No. 12*, Department of Families, Housing, Community Services and Indigenous Affairs, <www.facsia.gov.au>, accessed 25 October 2002.

AUSTRALIAN GOVERNMENT 2007a, *Citizenship Act*, Commonwealth Consolidated Acts, <www.austlii.edu.au>, accessed 16 October 2008.

AUSTRALIAN GOVERNMENT 2007b, *Australian Citizenship Amendment (Citizenship Testing) Bill*, Commonwealth of Australia Bills, <www.austlii.edu.au>, accessed 16 October, 2008.

AUSTRALIAN GOVERNMENT 2007c, *History of the Citizenship Test*, Department of Immigration and Citizenship, Canberra, <www.citizenship.gov.au>, accessed 14 May 2008.

AUSTRALIAN GOVERNMENT 2008, *Temporary Business (Long Stay) – Standard Business Sponsorship (Subclass 457)*, Department of Immigration and Citizenship, Visas and Immigration, Canberra, <www.immi.gov.au>, accessed 14 May 2008.

BACCHI, C. 1980, 'The Nature-Nurture Debate in Australia, 1900–1914', *Historical Studies*, vol. 19, no. 75, pp. 199–212.

BERNSTEIN, A. & WEINER, M. eds 1999, *Migration and Refugee Policies: An Overview*, Continuum, London.

BIGO, D. 2002, 'Security and Immigration: Toward a Critique of the Governmentality of Unease', *Alternatives: Global, Local, Political*, vol. 27, no. 1, pp. 63–92,

BIRRELL, B. 1996, 'A Note on the New Rules Governing the Temporary Entry of Business People and Highly-Skilled Specialists', *People and Place*, vol. 4, no. 4, <http://elecpress.monash.edu.au/pnp/free/pnpv4n4/birtoend.htm>, accessed 14 May 2008.

COLEBATCH, T. 2000, 'Childless Future For Many Women', *The Age*, 22 March.

COLEBATCH, T. 2003, 'Our Greying Nation Can Offer Good News', *The Age*, 6 September.

COLEBATCH, T. & TAYLOR, K. 2002, 'The Quiet Revolution: Australia's Changing Face', *The Age*, 19 January.

COMMENT 2004, 'Populate or Perish With the Burnt Snags', *Sydney Morning Herald Online*, 12 May, <www.smh.com.au>, accessed 12 May 2008.

COSTELLO, P. 2002, 'Press Release: The Coalition's Baby Bonus – Helping 118,000 Australian Families and Counting', Canberra, <www.treasurer.gov.au>, accessed 17 July 2007.

DALTON, R. 2003, 'Shape of Things to Come', *The Australian*, 27 February.

DAVIDSON, A. 1997, *From Subject to Citizen: Australian Citizenship in the Twentieth Century*, Cambridge University Press, Cambridge.

DEAN, M. 1999, *Governmentality: Power and Rule in Modern Society*, Sage, London.

DELEUZE, G. 1988, *Foucault*, Trans. and ed. S. Hand, University of Minnesota Press, Minneapolis.

DEVER, M. 2005, 'Baby Talk: The Howard Government, Families, and the Politics of Difference', *Hecate*, vol. 31, no. 2, pp. 45–61.

DUNCAN, S. 2002, 'Policy Discourses on "Reconciling Work and Life" in the EU', *Social Policy and Society*, vol. 1, no. 4, pp. 305–14.

ESPING-ANDERSEN, G. 2002, 'A Child-Centred Social Investment Strategy', in *Why We Need a New Welfare State*, ed. G. Esping-Andersen, Oxford University Press, Oxford.

FORBES, M. 2007, 'Deal to Send Boat People Packing', *The Sydney Morning Herald*, 24 February, <www.smh.com.au>, accessed 14 May 2008.

FOUCAULT, M. 1979, *The History of Sexuality, Volume I, An Introduction*, Trans. R. Hurley, Allen Lane, London.

FOUCAULT, M. 1991, 'Governmentality', in *The Foucault Effect: Studies in Governmentality*, eds G. Burchell, C. Gordon & P. Miller, University of Chicago Press, Chicago.

FOUCAULT, M. 2003 [1976], 'Chapter 11: 17 March 1976' in *'Society Must Be Defended': Lectures at the Collège de France, 1975–76*, eds F. Ewald & A. Fontana, Trans. D. Macey, Penguin Books, London.

GARNAUT, J. 2006, 'Love Australia or Leave It, Costello Warns Violent Immigrants', *The Sydney Morning Herald*, 24 February.

GILLARD, J. 2002, 'The Plan Ruddock Won't talk About', *The Age*, 15 January.

GORNICK, J. & MYERS, M. K. 2004, 'More Alike than Different: Re-assessing the Long-Term Prospects for Developing "European-like" Work-Family Policy in the United States', *Journal of Comparative Policy Analysis: Research and Practice*, vol. 6, no. 3, pp. 251–73.

HINDESS, B. 2000a, 'Citizenship in the International Management of Population', *American Behavioral Scientist*, vol. 43, no. 9, pp. 1486–97.

JAMES, P. D. 1992, *Children of Men*, Faber, London.

JUPP, J. 1998, *Immigration*, Oxford University Press, Melbourne.

KEANE, A. 2002, 'Set Goals for Growth Over Two Decades', *The Advertiser*, 23 January.

KEMP, M. & WILLIAMS, N. 2002, 'Where Have all the Mothers Gone?' *The Advertiser*, 11 May.

KINNAIRD, B. 1996, 'Temporary-Entry Migration: Balancing Corporate Rights and Australian Work Opportunities', *People and Place*, vol. 4, no. 1, <http://elecpress.monash.edu.au/pnp/free/pnpv4n1/kinnaird.htm>, accessed 14 May 2008.

KINNAIRD, B. 2006, 'Fixing the 457 visa for Temporary Foreign Workers', Centre for Policy Development, 8 September, <http://cpd.org.au/article/fixing-visa457>, accessed 14 May 2008.

KROCKENBERGER, M. 2002, 'The Risk Now is to Populate *and* Perish', *The Age*, 23 February, emphasis in original.

LARNER, W. & WALTERS, W. 2004, 'Globalization as Governmentality', *Alternatives: Global, Local, Political*, vol. 29, no. 5, pp. 495–515.

LARNER, W. & WALTERS, W. eds 2006a, *Global Governmentality: Governing International Spaces*, 2nd edition, Routledge, London.

LARNER, W. & WALTERS, W. 2006b, 'Introduction: Global Governmentality', in *Global Governmentality: Governing International Spaces*, 2nd edition, eds W. Larner & W. Walters, Routledge, London.

LEGRAIN, P. 2007, *Immigrants: Your Country Needs Them*, Little, Brown Publishers, London.

LEIGH, A. 2006, 'Trust, Inequality and Ethnic Heterogeneity', *The Economic Record*, vol. 82, no. 258, pp. 268–80.

LIVE IN AUSTRALIA 2008, 'Company Sponsored "457" Visa to Australia', January, <www.liveinaustralia.com/457/>, accessed 14 May 2008.

LUI, R. 2006, 'The International Government of Refugees', in *Global Governmentality: Governing International Spaces*, 2nd edition, eds W. Larner & W. Walters, Routledge, London.

MALKIN, B. 2008, 'Financial Crisis: Australia May Cut Migrant Visas as Unemployment Grows', *Telegraph.co.uk*, 22 October, <www.telegraph.co.uk>, accessed 25 October 2008.

MANNE, A. 2002, 'Paid Maternity Leave Just a Start', *The Age*, 21 February.

McPHEE, H. 2002, 'Looking Beyond Economic Ambition', *The Age*, 9 March.

MILLER, P. & ROSE, N. 1990, 'Governing Economic Life', *Economy and Society*, vol. 19, no. 1, pp. 1–31.

MITCHELL, B. & QUIRK, V. 2005, *Skills Shortages in Australia: Concepts and Reality*, Centre for Full Employment and Equity, Working Paper No. 05–16, Newcastle.

MITCHELL, K. 2004, 'Geographies of Identity: Multiculturalism Unplugged', *Progress in Human Geography*, vol. 28, no. 5, pp. 641–51.

NMAC (NATIONAL MULTICULTURAL ADVISORY COUNCIL) 1999 *Australian Multiculturalism for a New Century: Towards Inclusiveness*, Department of Immigration and Citizenship, Canberra, <www.immi.gov.au>, accessed 15 May 2008.

ONG, A. 1999, *Flexible Citizenship: The Cultural Logics of Transnationality*, Duke University Press, Durham, North Carolina.

PACKHAM, B & MALINAUSKAS, R. 2007, 'A True Blue Test to be an Aussie', *The Advertiser*, 19 May.

PÉCOUD, A. & DE GUCHTENEIRE, P. 2005, *Migration Without Borders: An Investigation Into the Free Movement of People*, Global Commission on International Migration, Switzerland, <www.gcim.org>, accessed 10 May 2007.

POCOCK, B. 2005, 'Work/Care Regimes: Institutions, Culture and Behaviour and the Australian Case', *Gender, Work and Organization*, vol. 12, no. 1, pp. 32–49.

PRITCHETT, L. 2003, 'The Future of Migration: Part One', *YaleGlobal Online*, <http://yaleglobal.yale.edu>, accessed 4 May 2007.

ROJAS, C. 2006, 'Governing Through the Social: Representations of Poverty and Global Governmentality', in *Global Governmentality: Governing International Spaces*, 2nd edition, eds W. Larner & W. Walters, Routledge, London.

VALVERDE, M. & MOPAS, M. 2006, 'Insecurity and the Dream of Targeted Governance', in *Global Governmentality: Governing International Spaces*, 2nd edition, eds W. Larner & W. Walters, Routledge, London.

WALTERS, W. 2004, 'Secure Borders, Safe Haven, Domopolitics', *Citizenship Studies*, vol. 8, no, 3, pp. 237–60.

WILLIAMS, N. 2000, 'Why Child Care Should be Free: Professor's Plea at Forum', *The Advertiser*, 12 February.

WILSON, J., THOMSON, J. & MCMAHON, A. eds 1996, *The Australian Welfare State, Key Documents and Themes*, MacMillan Education Australia, Melbourne, <www.multiculturalaustralia.edu.au>, accessed 25 October 2008.

FURTHER READING

BIGO, D. 2000, 'When Two Become One: Internal and External Securitisations in Europe', in *International Relations Theory and the Politics of European Integration: Power, Security and Community*, eds M. Kelstrup & M. C. Williams, Routledge, London.

HINDESS, B. 2000b, 'Divide and Govern', in *Governing Modern Societies*, eds R. Ericson & N. Stehr, University of Toronto Press, Toronto.

HUGO, G. 2004, 'Temporary Migration: A New Paradigm of International Migration', *Research Note*, Parliamentary Library, Department of Parliamentary Services, 24 May, <www.aph.gov.au>, accessed 9 May 2008.

RAJCHMAN, J. 1999, 'Diagram and Diagnosis', in *Becomings: Explorations in Time, Memory and Futures*, ed. E. Grosz, Cornell University Press, Ithaca, New York.

The limits of equality: Anti-discrimination and 'special measures'

Chapter 8

SOME DIFFICULT TERRAIN

In Chapter 2 we had a brief introduction to the idea of contested concepts and to the importance of tracing the meanings of key terms within policies and policy debates (Q2). No term is more contested than equality. Western political philosophers have written numerous treatises on the topic. How then are we to understand the ways in which the term functions in public policy? And how can a WPR approach assist in this task?

The first section below clarifies what it means to talk about equality as a contested concept. It also alerts us to the key role played in Western public policy (and in policy elsewhere affected by Western laws and Western precedents) by a set of binaries – i.e. equality/difference, sameness/difference, equal treatment/different treatment, equal opportunity/equal results or outcomes – that rests upon specific meanings of equality (Q2). We then go on to investigate the role played by these dichotomies in anti-discrimination legislation. Particular attention is addressed to the ways in which norms implicit within equality policies set limits on visions of social change. As with the rest of the book, the point in identifying such limits is to suggest, not that nothing can succeed, but rather that 'everything is dangerous', and hence 'we always have something to do' (Foucault 1984, p. 343).

Our 'practical texts' for this exercise include: Australia's *Racial Discrimination Act 1975 (Cth)* (Australian Government 1975) and *Sex Discrimination Act 1984 (Cth)* (Australian Government 1984). I describe this chapter as 'difficult terrain' to provide fair warning that the equality jurisprudence discussed below can be difficult to follow and may require more than one reading.

Reminder

The six questions in a WPR approach can be followed systematically – addressing each question separately and in order – as in Chapters 3 and 4. More commonly, the questions form part of an integrated analysis, with specific questions applied where the analysis occasions their use. This chapter follows the second, integrated form of analysis, employing the notation **Q1, Q2,** etc. where a specific question has been applied. Until students are completely familiar with the questions in the approach, it is advisable to look back to the original list (either the abbreviated form in the Introduction and Chapter 1, or the expanded version at the end of Chapter 2) when such notation appears.

THINKING ABOUT 'EQUALITY'

According to Hoffman and Graham (2006, p. 58) the 'core idea of equality is that people should be treated in the same way'. To say that a term or key word is contested is to challenge the suggestion that there is any such thing as a 'core idea'. Rather, the approach to language adopted in a WPR approach puts the emphasis on the work that key terms do in political processes. As Tanesini says, concepts are not descriptive of anything; rather they are 'proposals about how we ought to proceed from here'. The purpose of concepts or categories is 'to influence the evolution of ongoing practices' (Tanesini 1994, p. 207). Hence, they can be defined to certain purposes and redefined to other purposes. In this form of analysis the focus therefore shifts from seeking 'true' meaning to interrogating the emergence of *competing* meanings of specific terms and how they function in shaping political possibilities. Attention is directed to the uneven power relations involved in shaping the meaning of concepts – 'the struggle for control of discourses' (Foucault 1991, p. 60) – and to the effects **(Q5)** that accompany the ways in which specific meanings become embedded in government practices.

It follows that, in this chapter, we are *not* trying to find out what 'equality' *really* means; rather, we are investigating the meanings it has acquired and the roles these meanings play in political decision-making. In this understanding 'language is not secondary to government; it is constitutive of it' (Rose 2000, p. 28). Therefore, let us proceed to investigate how equality has acquired a *taken-for-granted* meaning as treating people 'in the same way' (see Hoffman and Graham 2006, p. 58 above; **Q3**).

'Likes should be treated alike'

The idea that people should be treated *in the same way* is captured in what is commonly described as the anti-discrimination principle that 'likes should be treated alike' (also referred to as 'formal equality'). This idea can be traced back to the *Equal Protection Clause* of the Fourteenth Amendment of the American Constitution. This amendment was introduced in

1868 to enable the federal government to strike down the ignominious Black Codes or Slave Codes, which denied Black people the opportunity to own property, attend schools, or enter certain occupations. 'Equal protection' was interpreted to mean that 'those who are similarly situated' should be 'similarly treated'. Discrimination came to mean 'different treatment' of 'similarly situated people' (Bacchi 1990, pp. 157–8). The principle here, that the law needs to be consistent in the way it treats people, is captured in the well-known image of the blind-folded statue of justice. The rationale behind the image is that, if you cannot see whom you are judging, you will not be influenced by 'extraneous' factors like their 'race' or their sex. You will treat everyone *in the same way*, or consistently.

From its inception the openness of this dictum to interpretation caused problems for particular groups. For example, while it was generally accepted that members of 'races' were always 'similarly situated', most judges were convinced that innate differences between women and men prevented them from being 'similarly situated', and therefore justified treating them 'differently' – which is not to suggest that Black people were ever treated fairly. In a classic case in 1873, Myra Bradwell was denied access to the bar to practise as a lawyer on the grounds that she was a married woman and that 'the civil law, *as well as nature herself*, has always recognised a wide difference in the respective spheres and destinies of man and woman' (Goldstein 1988, p. 71; emphasis added).

A difficulty here is that, while the principle ('likes should be treated alike') appears logical, it 'begs the question of the level of abstraction from personal characteristics at which the comparison is to be made' (O'Donovan and Szyszczak 1988, p. 55). As a consequence, the slogan 'likes should be treated alike' can be used to argue any case, depending upon the criteria selected to identify 'likes' and/or the 'like treatment' they ought to be accorded (Westen 1982, p. 547). For example, I could argue simply that women and men are 'alike' in their human potential for development and that therefore they should be treated 'alike' by giving them every opportunity to develop that potential. Of course, the *specifics* of that treatment might be 'different'. On the other hand, as above, I could argue that by nature women and men have 'different' roles in life and hence it is acceptable to treat them 'differently', even if that means blocking some women from pursuing certain career paths.

It is somewhat disturbing to find that a central principle in Western political philosophy and Western jurisprudence gets reduced in the end to a matter of interpretation. However, given that this is the case, it becomes all the more important to trace just how interpretation has gone – which patterns can be detected in the jurisprudence surrounding 'equality'? We have already identified one such pattern – the tendency to see women and men as naturally separate categories, which then allows forms of 'different' treatment that can be restrictive and harmful. Another pattern (pursued further in the section below on 'Anti-discrimination and "special measures"') is the way in which the dictum 'likes should be treated alike' has been used either to block forms of affirmative/positive action – such as reserving jobs or educational places for members of identified 'target groups' — or to render such programs an 'exception' to the anti-discrimination principle and hence subject to close scrutiny and possible removal.

Westen (1982) provides an example to illustrate how this has worked. In *Sweatt v. Painter* (1950) the American Supreme Court found that it was unconstitutional to exclude Blacks from a Texas law school on the basis of 'race'. What this signified was an end to the historically established practice of excluding Black students. Some sixteen years after *Sweatt*, in 1976, an affirmative action policy to promote the inclusion of Black students in University of Washington's predominantly white law school came under legal challenge from a white student who had been denied entry. The court decision (*De Funis v. Odegaard*) overthrew the University's affirmative action program on the grounds that 'race is not a difference that is constitutionally allowed to make a difference'.

The court in the Washington case claimed to be upholding the same principle as that established in *Sweatt v. Painter*. Because 'likes should be treated alike', the judges in *De Funis v. Odegaard* (1976) argued, the law is supposed to be 'race-blind' and hence they could not deny admission to a white applicant. This decision loses sight of one critical factor, however. The goal in Texas had been to *reduce* racial segregation, whereas the outcome in *De Funis v. Odegaard* was to *perpetuate* racial segregation (Westen 1982, pp. 582–3). In this way, in the Washington case, a narrow interpretation that focused on '*different* treatment', regardless of the nature of that treatment, meant that the *substantive* harm caused by racial discrimination was ignored.

A number of political philosophers have attempted to confront head-on the limitations in this tendency to reduce matters of equality to quasi-mathematical formulae **(Q6)**. Weinzweig (1987) makes the case that the proposition that 'likes should be treated alike' is so open-ended that it could be interpreted to embrace any *substantive* right, such as the right to be free of certain kinds of injuries. As another form of intervention, Karst (1984) contends that the historical meaning of the word 'equality' in the USA is much broader than the notion that 'likes should be treated alike', encompassing 'the presumptive right of each person to be treated by society as a respected, responsible, participating member, regardless of the differences between persons' (Weinzweig 1987, p. 83). Dworkin's (1978, p. 227) argument that the right to treatment *as an equal* ought to be anterior to (ought to come before) the right to *equal treatment* expresses similar sentiments.

With meanings of 'equality' such as these, it is unlikely that the University of Washington's affirmative action program would have been struck down. However, the dictum 'likes should be treated alike' continues to dominate the way in which equality is understood in Western jurisprudence. Hence, it is important to pursue more closely the ways in which 'likes should be treated alike' represents the 'problem' of 'inequality' **(Q1)**.

Native Title and racial discrimination

We will be pursuing the topic of Native Title and racial discrimination later in the chapter. For the time being, consider:

In 1985 Queensland enacted the *Queensland Coast Islands Declaratory Act* which declared, retroactively to 1879, that, on the acquisition of the Murray Island group in that year, any native title was extinguished, with no entitlement to compensation. In *Mabo v. Queensland* (1988) the High Court ruled that the Queensland legislation contravened the *Racial Discrimination Act* (1975).

In 1981 the South Australian Government passed the *Anangu Pitjantjatjara Yankunytjatjara Land Rights Act* (APLRA), which authorised the government to provide for, and thus acknowledge, Anangu ownership of the land. In *Gerhardy v. Brown* (1984–85) the High Court ruled that the APLRA was, prima facie, discriminatory.

- **How do you think these two decisions could be seen as consistent?**

- **Do you see any reasons to question the 'equivalence' drawn in these cases?**

- **Should state native title legislation be considered discriminatory against non-Aboriginal Australians? Why or why not?**

For this Activity see Nettheim 1998.

Equal treatment/different treatment

In Chapter 2 we broached the crucial role played by binaries or dichotomies in modes of governance, and the need to examine the ways in which they oversimplify social relations and establish hierarchies based on implicit norms. A dichotomy is set up as an 'A/ not-A' relationship. That is, there is a presumed starting point, the unmarked term, from which the second marked term is differentiated, or set in contrast. Because of this arrangement, the second term is positioned as 'other' and lesser. Think, for example, of mind/body, man/ woman, reason/emotion. Feminists have been highly successful at identifying the gendered character of dichotomies such as these, which are foundational in Western philosophy (Bacchi 2005a, p. 184).

With the topic at hand, we might have expected an equality/inequality dichotomy to set the scene for discussions about equality. However, this seldom happens. Rather, the widely accepted dichotomy framing the issue of equality is equality/*difference*. This development is significant. In the term 'difference' the emphasis is not on a state of *lacking* equality, as it would be with *inequality*, but on a state of *being* different. The common use of sameness/difference as a parallel dichotomy to equality/difference confirms this point. Those who are 'equal' are held to be the 'same' in some way. They are the 'likes' in 'likes must be treated alike'.

This, of course, would not be a problem if we all agreed on what 'likeness' consisted of, but, as we have seen, the content of 'likeness' is contested. Indeed, many of the central disputes around the meaning of equality are exactly over this content. We had an example above where women are described as 'different' because they are assumed to fill a domestic role. This case illustrates nicely one of the major limitations in an equality/difference way of thinking about social relationships – the ability of those who hold positions of normative superiority to determine the content of 'alikeness' and 'difference'.

For example, marking women as 'different' because they are presumed to fill a domestic role constitutes the *unmarked* position as filled by men, who are then deemed to be unlikely to be nurturers or carers. As a more specific example, with relevance to the analysis of anti-discrimination legislation below, pregnant women in the United States seeking maternity leave have faced a rather unenviable 'choice' – a policy option of either 'equal treatment' (implicitly with men), in which case their pregnancy would be ignored, or 'different treatment', in which case they would be marked as anomalous, sacrificing any claim to 'equality' (Bacchi 1990, Chapter 5). Because of the history of 'different' treatment, which has served to constrain and harm many women (see Bradwell above), some American feminists have pursued a 'sameness' option, trying to have maternity leave covered by disability insurance. These feminists are trying to 'raise' the level of abstraction in 'likes should be treated alike' to something that women could claim to share with men (i.e. disability) – despite the inappropriateness of characterising pregnancy as a disability, and despite the inadequate insurance coverage available.

We have here an instance of what Minow (1990) calls the 'difference dilemma'. Basically, says Minow, the dictum, 'likes should be treated alike', stipulates a worthy goal – 'race' (or sex) should *not* matter. People ought to be judged on characteristics *other than* skin colour (or their sex, or ethnicity, etc.). However, she goes on, many people are harmed *on the basis* of their 'race' and, *if you ignore the harm caused by racism*, those marked by 'racial' categorisation will suffer. In an 'equal treatment' approach this harm is ignored; in a 'different' treatment approach the groups so marked are 'othered' and stigmatised.

Minow identifies part of the difficulty here in the way we tend to think of differences as parts of people's *essences*. For example, the suggestion above that women should take the primary role in domestic caring arrangements was assumed to be part of their very 'nature'. Minow suggests an alternative interpretation that understands 'difference' as a relational concept. In this interpretation, someone is 'different' only *in relation to* someone else. Someone either *labels* you as 'different' from them, or you *claim* to be 'different' from them.

'Differences' in this understanding are *attributions*, either welcomed or imposed, *not* essences. Hence, the emphasis shifts from what people 'naturally' are like to the *activity of attributing 'difference'* and to those involved in that activity. In large part, in equality jurisprudence, the determination of 'difference' has often rested in the hands of a select group of white upper middle-class men. It is this dynamic that allows pregnancy, as just one example, to be constituted a 'difference'. There is no suggestion of a malign intention in this claim. The point is, quite simply, that those who hold influence in shaping norms are likely to give them content that reflects their own lives and experiences. As ways forward Minow recommends:

■ putting all parties on the same side through policies that provide universal benefits, so that no group is singled out as 'different' and stigmatised;

■ exposing the norms in 'equal treatment' as selective rather than universal – showing, for example, that constituting pregnancy a 'difference' means that the normative position can be filled only by men.

Affirmative action for men?

In June 2002 the then Prime Minister, John Howard, was asked to comment on the ALP's (Australian Labor Party) quota for women nominees for electoral office. He said, 'I think that affirmative action rules are insulting to women. I think quotas are patronizing to women and most women don't want the patronizing existence of quotas' (News Room 2002).

On 10 March 2004 Howard explained why he thought it a simple matter to amend the *Sex Discrimination Act 1984 (Cth)* to allow the Catholic Education Commission to offer scholarships for men teachers only:

> I think you apply a test of commonsense . . . we've got a problem in relation to male teachers and if the *Sex Discrimination Act* is standing in the way of commonsense then we should alter the *Sex Discrimination Act* . . . Apparently, an ideological obsession about never changing a word of the *Sex Discrimination Act* is more important to Labor than helping boys with male role models. (News Room 2004)

● **What can we learn from these two quite different positions on affirmative action?**

● **Can you identify any implicit norms in the defence of men-only scholarships?**

For this Activity see Bacchi 2005b.

The way in which the equal treatment/different treatment distinction gets played out in liberal capitalist societies is pursued in the next section.

Equal opportunity/equal results

The 'likes being treated alike' rule forms part of a mode of governance that privileges the market (see Chapter 2; Q2). This is clear in the 1868 *Equal Protection Clause*, where the expressed concern is to enable Black people to own property, attend schools and enter a range of occupations. The premise grounding the Clause was that Black people, like white people, should have the opportunity to engage in competitive economic activity and have access to the institutions required to facilitate that engagement. This premise is captured in the concept of *equal opportunity*, which has become the dominant equality discourse in Western industrialised countries and, to a large extent, elsewhere (Bacchi 2006, p. 32).

To call 'equal opportunity' or 'equality of opportunity' a dominant discourse means acknowledging the major role it plays in shaping views about appropriate social relationships. The idea it encapsulates is that every individual should have the same chance to succeed, with an emphasis on *access* to opportunities. The notion of 'a fair go' echoes this sentiment. The fact that this phrase was put forward in the Australian Citizenship Test as a fundamental Australian value (see Chapter 7) indicates the authority that equal opportunity commands.

At the same time it is inappropriate and unwise to ignore the ambiguity and tensions within the discourse and hence to falsely homogenise views on equality (Bacchi 1992). As Billig *et al.* (1988, p. 140) argue, formal liberal theories such as 'equal opportunity' endorse both 'a fundamental human equality and an infinite human variety', which means that the extent of similarity or difference between persons always constitutes a 'potentially contestable issue'. Key notions like 'equality' and 'difference' are therefore open to multiple interpretations (Goot and Rowse 2007), as noted earlier. However, as we shall see shortly, this is not the way in which the matter tends to be represented.

The notion of equal opportunity is expressed through the metaphor of a running race. Disputes about equality in Australia and in many other industrialised and industrialising countries are largely over what constitute 'barriers' to 'opportunities' to do well in the race, and how to deal with these barriers. In some accounts equality of opportunity means little more than minimal formal equality (consistency). It is assumed that, if you are guaranteed 'equal treatment' before the law, you have every 'opportunity' you need to 'get ahead'. The means to 'advancement' in this understanding are talent and effort, often referred to as 'merit'. In other accounts, it is held to be important to confront the 'problem' of discrimination, which is seen as an unfair obstacle in the race. Recall, the law is *supposed* to be 'race-blind' and 'sex-blind', explaining why explicit discrimination is considered a 'problem'.

Still other accounts are willing to introduce forms of 'benefit' to ensure that 'runners' start the race from a more or less equal position. In this view those who have been 'held back' are deemed to need 'assistance' to achieve the goal of an equal starting place in the 'race'. It is in exactly these terms that President Johnson defended the introduction of affirmative action in the United States in 1965: 'You do not take a person who has been hobbled by chains and liberate him and then say, "You are free to compete with the others", and still believe [that you are] being fair' (Davis 1993, p. 5). In this account, affirmative action becomes justified as a form of 'special assistance', or 'special treatment', for those who have been 'held back' in the race, and who were presumably damaged in the process. These groups, it is argued, need 'help' so that they can perform adequately in the 'race'. In the terms of an equal opportunity discourse, because such 'assistance' is a form of *different* treatment, it is considered to be *discrimination*, either 'positive discrimination' or 'reverse discrimination' (Moens 1985), understood as an intrinsically 'bad' thing that can be tolerated only in exceptional circumstances.

There are other ways to understand the social relations requiring affirmative action, however. For example, a basic assumption underpinning equal opportunity is that background social rules are generally fair (Q2). Discrimination is seen as an aberration that can be corrected through complaint-based anti-discrimination legislation (see below). However, if inequality is more deeply entrenched than this, with social differentials among people affecting every aspect of their lives, treating discrimination as an aberration mystifies the nature of social inequality (Q4; see Black 1989).

Arguing along these lines, some theorists (Thalberg 1980; Wasserstrom 1976) make the case that, because procedures that are *ostensibly* fair often benefit some people more than others, affirmative action is neither 'assistance' nor 'discrimination' but, quite simply, acknowledgement that power and bias are at work in appointments and promotions. Saying that power and bias are at work in this way, constitutes a significant challenge to the basic premise of equal opportunity – the presumption that everyone automatically has a 'fair go'. The declared goal of those who challenge this 'truth' is to achieve more *substantive* equality.

The understanding of affirmative action in the dominant equal opportunity discourse as 'help' for the 'damaged' or 'disadvantaged' (see Chapter 3), determines the forms of positive/ affirmative action that are considered to be acceptable. The question becomes – how much 'help' do the 'disadvantaged' need? Outreach or training programs are considered acceptable to 'help' 'disadvantaged' people up to the starting line of the race, but then they are on their own. Policies that guarantee certain kinds of job or position are considered anathema to 'fair play' because they appear to 'fix' the 'race'. They are condemned for aiming at 'equal results', which is set in contradistinction to 'equal opportunity'.

In this vein opinion polls frequently set up 'equal opportunity' and 'equal results' as separate and incompatible alternatives. Respondents are compelled to make an unenviable choice, given the strength and status of the equal opportunity discourse (Q5; Q6). Almost inevitably, 'equal opportunity' receives overwhelming endorsement, allowing social scientists to create the impression of a homogeneous value community with no place for affirmative action (Bacchi 1992; Q6). As a result, those who wish to raise possible limitations in the way in which equal opportunity represents the 'problem' of inequality have difficulty being heard.

Poverty proves somewhat of an embarrassment in countries which prize themselves as committed to equal opportunity. One common way to divert attention from the uncomfortable topic is to debate poverty's very existence (see Bletsas 2007). Another option is to focus on identifiable 'obstacles', such as discrimination, on the road to success. At times, when the focus on 'racial' issues becomes too heated, as in American debates about affirmative action, it is always possible to return the focus to the 'poor', so long as the 'poor' are created as a particular kind of problem – an 'underclass' who needs 'assistance' to overcome their 'disadvantages' (Q1, Q2). This representation of the 'problem' bears a strong resemblance to President Johnson's commitment to 'liberate' 'through affirmative action' those 'hobbled by chains' (see above).

It is crucial to reflect on how political subjects are constituted within these representations of the 'problem' of 'inequality' (Q5). In each case members of outgroups – those located outside influence and recognition – are constructed as, in some way, lesser than the unspoken norm. Attempts to alter their status become 'handouts', to be severely restricted given their 'exceptional' nature and their contravention of a basic equal treatment rule. Given this starting point, it is not surprising that the 'dominant ordinary-language view' often identifies recipients, of both affirmative action and forms of welfare (see Chapter 3), as receiving 'assistance' beyond genuine 'need', and therefore paradoxically as advantaged (Radin 1991). Calling affirmative action *preferential* treatment' reinforces this perception (Bacchi 2004). This representation of the 'problem' sometimes produces 'a low sense of self-worth in victims of discrimination' and contributes to the public impression of them as inferior (Edelman 1988, p. 26; Q5). Fear of stigmatisation can then lead members of outgroups to disassociate themselves from initiatives such as affirmative action, entrenching the social status quo.

Importantly, however, targeting does not always lead to stigmatisation. It all depends on who is doing the targeting and who is being targeted. There are many forms of targeted benefits – for example, veterans' benefit schemes, industry subsidies, grants to private schools – that have no stigma attached (Bacchi 2005b; Q4). We return to the central importance of considering who is in a position to shape determinations about who is 'alike' and who is 'different', and about what forms of treatment the respective groups ought to receive.

Disabling policies?

Gillian Fulcher (1989) argues that the discourse surrounding education policy and disability construes disabled children as the 'problem', distracting attention from the disabling structures that surround them. She also notes that representing the disabled as the 'problem' allows government 'responses' to be seen as benevolent, generous and compassionate, reinforcing existing power relations.

Reflecting on Fulcher's argument, consider the following proposition: 'Lighting is affirmative action for the sighted'.

- **How does this proposition reframe the issue of affirmative action?**

- **What implications would accompany such a reframing of the 'problem'?**

With this background it is time to explore more closely the kinds of problems 'inequality' and 'discrimination' are represented to be through our selected 'practical texts'.

ANTI-DISCRIMINATION AND 'SPECIAL MEASURES'

Our 'practical texts' in this chapter are Australia's *Racial Discrimination Act 1975 (Cth)* and *Sex Discrimination Act 1984 (Cth)*, with particular attention to their 'Special Measures' provisions. Before we undertake this analysis we need to reflect more broadly on the development of anti-discrimination legislation in Western democracies, keeping in mind our WPR questions.

A genealogy of anti-discrimination legislation

The idea of a human rights policy, and the anti-discrimination ethic it produced, emerged after the Second World War, stimulated by the international struggle against fascism and the 'surge of egalitarian idealism which the war had generated' (Howe 1991, p. 787; Q3). Anti-discrimination legislation is similar in form in all Western industrialised states. There are either Acts condemning specific kinds of discrimination, most often racial or sex discrimination, or omnibus pieces of legislation with closed or open-ended lists of the forms of discrimination disallowed. Commonly enumerated grounds, depending on the country or jurisdiction, include sexual orientation, marital status, age and disability.

What is called '*direct* discrimination' focuses upon behaviours resulting ostensibly from malice or evil intent. Direct discrimination occurs when an employer adopts a practice that excludes or maltreats members of certain groups because of their 'race'/ethnicity, religion, sex, etc. There are two key premises in direct discrimination: first, that a malicious individual is the 'problem'; and second, that people are being treated unfairly because they are being judged by forms of unsubstantiated generalisation (Q1). To the extent that the 'problem' is considered to be a matter of individual prejudice, deeper, structural patterns of discrimination are discounted (Q4).

The concept of *indirect* discrimination widens considerably the impact of anti-discrimination legislation. It recognises that discrimination occurs beyond a (malicious) individual's behaviour or actions, and may lodge within the structures or practices of an organisation, or in society more generally (Ronalds 1987, p. 99). Indirect discrimination allows members of so-called 'equity groups' to challenge apparently neutral rules, such as height or weight requirements, not necessary for job performance, that adversely affect their group. However, 'disparate impact' claims, as they are called, are difficult to prove and can be disallowed if the courts decide there is a 'business necessity' for the practice or policy that has been challenged.

Moreover, as with direct discrimination, recognition of indirect discrimination relies upon a complaint being made. That is, recognition depends upon an individual having the time, resources and determination to use court processes to lodge a discrimination complaint. At its heart, therefore, an anti-discrimination approach to equality is individualistic (Q2). The law is further circumscribed by explicit and implicit reliance on a public/private dichotomy. Private institutions, such as private schools, religious groups and clubs, are usually considered outside the ambit of the legislation. In addition, because the target of the legislation is the 'public' world of work and 'public' institutions, the family and activities performed in the care of family are left unscrutinised (Thornton 1991; **Q4**).

There are other limitations to anti-discrimination law. As noted above, a focus on discrimination as the 'problem' leaves the impression that social rules are generally fair, which may not be the case (**Q4**). In addition, the listing of separate categories of discrimination can make it difficult for people to protest when their experience crosses the categories (**Q5**). For example, the experience of Black women is difficult to capture when racial and sex discrimination are treated as separate and discrete offences. Finally, in this understanding of equality people are abstracted from their particular circumstances (e.g. their colour, their sex, etc.) and treated 'equally', meaning the same – 'likes should be treated alike'. This makes it difficult to acknowledge people's *specific* circumstances, which can mean perpetuating inequalities in their status (**Q4**).

On these grounds Justice Rosalie Abella (1987, p. 2), the head of the Canadian Commission on Equality in Employment in 1985, challenged the adequacy of a simple 'equal treatment' rule:

> There is a difference between treating people equally as we do in civil rights and treating people as equals as we do in human rights. For purposes of the former, we treat everyone the same; for purposes of the latter we treat them according to their differences.

Abella's reasoning creates an opening for affirmative or positive action – called employment equity in Canada.

With affirmative action, rather than waiting upon a complaint of discrimination, companies and large public organisations are directed to become *proactive* in confronting the systemic barriers in their rules and practices that effectively bar members of 'equity groups' from access and promotion. The challenge for those supporting such positive action has been making interventions that target members of equity groups *consistent with* the 'race'-blind and sex-blind premises of the anti-discrimination principle ('likes should be treated alike').

In these debates you might have noticed some slippage between the idea of *discriminatory* treatment and *different* treatment. That is, under the equal treatment dictum – 'likes should be treated alike' – forms of 'different' treatment responding to people's *specific* circumstances are deemed to be *discriminatory* regardless of whether the treatment *harms* people or has some other goal, such as removing injustices or attempting to compensate for harms, be they historical or present-day. As we shall soon see, a range of deleterious effects accompanies this interpretation that any form of 'different treatment' is discrimination (**Q5**).

Racial discrimination and 'special measures'

Australia's 1975 *Racial Discrimination Act 1975 (Cth)* (*RDA*) takes as its model the *International Convention on All Forms of Racial Discrimination* (*CERD*) (1969). Alongside condemnation of racial discrimination (section 9) and endorsement of 'equality before the law' (section 10; 'equal treatment') Australia's legislation identifies as an 'exception' 'special measures' (section 8), based on Article 1, section 4 of *CERD*, which reads:

> Special measures for the sole purpose of securing the advancement of certain racial or ethnic groups or individuals requiring such protection as may be necessary in order to ensure such groups or individuals equal enjoyment or exercise of human rights and fundamental freedoms shall not be deemed racial discrimination, provided, however, that such measures do not, as a consequence, lead to the maintenance of separate rights for different racial groups and that they shall not be continued after the objectives for which they were taken have been achieved. (Office of the High Commission on Human Rights 2008)

Affirmative action, where it occurs, is generally 'permitted' as a 'special measure'.

How did this representation of the 'problem' of discrimination gain prominence? (Q3) In discussions leading to *CERD*, the representative from India explained that the principle of non-discrimination 'raised certain problems in the case of the particularly backward groups still to be found in many under-developed countries'. In his country, he said, 'the constitution and the laws provided for special measures ("reservations" or reserved places or positions) for the *social and cultural betterment* of such groups, called "backward classes"' (Craven 1995, p. 185; emphasis added). He explained further that he felt it necessary to make this case because the framework for the ICESCR (*International Covenant on Economic, Social, and Cultural Rights*) hinged upon a commitment to *formal equality*, or 'equal treatment', which appeared to render such *special* measures unlawful. In the end, the explanatory paragraph included in the text of Article 2 of the ICESCR met the needs of India. It specified that: 'Special measures for the advancement of any socially and educationally backward sections of society shall not be construed as "distinction" under this article' (Craven 1995, p. 185).

The understanding of affirmative action in this case represents the 'problem' to be the social and cultural 'backwardness' of particular social groups (Q1). 'Special measures' are to be allowed in order to bring these groups up to some assumed state of desirable social development (Q2). The 'backward classes' become the 'problem' and their assimilation, the postulated solution. They will be added to the status quo, which will remain largely unchanged (Q5). There are resonances here with President Johnson's reference to those 'hobbled by chains' (see above).

The word 'discrimination' came to replace 'distinction' because it 'seemed to convey more accurately the requirement that the distinction be of an unjustified nature or arbitrary'

(Craven 1995, p. 161). Still, the 'equal treatment' rule continues to mean that any policy which suggests drawing attention to categories of people, singling them out for 'different treatment', is treated with suspicion and hence listed as an 'exemption' or exception. As exceptions, special measures can quite easily be removed if they are considered to contravene some 'larger' goal.

The underlying individualistic character of anti-discrimination legislation explains in large part why positive action is considered to be a 'special measure' and an exception to the anti-discrimination rule (Q2). The 'dilemma' was clarified in other discussion leading to *CERD*. Concern was expressed that targeting particular *groups* undermined the non-discrimination principle, which upholds the equal treatment of *individuals*:

> It was made clear that the Convention should protect groups as well as individuals, although some representatives felt that groups as such should not be stressed, because the Convention should seek to accomplish the objective of the Universal Declaration of Human Rights to promote the rights and freedoms of all human beings, without distinction of any kind. The aim should not be to emphasize the distinctions between different racial groups, but rather to ensure that persons belonging to such groups could be integrated into the community. (Lerner 1980, p. 33)

'Special measures', then, are *allowed*, but only for the 'sole purpose of securing the advancement of certain racial or ethnic groups or individuals' and provided they are not maintained 'after the objectives for which they were taken have been achieved' (see above). By being so characterised, such programs are placed on the defensive and come under intense scrutiny to ensure that they have not moved 'too far' from conventional understandings of equality as 'treating likes alike' (Q5).

Returning to the *Pitjantjatjara Land Rights Act* (SA) considered earlier (see Activity on 'Native Title and racial discrimination'), while the Act was declared to be discriminatory (because people of one 'race' were treated 'differently'), it was 'saved' under the 'special measures' provision of Australia's Racial Discrimination legislation (section 8; see above). The South Australian Government tried to make the case that it was unnecessary to invoke the 'special measures' clause since 'discrimination' under *CERD* meant 'distinctions that were arbitrary or for an invidious purpose' (i.e. harmful treatment, not just 'different' treatment), while the government's goal was to achieve more substantive equality. The court rejected this argument, ruling that under *CERD* and hence under the *RDA*, 'any distinction based on race is discriminatory, and will therefore be prohibited unless it falls within the special measures exception' (Parliament of Australia 2000, section 4.102). There are echoes here of *De Funis v. Odegaard* (see above).

Here it is clear that there were two competing views (Q6). The South Australian government saw discrimination as *harmful* treatment and hence had no trouble accepting land rights legislation as *not* discriminatory, as aimed in fact at *redressing* harm, and hence as not requiring legitimation through the special measures provision of the *RDA*. By contrast the High Court understood discrimination strictly as any form of *different* treatment and hence insisted that South Australia's land rights legislation was indeed a form of discrimination, allowable only in exceptional circumstances. To date, the latter view has remained dominant in Australia, with all sorts of negative repercussions for Aboriginal peoples and Torres Strait Islanders (Q5).

For example, the 1993 *Native Title Act* reflects the view that the principle of equality – or non-discrimination – requires *formal equality*, with an *exception* for *special* measures. The Preamble to the Act specifies that 'the people of Australia intend . . . to rectify the consequences of past injustices by the *special measures* contained in this Act . . . for securing the adequate advancement and protection of Aboriginal peoples and Torres Strait Islanders' (Parliament of Australia 1993; emphasis added). In line with this position, the right to negotiate forms of native title was described as a *'special* right'. Because this was the case, it was then relatively easy for the Howard-led Coalition government to *remove* the right to negotiate in the amended *Native Title Act* of 1998. At the very same time the Howard government described the *Native Title Amendment Act* as *itself* a 'special measure' in order to escape criticism by *CERD* that the *Amendment Act* may have been discriminatory (Dick and Donaldson 1999, p. 5).

In an earlier attempt to remove the right to negotiate from the *Native Title Act*, the Attorney-General's Department clarified the government's position: 'The traditional legal position in Australia has been that any laws which deal with racial matters either have to provide formal equality – that means they have to treat people of different races *in the same way* – or have to be a special measure' (Parliament of Australia 1996, Section 4.2; emphasis added). In further clarification, the Department can be seen, somewhat ironically, to endorse the position developed in this chapter – that it is all a matter of interpretation:

> The *RDA*, whilst recognising special measures as a permissible exception to 'non-discrimination', and thus permitting *positive discrimination*, does not impose an obligation on governments to establish special measures or to continue them either in their current terms or with amendments. The necessity for such measures and their form are matters to be decided in the political arena. (Parliament of Australia 1996, Section 4.11; emphasis added)

The Parliamentary Joint Committee, convened to consider the matter, noted the alternative view that 'the acknowledgement of native title rights (including the right to negotiate) does not amount to a special measure but is in fact given to ensure substantive equality'. However, it concluded:

> The Attorney-General's Department has advised the Committee that the substantive equality approach has not yet been accepted in Australian law. Even were it accepted,

a substantive equality approach would not require governments to make laws with that objective; it would simply enable them to do so. (Parliament of Australia 1996, Section 4.15; **Q3**)

An understanding of 'discrimination' as (simply) 'different treatment' puts serious limitations on the forms of possible legislative intervention addressed to the substantive harms accompanying European territorial occupation and continuing racism. The provisional nature of 'special measures' implicitly accepts those harms, offering piecemeal and tentative 'compensation'. Nor are 'special measures' adequate 'to deal with the longer term, collective interests of indigenous peoples to retain their distinctiveness as peoples' (Nettheim 1998, p. 201). All the while, the composition and character of the 'unmarked' group, who in this instance get to define the limits of equality, go unscrutinised (**Q4**). Attempts to redress this situation highlight the 'intimate relationship between whiteness and asset accumulation' in Australian society (Moreton-Robinson 2001, p. 177; **Q6**).

The Northern Territory intervention and racial discrimination

The Northern Territory measures, referred to as 'the intervention', contain provisions exempting them from the protections of the *Racial Discrimination Act*. In the second reading speech on the Bills the government explained that: 'The provisions make it clear that the Northern Territory emergency response and related legislation are "special measures" for the purposes of the *Racial Discrimination Act 1975* and excluded from Part II of the Act' [the section prohibiting racial discrimination]. The government stated that the provisions were special measures 'taken for the sole purpose of securing the advancement of Indigenous Australians' (Brough 2007).

- **How does this case help us understand the ambiguity and hence potential for manipulation in the 'special measures' provision?**

For this Activity refer back to Chapter 5 and see Calma 2007.

Sex discrimination and 'special measures'

Australia's 1984 *Sex Discrimination Act* (*SDA*) takes its lead from the *International Convention on the Elimination of All Forms of Discrimination Against Women* (*CEDAW*, 1979), Article 4(1), which in turn follows the principles established in *CERD*. As a result, 'temporary special measures' are allowed as an exception to the Convention:

Adoption by States Parties of temporary special measures aimed at accelerating de facto equality between men and women shall not be considered discrimination as defined in the present Convention, but shall in no way entail as a consequence the maintenance of unequal or separate standards; these measures shall be discontinued when the objectives of equality of opportunity and treatment have been achieved. (United Nations 2007)

Along similar lines, Section 33 of the original *SDA* provided that 'special measures' were not unlawful, if the purpose was to provide 'equal opportunities' for specified groups, including 'persons of a particular sex', or of a particular marital status, or pregnant women (Ronalds 1987, p. 153). This clause allowed the then Labor Government to introduce an *Affirmative Action (Equal Employment Opportunity for Women) Act* in 1986 as a 'special measure'.

Because of the furore over affirmative action in the United States at the time, the government did its best to distance Australia's legislation from the idea of 'quotas'. Public debate was framed in terms of equal opportunity *versus* equal results (quotas), with the latter marked as the negative term (Q2). Government statements made the case that a reform which called for 'results' would impose unfair economic constraints on industry (Q3, Q6). For example, in 1977 Peter Wilenski, one of the architects of affirmative action in New South Wales, insisted that 'affirmative action plans which require quotas . . . can be regarded as inconsistent with the principle of open competition and can result in the *hiring of less efficient workers*' (Wilenski 1977, p. 233; emphasis added). Along similar lines, in 1984 the NSW Department of Premier and Cabinet issued a statement that:

> The imposition of quotas would have a negative effect for organizations in general and for women employees in particular. It would create a 'second stream' of jobs which are only to meet the quota requirements. Such an approach would do nothing to raise women's labour market participation in an effective and long term way, and *would impose unreasonable and uneconomic requirements on organizations*. (Kramar 1987, pp. 175–6; emphasis added)

In this understanding it is implied that attempts to increase women's representation through forms of affirmative action, such as 'quotas', means hiring *unqualified* women – 'less efficient workers' – foreclosing discussion of what the term 'qualified' means (Q4). In line with this position, Section 3(4) of the *Affirmative Action Act* specifies that: 'Nothing in this Act shall be taken to require a relevant employer to take any action incompatible with the principle that employment matters should be dealt with on the basis of merit' (Ronalds 1987, p. 63; Q2). Contesting this position Burton (1987) argues that 'merit' and qualifications are *not* objective criteria, free from cultural determination. She introduces the concept of 'homosocial reproduction' to explain why in many cases those who are hired or promoted tend to be similar to those doing the hiring or promoting (Q4, Q6).

Linking affirmative action to economic (in)efficiency, in the way Wilenski and the NSW Department of Premier and Cabinet do above, has other effects (**Q5**). It leaves the reform susceptible to economic fluctuations and to 'what the market will bear'. It also leaves little room for demanding that industry accept social responsibility for its hiring and promotion policies.

Forms of affirmative action, such as training programs and 'outreach' (soliciting applications from women), meanwhile are permitted on the grounds that some groups in society need limited 'assistance' in order to compete. The first serious defence of affirmative action in Australia, a 1974 piece by Gareth Evans (1974, pp. 26–28; emphasis added), a Labor Senator in 1995, defined 'benign discrimination' as 'the singling out by the state of a designated group for *more favourable* treatment than is accorded the others'. The rationale offered was that 'groups suffering *special disabilities*' need to be '*specially helped*' (**Q2**, **Q3**).

There is a distinct resonance here with President Johnson's endorsement of affirmative action for those described as 'hobbled by chains' (see above), and with much the same effect. Women are constituted as 'disadvantaged', as 'needy', and as needing '*preferential* treatment' in order to 'succeed' (**Q5**). They are offered 'protection', a justification that mystifies the state's role in reproducing the current gender order (**Q4**). Moreover, as Eveline (1994) points out, representing the 'problem' as women's 'disadvantage' leaves no room for reference to, or accounts of, men's *advantage*. The fact that men's advantage is contingent on women's 'disadvantage', then, is obscured by liberal notions of equal opportunity (**Q2**, **Q4**; see Chapter 3).

Somewhat puzzlingly Article 4(1) of *CEDAW* (see above) endorses 'de facto equality' (i.e. *substantive* equality) as an objective *alongside* the commitment to 'equality of opportunity and treatment'. The *travaux préparatoires* (official record of the negotiation) explain the paradox: the reference to 'de facto equality' came from the then Union of Soviet Socialist Republics while the endorsement of equal opportunity was drafted by the United States (Renouf 1993, pp. 66–76; **Q3**). The tension between the two positions is resolved in the production of 'special measures' as exceptional and as limited in duration.

Australia made an important alteration to the *SDA* in 1993. Section 33 was repealed and section 7D on 'Special measures intended to achieve equality' was added. Significantly, the new section stipulated that special measures 'for the purpose of achieving *substantive* equality' did not constitute discrimination (Commonwealth Consolidated Acts 1984). The Australian Government Solicitor (1996) explained the rationale for the new section: 'The new "special measures" provision reflects the view that a narrow and formalistic approach to equality will not produce equality in fact and may entrench existing discrimination or create new discriminatory situations.'

Despite this endorsement of *substantive* equality, the focus of attention in the amended legislation remains on the 'special' and 'temporary' character of 'special measures'. Indeed, as an illustration of the new approach, the Government Solicitor used a decision made under Section 33 which disallowed a challenge to specialist women's health services that they discriminated against men, on the grounds that the services were 'special measures':

> The decision that provision of the service constituted a special measure was based on a consideration of the particular health needs women have, and their disadvantaged state. Mention was made of the distinctive health needs of women arising from particular circumstances, for example, the need for appropriate services to treat women subjected to violence. (Australian Government Solicitor 1996)

Recalling Minow's concern about the stigma attached to those designated 'different', it is important to identify the invisible male norm that leads to the labelling of women's health needs as 'special' or 'distinctive'.

Pregnancy and discrimination

Under the 'exemptions' in the 1984 *Sex Discrimination Act*, Section 31 specifies that 'Nothing in Division 1 or 2 renders it unlawful for a person to discriminate against a man on the ground of his sex by reason only of the fact that the first-mentioned person grants to a woman rights or privileges in connection with pregnancy or childbirth' (Human Rights and Equal Opportunity Commission 2007).

- **Is there an unspoken norm in an anti-discrimination law that deems pregnancy an exemption?**
- **What effects follow from constituting pregnancy an exemption to discrimination?**

For this Activity see Eisenstein 1988.

The interpretation of Article 4(1) of the *CEDAW* Convention continues to be contested (Q6). The dominant view, put by the Special Rapporteur to the United Nations, Mark Bossuyt, identifies three forms of affirmative action: programs of 'affirmative mobilization' such as 'job-training programs to enable members of minorities to *acquire the skills* that would allow them to compete for jobs and promotion'; programs of 'affirmative fairness', which guarantee that 'the "*best qualified*" ought always to be hired'; and programs of 'affirmative *preference*'. These last, in Bossuyt's view, are 'not objectionable as long as *preference* is given to members of the targeted group only if they are as *equally qualified* as others not belonging to that group' (Bossuyt 2002, paragraph 102; emphasis added). The suggestion that 'everything else being equal' (i.e. that women are '*equally qualified* as others'), women should be appointed or promoted has been taken up in a number of European countries (Bacchi 2004, p. 136). Implicitly this way of representing the 'problem' accepts that standard methods of assessment are fair (Q2) and that women need a 'special' boost.

A very different position on positive action was put forward at a 2003 expert meeting organised to develop building blocks for a General Recommendation on Article 4(1) **(Q6)**. The Rapporteur, Rikki Holtmaat (2003, p. 14), advised:

> The drafters must carefully choose their words to overcome the dominant view of 'positive action' or 'affirmative action' as special favours or preferential treatment of women, or which otherwise portray women as the problem and as the ones needing to change. To avoid these understandings the term disadvantage should be used judiciously in the GR [General Recommendation]. More accurate language, e.g. 'underrepresented' or 'excluded' ought to be used where appropriate. The GR should clearly reflect that the central problem is the existing privilege of men, rather than the 'disadvantage' (too often constructed as the 'impairment') of women.

In this alternative representation of the 'problem' **(Q4)** measures to redress men's advantages become necessary to substantive equality. These measures may be 'different' treatment but they are *not* discrimination. Nor should they be characterised as 'special', meaning exceptional.

SUMMARY

In this chapter we explored the ways in which anti-discrimination law constitutes equality as *formal* equality, entailing 'equal treatment' of those deemed to be 'alike'. Based on this understanding, attempts to achieve substantive equality are characterised as 'special measures', subject to the discretion of people with influence and authority. The accompanying creation of recipients as 'different' and 'lesser' reinforces the social and political status quo. To the extent that equality initiatives remain tied to this diagram of rule, the possibility of redressing asymmetrical power relations is limited.

QUESTIONS

1. How does the aphorism 'likes should be treated alike' represent the 'problem' of inequality?
2. What assumptions underpin this representation of the 'problem'?
3. How has this representation of the 'problem' achieved dominance in Western jurisprudence?
4. Are there any silences in this representation of the 'problem'?
5. Is it possible to contest this representation of the 'problem'? Which strategies are available?

REFERENCES

ABELLA, R. S. 1987, 'Employment Equity – Implications for Industrial Relations', *Industrial Relations Centre Reprint Series* No. 73, Queen's University, Kingston.

AUSTRALIAN GOVERNMENT 1975, *Racial Discrimination Act*, Attorney-General's Department, Australian Law Online, <http://scaleplus.law.gov.au>, accessed 16 October 2008.

AUSTRALIAN GOVERNMENT 1984, *Sex Discrimination Act*, Attorney-General's Department, Commonwealth of Australia Law, <www.comlaw.gov.au>, accessed 16 October 2008.

AUSTRALIAN GOVERNMENT SOLICITOR 1996, 'Significant Changes to the Sex Discrimination Act', *Legal Practice Briefing*, no. 25.

BACCHI, C. 1990, *Same Difference: Feminism and Sexual Difference*, Allen & Unwin, Sydney.

BACCHI, C. 1992, 'Affirmative Action – Is it Really Un-American?' *International Journal of Moral and Social Studies*, vol. 7, no. 1, pp. 19–31.

BACCHI, C. 2004, 'Policy and Discourse: Challenging the Construction of Affirmative Action as Preferential Treatment', *Journal of European Public Policy*, vol. 11, no. 1, pp. 128–46.

BACCHI, C. 2005a, 'Policy', in *A Companion to Gender Studies*, eds P. Essed, D. T. Goldberg & A. Kiobayashi, Blackwell Publishing, Oxford.

BACCHI, C. 2005b, 'Affirmative Action for Men: "A Test of Common Sense?"', *Just Policy: A Journal of Australian Social Policy*, vol. 36, pp. 5–10.

BACCHI, C. 2006, 'Arguing for and Against Quotas: Theoretical Issues', in *Women, Quotas and Politics*, ed. D. Dahlerup, Routledge, London.

BILLIG, M., CONDON, S., EDWARDS, D., GANE, M., MIDDLETON, D. & RADLEY, A. 1988, *Ideological Dilemmas: A Social Psychology of Everyday Thinking*, Sage, London.

BLACK, D. 1989, *Sociological Justice*, Oxford University Press, New York.

BLETSAS, A. 2007, 'Contesting Representations of Poverty: Ethics and Evaluation', *Policy and Society*, vol. 26, no. 3, pp. 63–81.

BOSSUYT, M. 2002, *Prevention of Discrimination: The Concept and Practice of Affirmative Action*, Final Report by the Special Rapporteur in accordance with Sub-Commission Resolution 1998/5, Economic and Social Council, E/CN/Sub.2/2002/21.

BROUGH, M. 2007, Second Reading Speech, *Northern Territory Emergency Response Bill 2007*, House of Representatives, *Official Hansard*, No. 11, 7 August.

BURTON, C. 1987, 'Merit and Gender: Organisations and the Mobilisation of Masculine Bias', *Australian Journal of Social Issues*, vol. 22, no. 2, pp. 424–35.

CALMA, T. 2007, *Social Justice Report*, Human Rights & Equal Opportunity Commission, Canberra, <www.hreoc.gov.au>, accessed 28 May 2008.

COMMONWEALTH CONSOLIDATED ACTS 1984, *Sex Discrimination Act 1984* – Section 7D, <www.austlii.edu.au>, accessed 3 August 2008.

CRAVEN, M. C. R. 1995, *The International Covenant on Economic, Social, and Cultural Rights: A Perspective on its Development*, Clarendon Press, Oxford.

DAVIS, F. E. 1993, *Affirmative Action in the United States and its Application to Women in Employment. Equality for Women in Employment: An Interdepartmental Project*, Working Paper, International Labour Office, Geneva.

DICK, D. & DONALDSON, M. 1999, 'The compatibility of the amended Native Title Act 1993 (Cth) with the United Nations Convention on the Elimination of All Forms of Racial Discrimination', *Land, Rights, Laws: Issues of Native Title*, Issues paper no. 29, Native Title Research Unit, Australian Institute of Aboriginal and Torres Strait Islander Studies, <http://ntru.aiatsis.gov.au,>, accessed 14 December 2008.

DWORKIN, R. 1978, *Taking Rights Seriously*, Duckworth, London.

EDELMAN, M. 1988, *Constructing the Political Spectacle*, University of Chicago Press, Chicago, Illinois.

EISENSTEIN. Z. 1988, *The Female Body and the Law*, University of California Press, Berkeley, CA.

EVANS, G. 1974, 'Benign Discrimination and the Right to Equality', *Federal Law Review*, vol. 6, pp. 26–83.

EVELINE, J. 1994, 'The Politics of Advantage', *Australian Feminist Studies*, special issue: *Women and Citizenship*, vol. 19, pp. 129–54.

FOUCAULT, M. 1984 [1983], 'On the Genealogy of Ethics: An Overview of Work in Progress', in *The Foucault Reader*, ed. P. Rabinow, Pantheon, New York.

FOUCAULT, M. 1991 [1968], 'Politics and the Study of Discourse', in *The Foucault Effect: Studies in Governmentality*, eds G. Burchell, C. Gordon & P. Miller, University of Chicago Press, Chicago.

FULCHER, G. 1989, *Disabling Policies? A Comparative Approach to Education Policy and Disability*, The Falmer Press, London.

GOLDSTEIN, L. 1988, *The Constitutional Rights of Women: Cases in Law and Social Change*, 2nd edition, University of Wisconsin Press, Madison.

GOOT, M. & ROWSE, T. 2007, *Divided Nation? Indigenous Affairs and the Imagined Public*, Melbourne University Press, Melbourne.

HOFFMAN, J. & GRAHAM, P. 2006, *Introduction to Political Concepts*, Pearson Education, Harlow, England.

HOLTMAAT, R. 2003, 'Building Blocks for a General Recommendation on Article 4(1) of the *CEDAW* Convention', in *Temporary Special Measures: Accelerating De Facto Equality for Women Under Article 4(1) UN Convention on the Elimination of All Forms of Discrimination Against Women*, eds I. Boerefinj, F. Coomans, J. Goldschmidt, R. Holtmaat & R. Wolleswinkel, Intersentia, Antwerpen.

HOWE, R. B. 1991, 'The Evolution of Human Rights Policy in Ontario', *Canadian Journal of Political Science/Revue Canadienne de Science Politique*, vol. 24, no. 4, pp. 783–802.

HUMAN RIGHTS AND EQUAL OPPORTUNITY COMMISSION 2007, *Sex Discrimination Act 1984*, <www.hreoc.gov.au>, accessed 3 August 2008.

KARST, K. 1984, 'Woman's Constitution', *Duke Law Journal*, vol. 3, pp. 447–509.

KRAMAR, R. 1987, 'Affirmative Action: A Challenge to Australian Employers and Trades Unions', *Journal of Industrial Relations*, vol. 29, no. 2, pp. 169–89.

LERNER, N. 1980, *The UN Convention on the Elimination of All Forms of Racial Discrimination*, Sijthoff & Noordhoff, Alphen aan den Rijn, The Netherlands.

MINOW, M. 1990, *Making All the Difference: Inclusion, Exclusion, and American Law*, Cornell University Press, Ithaca, New York.

MOENS, G. 1985, *Affirmative Action: The New Discrimination*, Centre for Independent Studies, Sydney.

MORETON-ROBINSON, A. 2001, 'A Possessive Investment in Patriarchal Whiteness: Nullifying Native Title', in *Left Directions: Is There a Third Way?* eds P. Nursey-Bray & C. Bacchi, University of Western Australia Press, Perth.

NETTHEIM, G. 1998, 'The International Law Context', in *Citizenship and Indigenous Australians*, eds N. Peterson & W. Sanders, Cambridge University Press, Cambridge.

NEWS ROOM 2002, *Transcript* of the Prime Minister, the Hon John Howard, Doorstop interview, Dunmore Lang College, Sydney 6 October, <www.pm.gov.au>, accessed 7 June 2004.

NEWS ROOM 2004, *Transcript* of the Prime Minister, the Hon John Howard, Interview with David Speers, Sky News, 10 March, <www.pm.gov.au>, accessed 7 June 2004.

O'DONOVAN, K. & SZYSZCZAK, E. 1988, *Equality and Sex Discrimination Law*, Basil Blackwell, Oxford.

OFFICE OF THE HIGH COMMISSION ON HUMAN RIGHTS 2008, *International Convention on the Elimination of All Forms of Racial Discrimination 1969*, United Nations, <www.unhchr.ch>, accessed 3 August 2008.

PARLIAMENT OF AUSTRALIA 1993, *Native Title Act*, <www.austlii.edu.au>, accessed 28 May 2008.

PARLIAMENT OF AUSTRALIA 1996, *Joint Committee on Native Title and the Aboriginal and Torres Strait Islander Land Fund, Seventh Report*, Canberra, <www.aph.gov.au>, accessed 26 May 2008

PARLIAMENT OF AUSTRALIA 2000, *Joint Committee on Native Title and the Aboriginal and Torres Strait Islander Land Fund, Sixteenth Report*, Canberra, <www.aph.gov.au>, accessed 16 October 2008.

RADIN, M. 1991, 'Affirmative Action Rhetoric', *Social Philosophy & Policy*, vol. 8, no. 2, pp. 130–49.

RENOUF, L. A. 1993, *Guide to the Travaux Préparatoires of the United Nations Convention on the Elimination of All Forms of Discrimination Against Women*, M. Nijho Pubs., Dordrecht.

RONALDS, C. 1987, *Affirmative Action and Sex Discrimination: A Handbook on Legal Rights for Women*, Pluto Press, Sydney.

ROSE, N. S. 2000, *Powers of Freedom: Reframing Political Thought*, 1st edition 1999, Cambridge University Press, Cambridge, UK.

TANESINI, A. 1994, 'Whose Language?' in *Knowing the Difference: Feminist Perspectives in Epistemology*, eds K. Lennon & M. Whitford, Routledge, New York.

THALBERG, I. 1980, 'Themes in the Reverse-Discrimination Debate', *Ethics*, vol. 91, no. 1, pp. 138–50.

THORNTON, M. 1991, 'The Public/Private Dichotomy: Gendered and Discriminatory', *Journal of Law and Society*, vol. 18, no. 4, pp. 448–63.

UNITED NATIONS 2007, *Convention on the Elimination of All Forms of Discrimination Against Women*, Division for Advancement of Women, Department of Economic and Social Affairs, <www.un.org>, accessed 3 August 2008.

WASSERSTROM, R. 1976, 'The University and the Case for Preferential Treatment', *American Philosophical Quarterly*, vol. 13, no. 2, pp. 165–70.

WEINZWEIG, M. 1987, 'Pregnancy Leave, Comparable Worth, and Concepts of Equality', *Hypatia*, vol. 2, no. 1, pp. 71–101.

WESTEN, P. 1982, 'The Empty Idea of Equality', *Harvard Law Review*, vol. 95, no. 3, pp. 537–88.

WILENSKI, P. 1977, *Directions for Change: Review of the New South Wales Government Administration*, P. West, Sydney.

FURTHER READING

BUMILLER, K. 1988, *The Civil Rights Society: The Social Construction of Victims*, Johns Hopkins University Press, Baltimore, MD.

SIMONS, J. 1995, *Foucault & the Political*, Routledge, London.

The ambivalence of education: HECS and lifelong learning

Chapter 9

CLOSE TO HOME

Education as a topic brings us 'close to home' in several senses. Besides the obvious meaning – that we are approaching the end of the book – this chapter is centrally concerned with what many of us do. That is, many of the readers of this book are located in educational institutions. I am also so located. Moreover, the book is designed as a textbook and hence is intended to be 'educational'. Therefore, it is important to reflect on what exactly this means both in the wider context and in the specific instance of a WPR approach. In addition, a key term in education policy is 'knowledge', a clear point of reference in a WPR analysis. Relationships between power and knowledge have been pursued in earlier chapters and become the central problematic in the concluding chapter (Chapter 10).

The 'practical texts' for this chapter are: the *Higher Education Contribution Scheme* (HECS), introduced in 1989, and the *Student Learning Entitlement* (SLE), introduced in 2003, with its commitment to an 'entitlement' for 'lifelong learning'.

While there appears to be a tension between these concurrent policies, with HECS demanding *forms of economic commitment* in order to access higher education, and the SLE promising *entitlement* (implying a *right*) to higher education, including 'lifelong learning', the two are reconciled in the production of a particular kind of political subject – entrepreneurial subjects who invest in themselves and in their futures. This chapter explores how this reconciliation occurs and reflects on the implications associated with this conception of the individual (Q2, Q5).

Reminder

The six questions in a WPR approach can be followed systematically – addressing each question separately and in order – as in Chapters 3 and 4. More commonly, the questions form part of an integrated analysis, with specific questions applied where the analysis occasions their use. This chapter follows the second, integrated form of analysis, employing the notation Q1, Q2, etc. where a specific question has been applied.

THINKING ABOUT 'EDUCATION'

There is ambivalence, or tension, at the heart of the education project, linked closely to the issue of how the subject is imagined within it. On the one hand, there are those theorists (the vast majority) who see education as the great equaliser, the key to promoting social mobility; on the other hand, some others consider education to be the ultimate normalising institution (see Chapter 2), taming 'the feral working class' (Thomson 2001, p. 180) and (re)producing social hierarchies (Connell 1993, p. 27). For the former group of theorists, education holds out the promise of smoothing over social distinctions, allowing the poor to 'do well' and to 'make good'. For the latter, an education dominated by an elite group will necessarily serve that elite group by producing well-disciplined and law-abiding citizens who believe, mistakenly, that they will indeed 'make good'. For the former, education promises liberation; for the latter, it mystifies the reality of domination.

For those who see education as social equaliser, the 'problem' is represented to be *lack of* access or *inadequate* access to educational institutions, marking a clear link with the dominant understanding of equality as a matter of access to opportunities (see Chapter 8). For those who see education as oppressor, the 'problem' is represented to be the nature of the education on offer, which reinforces asymmetrical social roles and disguises this outcome through the idea of equal opportunity. In this latter tradition, critical pedagogy scholars such as Paulo Freire (1973, 1976) and Henry Giroux (2005; see also Giroux and McLaren 1989) are committed to producing a form of education that is *truly* liberating.

Poststructuralist education scholars position themselves outside this debate. In their view, since all knowledge is implicated with power, all pedagogical discourses, including those put forward by critical pedagogy scholars, need to be subjected to questioning. The key question for poststructuralist analysis is how these discourses position the subject – how the subject is constituted within discourse/s (Q5). In other words, the interest for poststructuralists is in exploring what kinds of individuals come to be 'made up' within the different narrative accounts of education.

In this vein, Popkewitz (1998) highlights the way in which the focus in much critical pedagogy on 'voice' and 'participation' for members of marginalised social and economic groups positions these groups as 'agents of their own emancipation and liberation'. This 'culture of redemption', as he describes it, 'embodies norms about dispositions and capabilities that are not equally available to all' (Popkewitz 1998, p. 14, 19). In effect, therefore, this project introduces a form of discipline that invokes self-regulation among the marginalised, though the goal of this regulation may appear to be a worthy one.

This kind of critical problematisation of all 'expert' discourses may sound a little self-defeating, and poststructuralism is certainly subject to critiques of this nature. However, the larger message – that any person may inadvertently invoke precepts that subvert their declared goals – is certainly one worth considering. Such a stance highlights the importance of identifying and historicising principles central to thinking about education, such as notions of rationality and individual autonomy, and tracing how these principles are in fact the results of particular power relations (Q3).

This approach also makes it easier to identify links between past discourses that might appear to be benign or even progressive, and present ones that we might find problematic, links that might well incline us to reflect more critically on those past discourses. In this vein, Popkewitz (1998, pp. 7–8) notes that the current dominant view that the primary goal of education policy is to produce citizen-workers can be identified even in the work of the well-known early twentieth-century education reformer, John Dewey. Here we can see that the close alignment between education policy and labour market policy, which we proceed to explore in this chapter, has deep roots, though it is not and has never been the only way to imagine the education project.

What kind of a policy is 'education' policy?

As a 'field', education policy bears some similarity to health policy. You may recall that, in Chapter 6, we discussed how a whole range of social issues become health 'problems'. The suggestion there was that the concept of 'health policy' provided a form of diversion from political issues such as wealth distribution and corporate exploitation of both workers and the environment.

It is likewise the case that education is seen as the 'solution' to a swathe of social 'problems'. Schooling, for example, with an increasing emphasis on nutrition and sex education, is seen as an investment in *public health* (Popkewitz *et al*. 2007, p. 23). Education is connected to *crime prevention* through the premise that a good education provides the 'best start in life'. The current focus on drugs education (see Chapter 1, Activity on 'Approaches to drug education') indicates a conviction that 'proper' education will reduce the drug 'problem'. Faith in education as the 'solution' to numerous social 'problems' enables truancy to itself be considered a crime, at least for those parents who fail to prevent its occurrence (see Chapter 5, Activity on 'School enrolment and attendance initiatives').

Education is also put forward as the 'solution' to 'disadvantage', as in the 1990 policy document, *A Fair Chance for All* (Commonwealth of Australia 1990, p. iii; see Activity below): 'Education and training are vital factors in providing opportunities for people from disadvantaged groups'. Since education is put forward as the 'solution' to 'disadvantage', *lack of* education is represented to be the 'problem' (**Q1**) – a view that ignores deep structural asymmetries of power both within educational institutions and in the wider society (**Q4**). It is this view of education, of course, that underpins both the discourse of equal opportunity (see Chapter 8) and the conviction that education, through facilitating access to the labour market, is both equalising and liberating. Policy approaches to girls' education are a case in point.

In the 1970s, the period in which 'girls' became a category of significance in educational deliberations, there was a concerted effort to encourage girls to enter non-traditional study areas. In this policy the 'problem' is represented to be girls' subject choices in secondary schools and at university. The fact that girls tended to select humanities and arts subjects, while boys tended to dominate science and mathematics, produced, it was argued, 'restrictive post-school options' (**Q1**).

Without denigrating the desirability of integrating girls into non-traditional study areas, it is useful to identify the presuppositions underlying this problem representation (**Q2**). First, this agenda understands women's inequality to be a matter of their lack of access to the labour market. Second, the focus on 'non-traditional' areas of study and work, privileges boys' choices. The suggestion that the 'problem' might be the other way around, that boys are not choosing to study the arts, for example, finds few advocates (**Q4**). Finally, the emphasis upon encouraging girls to study science and technology comfortably fits a discourse that emphasises technological innovation as the key to national economic 'security' and international competitiveness.

Such a representation of the 'problem' produces a number of silences (**Q4**). It ignores the many women who have long had access to labour market participation and who do not find the experience 'liberating'. This is emphatically the case for many women in so-called 'underdeveloped' countries. The suggestion that labour force participation is a necessary 'good' also leaves unaddressed the 'good' of the lives we lead when we are *not* in paid labour. Despite all the rhetoric about reconciling family responsibilities and paid labour in many current policy proposals (see Chapter 7), the emphasis remains upon minimising the former (family responsibilities) in order to maximise the latter (labour force participation), or upon transforming family responsibilities into marketable services, such as institutional child care.

A Fair Chance for All

This 1990 Discussion Paper declared a commitment 'to the achievement of a fairer and more just society' to be accomplished by 'working towards the removal of the barriers which prevent people from many groups in our society from participating fully in the life of our community'. The government declared a commitment to 'achieving equity in higher education', the softer language of 'equity' replacing 'equality'. This commitment involved:

■ An increase in the proportion of women in non-traditional courses other than engineering from their current level to at least 40 per cent by 1995;

■ An increase in the proportion of women in engineering courses from 7 per cent to 15 per cent by 1995;

■ An increase in the number of women in postgraduate study, particularly in research, relative to the proportion of female undergraduates in each field by 1995. (Commonwealth of Australia 1990)

• **What understanding of equality (or 'equity') is supported in this document?** *(see Chapter 8)*

• **What is the 'problem' of women's inequality represented to be in these proposals?**

• **Can you identify any silences?**

The close alignment between education policy and labour market policy, noted in the case of girls' education, is nowhere clearer than in the departmental and ministerial location of education policy. John Dawkins, who produced the Foreword for *A Fair Chance for All*, was the Minister for Employment, Education and Training. More recently, in the new Rudd Labor government, Julia Gillard heads up the 'super-ministry' of Education, Employment and Workplace Relations. When this appointment was announced, Heather Ridout of the Australian Industry Group supported the combination of portfolios by declaring 'they have synergies, clear synergies'. The spokesperson for the Minerals Council agreed, arguing that the super-ministry 'is the solution to the long-term skills crisis, while skilled immigration will continue to offer a band-aid solution in the short-term' (see Chapter 7 for discussion of the 'skills shortage' and 457 visas). He added: 'The (incoming Labor) government is looking to approximate what industry is doing, what businesses are doing and that is moving to direct relationships, moving to a better understanding of what the market needs in terms of the range of skills across the professions and the trades' (Vincent 2007).

At the 2020 Summit, a gathering of 1000 of the country's 'best' minds to generate new ideas for the Rudd government, education was located as part of the 'Productivity agenda stream', alongside skills, training, science and innovation. Headed by Gillard and Warwick Smith, who among other roles acts as Chair of the Advisory Board of Australian Capital Equity Pty Ltd., the stream agreed on three goals and ambitions:

- maximising wealth, excellence and equity by *driving up productivity* to the leading edge of developed countries;
- focusing on *human capital* through early childhood development, world-class education, skills formation and innovation;
- encouraging all Australians to realise their potential. (Gillard and Smith 2008; emphasis added)

We have here a long-standing and familiar narrative of education as the key to economic growth and international competitiveness. It is also a narrative that currently dominates Western industrialised views about education. In the sections to follow we shall see that lifelong learning and student-funded higher education, policies endorsed by many Western industrialised states, are both linked to this narrative. Asking how the 'problem' is represented in select contexts allows us to identify 'discursively constructed practices' that extend beyond singular geographical sites while keeping space open to reflect on contextual variation (see Popkewitz 1998, p. 12). In this way, a WPR approach offers a new kind of comparative policy study. Instead of looking to compare employment rates or labour force participation rates, for example, the focus is on how these issues are conceptualised and with what effects in different sites.

A WPR approach also encourages us to put in question singular narratives such as the one we have just identified about education. It does this by asking: if education is posed as the 'solution' to economic growth and international competitiveness, what is represented to be the 'problem'? And, what follows from this particular representation of the 'problem'? Here, as we shall see, the 'problem' is represented to be specific political subjects (people), and the need for them to attend to their 'skill' development and their 'flexibility'. The effects of this problem representation include dividing practices, both internally between those who are considered to have achieved this goal and those who are marked as 'failures', and externally in competition for international students (Q5).

Education and the 'culture wars'

While our focus in this chapter is *higher education* in Australia, it is important to extend our vision to other parts of the education sector. Consistently, as we saw above in our brief discussion of the location of education as a ministerial portfolio, higher education is positioned alongside 'training'. Past debates about whether or not education should be 'vocational' are bypassed in this creation of education and training as a singular and seamless field, dedicated to the production of 'citizen-workers'. The subject of this education (i.e. the one who receives it) is targeted in primary and secondary schooling with a renewed emphasis on 'core competencies' (Muller 1998) and 'literacy' (see Activity on '*Literacy for all*').

This particular representation of the 'problem' of education is soundly contested (Q6). Indeed, the extent of the contestation has led to the labelling of the debates around these topics as the 'culture wars'. On the one side there are expressed concerns about the 'lack of relevance' of course material that is not clearly instrumental (i.e. 'useful'). In this vein, former Prime Minister John Howard claimed that a revised national history curriculum that taught 'the central currents of our nation's development' was a victory over a 'postmodern culture of relativism' and the 'excesses of multiculturalism' (Grattan 2006; see Chapter 7). On the other side there are expressed concerns about the narrowness of an agenda focused almost exclusively on the three 'Rs' — reading, writing and (a)rithmetic.

'[T]he New Right has waged a cultural war against schools as part of a wider attempt to contest the emergence of new public cultures and social movements that have begun to demand that schools take seriously the imperatives of living in a multiracial and multicultural democracy. The contours of this cultural offensive are evident in the call by the Right for standardized testing, the rejection of multiculturalism and the development of curricula around what is euphemistically called a "common culture"' (Giroux 1996, p. x).

These debates carry over to discussions about the nature of educational research. The dominant and conventional narrative of 'useful' education aligns itself with an 'evidence-based approach', while those who are committed to a broader and less instrumental education invoke research techniques such as case-studies and action research. Importantly, as St Pierre (2006, p. 248) notes, the disagreement over research involves more than a dispute over methodologies. She identifies SBR (scientifically-based research), another name for EBR (evidence-based research), as a *form of governmentality*, 'a mode of power by which state and complicit nonstate institutions and discourses produce subjects that satisfy the aims of government policy' (St Pierre 2006, p. 259).

St Pierre's argument is supported in this text. Previous chapters (5 and 6) describe how difficult it has become for researchers to step outside of an 'evidence-based' discourse, and raise qualms about the narrowing of research agendas as a result. In effect, evidence-based approaches have become a form of 'knowledge', a 'truth'. Hence, it is not surprising to find the Productivity Stream agenda from the 2020 Summit, chaired by Gillard and Smith (2008, section 1.1), strongly endorsing *evidence-based* educational research and *evidence-based* policy: 'Better evidence: education policies should be guided by the principle of "what works?", and are underpinned by rigorous and scientific evaluations'. The way in which a WPR approach to policy constitutes itself in direct opposition to evidence-based policy is pursued in Chapter 10.

To understand the current ascendency of evidence-based policy and research, and of conventional 'competency-based' education we need to explore the ways in which governing practices work to shape subjectivity. As stated in earlier chapters, policy needs to be understood as *creative*, not as *reactive*, as creating both (understandings of) 'problems' and particular subjectivities. A WPR approach provides a methodology for mapping how this occurs (Q3) and for speculating on the consequences that accompany particular modes of governance (Q5). It allows us to identify the subjects we have become and to speculate about whether or not these are the subjects we wish to be. This kind of interrogation requires willingness to put in question categories of analysis that have become commonsense, such as 'evidence' and 'competence'. Other key terms, including 'human capital', 'lifelong learning' and 'literacy', need to be subjected to close scrutiny. The form of analysis offered here is an analysis of discourses (Q2).

Literacy for All

In 1998 the Howard-led Coalition government followed up its *National Literacy and Numeracy Plan* (1997) with *Literacy for All: the challenge for Australian Schools* (DEETYA 1998), which elaborated nine principles underpinning the Commonwealth Literacy Policies for Schools. Two of these principles were:

'All students will be given an equal opportunity to learn
If schooling fails to overcome educational disadvantage the Commonwealth bears the cost of this failure through its budgetary provision for unemployment benefits and social programmes. The Commonwealth will continue to provide targeted funding for educationally disadvantaged students by supplementing the funding of Australian schools to achieve specific national objectives. The major factors which are usually seen as placing educational outcomes at risk include socio-economic disadvantage, poverty, low parental expectation, disability, language background other than English, family or personal difficulties, geographic isolation, Indigenous background and gender.

Literacy for all
Australia will go a long way towards countering other forms of educational and social disadvantage if strong foundational literacy and numeracy skills are successfully taught to all children' (DEETYA 1998, Section 1.1).

- **How is the 'problem' of 'disadvantage' understood in these statements?**

- **How is 'equity' understood?**

- **Who and what is held responsible for a lack of 'literacy'?**

- **Are there any silences in this representation of the 'problem'?**

For this Activity see McInerney 2007.

Discourse and subjectification

Chapter 2 outlined in brief how discourse is understood in a WPR approach. There the point is made that discourses are not the same as speech or language. Rather discourses are well-bounded areas of social 'knowledge' (i.e. knowledges) that rely upon specific conceptual logics. Human sciences, such as psychiatry and political 'science', are discourses in this sense. Such 'disciplines' generally accept a conception of the individual as separate, independent and rational, as 'choice maker', unless of course some fail to meet that standard, in which case they become 'failed subjects' (Q2).

Importantly, discourses are not benign. Rather, they make things happen, most often through their wide acceptance as forms of 'truth'. One way to identify discourses, therefore, is to look for truth claims. Since 'evidence-based research' has achieved the status of 'truth' in this sense, it is helpful to think about it as a discourse. Asserting a sceptical stance in relation to claims to 'truth', a WPR approach encourages questioning such claims.

Genealogy provides a useful methodology to open up discourses to critical scrutiny (Q3). By tracking the emergence of a particular way of thinking – seeing when and where it was endorsed, and noting the institutional developments that marked and accompanied its acceptance – it becomes possible to see its accomplishment as a historical *event*. It follows that things could have been otherwise and hence that it is possible to think differently. As Bové explains, genealogy tries to locate:

> ... the power to produce statements which alone can be judged 'true' or 'false' within the knowledge/power system that produces 'truth' and its criteria within a culture ... [I]t is by recognizing this effect of power that genealogy does its work. Indeed, genealogy lets us confront how power constructs truth-producing systems in which propositions, concepts and representations generally assign value and meaning to the objects of the various disciplines that treat them. (Bové 1990, p. 57)

Genealogies require long, detailed records of decision-making and claims-making, together with the identification of specific institutional developments that support particular claims, or ways of seeing. In a book such as this one, as noted elsewhere, it is possible only to suggest the forms of questions and kinds of areas that require close scrutiny. Along similar lines St Pierre (2006, p. 243) notes that she will not attempt a 'careful genealogy' of evidence-based research, 'though no doubt that work needs to be done'. Rather, akin to the approach taken in this book, St Pierre undertakes to track 'to some extent, the discursive, juridical, and material formation of the truth of the concept SBR'.

This kind of study needs to be distinguished from a study of rhetoric, an important distinction given the increasing interest in rhetoric among policy scholars (e.g. Majone 1989). Policy scholars interested in the study of rhetoric are careful to distance themselves from the type of commonplace implication that rhetoric is *manipulation* of language use for political, or propaganda, purposes (i.e. 'just rhetoric'). Rather, rhetoric is described as 'acts of *persuasion*' which are inherent 'in policy and political processes, just as they are within all communications' (Nicoll and Edwards 2004, p. 45–6; emphasis added). In this view it is unsurprising, for example, that government policy statements lay claim to have, as objectives, to produce 'a fairer and more just society' (see Activity, '*A Fair Chance for All*', above), and to counter 'forms of educational and social disadvantage' (see Activity, '*Literacy for All*' above). Comments like these are clearly intended to incline people to accept that these interventions are positive, rather than negative, developments.

While acknowledging the usefulness of this kind of study of rhetoric, the analysis of discourses in a WPR approach asks different questions, such as – what makes it possible for governments to make these sorts of statements? What understandings of the key terms, 'fairness', 'justice' and 'disadvantage', for example, are assumed in these statements? Where do these understandings come from? And, have they been contested? Are there other meanings of these or related terms that have some status historically or currently? In a discourse analysis of this kind, moreover, political subjects are understood as *products of discourse*, rather than as discourse *users*. Studies of rhetoric, by contrast, even when not focused on language *manipulation*, still assume political subjects who are active in the *deliberate* task of persuasion. As explained in Chapter 2, a WPR approach is not interested in intentionality; hence, it does not study efforts to persuade.

This point of difference is important primarily because of the tendency to dismiss some government policy statements as 'rhetorical'. That is, if it is assumed that the government is involved in a project of persuasion, the way in which a 'problem' is represented might come to be seen simply as a part of that exercise. With this understanding, a WPR approach might be employed to *expose* 'problem representations' that were never meant to be fully supported. This would be a misuse of the methodology. To repeat, the objective is not to discern examples of persuasive language, but to identify and elaborate the deep conceptual underpinnings that allow certain kinds of claim to be made.

The key distinction here is the different way in which political subjects are conceptualised. The goal in a WPR approach is to understand the kind of subject we have (been encouraged to) become, not through deliberate attempts at persuasion, but through the full complex of knowledges brought to bear on how we think about ourselves. A quote from Rose (2000, p. 162; emphasis added), directly relevant to the topic in this chapter, assists us here. He states that national and international competitiveness are:

> … recoded, at least in part, in terms of the psychological, dispositional and aspirational capacities of those that make up the labour force . . . Personal employment and macro-economic health is to be ensured *by encouraging individuals* to 'capitalize' themselves, to invest in the management, presentation, promotion, and enhancement of their own economic capital as a capacity of their selves and as a lifelong project.

While Rose uses the term 'encouraging', he does *not* mean that it is possible to identify specific political actors who decided one day to *encourage* people to think about themselves as investors in (their own) human capital, to *persuade* them to think in this way (as in studies of rhetoric). Rather, the processes by which this particular type of individual emerges are complex – embedded in social and political practices, and in a multiplicity of sites, including professions such as psychology.

The concept of 'subjectification' (or subjectivisation) has been introduced to capture these broad processes (see Chapter 2). Subjectification is not the same as socialisation, which is a process of subject formation commonly associated with education. In socialisation, there are a number of people or institutional 'forces', such as teachers and schools, who act as 'socialisers', teaching students how to behave in ways deemed to be acceptable. Schools are commonly described as agents of socialisation in this sense, and it is a concept with which we are well familiar.

Subjectification operates at a deeper level than socialisation. The very concepts through which we think about ourselves and others play a part in subjectification. Hence, the whole of our intellectual tradition is implicated. There is no outside and no identifiable agent working on us in the way socialisation implies. Davies (1994, p. 75) describes a shift from the *humanist* concept of socialisation to the *poststructuralist* concept of subjectification in the following way: 'this then is a challenge to the humanist vision of one who essentially is, rather than being positioned as one who can or cannot speak in this way or that'. In this quote Davies is highlighting the distinction between a humanist conception of human beings as essences and the poststructuralist idea that human beings are shaped by their discursive positioning, by what discourses allow them to say and also block them from saying. For poststructuralists, therefore, the analytic task becomes identifying the *a priori* of talk (what comes before talk), the 'concepts, objects, strategies and subject positions that organize statements prior to individual reception' (Blackman 2001, p. 84). These broad historical systems of meaning constitute what Burchell describes as 'the contours of the "goldfish bowl" we inhabit' (Burchell 1993, p. 277 in Shore and Wright 1997, p. 17).

This conception of a 'discoursing subject' produced *within* rather than standing *outside* discourse requires a rethinking of 'agency' and of resistance, as noted in Chapter 2. On this topic the discourse theorist, Stephen Ball (1993), draws a distinction between 'policy as *discourse*' and 'policy as *text*'. The former is meant to highlight the limits imposed on what can be said, while the latter opens up a space for interpretation, and hence for contestation, in the process of implementation. While a WPR approach is also keenly interested in the possibility of contestation, it finds this distinction unviable since the whole point of an analysis of discourses, in poststructuralist analysis, is to emphasise the *lack of outside* to discourse and to discursive practices. Contestation in a WPR approach, therefore, does not involve *deliberate* undermining of policies we dislike through implementing them in ways that compromise their original intent, as is implied in Ball's 'policy as text' (in the same way that rhetoric implies *consciously* using language to persuade). Rather, in a WPR approach, contestation means reconsidering the basic concepts through which we organise our ways of thinking.

While there is no doubt that strategic intransigence does take place among some who have been charged with 'implementing' policies they dislike, as Ball identifies, these behaviours are not the focus of study here. Rather the key task in a WPR approach is to identify and scrutinise the forms of 'truth' we tend to take for granted, asking where these forms of truth come from (**Q3**) and whether or not it is useful to (try to) identify and reflect upon them critically (**Q4, Q6**). Clearly, this is no easy task. Still, it is possible to achieve a kind of reflexive introspection (see Chapter 2 on reflexivity) on who we have (been encouraged to) become. It is this task we now undertake through examining our selected 'practical texts':

- first, the *Higher Education Contribution Scheme* (HECS), introduced in 1989; and, second,
- the *Student Learning Entitlement* (SLE), introduced in 2003, with its commitment to an 'entitlement' for 'lifelong learning'.

WHO PAYS? *THE HIGHER EDUCATION CONTRIBUTION SCHEME*

On 23 August 1988, the Hawke Labor government endorsed an annual *Higher Education Contribution Scheme* (HECS), requiring students to pay a portion of the cost of university study. The scheme established loans which students had to pay back once they had graduated and were earning a specific level of income (see below). The statutory authority for the scheme is the *Higher Education Funding Act* (Australian Government 1988), which made grants of financial assistance to universities contingent on compliance with the requirement of HECS.

Applying Question 1 of a WPR approach, we ask – if HECS is the policy or proposal, what is the 'problem' represented to be? At the most basic level, HECS, which requires fees for university study, constitutes the 'problem' as *free* university education. In order to understand the basis of this problem representation, we need to proceed to ask Question 2 – what assumptions and preconceptions underpin this representation of the problem? We also need to reflect on how this representation of the 'problem' came to gain support (**Q3**).

To address Questions 2 and 3 it is necessary to consider context of several kinds:

- a 'long view' of developments in relation to university education and fees in Australia;
- background on fees and tertiary education in other Western industrialised countries;
- other changes in the higher education sector and their relationship to HECS.

Importantly, in Australia education is generally a state (as opposed to a federal) responsibility. However, the Commonwealth gives grants to universities, essential to their functioning. From their establishment, universities in every state other than Western Australia charged tuition fees until they were abolished by the Whitlam Federal Labor government in 1974. Whitlam and his Education Minister, Kim Beazley, put the case that university education was a public good, not a private benefit, and should therefore be publicly funded (Bessant *et al.* 2006, p. 317).

In 1987 the Hawke Labor government introduced an up-front administrative charge of $250 to be paid by all full-time students. The following year the Education Minister, John Dawkins, commissioned a review of higher education funding. The review committee (Wran 1988) recommended that students should contribute about one third of the cost of their course, but that this contribution should be deferrable and repaid as a levy (tax) once students earned better than average incomes.

This idea of income-contingent loans had been proposed by the American economist Milton Friedman in 1955. Most **OECD** countries either had or were considering student financing ('user pays') of higher education at the time of the Wran Committee. An economist at the Australian National University, Bruce Chapman, sat on the Wran Committee and played a pivotal role in the design of HECS.

HECS formed part of a larger package of reforms to the higher education sector introduced at this time. Commonly referred to as the 'Dawkins Revolution', the reforms included:

■ the conversion of all Colleges of Advanced Education (CAEs) into universities;
■ many mergers between universities and former CAEs;
■ a series of provisions requiring universities to provide plans, profiles and statistics justifying courses and research;
■ a shift in the funding mix for higher education institutions, reducing public funding and insisting that universities solicit funds from sources other than the government (e.g. consultancies, grants, etc.).

The backdrop to these changes was the economic situation in the mid-1980s and the political priority of the Hawke Labor government to appear fiscally sound. There was high unemployment at the time and the government wished to establish its economic credentials.

Question 2 of a WPR approach requires more in-depth reflection on the rationales and conceptual logics underpinning selected policies. Two concepts dominated the discussion surrounding the higher education reform package, including HECS: efficiency and equity. That is, the 'problem' requiring the introduction of HECS is represented to be both *in*efficiency and *in*equity in higher education. The argument ran thus:

■ Australia has to become internationally competitive.
■ Changes in the economy require a workforce with higher skill levels.
■ Therefore, a mass education system is required.
■ To fund expansion more resources are needed.
■ It is unfair for the 'middle class' and the 'wealthy', who fill the universities, to benefit from

a free university education funded by the taxes of ordinary workers (Bessant *et al.* 2006, p. 327).

■ Since students stand to benefit financially from higher education it is fair to get them to contribute towards that education.

These propositions reveal a number of assumptions that require analysis and reflection: first, that international competition should determine the shape of Australia's education system; second, that 'higher skills' will indeed make Australia internationally competitive; third, that financial benefit to students justifies 'user pays'; and fourth, that other options for funding university expansion, such as public funding, are neither viable nor equitable. These assumptions have become so commonplace that it is difficult to think outside them. A way forward is to identify key precepts underpinning these assumptions (**Q2**) and to trace their origins through conducting genealogies (**Q3**). Two key precepts that require scrutiny include: Becker's idea of 'human capital' and Reich's concept of 'symbolic workers'. Let us examine each in turn and how they are linked.

The notion of 'human capital' is currently ubiquitous in education and labour market policy, constituting a taken-for-granted 'truth'. For example, the Productivity stream at the 2020 Summit listed as a significant principle, to release the 'latent value in our human capital' (Gillard and Smith 2008, section 1.20; see above). The idea of human capital can be traced back to Mincer's 1958 article in *The Journal of Political Economy*, entitled 'Investment in Human Capital and Personal Income Distribution' (Mincer 1958). Becker (1964), of the '**Chicago School**' of economics, made the concept popular through his 1964 book, *Human Capital*. In Becker's view people 'invest' in their personal 'human' capital much in the same way as they invest in the physical means of production, such as factories and machines. Your 'rate of return' depends on how much you 'invest'. Education is considered to be a form of investment. This idea of education as investment in the self lies behind the proposition that students should pay part of their education costs. As the Wran Committee stated:

> Higher education in Australia provides its users with the opportunity to improve their social and economic circumstances. Graduates can expect higher lifetime incomes, on average, than the rest of the population because of higher starting wages, better promotion prospects and a reduced chance of being unemployed. They can also expect higher social status and enhanced personal fulfilment. (Wran 1988, p. 12)

To draw attention to the terms of this discussion is not to challenge their *accuracy*. That is, it is quite likely that tertiary education translates into higher wages, though some of the other claims in the quote (e.g. regarding 'personal fulfilment') are clearly more speculative. However, there is a need to think about the way in which the proposition about anticipated higher wages is used to justify 'user pays'. For example, there are questions to be asked about the kind of political subject assumed in human capital logic (**Q2**). Do people really 'stockpile' experiences, educational and otherwise, in this way? Or, are lives lived differently, with more complex reasons for seeking education and with a broader range of possible benefits?

In human capital theory, 'knowledge' is conceived of as a particular kind of 'product' (see Chapter 10). It is seen as expandable and self-generating, transportable and tradeable. There are links here to Reich's (1991) concept of 'symbolic workers'. Reich divides American jobs into three broad categories:

- routine production jobs, such as old blue-collar jobs and routine supervisory jobs;
- in-person service jobs, such as waiters, police, dentists and doctors;
- symbolic analytic services provided by people who manipulate symbols, e.g. data, words, audio and visual images, and who can be either professionals or technicians.

In the new 'knowledge economy', Reich argues, symbolic workers are privileged because of the demand internationally for their 'skills'. Moreover, in his view, because this group is highly mobile, they pose a challenge to conventional national economies. Reich is particularly concerned that public policy addresses the deepening economic divisions between 'symbolic workers' and other workers. To this end he suggests: a genuinely progressive income tax; providing for *all* Americans to become symbolic analysts by investing in education at all levels; and addressing the plight of the long-term poor. In his view:

> . . . human capital can be developed and competitive advantage can be acquired if a group of people in a nation gain experience doing complex things, such as research development, applications engineering, fabrications, or other complex knowledge-intensive activities . . . The skills people need to develop have to do with *problem solving* and identification, developing critical facilities, understanding the value of experimentation and the ability to collaborate. (Morrison 1991, p. 5; emphasis added)

To date, the idea of a *genuinely* progressive income tax finds few supporters. Reich's second and third proposals, however, underpin the thinking behind the Dawkins reforms. Mass higher education is seen to provide the (analytic) skills to allow Australians to compete in the new 'knowledge economy'. As stated at a 1988 *Intergovernmental Conference on Education and the Economy in a Changing Society*, 'the skills and qualifications of workers are coming to be viewed as critical determinants of effective performance of enterprises and economies' (OECD 1989, p. 18). Dawkins, who chaired the conference, concluded: 'We recognise that failure in education and training – in the form of drop-out, low skills or poor retention – represents a wasted investment and a cost to society' (Dawkins 1989, p. 111).

Within this 'new' global economic discourse, Becker's concept of human capital is retained but significantly *reframed*. It is no longer *precise* skills that are prized, but *adaptability*. People are told they need to learn *how to learn* so that they will be flexible enough to keep pace with rapidly changing economic factors (Alheit and Dansien 2002). This emphasis on making workers *flexible* assumes, of course, that workers have to fit the needs of employers (**Q2**). The work context is taken as given and *in*flexible (**Q4**). As Rose (2000, p. 161) explains, 'The new citizen is required to engage in a ceaseless work of training and retraining, skilling and reskilling, enhancement of credentials and preparation for a life of incessant job seeking: life is to become a continuous economic capitalization of the self'. There are clear links here with the concept of 'lifelong learning', which has become shorthand for the proposition that political subjects ought to undertake a lifelong commitment to reskill when necessary – a topic pursed through our second selected text, later in the chapter.

The Dawkins' Revolution

In December 1987 John Dawkins, the Education Minister, released a Green Paper, *Higher Education: A Policy Discussion Paper*, explaining the rationale for the package of reforms planned for the higher education sector. It read:

'An expansion of the higher education system is important for several reasons. A better educated and more highly skilled population will be able to deal more effectively with change. A major function of education is, after all, to increase individuals' *capacity to learn*, to provide them with a framework with which to *analyse problems* and to increase their capacity to *deal with new information*. At the same time, education facilitates *adaptability*, making it easier for individuals to learn skills related to their intended profession and improve their ability to learn while pursuing their profession' (Dawkins 1987, p. 1; emphasis added).

- **How are workers conceptualised in this representation of the 'problem'?**

- **Are there any silences?**

The Dawkins 'revolution' included proposals to deal with the 'long-term poor' in the 1990 Discussion Paper, *A Fair Chance for All*. Remembering that a WPR approach requires repeated interrogation of policy proposals (see 'nesting' in Chapter 1), we need to ask – what kind of a 'problem' is 'inequity' represented to be in a *Fair Chance*? Above (see Activity on '*A Fair Chance for All*') we reflected upon the *meaning of* equity within this Discussion Paper and how it constituted 'disadvantaged' groups, specifically women, as 'citizen-workers'. In terms of *diagnosing* the 'problem' of 'inequity', a *Fair Chance* (Commonwealth of Australia 1990, p. vi) noted that 'much progress towards achieving equity goals can be made without the need for the institution to commit substantial resources, but instead by working towards behavioural changes on the part of academic and administrative staff'. Here 'inequity' is constituted as a behavioural, rather than as a structural, 'problem'.

Developments since that time suggest the *limitations* of this problem representation (**Q4**). Public funding of education has declined significantly while HECS has consistently been increased (see 'Education at a Glance' and 'A History of Fees' below). The prospect of a large HECS debt acts as a deterrent to particular groups of students – women, Aboriginal students, the poor – reinscribing dividing practices among the student population. Universities, starved of funds, have been compelled to commercialise their activities by seeking international fee-paying students and by impelling university staff to seek outside funding. Class sizes have risen significantly, with the quality of teaching falling, despite the best efforts of dedicated staff (Stretton 2005, p. 175). The shift in financing also creates 'a new dynamic in the learning process, as it moves towards a fee-for-service, client relationship' (Allport 2000, p. 42). As University of Melbourne Vice-Chancellor Glyn Davis (2006, p. 10) describes, the effects (**Q5**) are ironic: 'the system growth that has improved their chances of getting to university simultaneously produced a more crowded and less well resourced institution than the university fondly remembered by parents'. The 'race' for international students, meanwhile, puts us in mind of 457 visas and international competition for skilled labourers (see Chapter 7), introducing dividing practices at the international level.

Education at a Glance

The OECD's 2007 Report, *Education at a Glance*, identifies the following patterns in higher education spending:

- Australia is 25th of 29 OECD countries in the level of public funding of tertiary education as a proportion of GDP;
- Australia is the only OECD country where the total level of public funding of tertiary education *decreased* between 1995 and 2007;
- Total public funding in Australia fell by 4 per cent over this period, while the average OECD country public funding of tertiary education rose by 49 per cent;
- In Australia 52.8 per cent of tertiary funding was from *private* sources in 2004, the third highest level in the OECD after Korea, the USA and Japan, having increased from 35.2 per cent in 1995;
- Tuition fee levels in Australia's public universities are the third highest in the OECD after the USA and Japan;
- The fall of 4 per cent in public investment in tertiary education in Australia occurred while tertiary student numbers increased by 31 per cent

(Marginson 2007; OECD 2007).

At the discursive level it has become difficult, but not impossible, to talk about the broad public benefits of university education, such as the sharing and testing of ideas. A significant obstacle blocking this alternative view of education is the way in which the accumulation of a HECS debt produces subjects who (have to) think of themselves as 'entrepreneurs of themselves'. Recognising that policy is a creative, rather than a reactive, process means recognising the ways in which

HECS produces the subjects it assumes – individuals intent on education as an investment in their own economic success, which becomes necessary to pay off their HECS debt **(Q5)**.

Importantly, there remain spaces for contestation. While many students go to university to acquire credentials to secure their economic futures, at times they seek out courses for other than instrumental goals. Policy is formative rather than determinative **(Q6)**. Still, voices defending the idea of education as a public service and as a community good are muted. The dominant paradigm has become an education market, steered from the background by governments, in which students and parents are consumers, teachers and academics are producers, and educational administrators are managers and entrepreneurs.

> 'When governments imagine students to be financial investors in their own economic futures, and consistent with this vision, provide student financing in the form of student loans repayable after education, forcing students to take into account their future earnings when choosing their course, more of those students *become* self-managing investors in themselves. These economic behaviours are never as complete as the theory imagines. The student subjects also have other identities and behaviours, and no one is ever completely "governed". Nevertheless, the point is that joined to government, the economics of education forms the objects of which it speaks. It produces itself as true' (Marginson 1997, p. 225; emphasis in original).

'A course to nowhere'

In a newspaper article former editor and publisher Hilary McPhee describes her experience of speaking to year 12 students about their possible futures. She wanted, she explained, to excite them, to suggest that 'A life designed around money-making was an impoverished life'. Her comments, she reports, fell flat. McPhee notes that the vast majority of the 16- and 17-year-olds in her audience had decided to study subjects such as economics, accountancy, legal and computer studies. She explains the focus on vocational subjects thus:

'HECS, a teacher explained to me afterwards, concentrates the minds of final-year students. They know they will be graduating with sizeable debts, or beholden to parents who paid up front. Their real choices lie with salaries and career paths' (McPhee 2001).

- **What does it mean to say that policy is a creative rather than a reactive process?**

- **How would you describe the subjectification effects of HECS?**

- **Is there space for contestation? What would contestation involve?**

Volunteering for education?

One of the proposals put forward by the Productivity stream of the 2020 Summit was to allow students to undertake volunteer work to start paying off their HELP (formerly HECS) debt. The proposal was to establish 'Community Corps', an idea borrowed from the volunteer network called AmeriCorps in the United States.

- **How does the idea of volunteer work to pay off HECS represent the 'problem' of education? Of HECS? Of volunteering?**

- **Are there any silences?**

For this Activity see Warburton and Smith 2003.

A History of Fees

1989   The Hawke government introduces a deferred loan scheme, called the Higher Education Contribution Scheme (HECS);

1997   So-called differential HECS introduced, which charges different HECS fees for different courses; fees are increased;

1998   Full fee places introduced for domestic undergraduate courses, capped at 25 per cent of a course;

2005   Individual universities allowed to increase HECS fees by 25 per cent, with the exception of teaching and nursing courses. Institutions allowed to increase the quota of fee-paying students in a course from 25 per cent to 35 per cent. A new deferred loan scheme (FEE-HELP) for fee paying domestic undergraduate students is introduced, capped at $50 000. A Student Learning Entitlement (SLE) of 7 years maximum full-time or 14 years part-time is introduced (see discussion below). Post 2007 HECS loans are called HECS-HELP.

2007   The cap is 'lifted on how many full-fee places universities can offer. Full-fee degrees cost up to $250 000.' (Morton 2007)

LIFELONG LEARNING: AN EDUCATIONAL 'ENTITLEMENT'?

Our second 'practical text', the *Student Learning Entitlement* (SLE), bears a direct connection to HECS. Indeed it forms part of the changes to HECS introduced by the Howard-led government in 2005 (see 'The History of Fees'). However, it adds a new element to the mix – lifelong learning, which will be the particular focus in this section.

The SLE gives eligible students access to seven years' equivalent full-time study as a 'Commonwealth supported student'. This means that the Australian government provides a *contribution* towards study costs via the Commonwealth Grants Scheme, with students paying the remaining fee amount, known as their *Student Contribution*. Students can access HELP (formerly HECS) to cover their proportion of the costs with income-contingent loans. Commonwealth-supported students also receive a Lifelong Learning Entitlement to use towards upgrading their qualifications or re-training: 'Once a person is eligible to accrue Lifelong SLE, they receive the equivalent of 1 EFTSL [Equivalent full-time study load] of Lifelong SLE in the first year, and 0.125 EFTSL of Lifelong SLE each following year' (Australian Government 2008).

As with many of the key terms introduced in this book, the concept of 'lifelong learning' has a history. Its roots can be traced back to the 1960s and 1970s, when non-governmental organisations like UNESCO (United Nations Educational, Scientific and Cultural Organization) initially promulgated lifelong learning as concerned with 'the holistic formation of a well-rounded, civically aware, personally fulfilled and critically minded citizen' (Mitchell 2006, p. 391). The term more commonly used at that time was 'recurrent education', with connections to education reformers like Freire and to the idea of de-institutionalising education (Tuschling and Engemann 2006, p. 460).

Currently, a distinction is drawn between minimalist and maximalist approaches to lifelong learning: the former, with links to 'recurrent education', concentrates on voluntary, accessible, adult educational facilities, and demands sufficient funding to provide such learning; the latter, while it also stresses the importance of learning outside of traditional educational contexts, places the individual at the centre of the process, responsible for their educational prospects and for co-financing education (**Q2**). The minimalist position, sometimes referred to as the 'first career' of lifelong learning, is closely tied to Becker's original concept of human capital as skill acquisition. The 'maximalist' model is linked to the reframed understanding of human capital as adaptability, associated with Reich. It is based on a paradigm of knowledge as 'know *how*' (rather than 'know *what*') – in effect, it is about learning *how* to learn (see discussion above).

The distinction between minimalist and maximalist versions of lifelong learning should not be drawn too sharply. In fact, the move from Becker's human capital to Reich's adaptable 'symbolic workers' is a relatively easy one, based on the common premise that human subjects are investors in themselves. This deep-seated conceptual logic (**Q2**) lies at the heart of the ambivalence around the education project, discussed at the outset of this chapter. A vision of education as *improvement* assumes subjects who need to be improved, leaving undiscussed the meaning of 'improvement' (**Q4**).

Still, the more recent, maximalist incarnation of the reform is much more explicitly instrumentalist. For example, EU funding for lifelong learning typically goes into workplace training programs rather than into curricula emphasising social or civic education, as had happened previously. Expenditure on lifelong workplace training represents the 'problem' to be the need to make workers 'job ready' and mobile (Q1). In the European context this representation of the 'problem' emerges due to the expressed need to ease the flow of labour across (internal) European borders (Q3). To this end it is held to be crucial that training and education qualifications be comparable and transparent. Labour mobility and flexibility is contrasted with 'labour market rigidity', referring to labour standards and trade union activity (Ainley and Corbett 1994, p. 369), which come to be understood as part of the 'problem' (Q2). Through mechanisms such as the Europass, which make it easier for individual European migrants to be assimilated into the labour market (Mitchell 2006, pp. 392, 398; see Chapter 7), people become 'secretaries of their own being', producing a new 'regime of documentation of oneself' (Tuschling and Engermann 2006, pp. 461–4; Q5).

Towards a European Qualifications Framework for Lifelong Learning

In July 2005 the European Commission produced a paper outlining the main features of a possible future European Qualifications Framework (EQF) as a 'meta-framework that will enable qualifications frameworks at national and sectoral level to relate and communicate to each other thus developing transparency at the European level':

'A principal function of an EQF would be to strengthen mutual trust and co-operation between the different stakeholders in lifelong learning. This is important for reducing barriers to recognition of learning and for enabling learners to make better use of available knowledge, skills and competences. Its role would furthermore be to enable and promote mobility of learners and labour market mobility' (European Commission 2005, p. 8).

- **What is the 'problem' of 'lifelong learning' represented to be in this proposal?**

- **Are there any silences?**

For this Activity see Cort 2008.

The current dominant understanding of 'lifelong learning' as extended investment in the self sits alongside a cluster of related concepts – the 'knowledge-based economy', 'knowledge cities', the 'learning society', the 'information society', 'knowledge production' (see Chapter 10) – a cluster firmly established in contemporary international educational discourse. This 'colonisation of education policy by economic policy imperatives', as Ball (1998, p. 122) describes it, 'travels' via several routes (Q6):

- the 'inter-national circulation of ideas' (Popkewitz 1998);
- processes of policy 'borrowing' (Halpin and Troyna 1995);

■ the role of policy entrepreneurs who sell their ideas through journals and books;

■ the enforcement of particular policy 'solutions' by multinational agencies, in particular the World Bank;

■ the proliferation of support professionals and the development of conceptually friendly sub-disciplines, such as behavioural industrial psychology (Ainley and Corbett 1994, p. 369).

Sidhu and Matthews (2005, p. 6) highlight the role played by the 'cultural circuit of capital', the trinity of business schools, management consultants and business gurus, in the process of disseminating this particular way of thinking about education. They also mention that the media 'promote the idea of the naturalness of the knowledge based economy' (see Chapter 10), portraying education as a 'tradeable commodity' driven by consumer choice. As Sidhu and Matthews (2005, p. 9) point out, this version of events silences 'the active role of governments in driving demand by reducing funding for national educational institutions and developing educational export industries' (Q3, Q4).

In a WPR approach there is no suggestion of a plot, perhaps of evil capitalists, in these developments. Rather, the contention is that the combination of circumstances leading to the present is unpredictable and fluid, taking place through *assemblages* of people and institutions. Importantly, through subjectification processes, we all become *part* of these assemblages and hence of these developments. This idea makes it easier to understand why it is so difficult to contest the notion of lifelong learning, which has become something of a motherhood statement. Still, it remains important to reflect on how particular incarnations of the proposal represent the 'problem' quite differently and with differential effects for particular groups of political subjects. A WPR approach encourages exactly this kind of analysis, seeking out competing problem representations and comparing their effects (Q5) in order to decide which scenario accomplishes most good and does least harm for different social groups.

Lifelong learning in Australia

In Australia, as elsewhere, the discourse of lifelong learning has its roots in the 1970s idea of 'recurrent education', but has since become tied more and more closely to a *market-oriented* agenda. As Axford and Sneddon (2006, p. 170) describe, lifelong learning is now part of a wider discursive formation that privileges an 'individuation of society'. More precisely, the focus has shifted 'from individuals as citizens with citizen rights to individuals as consumers with consumer rights' (Axford and Sneddon 2006, p. 167). There is no call to dismantle educational institutions, but there is a symbolic 'outsourcing of learning from the education system into the lives of individuals' (Tuschling and Engemann 2006, p. 457). To date, the Lifelong Student Entitlement is the closest that Australia has come to a *formal* lifelong learning policy. Support for the concept is bi-partisan, however, and therefore further developments can be anticipated.

The idea of a Student Learning Entitlement can be traced back to the West Report of 1998, named after the chair, Roderick West (Q3). On the one hand, West endorsed the dominant narrative that we have already identified, of individual responsibility for 'learning and choosing when to learn': 'The individual should be prepared to explore learning options and to invest time, money and effort' (West 1998, p. 44). On the other hand, the West Committee argued that 'the Government should aim to provide all school leavers, and mature age students who are seeking access to postsecondary education for the first time, with *an entitlement to tuition funding*' (West 1998, p. 120; emphasis added). West (1998, p. 132) identified the 'duration of any entitlement' as 'one important mechanism for controlling government outlays'.

The current SLE follows West's last piece of advice: by imposing strict limits on both the SLE and the Lifelong Learning 'entitlement', government outlays are limited. However, it does *not* adopt his first recommendation – that students have an *entitlement to tuition funding*. Rather, students are 'entitled' to seven years of equivalent full-time study load, *for which they will pay fees*, and will accrue limited amounts of Lifelong Study Entitlement, *also to be self-funded* (Q3).

Our Universities: Backing Australia's Future (Commonwealth of Australia 2003, p. 19; emphasis added) claims that the 'Learning Entitlement will provide greater opportunities for more students to gain access to Commonwealth supported higher education places as new entrants occupy places freed by students who have *consumed their entitlement*'. This idea of a learning 'entitlement' that will be 'consumed' sits in direct opposition to the more expansive idea of lifelong learning endorsed in earlier (minimalist) versions of the reform as on-going, accessible and *publicly* funded. Rather, lifelong learning under the SLE will be largely *self-funded*, reinforcing the dynamic described above where students come to see education as a market product and an economic 'investment'. An additional effect is that distinctions between those who have the necessary funds to 'invest' in lifelong learning, and those who do not have those funds will be sharpened. Only some, it seems, will be lifelong learners, acquiring the 'skills' necessary to compete in the 'new' global economy (Q5).

Based on this analysis it is possible to challenge the market-oriented, self-funded lifelong learning model. The argument, however, does not take up a position for or against lifelong learning. Rather, as with the ambivalence at the heart of the education project introduced at the beginning of this chapter, the point of intervention is reflection on the kinds of subjects particular strategies of governing (here, particular models of lifelong learning) produce. There is no suggestion that these modes of governance can be escaped but that, due to variability in their specifics, some are more harmful than others.

In this chapter it has been suggested that a *self-funded* model of lifelong learning produces subjects who view the world through an economic lens, and is therefore less likely to encourage interpersonal recognition and cultural sharing than a *publicly-funded* model. The same can be said of self-funded higher education generally. It has also been suggested that it is important to think through how we have arrived at a point where self-funded higher and 'lifelong' education is widely accepted as 'truth' **(Q3)**. The role played by the concept of human capital as a linchpin between earlier, more expansive versions of lifelong learning, sometimes called progressive, and recent market-oriented versions has been emphasised. This kind of analysis highlights the importance of subjecting taken-for-granted precepts in our intellectual heritage to genealogical and reflexive scrutiny.

SUMMARY

In this chapter we explored a number of current debates about education and education policy. We identified ambivalence at the heart of the education project between a desire to 'liberate' political subjects and an imperative to produce them as well-behaved citizens. This ambivalence hinges on the kind of political subject imagined in the education project. Our 'practical texts', HECS and the SLE, including lifelong learning, constitute the political subject as independent, self-produced and self-regulating **(Q5)**. The extent to which this model of political subjectivity ignores embodied and social relationships, and sets up dividing practices, which tend to exclude specific social groups, raises questions about its desirability. The complexities involved in contesting this educational narrative, given its discursive dominance and our positioning as 'discoursing subjects', are also discussed.

QUESTIONS

1. What norms are currently encouraged in Australian institutions of higher education through policies such as HELP (formerly HECS) and SLE?
2. Do these norms exclude some people? If so, who is likely to be excluded?
3. To what extent is the normative position filled by 'economic man'?
4. Is education necessarily normalising?

REFERENCES

AINLEY, P. & CORBETT, C. 1994, 'From Vocationalism to Enterprise: Social and Life Skills Become Personal and Transferable', *British Journal of Sociology of Education*, vol. 15, no. 3, pp. 365–74.

ALHEIT, P. & DANSIEN, B. 2002, 'The "Double Face" of Lifelong Learning: Two Analytical Perspectives on a "Silent Revolution"', *Studies in the Education of Adults*, vol. 34, no. 1, pp. 3–21.

ALLPORT, C. 2000, 'Thinking Globally, Acting Locally: Lifelong Learning and the Implications for University Staff', *Journal of Higher Education Policy and Management*, vol. 22, no. 1, pp. 37–46.

AUSTRALIAN GOVERNMENT 1988, *Higher Education Funding Act*, Attorney-General's Department, Canberra, <www.comlaw.gov.au>, accessed 27 October 2008.

AUSTRALIAN GOVERNMENT 2008, 'Being Eligible & Student Learning Entitlement', Department of Education, Employment and Workplace Relations, Canberra, <www.goingtouni.gov.au>, accessed 4 June 2008.

AXFORD, B. & SNEDDON, T. 2006, 'Lifelong Learning in a Market Economy: Education, Training and the Citizen-Consumer', *Australian Journal of Education*, vol. 50, no. 2, pp. 167–184.

BALL, S. J. 1993, 'What is Policy? Texts, Trajectories and Toolboxes', *Discourse: The Australian Journal of Educational Studies*, vol. 13, no. 2, pp. 10–17.

BALL, S. J. 1998, 'Big Policies/Small World: An Introduction to International Perspectives in Education Policy', *Comparative Education*, vol. 34, no. 2, pp. 119–30.

BECKER, G. S. 1964, *Human Capital: A Theoretical and Empirical Analysis, with Special Reference to Education*, National Bureau of Economic Research, distributed by Columbia University Press, New York.

BESSANT, J., WATTS, R., DALTON, T. & SMYTH, P. 2006, *Talking Policy: How Social Policy is Made*, Allen & Unwin, Sydney.

BLACKMAN, L. 2001, *Hearing Voices: Embodiment and Experience*, Free Association Books, London.

BOVÉ, P. A. 1990, 'Discourse', in *Critical Terms for Literary Study*, eds F. Lentricchia & T. McLaughlin, University of Chicago Press, Chicago.

BURCHELL, G. 1993, 'Liberal Government and Techniques of the Self', *Economy and Society*, vol. 22, no. 3, pp. 267–82.

COMMONWEALTH OF AUSTRALIA 1990, *A Fair Chance for All: National and Institutional Planning for Equity in Higher Education*, A Discussion Paper, Department of Employment, Education and Training, National Board of Employment, Education and Training, Australian Government Publishing Services, Canberra.

COMMONWEALTH OF AUSTRALIA 2003, *Our Universities: Backing Australia's Future*, Policy Paper, Department of Education, Science and Training, Australian Government Publishing Services, Canberra.

CONNELL, R. W. 1993, *Schools and Social Justice*, Temple University Press, Philadelphia.

CORT, P. 2008, 'VET Policy Formation and Discourse in the EU: A Mobile Work Force for a European Labour Market?', in *Divergence and Convergence in Education and Work*, eds V. Aarkrog & C. H. Jorgensen, Peter Lang, Berlin.

DAVIES, B. 1994, *Poststructuralist Theory and Classroom Practice*, Deakin University, Geelong, Victoria.

DAVIS, G. 2006, 'Campus Unrest', *Australian Financial Review*, 10 February, pp. 1 & 2, 10 & 11.

DAWKINS, J. 1987, *Higher Education: A Discussion Paper*, AGPS (Australian Government Publishing Service), Canberra.

DAWKINS, J. 1989, 'Conclusions of the Chairman', *Intergovernmental Conference on Education and the Economy in a Changing Society*, OECD, Paris.

DEETYA (Department of Education, Employment, Training and Youth Affairs) 1998, *Literacy for All: The Challenge for Australian Schools*, DEETYA, Canberra.

EUROPEAN COMMISSION 2005, *Towards a European Qualifications Framework for Lifelong Learning*, Council of the European Union, Geneva, <www.tsu.ge/qa/doc/eqf.pdf>, accessed 16 October 2008.

FREIRE, P. 1973, *Education for Critical Consciousness*, Seabury Press, New York.

FREIRE, P. 1976, *Education, the Practice of Freedom*, Writers and Readers Publishing Cooperative, London.

GILLARD, J. & SMITH, W. 2008, *The Productivity Agenda: Education, Skills, Training, Science and Technology*, Final Report, 2020 Summit, Canberra, <www.australia2020.gov.au>, accessed 7 June 2008.

GIROUX, H. A. & McLAREN, P. L. 1989, *Critical Pedagogy, the State and Cultural Struggle*, State University of New York Press, New York.

GIROUX, H. A. 1996, 'Series Foreword', in *Poststructuralism, Politics and Education*, M. Peters, Bergin & Garvey, Westport, CT.

GIROUX, H. A. 2005, *Border Crossings: Cultural Workers in the Politics of Education*, Routledge, New York.

GRATTAN, M. 2006, 'Howard Claims Victory in National Culture Wars', *The Age*, 26 January.

HALPIN, D. & TROYNA, B. 1995, 'The Politics of Education Borrowing', *Comparative Education*, vol. 31, no. 3, pp. 303–10.

MAJONE, G. 1989, *Evidence, Argument and Persuasion in the Policy Process*, Yale University Press, New Haven, CT.

MARGINSON, S. 1997, 'Subjects and Subjugation: The Economics of Education as Power-Knowledge', *Discourse: Studies in the Cultural Politics of Education*, vol. 18, no. 2, pp. 215–27.

MARGINSON, S. 2007, 'The 2007 Edition of Education at a Glance: Where Does Australia Sit in the OECD Comparison?', University of Melbourne, Centre for the Study of Higher Education, Seminar Series, 'Ideas and Issues in Higher Education', 15 October, <www.cshe.unimelb.edu.au>, accessed 10 June 2008.

McINERNEY, P. 2007, 'The Ethics of Problem Representation in Public Education Policy: From Educational Disadvantage to Individual Deficits', *Policy and Society*, Special Issue: *Ethics and Public Policy*, eds C. Bacchi & P. Jewell, vol. 26, no. 3, pp. 83–96.

McPHEE, H. 2001, 'A Course to Nowhere', *The Age*, 4 August.

MINCER, J. 1958, 'Investment in Human Capital and Personal Income Distribution', *The Journal of Political Economy*, vol. 66, no. 4, pp. 281–302.

MITCHELL, K. 2006, 'Neoliberal Governmentality in the European Union: Education, Training, and Technologies of Citizenship', *Environment and Planning D: Society and Space*, vol. 24, no. 3, pp. 389–407.

MORRISON, T. 1991, 'Interview with Robert B. Reich', Aurora Online, <http://aurora.icaap.org>, accessed 6 August 2008.

MORTON, A. 2007, 'Degree in Debt is Students' Reality', *The Age*, 29 September.

MULLER, J. 1998, 'The Well-Tempered Learner: Self-Regulation, Pedagogical Models and Teacher Education Policy', *Comparative Education*, vol. 34, no. 2, pp. 177–93.

NICOLL, K. & EDWARDS, R. 2004, 'Lifelong Learning and the Sultans of Spin: Policy as Persuasion', *Journal of Education Policy*, vol. 19, no. 1, pp. 43–55.

OECD 1989, *Education and the Economy in a Changing Society*, OECD, Paris.

OECD 2007, *Education at a Glance*, <www.oecd.org>, accessed 10 June 2008.

POPKEWITZ, T. S. 1998, 'The Culture of Redemption and the Administration of Freedom as Research', *Review of Educational Research*, vol. 68, no. 1, pp. 1–34.

POPKEWITZ, T. S., OLSSON, U. & PETERSSON, K. 2007, 'The Learning Society, the Unfinished Cosmopolitan, and Governing Education, Public Health and Crime Prevention at the Beginning of the Twenty-First Century', in *The Learning Society from the Perspective of Governmentality*, eds J. Masschelein, M. Simons, U. Brockling & L. Pongratz, Blackwell Publishing, Oxford.

REICH, R. B. 1991, *Work of Nations: Preparing Ourselves for 21st-Century Capitalism*, A. A. Knopf, New York.

ROSE, N. S. 2000, *Powers of Freedom: Reframing Political Thought*, 1st edition 1999, Cambridge University Press, Cambridge, UK.

SHORE, C. & WRIGHT, S. 1997, *Anthropology of Policy: Critical Perspectives on Governance and Power*, Routledge, New York.

SIDHU, R. & MATTHEWS, J. 2005, 'International Education for What? Under What Conditions? The Global Schoolhouse Project', *Social Alternatives*, vol. 24, no. 4, pp. 6–12.

ST PIERRE, E. A. 2006, 'Scientifically Based Research in Education: Epistemology and Ethics', *Adult Education Quarterly*, vol. 56, no. 4, pp. 239–66.

STRETTON, H. 2005, *Australia Fair*, University of New South Wales Press, Sydney.

THOMSON, P. 2001 'The Sound of One Hand Grasping at Straws? Struggles for Quality and Equity in Public School Education', in *Left Directions: Is There a Third Way?* eds P. Nursey-Bray & C. Bacchi, University of Western Australia Press, Perth.

TUSCHLING, A. & ENGEMANN, C. 2006, 'From Education to Lifelong Learning: The Emerging Regime of Learning in the European Union', *Educational Philosophy and Theory*, vol. 38, no. 4, pp. 451–69.

VINCENT, M. 2007, 'Gillard's Super-Ministry a "Very Ambitious Task"', *ABC News*, 30 November, <www.abc.net.au>, accessed 7 June 2008.

WEST, R. 1998, *Learning for Life: Final Report. Review of Higher Education Financing and Policy*, Higher Education Financing and Policy Review Committee, Department of Employment, Education, Training and Youth Affairs, Canberra.

WARBURTON, J. & SMITH, J. 2003, 'Out of the Generosity of Your Heart: Are We Creating Active Citizens Through Compulsory Volunteer Programmes for Young People in Australia?', *Social Policy and Administration*, vol. 37, no. 7, pp. 772–86.

WRAN, N. 1988, *Report of the Committee on Higher Education Funding*, Department of Employment, Education and Training, Commonwealth Government, Australian Government Publishing Services, Canberra.

FURTHER READING

MASSCHELEIN, J., SIMONS, M., BRÖCKLING, U. & PONGRATZ, L. eds 2007, *The Learning Society from the Perspective of Governmentality*, Wiley-Blackwell, London.

MILLER, P. 1986, *Long Division: State Schooling in South Australia*, Wakefield Press, Adelaide.

POPKEWITZ, T. S. 1996, 'Rethinking Decentralisation and State/Civil Society Distinctions: The State as a Problematic of Governing', *Journal of Education Policy*, vol. 11, no. 1, pp. 25–48.

WATSON, L. 2003, *Lifelong Learning in Australia*, Department of Education, Science and Training, AGPS, Canberra, <www.dest.gov.au>, accessed 12 June 2008

WILLIS, P. & CARDEN, P. eds 2004, *Lifelong Learning and the Democratic Imagination: Revisioning Justice, Freedom and Community*, Post Pressed, Flaxton, Queensland.

'Knowledge production' in the 'information society': Media and research policy

Chapter 10

WE ARRIVE . . . AND HOPEFULLY KEEP GOING

It is appropriate that the question of 'knowledge' should be our final port of call. Chapter 9 prefigured some of the issues that need pursuing: What is a 'knowledge economy'? What or who are 'knowledge workers'?

Central to these concepts is a particular understanding of 'knowledge', also introduced briefly in Chapter 9 – 'knowledge' as expandable and self-generating, transportable and tradeable. In this view, the education reforms examined in Chapter 9, in particular lifelong learning, represent 'knowledge' as a particular kind of 'problem' – a 'problem' of access to 'information'. 'Knowledge' and 'information' are oftentimes treated as interchangeable concepts. Think, for example, of the 'knowledge society' and the 'information society', which both sit alongside the 'learning society'.

The goal of this chapter is to sort through some of these links in meaning, in the process reflecting critically:

- on the issues raised in Question 6 of a WPR approach – how/where are specific problem representations produced, disseminated and defended? How, if deemed to be appropriate, could they be questioned, disrupted and replaced?
- on the directive that follows Question 6 – to apply the list of questions in a WPR approach to one's own problem representations.

The roles played by the mass media and by academic research in the process of 'knowledge production' are our central focus.

In an opening section the chapter reviews and expands some key themes:

- the relationship between 'knowledge' and power;
- the place of the human sciences in governing;
- the meaning of 'subjugated knowledges'.

This first section explores connections between these themes and the cluster of concepts mentioned above, 'knowledge economy', 'information society', etc. It introduces the argument that an instrumental understanding of 'knowledge' as 'information' dominates contemporary public policy in Western liberal states and that this dominance is illustrated in the widespread endorsement of 'evidence-based policy' (a theme addressed in several chapters already). Particular attention is directed to the creation of the 'problem-solving' political subject as a part of this understanding. The case is made that a 'problem-solving' paradigm is gaining hegemonic status in contemporary reflections on 'knowledge', highlighting the importance of the challenge to this paradigm posed by a WPR approach.

The second section of the chapter follows a standard format, applying the questions in a WPR approach to a selection of 'practical texts'. In order to reflect on the place of the media in relationship to 'knowledge production', three 'practical texts' are scrutinised:

- *Australia's Strategic Framework for the Information Economy 2004–2006* (Australian Government 2004);
- *The Broadcasting Services Amendment (Media Ownership) Act 2006 (Cth)* (Australian Government 2006a);
- *Classification (Publications, Films and Computer Games) Amendment (Terrorist Material) Act,* 2007 (Commonwealth Numbered Acts, no. 179, 2007).

The last section of the chapter takes a slightly different tack. Through exploring the ways in which approaches to policy studies represent the 'problem' of policy, it illustrates that a WPR approach has an ambit beyond analysing policy, that it can be used to interrogate theoretical stances more generally. The point of this exercise is to highlight the *political implications* of theoretical 'knowledges'.

Reminder

The six questions in a WPR approach can be followed systematically – addressing each question separately and in order – as in Chapters 3 and 4. More commonly, the questions form part of an integrated analysis, with specific questions applied where the analysis occasions their use. This chapter follows the second, integrated form of analysis, employing the notation **Q1, Q2,** etc. where a specific question has been applied.

Thinking about 'knowledge'

Somewhat confusingly, the concept 'knowledge production' can have two meanings:

- on the one side, it appears alongside the cluster of 'knowledge' concepts problematised in this chapter (e.g. 'knowledge economy') and refers to the production of 'knowledge' as a marketable 'product', to be *produced* like other *products*;
- on the other side, the phrase 'knowledge production' is commonly associated with the sociology of knowledge and the social construction of knowledge – the suggestion that 'knowledge' is a *social* product.

On the one side is the idea that knowledge is produced like any other commodity; on the other, the social context in which what gets to count *as* knowledge becomes the focus of analysis.

The term 'knowledge production' has been placed in inverted commas in the title to this chapter to signal the contested usage of the term. The chapter applies the second meaning of 'knowledge' (as *social* product) to the first meaning of 'knowledge' (as *marketable* product), arguing that the latter meaning is a (social) product of late twentieth century, early twenty-first century ways of thinking in Western liberal states. To keep the perspective adopted in the chapter clear, I use the term 'knowledge *construction*' (as in the social construction of knowledge), rather than 'knowledge *production*', when referring to the malleable and contested nature of 'knowledge'.

Interrogating 'knowledges'

As indicated early in the book, a WPR approach adopts a sceptical stance to 'knowledge'. This scepticism does not mean arguing that some claims to knowledge are false and that others are true. Rather, it means exploring the *forms of knowledge* that are 'in the true', and the effects they have on how society is organised and governed.

The study of governmentality (see Chapters 2 and 7) highlights the point that 'knowledge' is crucial to governing. This is because, in order to rule or govern, it is necessary to have 'knowledge' about whom or what is to be governed. Here it is worth repeating a key quote from Foucault, explaining this point with specific reference to 'knowledge' about sexual behaviours:

> It was essential that the state know what was happening with its citizens' sex, and the use they made of it, but also that each individual be capable of controlling the use he made of it. Between the state and the individual, sex became an issue, and a public issue no less; a whole web of discourses, *special knowledges*, analyses, and similar injunctions settled upon it. (Foucault 1979, p. 26; emphasis added)

Following Foucault, a WPR approach is crucially interested in investigating the role of the human sciences in supplying 'special knowledges' and 'analyses' of 'population'. Recalling the broad understanding of governance in a governmentality approach, the human sciences are identified as engaged in the governance project. This stance contests the common understanding of academic or theoretical contributions to 'knowledge' as objective resources for the government to 'draw upon' to assist in governing. Rather, we are seen as governed, in part, through the ways in which 'scientific' theories construct us as particular kinds of being, through the kinds of 'truth' they produce. The way in which the notion of human capital creates political subjects as investors in themselves is one example of this relationship (see Chapter 9).

A key point here, pursued later in the chapter, is that researchers are central to this relationship since 'our research is itself a process of governing and constituting subjects' (Marston and MacDonald 2006, p. 225). Research is powerful 'knowledge'. The notion of power invoked here is the Foucauldian sense of power as productive. That is, research 'knowledge' *produces* specific kinds of political subjects and is powerful in this sense.

Psychiatry and social knowledge: 81 Words

Up until 1972 homosexuality was listed under 'sexual deviations' in the *American Psychiatric Association's Diagnostic and Statistical Manual of Mental Disorders* (*DSM*), a volume that contains all the recognised psychiatric disorders and symptoms. First published in 1952 (American Psychiatric Association 1952), it is currently in its fourth edition (*DSM-IV*) (American Psychiatric Association 1994). In the 1952 edition homosexuality was described as a psychiatric 'problem' called 'sexual deviance'. In 1974 the 'diagnosis' of homosexuality as 'sexual deviance' was modified and now referred to 'sexual orientation disturbance' or 'ego-distonic homosexuality', which described homosexuality as pathological only if it caused 'subjective distress'. This reference to homosexuality was removed in 1987. The fifth edition of the *Manual* is due for publication in 2012.

- **How does this abbreviated history of the shifting definition of homosexuality in psychiatric terms contribute to understanding the notion of *social* knowledge (knowledge as socially constructed)?**
- **What does it contribute to the broad understanding of governance developed in a WPR approach?**

For this Activity see Spiegel's (2002) documentary '81 Words'.

There is another aspect of the knowledge-power relationship that needs exploring – the issue of who is best placed to produce 'knowledges' that will count as 'truth', and how they secure their position/s of influence. Foucault was expressly concerned with this issue, as we saw in Chapter 1. He asks: 'What individuals, what groups or classes have access to a particular kind of discourse? How is the relationship institutionalized between the discourse, speakers and its destined audience?' (1991c, p. 60).

A recommended way to proceed in addressing these questions is to chart the 'rules of formation' of discursive practices (see Chapter 2) – to identify 'the conditions of exercise, functioning, and institutionalization of scientific discourses' (Foucault 1991, p. 65). Questions 3 and 6 of a WPR approach undertake these tasks. Question 3 directs attention to the institutional processes by which specific problem representations become ensconced as 'truth'. Question 6 calls more directly for exploration of the means used to produce, disseminate and defend these problem representations.

There is doubtless a suggestion of instrumentality in relation to Question 6 that appears to sit uneasily with the rest of a WPR approach. Question 6 reads: How/where has this representation of the 'problem' been produced, disseminated and defended? How could it be questioned, disrupted and replaced? There is a sense here of people *with* more or less power setting out deliberately to defend (or contest) problem representations that serve their purposes, or even their 'interests'. And yet, a WPR approach works explicitly at a level deeper than intentionality, in uncovering the conceptual logics that underpin specific problem representations (Q2).

This apparent inconsistency is reconciled through an emphasis on plurality of meanings, and on recognising that none of us exists outside power. For example, while it may be possible and indeed relevant to point to the ways in which large corporations deliberately promote brand images in an attempt to sway consumers, a WPR approach directs attention to the complex interactions between these messages and the subjectivities both of marketers and of consumers. As another example, while it is possible to identify ways in which researchers sometimes produce research that serves the needs and hence the 'interests' of those who employ them, as consultants perhaps, the kinds of researcher–institutional relationship that are of interest in this study are both more complicated and less explicit than the notion of 'interests' implies. The concern is with the ways in which researchers become 'unconsciously' implicated, through the 'knowledges' they produce – in particular, modes of governance.[1]

It is this 'unconscious' involvement that makes reflexivity, introduced in Chapter 2, so necessary and so very difficult. That is, if we are indeed created as particular kinds of subjects, there is an urgent need to reflect critically upon the concepts and practices that so shape us. Again, human capital was put forward in the last chapter as a concept that demanded this kind of critical scrutiny. Poststructuralist psychology, also discussed in Chapter 2, provides some tools for undertaking this kind of investigation – identifying the subject positions available in specific discourses, and reflecting on the tensions and contradictions among them (Davies 1994; Davies *et al.* 2006; Walkerdine 2001).

In summary, it is useful to think about *both* the power *of* discourses to limit the meanings of topics of analysis, *and* the power to *make* and/or to *deploy* discourses. As Ball (1990, pp. 17–18) puts it, discourses are 'about what can be said, and thought, but also about who can speak, when, where and with what authority'. On the first dynamic – the power *of* discourses – Ball explains: 'discourses construct certain possibilities for thought. They order and combine words in particular ways and exclude or displace other combinations'. On the second dynamic – the power to *make* and deploy discourses – he states: 'Meanings thus arise not from language, but from institutional practices, from power relations, from social position. Words and concepts change their meaning and their effects as they are deployed within different discourses'. This dual perspective on discourse has been maintained throughout the book – recognising both the power that concepts and categories accrue through being embedded in governmental practices and programs (limiting what can be talked about), and the uneven power relations involved in the production of discourse/s.

On this last issue – the uneven power relations involved in the production of discourse/s – it is important not to assume that social and/or political elites are the only ones who can marshal and deploy discourses for instrumental purposes. There is a tendency in some policy-as-discourse theory to speak about discourse in this way. The accompanying tendency is to portray the 'common people' as the ones constituted *within* discourses and, therefore, as lacking the power to challenge repressive and dominant meanings. By contrast, in a WPR approach, we are *all* recognised as subjects constituted in discourse/s. While acknowledging the constraints imposed by dominant discourses, this position makes it possible to theorise the 'space for challenge' (see Bacchi 2000 and below).

On this point, Foucault directs attention to the importance of what he calls 'subjugated knowledges'. As we saw in Chapter 2 he identifies two classes of subjugated knowledges:

- erudite knowledges that have been buried, e.g. 'knowledges' recuperated through books such as Dale Spender's (1982) *Women of Ideas*;
- 'local popular' or 'indigenous knowledges', 'regional knowledges', those that survive 'at the margins'.

Together erudite and local knowledges create the grounds for struggle and contestation (Foucault 1980, p. 83).

Importantly, Foucault eschews the temptation of endorsing a specific political program. He quite famously said: 'My position is that it is not up to us to propose. As soon as one "proposes" – one proposes a vocabulary, an ideology, which can only have effects of domination. What we have to present are instruments and tools that people might find useful' (Foucault 1988, p. 197). This kind of comment has led some critics to describe Foucault's analysis as nihilistic, claiming that it leads nowhere and is therefore politically useless. However, Foucault's position is more complicated than this indictment suggests and it certainly has political implications. Foucault makes the case that it is impossible to *deny* knowledge, 'to act apart from and experience the world from outside of the mediating effects of knowledge and discursive practices' (White and

Epston 1990, p. 27). It is this location *within* governing knowledges that makes critical analysis and attempts at change both so challenging and so necessary.

Foucault's way forward here is to pay less attention to the *contents* and *sources* of discourse/s and more attention to their *effects*. As he says, because there is no 'outside' to 'knowledge', the 'insurrection' of subjugated knowledges he recommends is 'opposed primarily not to the *contents*, methods or concepts of a science, but to the *effects* of the centralising powers which are linked to the institution and functioning of an organised scientific discourse within a society such as ours' (Foucault 1980, p. 84 in White and Epston 1990, p. 84; emphasis added). In tune with this form of analysis, a WPR approach recommends that policies be evaluated primarily *in terms of the effects* that accompany the identified problem representations they produce **(Q5)**.

As asserted in Chapter 2, in the struggle for 'control of discourses', a WPR analysis, with Foucault, affirms the perspective 'of those who resist' (Simons 1995, p. 91). Therefore, Question 6 creates the opportunity to consider how resistance can be conducted. As seen in other chapters, there are several possible ways to do this.

- Remembering that discourses are uneven and contradictory, it is possible to find spaces for interrogation and indeed for 'correction'.
- Remembering that discourse is an 'asset', not an innocent mode of communication (Shapiro 1988, p. 12), discourses can be treated as resources for re-problematisation. A discourse of power, for example, can 'be reversed into one of resistance' (Simons 1995, p. 83).

A WPR approach therefore does not suggest that particular problem representations can be dispensed with, but rather that a sharp eye to their *effects* can provide a basis for interacting with them, working with and within them. In this sense, the approach advocates a kind of guerrilla warfare on problem presentations judged to have deleterious consequences. It encourages those who wish to contest these problem representations to work carefully within contextual constraints to frame problems in ways that produce effects deemed to be more helpful and less destructive than those produced by problem representations judged to be harmful.

This proposal differs from conventional strategic framing that focuses on choosing ideas and concepts likely to win supporters to one's cause. Here, the task is to reflect on one's own conceptual frameworks to identify and rethink problem representations that are judged to do harm. While there is clearly an element of 'intentionality' involved in this recommendation, the emphasis is on internal critique and reflection (reflexivity) rather than on immediate political strategy (see Bacchi 2009).

'Discovering' the 'knowledge economy/society'

Above we considered the way in which contested meanings of 'knowledge production' create the idea of 'knowledge' quite differently, as either a *marketable* product or as a *social* product.

'Knowledge' itself therefore can be considered to be a contested concept. It is time to pursue this idea further, developing the argument that current references to 'knowledge' in terms such as the 'knowledge economy' and the 'knowledge society' produce 'knowledge' in narrow, instrumental ways that have a range of important political effects **(Q5)**:

- depoliticising the process of 'knowledge' construction (ignoring/silencing the power-knowledge links identified above);
- re-inscribing objectivist criteria for identifying 'knowledge';
- privileging some 'knowledges' – e.g. scientific, evidence-based – over other (subjugated) 'knowledges' – e.g. contextualised, embodied, lay 'knowledges' (Popay *et al.* 1998).

So, where does the idea of the 'knowledge economy' come from? **(Q3)** Peters (2001, pp. 4–5) identifies a number of discourses as having contributed to 'shaping the present policy narrative of the "knowledge economy"':

- several strands of discourse from the discipline of economics, including the 'economics of the production and distribution of knowledge' (Machlup 1962) and the 'economics of human capital' (Becker 1964; see Chapter 9);
- old and new management theories, including Taylorism, just-in-time production systems and 'knowledge management';
- sociological studies of the nature of work, such as Braverman's (1974) writing on deskilling;
- other sociological texts such as Masuda's (1981) *Postindustrial society as information society*, and Touraine's (1974) *Post-industrial society*;
- futurology and futures research; and
- the body of literature on communications and IT [Information Technology].

While some of the sociology material (e.g. Touraine 1974) stands as critique of the positivist economics strand, there is confluence in the idea that the nature of work and 'knowledge' *has changed*. It is this belief or conviction that supports the dominant singular narrative we have already identified in Chapter 9, that *people* need to change (themselves) to 'keep up' with 'the times', that they have to recreate themselves to 'fit' the 'changed circumstances'.

The 'knowledge economy' is a key part of this narrative. It is one of those travelling ideas, like lifelong learning (see Chapter 9), that appears currently in most Western industrialised countries. For example, Peters examines definitions of the 'knowledge economy' within policy documents emanating from the UK and New Zealand. The idea (or, more precisely, the problem representation) is also well entrenched in Australian public policy (see Vaile 2000). According to Peters (2001, p. 3), the concept reflects the mode of governance Rose (2000, p. 12) describes as 'advanced liberalism', a mode of governance common to liberalism and to neoliberalism that emphasises individual responsibility and independence. Another characteristic of this mode of governance ('advanced liberalism') is a particular conception of 'knowledge' – 'a narrow, instrumental approach to the economics of knowledge and to intellectual culture in general' (Peters 2001, p. 13). Peters is particularly concerned at the way in which 'knowledge *economy*' and 'knowledge *society*' are considered synonymous, so that an *economic* definition of knowledge displaces a more general understanding of knowledge as a *global public good* (Peters 2001, p. 15).

To say that an approach to knowledge is 'instrumental' means that 'knowledge' is seen (solely) as a means to an end, as 'useful' or 'relevant' for particular purposes rather than for its own sake. To challenge this understanding does not mean instituting a view of 'knowledge' as *non*-useful or *ir*relevant. Nor does it mean a wish to install some apolitical meaning of 'knowledge' as 'truth'. Rather the intention is to highlight the particular *kinds of knowledge* that are considered 'useful' and the ways in which this 'knowledge' is offered as 'fact'.

On this issue, Peters (2001, p. 13) notes the slippage between 'knowledge' and 'information'. The terms, as already mentioned, are often used interchangeably (e.g. 'information society', 'knowledge society'). The word 'information' has gained status due, in part, to technological developments like the internet, referred to as '*information* technologies' or ICTs (*information* and communication technologies). The way in which computers produce 'information' as 'bits' of 'data' encourages an understanding of 'knowledge' as *information*, measurable and transferable, 'intellectual *property*' to be protected legally and marketed.

As Peters explains, there 'are benign and less benign versions of these concepts'. Within the social democratic tradition, he suggests, the economy is positioned as subordinate to the state, allowing the idea of a 'knowledge society' to ground recognition of '*knowledge rights* as a basis for social inclusion and informed citizenship'. By contrast, within the 'neoliberal paradigm of globalisation', 'the term stands for a "stripped down" functionalist view of education in service of the multinationals' (Peters 2001, pp. 12–13; emphasis in original). We saw exactly this point in Chapter 9 in the current enthusiasm for lifelong learning as the means to produce *flexible* and *mobile* workers.

Despite the differences between the social democratic and neoliberal interpretations, the ubiquity of the concept 'knowledge economy' and the way in which it reduces 'knowledge' to 'information' is a development that has important *broad* political implications (Q5). Part of a rationalist and positivist paradigm, it removes political and power dimensions from policy deliberation, as we shall see later in the chapter in our consideration of two key sites of 'knowledge' construction, the media and academic research. Before we undertake that analysis, it is important to draw attention to the academic legitimacy that has been granted to this particular, restricted understanding of 'knowledge' as (useful) 'information'. To this end I take a brief look at the provocative proposals in the landmark text produced by Gibbons *et al.* (1994) that currently we are experiencing dramatic shifts from 'the traditional discipline-centred mode of knowledge that they characterise as Mode 1, towards a broader conception of knowledge production described as Mode 2' (Hanney *et al.* 2003, p. 6).

According to Gibbons *et al.* (1994, p. 10, 6), as a result of what they describe as 'the massification of higher education' – the production of numbers of graduates 'too large for them all to be absorbed within the disciplinary structure' – there has been 'an increase in the number of sites where knowledge can be created', extending beyond universities and colleges, and a proliferation of 'knowledge' 'users'. This new 'socially distributed knowledge production system', they say, blurs the old distinction between 'pure and applied science, between what is curiosity-oriented and what is mission-oriented'. Emphasis moves away, in their view, 'from free inquiry to *problem solving* and more generally in the direction of *problem-oriented research*', knowledge in the 'context of application', with quality assessed in terms of *usefulness* (Gibbons *et al.* 1994, pp. 14, 33; emphasis added): 'Such knowledge is intended to be *useful* to someone whether in industry or government, or society more generally, and this imperative is present from the beginning' (Gibbons *et al.* 1994, p. 4; emphasis added).

In Mode 2 knowledge production, the authors distinguish between '*tacit* knowledge', either 'residing in the heads of those working on a particular transformation process' or 'embodied in a particular organisational context', and '*codified* knowledge', which 'needs to be systematic enough to be written down and stored'. This second sense of knowledge as fixed and transferable is captured in their definition of 'knowledge industries' as 'Industries in which knowledge itself is the *commodity* traded' (Gibbons *et al.*, 1994, p. 167; emphasis added). The idea that 'knowledge' is a commodity conveys that sense of knowledge as fixed and transferable *bits of data*, as 'information', discussed above.

The specification that 'knowledge' in Mode 2 needs to be 'useful', to be judged in the 'context of application', reflects the current utilitarian emphasis on 'what works' in public policy, an emphasis we have identified in approaches to crime reduction (Chapter 5) and in health care (Chapter 6). In effect, it is the idea that stands behind and legitimates *evidence*-based policy approaches (see *What Works Clearinghouse* 2005). As Solesbury (2001, p. 4) explains, this turn to '*useful*' research has been driven, to a large extent, 'by the funders of social science' and by 'the demands of government science policy that views academic research as a means to economic and social development much more than as a cultural end in itself' **(Q2, Q3)**.

Solesbury (2001, p. 8; **Q4)** identifies how this instrumental approach to research produces a *narrow* understanding of relevance, bypassing a range of important and often prior questions, such as 'What is going on? What's the problem? Is it better or worse than . . ? What causes it? What might be done about it? At what cost? By whose agency?' In tune with Solesbury and as argued throughout this book, the focus on 'problem' *solving* (on 'what works') forecloses consideration of what the 'problem' is *represented to be*. There is a presumption that the nature of 'problems', designated as the starting place for research, is clear-cut and uncontroversial. Hopefully, by this stage in the book, this presumption can be debated.

The political subject constituted in this narrative is the 'problem-solving subject', whom we met in Reich's (1991) writing on 'symbolic workers' (see Chapter 9). These workers who know how to manipulate symbols (e.g. data, words, audio and visual images) are, according to Reich, the new elite and those most economically useful to the nation. Hence, the emphasis in education, he argues, needs to shift to teaching 'know *how*', rather than 'know *what*', to impart the skill of '*how* to learn'. In the previous chapter we saw how this political subject is expected to be flexible and mobile in suiting the needs of industry, and is held responsible for upgrading their specific 'skills' on a regular basis through lifelong learning (Q2).

Considered together, the focus on 'problem-oriented' research and on 'problem-solving' learners/subjects constitutes a powerful 'problem-solving' paradigm at the heart of contemporary social and intellectual life. This paradigm is positivist – a schism created between 'knowledge' and 'subject' is supposed to guarantee objectivity (Q2). That is, we have here an image of (disinterested) students and researchers doing their best to 'solve' 'problems', precluding consideration of the ways in which 'problems' are constituted. By way of contrast, because a WPR approach to policy analysis describes policy as a *creative*, as distinct from a *reactive* process which responds to or 'addresses' problems (see Chapter 1), it offers a counter-discourse to this 'problem-solving' paradigm. Hence, it puts in question the basic premises of evidence-based policy – that 'knowledge' is (simply) 'information, and that in order to sort through society's ills we need (only) to assess which 'evidence' best '*addresses*' the 'problem'.

In the following sections we explore further the political effects (Q5) of this increasingly authoritative 'problem-solving' paradigm, and of the creation of 'knowledge' as 'information' within media policy and academic research.

MEDIA, DEMOCRACY AND 'TRUTH'

The media has already featured as a significant political player in previous chapters. For example, the role the media plays in creating and disseminating particular images of 'welfare cheats' (Chapter 3), 'gambling addicts' (Chapter 4), 'damaged' Aboriginal people (Chapter 5) and 'recalcitrant' mothers (Chapter 7) has been mentioned in passing.

In a WPR approach, the media is a significant site of 'knowledge' construction. That is, the media is considered to be a dominant force in influencing how issues are perceived and how political subjects come to think about themselves. In this view, the media in their diversity do not simply 'report' news or 'reflect' audience preferences. Rather, they are active in the creation of 'problems' and people. Hence, they play a significant role in governing – co-constituting problem representations and influencing citizen subjectivities.

Media and the social construction of 'youth'

The following two headlines are representative of a vast amount of similar reporting on the topics of 'youth' 'binge-drinking' and 'youth' violence.

Headline: 'Drink puts youth on deadly trail'

Sub-heading: 'Police question Melbourne licensing policy as alcohol fuels "anarchy" and brain damage'

(Stark and Houston 2007)

Headline: 'Teen knife violence surge'

Sub-heading: 'Youths caught in vicious turf war, 8 stabbed'

(Sexton 2007)

- **What is the 'problem' of 'youth' represented to be in these headlines?**

- **How is 'youth' constituted in these problem representations?**

- **How do the media and government 'co-constitute' problem representations and 'youth' subjectivities?**

- **Are there any silences in these problem representations?**

For this Activity refer to Chapter 3 and to Sercombe 2005.

To explore this topic we interrogate three 'practical texts':

■ *Australia's Strategic Framework for the Information Economy 2004–2006*;

■ *The Broadcasting Services Amendment (Media Ownership) Act*, 2006;

■ *Classification (Publications, Films and Computer Games) Amendment (Terrorist Material) Act*, 2007.

These texts have been selected because they highlight connections between national and international policy, and between policy that regulates the *form* (structure) of the media industry and policy that regulates *content*. The objective is to see how these texts constitute knowledge as 'information'– ignoring the power-knowledge relationships described above – and the political effects (**Q5**) that follow, including:

■ 'securitisation' of media sources;

■ deregulation of media ownership; and,

■ censorship.

Making 'knowledge' safe

In 2004 the Australian government produced *Australia's Strategic Framework for the Information Economy 2004–2006*. The *Framework* identified the following priorities:

- Priority 1: Ensure that all Australians have the capabilities, networks and tools to participate in the benefits of the information economy;
- Priority 2: Ensure the security and interoperability of Australia's information infrastructure, and support confidence in digital services;
- Priority 3: Develop Australia's innovation system as a platform for productivity growth and industry transformation;
- Priority 4: Raise Australian public sector productivity, collaboration and accessibility through the effective use of information, knowledge and ICT [Information and Communications Technology] (Australian Government 2004).

The *Framework* lays out Australia's policy for internet and other IC developments. It was presented to the second meeting of the World Summit on the Information Society (WSIS) in October 2004 as part of Australia's contribution to the **World Trade Organization** (WTO) **GATT (General Agreement on Tariffs and Trade)** deliberations on free trade in services.

While it is possible to describe the *Framework* as an exercise in obfuscation, replete with numerous 'motherhood' statements (Philipson 2004) – that is, as an exercise in rhetoric – it is also possible to use it as an entry point to reflect on the conceptual logics underpinning the 'information economy' (**Q2**). The Executive Summary defines the 'information economy' as:

> ... the term adopted by the Australian Government in 1997 to describe the transformation of economic and social activities by information and communications technologies (ICT). An information economy is one where information, knowledge and education are *major inputs* to business and social activity – it is an economy in which the rapid development and diffusion of ICT-based innovation is transforming all sectors and all aspects of society. (Australian Government 2004, p. 6; emphasis added)

'Information', we are told, 'makes an increasingly important contribution' to the 'different dimensions of national power – diplomatic/political, information, military, economic, and socio-cultural'. Unless 'we succeed in applying the *power of information* and technology to our economic and social goals', 'we will lose ground to the other nations who succeed' and 'it will be difficult to maintain Australia's relative growth and social development' (Australian Government 2004, p. 13; emphasis added). The 'Policy Response' to the challenges posed by moving towards 'an open, adaptable economy and society', the declared goal of the GATT negotiations, is expressed in these terms:

Future economic growth and community development are required to meet future challenges. Increasingly we need to create and mobilise new capabilities and bring them to bear in a focused way. This will be an innovative, *problem-solving* society: in other words, an '*information*' economy and society. (Australian Government 2004, p.10; emphasis added)

The understanding in this document of 'information' and 'knowledge' as 'inputs' produces them as fixed, measurable 'givens', separate from contestation and from power (**Q2**). There is acknowledgement that knowledge *has* power ('the power of information'), but not that power *produces* knowledge. The use of the term 'problem-solving' locates the *Framework* within the 'problem-solving' paradigm identified earlier in the chapter — a paradigm in which political subjects learn to learn, and in which 'information' provides the key to national growth, international competitiveness and individual success. The four key priorities listed at the outset confirm this interpretation. Australian citizens are offered the 'capabilities' to 'participate'. They are 'information *users*'. 'Productivity' depends on 'the effective *use* of information, knowledge and ICT' (see above; emphasis added).

The term 'security' appears some sixty times in this fifty-seven page document, locating 'knowledge' as a key part of a securitisation discourse (**Q2**; see Chapter 7). Priority 2 states: 'Ensure the security and interoperability of Australia's information infrastructure'. The strategies listed to deliver on Priority 2 include:

■ Strategy 2.2: Improve the culture of security in both public and private organisations;
■ Strategy 2.3: Promote security research and development and improve capabilities for analysis of security threats and vulnerabilities (Australian Government 2004, p. 11).

In this account, knowledge as 'information' becomes something to be 'secured' and protected, providing a rationale for censorship (see *Classification Act* below). The 'securitisation' of 'knowledge' also guarantees a privileged role for security professionals and researchers (see Bigo 2002 in Chapter 7).

We have here a sanitised version of 'knowledge', constructed as separate from those who produce it and from its crucial influence in shaping social relationships and social priorities (**Q4**). This depoliticising effect (**Q5**) is illustrated again in the next text.

Protecting 'diversity'

On 4 November 2006 the *Broadcasting Services Amendment (Media Ownership) Act* became law. In brief, it made two important changes to Australia's media regulatory regime:

■ removing the restrictions on cross-media ownership that existed in the *Broadcasting Services Act* (Commonwealth Consolidated Acts 1992), which had prevented the common ownership of newspapers, television and radio broadcasting licences that serve the same region. Under the new legislation, media companies are able to own print (e.g. newspapers), radio and television interests in the one market. Safeguards are in place to ensure that no fewer than five commercial media groups operate in Australian capital cities and four in regional areas. Also, a minimum of local content is legislated on regional commercial television and radio – four and a half hours initially, subsequently lowered to three and a half hours (Australian Government 2008).

■ removing restrictions on foreign media ownership, as well as restrictions in the *Foreign Acquisitions and Takeovers Act* (Commonwealth Consolidated Acts 1975) that relate specifically to newspapers. The media sector remains a 'sensitive sector' under the government's *Foreign Investment Policy* and all investments are subject to final approval by the Treasurer.

To understand the significance of these changes it is necessary to have a little background. In Australia diversity in ownership of the media has, historically, been defended on two grounds: first, that concentrated ownership in the hands of the few threatens the plurality of views that is considered important in a democracy; second, that foreign ownership ought to be controlled because Australians need a space to cultivate their own culture and their own media, including actors, screen writers, etc.

In the lead-up to the new Act the government issued a Discussion Paper on media reform options: *Meeting the Digital Challenge: Reforming Australia's media in the digital age* (Australian Government 2006b). The then Minister for Communications, Information Technology and the Arts, Helen Coonan, introduced the Discussion Paper in a speech to the Committee for Economic Development of Australia (CEDA):

Traditional media services are being challenged by new digital technologies and this is resulting in the emergence of new players, new content, new services and new platforms. For the consumer, this means an ever-increasing number of new sources of information and entertainment. For the media sector, while this evolution poses challenges as audiences are attracted away from traditional media sources, it also presents significant opportunities to embrace new ways of doing business. For the government, the impact of digital technologies means the current regulatory settings, which are largely designed for an analogue world, risk becoming outdated …

The current media laws increasingly inhibiting the growth of new services, limiting media companies from obtaining economies of scale and scope, constraining them in addressing the challenges posed by emerging media forms and foreclosing future developments in the marketplace. As a result, investment and innovation in Australian media is outdated. (Coonan 2006)

In this Discussion Paper the 'problem' is represented to be the need for Australia to keep up with technological developments worldwide (the digital age) in order to compete economically (**Q1**). There are assumptions that a free market in communications technology is a prerequisite for this goal (**Q2**). There are concerns that conventional media forms need an opportunity to consolidate in order to prepare for more open competition, and an expressed willingness to compensate them for the challenges of greater competition. The promise to 'consumers' is that the plurality of new services and media forms will guarantee diversity: 'By allowing new entrants into the Australian media industry, the government will encourage increased *diversity* and new sources of *information* and entertainment' (Coonan 2006; emphasis added).

We have here a particular interpretation of 'diversity', tied to the focus on 'information'. In effect, as Curtis (2006, p. vii) describes, 'the concept of diversity has been refashioned to refer to a multitude of pieces of information – a proliferation of data' (**Q2**). Silenced are concerns that large media conglomerates offer a restricted range of positions and views. The safeguard of no fewer than five commercial media groups in capital cities and four in regional areas ignores differences in size and influence among these groups (**Q4**).

Changes to the media laws therefore were made possible by producing knowledge as 'information', as something separate and apart from power dynamics, something you can simply 'access' and 'use' (**Q2**). Meanwhile, expressed anxiety about the 'security' of 'information' provides the grounds for restricting Australians' 'right to know'.

Silencing dissent

In early 2007 the Commonwealth Government passed the *Classification (Publications, Films and Computer Games) Amendment (Terrorist Material) Act*. The purpose of the Act is to expand the government's powers to deny classification of (i.e. to ban) any material deemed to indirectly advocate terrorism. The Act specifies that 'a publication, film or computer game *advocates* the doing of a terrorist act if:

(a) it directly or indirectly counsels or urges the doing of a terrorist act;

(b) it directly or indirectly provides instruction on the doing of a terrorist act; or

(c) it directly praises the doing of a terrorist act in circumstances where there is a risk that such praise might have the effect of leading a person . . . to engage in a terrorist act. (Commonwealth Numbered Acts, no. 179, 2007; emphasis in original)

Prompted by dissatisfaction with the way in which the Office of Film and Literature Classification (OFLC), an independent review board, had dealt with certain materials that the government believed should be denied classification, the Act folded the OFLC's administration and policy functions into the Attorney-General's Department.

It is important to see this legislation in the context of earlier 2005 anti-sedition laws (Australian Government 2006c; **Q3**) and increased restrictions on journalists in Australia (Marr 2007), including:

■ increased use of suppression orders;
■ increased demands that journalists reveal their sources;
■ the high costs of getting information under Freedom of Information legislation;
■ lack of protection for 'whistleblowers' (see Calland and Dehn 2004; Martin 1999).

Defending the new Classification proposals, the then Attorney-General, Phillip Ruddock, made the case that 'it's important to protect the Australian community and there's much uncertainty whether the existing laws adequately capture material that advocates the doing of terrorist acts' (Media Report 2007b).

The ability to pass such a piece of legislation rests upon the creation of 'information' as a 'security' issue, accomplished so successfully in *Australia's Strategic Framework for the Information Economy* (**Q2, Q3**; see above). Terrorism is clearly represented to be the 'problem' (**Q1**). Importantly, Norris *et al.* (2003, p. 6) make the case that terrorism is a contested concept, 'value-laden, and open to multiple meanings located within broader cultural frames, so that, to some extent, terrorism is in the eye of the beholder' (**Q4, Q6**).

A number of commentators expressed concerns about the new Classification proposals (**Q6**). Fisher, of the Australian Society of Authors, argued that 'Unless they expressly promote, incite or instruct in matters of crime or violence we cannot see why a liberal, democratic society would seek to ban expression of ideas and opinions' (ASA 2007). Under pressure from critics, the Act was amended to stipulate that a publication does not advocate the doing of a terrorist act if the depiction could reasonably 'be considered to be done as part of public discussion or debate or as entertainment or satire' (Commonwealth Numbered Acts, no. 179, 2007).

In reaction against perceived restrictions on access to information, in May 2007 a coalition of media organisations, including *News Ltd.*, the *Australian Broadcasting Corporation* (*ABC*), *Fairfax*, *SBS* (*Special Broadcasting Service*) and *AAP* (*Australian Associated Press*) launched a campaign calling for *Australia's Right to Know* (**Q6**). The coalition pointed out that Australia had slipped to thirty-fifth place on the Worldwide Press Freedom Index, produced by Reporters Without Borders (Media Report 2007a).

By defending a 'right to know', the coalition represents the 'problem' to be lack of *access* to 'information' (**Q1**) – a useful if conventional 'response' to state censorship. This particular representation of the 'problem', however, makes it difficult to put in question the meaning of key concepts, such as terrorism (**Q4**). A more constitutive approach to 'knowledge' enables a more fundamental critique (**Q6**).

As an example it is useful to revisit the work of Henry and Milovanovic (1996), introduced in Chapter 5. They make the case that meaningful change requires the creation of *different* 'news', *counter*-narratives, and *replacement* discourse. You may recall that they redefine crime as harm in order to shift the focus away from street crime to the crimes of the powerful.

Henry and Milovanovic (1996, p. 217) are not content to leave the matter there, however – as an academic exercise in deconstruction. Instead, they make the case that criminologists have to become activists, claiming control of the 'crime news space'. With Barak (1988, 2007) they describe this form of intervention as 'newsmaking criminology' **(Q6)**. By drawing attention to the ways in which academic disciplines play pivotal roles in shaping, and possibly reshaping, representations of 'problems', Henry and Milovanovic set the scene for considering relationships between theory, power and 'knowledge', our final topic.

THE POLITICS OF POLICY STUDIES

It is time to consider the full ramifications of a WPR approach for policy studies and for academic research generally. The sceptical stance toward 'knowledge', mentioned at the outset, means a willingness to put under scrutiny all claims to 'knowledge', including academic research. It means recognising that researchers do not stand outside the **knowledge-power nexus**, but rather that 'our research is itself a process of governing and constituting subjects' (Marston and MacDonald 2006, p. 225). In this view, theory is inherently 'a political practice always and inescapably implicated with power' (McClure 1992, p. 365). To remind us of this point, McClure (1992, p. 365) usefully suggests that we think about theory as a verb rather than as a noun, drawing attention to those who practice theoris*ing* and their necessary positioning as political actors.

To repeat a point made in Chapter 5, because theories are forms of explanation – offering particular representations of the 'problem' – they can be subjected to a WPR analysis. In this way it becomes possible to tease out grounding assumptions (paradigms) **(Q2)**, sources and influences **(Q3)**, lacunae (silences) in explanation **(Q4)**, and political, including subjectification, effects **(Q5)**. If, as is claimed here, theory is non-innocent, this kind of careful scrutiny of theoretical premises becomes politically imperative.

The book has prepared us to take this leap forward in analysis from studying policies as 'practical texts' to analysing theories more generally. From the outset the role of the human/ social sciences in governing has been a central concern. We have spent some considerable time reflecting on the place of social science 'knowledges' in conceptualising 'problems'. Chapter 5, for example, details the connections between a range of criminal justice theories and specific policy recommendations. Similarly Chapter 6 reflects on the wide range of theories concerning the nature of 'health' and the causes of ill-health, and shows how these theories impact on the ways in which health policy is conceptualised and delivered.

In a similar vein, McMillen (1996) has produced an analysis of approaches to the study of gambling policy that highlights connections between theoretical premises, forms of analysis and policy developments. Her main argument is that studies of gambling have been dominated by 'normative and culturally specific theories of liberal social science', which rest upon individualist presuppositions (Q2). In the United States, for example, analysis of gambling practices in the post-World War II era has been dominated 'by the domain assumptions and methods of positivism' and by public choice theory, which is grounded in free market premises (Q2; see below). As a result, the focus in gambling studies has been primarily on *individual* behaviours and on 'quantifiable concepts and propositions in theory and research' (McMillen 1996, pp. 8, 20–21), with marked effects on gambling policy:

> The preference of US analysts for this view has been a major influence in the formulation and direction of casino policy. The trend to *laissez-faire* developments in Nevada, for example, reflects the concern of economists and policy-makers about the distorting effects of government regulation on the market and on governments themselves. (McMillen 1996, p. 27; Q3, Q5)

McMillen identifies the limits (Q4) on analysis imposed by remaining within this liberal, individualistic paradigm:

- The focus on individuals 'avoids conceptions of power and structure' (McMillen 1996, p. 21).
- Such analyses have failed to develop 'the categories for a critical account of private ownership or of capital-state relations'. Instead, large commercial casinos are 'represented as natural and, therefore, not modifiable' (McMillen 1996, p. 28–29).
- 'Contextual factors, such as the emergence of transnational gambling corporations and the state's varied and contradictory role in the transition of gambling from illegality to legality, are rarely brought into the discussion' (McMillen 1996, p. 22).

> 'Understandings of gambling are determined more by the perspectives and purposes of the analyst than by the inherent nature of the subject. All commentaries on gambling, even the most determinedly "objective", proceed from a particular historically and socially determined point of view.' (McMillen 1996, p. 7)

What McMillen has accomplished for *gambling* studies needs also to be undertaken for *policy* studies. That is, it is necessary to see how the theoretical premises within a range of approaches to policy analysis rest upon assumptions (Q2) that limit analysis (Q4) in ways that are important politically (Q5). To this end we ask – what kind of a 'problem' is *policy* represented to be?

Parsons (1995) offers valuable insights into the genesis of the notion of 'policy' and the relationships generated between governments and social scientists around 'policy'. As he explains, 'policy' has a neutral connotation, suggesting that it is cut off from 'politics': 'The language and rhetoric of "policy" thus became the main instrument of political rationality' (Parsons 1995, p. 16). Social and political scientists bolster this image of 'policy' as rational by offering 'information' on which to base 'knowledgeable governance' (Lasswell 1951). In this understanding, policy analysts serve the role of 'speaking truth to power' (Wildavsky 1979; **Q2**). Evidence-based policy continues in this rationalist tradition which says that policy-makers make 'good' decisions when they have 'knowledge' ('evidence'). 'Knowledge' in this view is decontextualised and sanitised 'information' (**Q2**). A WPR approach, which puts in question the nature of 'truth' and of social science 'knowledges', is designed to return politics to policy analysis (**Q6**). To this end I offer the approach as a replacement discourse for evidence-based policy, as developed below.

Policy science

'The word "policy" is commonly used to designate the most important choices made either in organized or in private life . . . "policy" is free of many of the undesirable connotations clustered about the word political, which is often believed to imply "partisanship" or "corruption"' (Lasswell 1951, p. 5).

- **How is policy understood in this quote?**

- **What does it mean to suggest that policy is 'free of' politics?**

- **Are there any silences in this representation of the 'problem'?**

Guide to paradigms in major policy approaches

- 'Comprehensive rational' or 'authorized choice' (Colebatch 1998) approaches to public policy fit a positivist paradigm. The emphasis is on providing technical expertise to 'address' identified 'problems'. Values are believed to be exogenous to the process of policy analysis. There is an agreed upon 'public interest' that gets sorted out in a 'decision space' before the policy-making process begins. Postulating a 'real world' that only needs 'describing', objectivity is considered to be possible.

- Political rationalists (a 'structured interaction' approach to policy analysis) are also positivists, though they acknowledge the role of values in public policy-making. They position themselves as democrats who are discontented with handing over political processes to bureaucrats, as per comprehensive rationalism. They believe that values are involved in shaping policy, but that effective policy analysts can take values into account and still offer 'good' policy advice. Value disagreements in this view can be worked through rationally. Political rationalists are pluralists and incrementalists, endorsing movement towards desired goals in small, incremental steps. They believe that authority needs to be diffused through acknowledgement of interest groups and that good outcomes require a plurality of voices. Pragmatically, the role of policy analysts is to define 'problems' in terms that make 'solutions' feasible (Bacchi 1999, p. 24–30).

■ Heavily reliant on quantitative studies and methodologies borrowed from operations research and management, public choice models of policy analysis can also be characterised as positivist. They rest on a view of human nature as naturally self-interested (Q2). Because bureaucrats are assumed to want ('naturally') to expand their area/s of influence, government itself is seen to be the 'problem'. The approach is anti-statist. There is a view that governments make 'problems' worse and that 'free' markets create more effective and efficient societies (Parsons 1995, p. 76).

■ Critical policy analysis derives from Marxist roots and emphasises the role of dominant interest groups, particularly class interest groups, in shaping outcomes that serve their interests. There is some slippage across the positivist-postpositivist divide given the sharp awareness of the role of culture (**superstructure; Ideological State Apparatuses**) in shaping people's perspectives.

■ Post-positivist approaches to policy are diverse, due largely to disagreements about what post-positivism means. Interpretive approaches (Hajer and Wagenaar 2003; Yanow 2000) stress the need to take into account the myriad ways in which different populations understand the full range of policy issues. Approaches that focus on rhetoric (Fischer 1980; Majone 1989) emphasise the role played by language and meaning-making in policy. Some in this grouping stress the use of metaphors and frames in shaping arguments, with the hope that awareness of these issues will facilitate 'frame reconciliation' (Rein and Schon 1996). Social constructionists are less interested in offering 'policy advice' or recommendations about how to reconcile frames than in identifying underlying conceptual logics (or ways of thinking) that shape understandings of policy issues.

The politics of evidence-based policy

The book has paid a good deal of attention to evidence-based policy approaches, due to their current near-hegemonic status in a wide range of policy areas, including health, criminal justice and education. Freedman (2006, p. 918) describes how evidence-based approaches are also gaining influence in *media policy*, 'using techniques like consumer research, market intelligence and technology research, even for rather amorphous concepts like "public value" and of course "public service"'. In concert with the arguments developed in this book, he expresses dismay at this development:

> The privileging of highly selective empirical and evidence-based approaches to policy-making fails both to de-politicize and to make any more objective the decision-making environment. Policy-making in a sphere of such cultural and political significance [the media] is bound to be highly political and the fetishizing of 'scientific' data is one means of marginalizing the public from the public policy process and safeguarding it for the economists, lawyers and executives who are in a prime position to furnish the sort of information that policy-makers are demanding. (Freedman 2006, pp. 920–1)

In contesting evidence-based policy approaches, it is important to be aware of the genesis of the approach and of the reasons so many researchers currently endorse the methodology (Q3). In Chapter 6 we considered how, at least initially, researchers saw an insistence on the importance of 'evidence' as one way of demanding accountability from governments. At the same time we saw how governments have been able to use this idea to insist that research be *relevant*. The question that tends to fall through the cracks of these different positions is – relevant *for what*?

Large numbers of researchers are concerned about the ways in which evidence-based approaches displace more contextual and interpretive forms of research (Q6; see, for example, St Pierre 2006; Marston and Watts 2003; Davies 2003). Counter to these criticisms, the MEKN Report on the social determinants of health (discussed in Chapter 6) insists that an evidence-based methodology does *not* necessarily presume an objectivist epistemology (MEKN 2007, p. 95): 'There is no such thing as value neutral science' (MEKN 2007, p. 99). However, in evidence-based policy, objective 'problems' *are* presumed to exist, separate from power and contestation, waiting only upon 'evidence' about 'what works'. So long as 'problems' are considered to sit outside the political process (exogenous) in this way, waiting to be 'solved' through 'relevant' 'evidence', the necessarily political contestation around competing representations of 'problems' is displaced and hence ignored (Q4).

Within an evidence-based paradigm, where social and other scientists are positioned as (simply) delivering 'evidence' on questions and priorities set by governments, it becomes extremely difficult to put those questions and priorities under scrutiny. In effect, these questions and priorities presume the nature of the 'problem'. As a result, by producing 'knowledge' for pre-set questions, researchers become implicated in particular modes of governance (Q3, Q4; Bacchi 2008). In this way, the processes of policy-making and research production are depoliticised. In direct opposition to this position, a WPR approach insists that space needs to be created to interrogate and to challenge representations of 'problems' that are judged to have deleterious consequences (Q5, Q6).

This kind of critical scrutiny of the problem representations within policy proposals, developed and applied in preceding chapters, marks a significant departure from conventional conceptions of the role of policy analysis. Regardless of paradigm, the vast majority of policy analysis literature articulates, as a primary objective, helping policy analysts to offer 'useful' advice. Even our more interpretive strands tend to do this (see 'Guide to paradigms in major policy approaches' above). By contrast, a WPR approach aims to create space for reflecting more broadly on how we are governed.

One way in which we are governed, I suggest (Bacchi 2007), is through the production (representation) of 'policy' as neutral, technical and as separate from politics. This view of policy encourages the conclusion that public policy is best left to politicians and to other 'experts', creating the conditions that encourage citizen disaffection (Q5). Why should citizens get involved, it implies, since the issues are clearly beyond them and are already handled 'efficiently'? By contrast, highlighting the political ramifications of problem representations *within* policies, as per a WPR approach, reveals the inherent contestation in policy-making (Q6). Hence, such an approach stands to invigorate citizen engagement and debate (Q5, Q6).

Here we can see that so-called neutral and apolitical policy theory is actually *highly political* and politically dangerous, encouraging quiescent behaviour among citizens (Q5). Given that this is the case, such approaches to policy need to be *challenged* rather than simply accepted as *complementary* forms of study. A WPR approach has this objective as its ultimate goal.

The distinction between more conventional approaches to policy analysis and a WPR approach is nowhere clearer than in the pedagogical practices it recommends. Keeping in mind the hesitation about whether or not education can ever mean 'liberation' (see Chapter 9), it is possible to draw sharp contrasts between positivist and poststructuralist approaches to teaching policy analysis. Illustrating the pragmatism of political rationalism (see 'Guide to paradigms in major policy approaches' above), Wildavsky recommends that policy should be 'taught backwards':

> Instead of beginning by formulating a problem, considering alternative solutions, developing criteria, applying criteria to data, and so on, students' work improved when exercises went the other way around. The best way to begin learning was to apply strong criteria to good data, go on to create criteria and discover alternatives, and, after numerous trials, formulate a problem at the very end . . . formulating the problem was more like the end than the beginning of the analysis. (Wildavsky 1979, p. 3)

Because a WPR approach also talks about 'working backwards' – starting with a policy and working backwards to identify problem representations – it is crucial to clarify how this position *differs from* Wildavsky's. For Wildavsky, the analyst's task is to define policy problems according to what is *feasible*, according to what is (considered to be) do-able, given political and financial constraints. A WPR approach, by contrast, wants to invigorate imaginations to consider alternative futures, to speculate on how we could be *governed* differently. Here it takes its cue from Foucault: 'as soon as people begin to have trouble thinking things the way they have been thought, transformation becomes at the same time very urgent, very difficult, and entirely possible' (Foucault 1994, p. 457).

Ultimately, then, a WPR approach to policy analysis poses a challenge to the 'problem-solving' paradigm currently dominating our intellectual and policy landscape. Attesting to the ascendancy of this paradigm, generic 'problem-solving skills' now appear regularly among the desired Graduate Attributes right across the Australian university sector, often alongside lifelong learning (University of New England 2007; see also University of Adelaide 2008, UNSW 2008, USYD 2008, UTAS 2008, etc.). Reflecting upon the ways in which these key terms represent the 'problem' – positioning individual students as ciphers whose task is to 'address' 'problems' set by others – it may well be worthwhile to consider replacing 'problem-*solving*' with 'problem-*questioning*' as a desirable attribute. The argument here is that critical thinking involves *probing*, rather than 'solving', 'problems'. In this view, it is high time we demanded a 'right to the problems' (Deleuze 1994, p. 158).

Summary

In this chapter we concentrated on relationships between power and 'knowledge', showing how the latter is a contested term. Through examining 'practical texts' in media policy we saw how creating 'knowledge' as 'information' produces three effects: securitisation of 'knowledge', media concentration, and censorship. We also explored the dominance, limitations and depoliticising effects of a problem-solving paradigm in three sites: conventional approaches to policy, evidence-based policy, and university 'knowledge' policy.

Questions

1. Are 'knowledge' and 'information' synonymous? How would you differentiate them?
2. What political consequences can be traced to the current tendency to reduce 'knowledge' to 'information'?
3. Is evidence-based policy apolitical?
4. What is meant by a problem-solving paradigm?
5. How does a WPR analysis put such a paradigm in question?

---

1 The term 'unconscious' is problematised because it works within accepted psychological premises, indicating how difficult it is to think outside of and find language to move beyond those premises.

REFERENCES

AMERICAN PSYCHIATRIC ASSOCIATION 1952, *Mental Disorders: Diagnostic and Statistical Manual*, Amer Psychiatric Pr, Washington, DC.

AMERICAN PSYCHIATRIC ASSOCIATION 1994, *Diagnostic and Statistical Manual of Mental Disorders*, Fourth Edition, American Psychiatric Pub. Inc., Washington, DC.

AUSTRALIAN GOVERNMENT 2004, *Australia's Strategic Framework for the Information Economy 2004–2006*, Department of Communications, Information Technology and the Arts, Canberra, <www.dbcde.gov.au>, accessed 23 June 2008.

AUSTRALIAN GOVERNMENT 2006a, *The Broadcasting Services Amendment (Media Ownership) Act*, Commonwealth of Australia Law, No. 129, <www.comlaw.gov.au>, accessed 16 October 2008.

AUSTRALIAN GOVERNMENT 2006b, *Meeting the Digital Challenge: Reforming Australia's Media in the Digital Age*, Discussion Paper on Media Reform Options, <http://webdiary.com.au>, accessed 6 August 2008.

AUSTRALIAN GOVERNMENT 2006c, *The Anti-Terrorism Act (No. 2) 2005*, <www.ag.gov.au>, accessed 27 June 2008.

AUSTRALIAN GOVERNMENT 2008, *Media Reform—Local Content and Local Presence Requirement for Commercial Radio Fact Sheet*, Australian Communications and Media Authority, <www.acma.gov.au>, accessed 27 June 2008.

ASA (Australian Society of Authors) 2007, 'Response to Attorney-General on material that advocates terrorism', <www.asauthors.org>, accessed 27 June 2008.

BACCHI, C. 1999, *Women, Policy, and Politics: The Construction of Policy Problems*, Sage, London.

BACCHI, C. 2000, 'Policy as Discourse: What Does it Mean? Where Does it Get Us?' *Discourse: Studies in the Cultural Practices of Education*, vol. 27, no. 1, pp. 45–57.

BACCHI, C. 2007, 'The Ethics of Problem Representation: Widening the Scope of Ethical Debate', *Policy & Society*, vol. 26, no. 3, pp. 5–20.

BACCHI, C. 2008, 'The Politics of Research Management: Reflections on the Gap Between What We "Know" [about SDH] and What We Do', *Health Sociology Review*, vol. 17, no. 2, pp. 165–76.

BACCHI, C. 2009, 'The Issue of Intentionality in Frame Theory: The Need for Reflexive Framing', in *The Discursive Politics of Gender Equality: Stretching, Bending and Policymaking*, eds E. Lombardo, P. Meier & M. Verloo, Routledge, London.

BALL, S. J. 1990, *Politics and Policy Making in Education: Explorations in Policy Sociology*, Routledge, New York.

BARAK, G. 1988, 'Newsmaking Criminology: Reflections on the Media, Intellectuals, and Crime', *Justice Quarterly*, vol. 5, pp. 565–87.

BARAK, G. 2007, 'Doing Newsmaking Criminology From Within the Academy', *Theoretical Criminology*, vol. 11, no. 2, pp. 191–207.

BECKER, G. S. 1964, *Human Capital: A Theoretical and Empirical Analysis, With Special Reference to Education*, National Bureau of Economic Research, distributed by Columbia University Press, New York.

BIGO, D. 2002, 'Security and Immigration: Toward a Critique of the Governmentality of Unease', *Alternatives: Global, Local, Political*, vol. 27, no. 1, pp. 63–92.

BRAVERMAN, H. 1974, *Labor and Monopoly Capital: The Degradation of Work in the Twentieth Century*, Monthly Review Press, London.

CALLAND, R. & DEHN, G. eds 2004, *Whistleblowing Around the World: Law, Culture & Practice*, Open Democracy Advice Centre and Public Concern at Work, Cape Town/London.

COLEBATCH, H. K. 1998, *Policy*, Open University Press, Buckingham.

COMMONWEALTH CONSOLIDATED ACTS 1975, *Foreign Acquisitions and Takeovers Act*, <www.austlii.edu.au>, accessed 26 October 2008.

COMMONWEALTH CONSOLIDATED ACTS 1992, *Broadcasting Services Act*, <www.austlii.edu.au>, accessed 27 October 2008.

COMMONWEALTH NUMBERED ACTS 2007, *Classification (Publications, Films and Computer Games) Amendment (Terrorist Material) Act 2007 (No.179 2007)* – Schedule 1 Amendments. Minister's second reading speech, House of Representatives, 21 June, <www.austlii.edu.au>, accessed 27 June 2008.

COONAN, H. 2006, 'Meeting the Digital Challenge: Reforming Australia's Media in the Digital Age', Speech to CEDA (Committee for Economic Development of Australia), <www.dbcde.gov.au>, accessed 24 June 2008.

CURTIS, S. 2006, 'Content, Consolidation and Clout: How will Regional Australia be Affected by Media Ownership Changes?' Communications Law Centre, Melbourne, <http://search.informit.com.au>, accessed 27 June 2008.

DAVIES, B. 1994, *Poststructuralist Theory and Classroom Practice*, Deakin University Press, Geelong.

DAVIES, B. 2003, 'Death to Critique and Dissent? The Policies and Practices of New Managerialism and of "Evidence-based Practice"', *Gender and Education*, vol. 15, no. 1, pp. 91–103.

DAVIES, B., BROWNE, J., GANNON, S., HOPKINS, L., McCANN, H. & WIHLBORG, M. 2006, 'Constituting the Feminist Subject in Poststructuralist Discourse', *Feminism & Psychology*, vol. 16, no. 1, pp. 87–103.

DELEUZE, G. 1994, *Difference and Repetition*. Trans. P. Patton, Columbia University Press, New York.

FISCHER, F. 1980, *Politics, Values and Public Policy: The Problem of Methodology*, Westview Press, Boulder, Colorado.

FOUCAULT, M. 1979, *The History of Sexuality, Volume I, An Introduction*, Trans. R. Hurley, Allen Lane, London.

FOUCAULT, M. 1980 [1976] 'Two Lectures', in *Power/Knowledge: Selected Interviews and Other Writings 1972–1977/Michel Foucault*, ed. C. Gordon, Trans. C. Gordon & others, Harvester Press, Sussex.

FOUCAULT, M. 1988 [1977] 'Confinement, Psychiatry, Prison', in *Michel Foucault: Politics, Philosophy, Culture: Interviews and Other Writings, 1977–1984*, ed. L. D. Kritzman, Trans. A. Sheridan & others, Routledge, New York.

FOUCAULT, M. 1991 [1968], 'Politics and the Study of Discourse', in *The Foucault Effect: Studies in Governmentality*, eds G. Burchell, C. Gordon & P. Miller, University of Chicago Press, Chicago.

FOUCAULT, M. 1994 [1981], 'So is it Important to Think?', in *Power: Essential Works of Foucault 1954–1984*, vol. 3, ed. J. D. Faubion, Trans. R. Hurley & others, Penguin, London.

FREEDMAN, D. 2006, 'Dynamics of Power in Contemporary Media Policy-making', *Media, Culture & Society*, vol. 28, no. 6, pp. 907–23.

GIBBONS, M., LIMOGES, C., NOWOTNY, H., SCHWARTZMAN, P. & TROW, M., 1994, *The New Production of Knowledge*, Sage, London.

HAJER, M. A. & WAGENAAR, H. eds 2003, *Deliberative Policy Analysis: Understanding Governance in the Network Society*, Cambridge University Press, Cambridge.

HANNEY, S. R., GONZALEZ-BLOCK, M. A., BUXTON, M. J. & KOGAN, M. 2003, 'The Utilisation of Health Research in Policy-Making: Concepts, Examples and Methods of Assessment', *Health Research Policy and Systems*, vol. 1, no. 2, pp. 1–28.

HENRY, S. & MILOVANOVIC, D. 1996, *Constitutive Criminology: Beyond Postmodernism*, Sage, London.

LASSWELL, H. D. 1951, 'The Policy Orientation', in *The Policy Sciences: Recent Developments in Scope and Method*, eds D. Lerner & H. D. Lasswell, Stanford University Press, Stanford, California.

MACHLUP, F. 1962, *Production and Distribution of Knowledge in the United States*, Princeton University Press, Princeton, New Jersey.

MAJONE, G. 1989, *Evidence, Argument and Persuasion in the Policy Process*, Yale University Press, New Haven, CT.

MARR, D. 2007, *His Master's Voice: The Corruption of Public Debate Under Howard*, Quarterly Essay, Issue 26, Black Inc., Melbourne.

MARSTON, G. & WATTS, R. 2003, 'Tampering With the Evidence: A Critical Appraisal of Evidence-Based Policy-Making', *The Drawing Board: An Australian Review of Public Affairs*, vol. 3, no. 3, pp. 143–63.

MARSTON, G. & MCDONALD, C. 2006, 'Conclusion: A Conversation Worth Pursuing?', in *Analysing Social Policy: A Governmental Approach*, eds G. Marston & C. McDonald, Edward Elgar, Cheltenham, UK.

MARTIN, B. 1999, *The Whistleblower's Handbook: How to Be an Effective Resister*, Envirobook, Sydney.

MASUDA, J. 1981, *The Information Society as Post-Industrial Society*, World Future Society, Washington, DC.

MCCLURE, K. 1992, 'The Issue of Foundations: Scientized Politics, Politicized Science and Feminist Critical Practice', in *Feminists Theorize the Political*, eds J. Butler & J. Scott, Routledge, New York.

MCMILLEN, J. 1996, 'Understanding Gambling: History, Concepts and Theories', in *Gambling Cultures: Studies in history and interpretation*, ed. J. McMillen, Routledge, London.

MEDIA REPORT 2007a, 'Australia's Right to Know', ABC Radio National, 31 May.

MEDIA REPORT 2007b, 'Australian Censorship Laws Tightened', ABC Radio National, 9 August.

MEKN (Measurement and Evidence Knowledge Network) 2007, *The Social Determinants of Health: Developing an Evidence Base for Political Action*, Final Report to the World Health Organization, Geneva, <www.who.int>, accessed 2 May 2008.

NORRIS, P., KERN, M. & JUST, M. 2003, *Framing Terrorism: The New Media, the Government and the Public*, Routledge, New York.

PARSONS, W. 1995, *Public Policy: An Introduction to the Theory and Practice of Policy Analysis*, Edward Elgar, Aldershot, UK.

PETERS, M. 2001, 'National Education Policy Constructions of the "Knowledge Economy": Towards a Critique', *Journal of Educational Enquiry*, vol. 2, no. 1, pp. 1–22.

PHILIPSON, G. 2004, 'IT – Lost in the Woolliness', *The Age*, 28 September.

POPAY, J. WILLIAMS, G., THOMAS, C. & GATRELL, A. 1998, 'Theorising Inequalities in Health: The Place of Lay Knowledge', *Sociology of Health and Illness*, vol. 20, no. 5, pp. 619–44.

REICH, R. B. 1991, *Work of Nations: Preparing Ourselves for 21st-Century Capitalism*, A. A. Knopf, New York.

REIN, M. & SCHON, D. 1996, 'Frame-Critical Policy Analysis and Frame-Reflective-Policy Practices', *Knowledge and Policy*, vol. 9, no. 1, pp. 85–105.

ROSE, N. S. 2000, *Powers of Freedom: Reframing Political Thought*, 1st edition 1999, Cambridge University Press, Cambridge, UK.

SERCOMBE, H. 2005, 'Media Representation, Policing Interventions: How Language and Discourse Shape the Policing of Young People', in *Youth, Otherness and the Plural City: Modes of Belonging and Social Life*, eds Andersson, M., Lithman, Y. & Särnhede, O., Daidalos, Gothenburg.

SEXTON, R. 2007, 'Teen Knife Violence Surge', *The Age*, 8 July.

SHAPIRO, M. J. 1988, *The Politics of Representation: Writing Practices in Biography, Photography and Policy Analysis*, University of Wisconsin Press, Madison.

SIMONS, J. 1995, *Foucault and the Political*, Routledge, New York.

SOLESBURY, W. 2001, 'Evidence-Based Policy: Whence it Came and Where it's Going', *ESRC Centre for Evidence-Based Policy and Practice: Working Paper 1*, <www.evidencenetwork. org>, accessed 10 October 2006.

SPENDER, D. 1982, *Women of Ideas and What Men Have Done to Them: From Aphra Behn to Adrienne Rich*, Routledge & Kegan Paul, London.

SPIEGEL, A. 2002, '81 Words', *This American Life*, Episode 204, Chicago Public Radio.

STARK, J. & HOUSTON, C. 2007, 'Drink Puts Youth on Deadly Trail', *Melbourne Age*, 9 June.

St Pierre, E. A. 2006, 'Scientifically Based Research in Education: Epistemology and Ethics', *Adult Education Quarterly*, vol. 56, no. 4, pp. 239–66.

TOURAINE, A. 1974, *The Post-Industrial Society: Tomorrow's Social History, Classes, Conflicts and Culture in the Programmed Society*, Trans. L. Mayhew, Wildwood House, London.

UNIVERSITY OF ADELAIDE 2008, *Graduate Attributes*, <www.adelaide.edu.au>, accessed 16 October 2008.

UNIVERSITY OF NEW ENGLAND 2007, *Attributes of a UNE Graduate*, <www.une.edu.au>, accessed 25 June 2008.

UNSW (UNIVERSITY OF NEW SOUTH WALES) 2008, *UNSW Graduate Attributes*, <www. unsw.edu.au>, accessed 16 October 2008.

USYD (UNIVERSITY OF SYDNEY) 2008, Graduate Attributes, Faculty of Economics and Business, <www.econ.usyd.edu.au>, accessed 16 October 2008.

UTAS (UNIVERSITY OF TASMANIA) 2008, *Generic Graduate Attributes*, <www.utas.edu.au>, accessed 16 October 2008.

VAILE, M. 2000, 'Australia and the Knowledge Economy', Speech, *The Economist Intelligence Unit*, Canberra, 31 October, <www.trademinister.gov.au>, accessed 6 August 2008.

WALKERDINE, V. ed. 2001, *Challenging Subjects: Critical Psychology for a New Millenium*, Palgrave, Basingstoke.

WHAT WORKS CLEARINGHOUSE 2005, 'Who we are', <www.whatworks.ed.gov/whoweare/ overview.html>, accessed 26 March 2007.

WHITE, M. & EPSTON, D. 1990, *Narrative Means to Therapeutic Ends*, W.W. Norton & Company, New York.

WILDAVSKY, A. 1979, *Speaking Truth to Power: The Art and Craft of Policy Analysis*, Little, Brown Publishers, Boston.

YANOW, D. 2000, *Conducting Interpretive Policy Analysis*, Sage, Thousand Oaks.

FURTHER READING

BARNETT, C. 2003, *Culture and Democracy: Media, Space, and Representation*, Edinburgh University Press, Edinburgh.

DAVIS, M. 1999, *Gangland: Cultural Elites and the New Generationalism*, St. Leonards, Allen & Unwin.

POYNTING, S. & MORGAN, G. eds 2007, *Outrageous!: Moral Panics in Australia*, ACYS, Hobart, Tasmania.

STREET, J. 2001, *Mass Media, Politics and Democracy*, Palgrave, Hampshire.

'A right to the problems'

Conclusion

This book, as declared at the outset, wants to contribute to an understanding of how we are governed, of how governing takes place. To this end it has two interrelated objectives:

- to introduce a methodology for analysing policies (a WPR approach);
- to challenge the problem-*solving* paradigm that dominates the current intellectual and policy landscape, most clearly in Western industrialised nations and in the international organisations that are their offspring, e.g. the IMF and the World Bank.

The two projects are united at a basic level. In both cases the purpose is to insist that 'problems' do not exist outside of the ways in which they are thought about or conceptualised. It follows that assuming that 'problems' *do* exist as discrete conditions (outside the way they are thought about) has serious political implications – removing necessary contestation from around the postulated nature and character of public policy 'problems'.

Chapter 1 introduces the 'what's the problem represented to be?' (WPR) approach to policy analysis, which consists of six interrelated questions and a directive to apply the questions to one's own problem representations. Chapter 2 provides the theory that underpins the methodology. The Introduction and Chapter 1 contain lists of the *basic* questions and the directive. At the end of Chapter 2 there is also an *expanded* list, which clarifies what is being sought in each question and in the directive. Chapters 3 through 10 apply the approach to a range of policy 'areas', developing the argument that policy analysis requires problem-*questioning* rather than problem-*solving*. Chapters 3 and 4 apply the six questions systematically, while subsequent chapters offer a more integrated analysis with use of a particular question signalled by the insertion of notation (Q1, Q2, etc.).

The principal contention of a WPR approach to policy analysis is that policies *are* problematisations. That is, because policies make proposals for change, by their very nature they imply what is held to be problematic. The approach, therefore, accepts Osborne's (1997, p. 174) insight about health policy – 'policy cannot get to work without first problematising its territory' – and applies this observation to policies generally.

The next step in the argument is that, through this process of problematisation, policies *create* particular understandings of what the 'problem' is. This proposal does not mean that all we are left with are *competing* conceptions or *definitions* of a 'problem', however. Rather, a WPR approach makes the case that policies create *representations* of 'problems' that *take on lives of their own* because they affect materially and symbolically how we are governed and how we live. Policies *constitute* 'problems', meaning that *they make a 'problem' exist* as a particular type of 'problem'.

Moreover, the argument continues, given the centrality of public policy to every dimension of our lives (see Activities in the Introduction), these *constituted* 'problems' significantly affect our lives on a day-to-day basis. This means that, effectively, **we are governed *through* problematisations.**

Problematisations are framing mechanisms; they determine what is considered to be significant and what is left out of consideration. As a result, public policies create 'problems' that channel and hence *limit* awareness of and sensitivity to the full range of troubling conditions that make up our existence. Because this is the case, it becomes crucially important to scrutinise the *ways in which 'problems' are represented in public policies*. To this end **we need to study problematisations rather than 'problems'.**

In order to accomplish this task, problematisations are 'opened up' for examination. By focusing on the proposal for change it is possible to identify how the 'problem' is understood. This is possible because what someone proposes to do about something reveals what they think needs to change, what is held to be problematic. I call these implied 'problems' *problem representations*, which become the focus of subsequent analysis.

To repeat an example from the Introduction that illustrates how the approach works, if you propose training programs for women in order to increase their representation in positions of influence, the 'problem' is *created* as their *lack* of training. Once the *problem representation* is clarified, attention shifts to examining its nature and character, and to considering what this examination can tell us about how we are governed. That is, in order to understand how governing takes place, **we need to problematise (interrogate) the problematisations uncovered in public policies through scrutinising the premises and effects of the problem representations they contain.**

A WPR approach facilitates this task. Adopting the notation form for referring to the questions in the approach, in applying a WPR approach, we get to ask: What is assumed to be the 'problem'? (Q1) Which meanings and presuppositions are necessary for this representation of the 'problem' to make sense or to be coherent? **(Q2)** How has this representation of the 'problem' come to prominence? **(Q3)** And, what does this representation of the 'problem' take for granted and leave unquestioned? **(Q4)** Since identified problem representations play such a significant role in how we are governed, we also get the opportunity to consider *more precisely* how they affect our lives and the lives of others **(Q5)**, how they influence who we are and our views of others **(Q5)**, who supports these problem representations, and how they could be challenged, if we are unhappy with them **(Q6)**. The final important recommendation in the approach follows from the insights generated by these questions: because we are governed through problematisations that influence who we are and how we think, it becomes necessary to apply the WPR approach to one's own proposals for change and to the problem representations they produce.

> 'If policies, arguments, analyses and prescriptions purport to provide answers, they do so only in relation to a set of questions. Their very status as answers is dependent upon the existence of such questions. If, for example, imprisonment, marketization, community care are seen as answers, to what are they answers? And, in reconstructing the problematizations which accord them intelligibility as answers, these grounds become visible, their limits and presuppositions are opened for interrogation in new ways.' (Rose 2000, p. 58)

To develop these arguments a WPR approach to policy analysis draws upon four intellectual traditions:

- social construction theory;
- poststructuralism, including poststructuralist discourse psychology;
- feminist body theory; and,
- governmentality studies.

From *social construction theory* a WPR approach accepts that things we often take for granted as forms of 'fixed' reality are products of particular times and places. A social constructionist perspective, therefore, encourages us to identify and examine categories and concepts that are embedded within particular policies and to see them, to an extent, as pliable and variable. Chapter 3, for example, identifies 'youth' as a socially constructed category, with differing meanings in different historical periods. 'Health' (Chapter 6), 'crime' (Chapter 5), 'unemployment' (Chapter 3) and 'knowledge' (Chapter 10) are other concepts that are treated as *social constructs*. By challenging the 'givenness' of such concepts and categories, social construction theory plays a useful destabilising role in the study of public policy. It makes us think about where concepts and categories come from, and opens up novel ways of exploring the governing practices to which they are attached.

Poststructuralism draws attention to the politics involved in the processes of assigning meaning to key terms. Starting from the premise, just established, that the meaning of concepts and categories is, to an extent, pliable and variable, poststructuralism directs us to track both the political influences that shape their content and how they function in political debate and political practice. Concepts are seen as *contested*, with disputes over their meaning related to competing political visions (see Chapter 1). Since our task in this book is to understand how we are governed, we track the usage of key concepts and categories that function to make certain forms of governing admissible and legitimate, while de-legitimising other forms of governing.

For example, in Chapter 3, we saw that (historical and variable) assumptions about the nature of 'youth' as a period of development and instability underpin and 'rationalise' policies and practices like youth wages and youth allowances, among other things. Chapter 4 draws attention to the ways in which a distinction between licit and illicit drugs dominates contemporary drugs/alcohol policy, despite some important anomalies in the distinction – e.g. the amount of harm to public 'health' associated with *licit* drugs such as alcohol and tobacco. In Chapter 6 we explore how a conception of 'health' as absence of disease contributes to the long-standing dominant focus on *curative* health policy, alongside a token nod to *prevention*. In Chapter 8 we trace how the notion of equality has come to be understood through dichotomies, such as equal treatment/different treatment, and how these understandings have translated into laws and policies that sustain the social status quo.

Reflecting the concerns of *poststructuralist discourse psychology*, a WPR approach emphasises how subjects (subjectivities) are constituted *within* policies – how policies incite us to feel about ourselves and others in particular ways. The focus throughout the book on dividing practices and subjectification effects, discussed below, indicates the influence of this perspective. *Feminist body theory* acts as a counter-balance to a focus on people's *perceptions* to ensure that lived materiality receives due recognition.

Governmentality studies – the fourth intellectual tradition informing a WPR approach – directs attention to broad patterns of thought within the ways in which governing takes place. These broad patterns of thought are called 'regimes of governance' or 'modes of governance' (govern-*mentalities*). The goal of this kind of study, associated with Foucault, is to explore the *thought in government*. Importantly, *thought* here is not what goes on in people's heads. Rather, it refers to the forms of thinking (rationalities or rationales) necessary to particular ways of governing. To get at the *thought in or behind government*, Foucault (1984) recommended studying problematisations, how 'problems' are conceived.

As was made clear in Chapter 2, a WPR approach takes the concept of problematisation and applies it somewhat differently from Foucault and from some other governmentality scholars (e.g. Garland 2001). In most governmentality studies there is an assumption that a particular confluence of circumstances provokes a *reaction* from governments in specific, relatively rare instances where the role of government is put into question (Dean 1999, p. 27). A WPR approach is uncomfortable with any suggestion that specific conditions *spark* governmental 'responses' in this way. Rather, emphasis is placed on the contested nature of 'problems' and on how specific policies have come to be *assumed* as necessary 'responses'.

Moreover, instead of specific instances where the role of government is put in question, a WPR approach directs attention to the problematising that necessarily takes place in *each and every* policy ('practical text'). The scope of the analysis, therefore, is broader than in most governmentality studies. While starting the analysis with specific public policies – which might seem to signal a narrow understanding of politics as to do with institutional decision-making – the concerns in a WPR analysis extend beyond the 'problem of government' to embrace a 'wider conceptualisation of politics as including struggles around identities and "difference", including issues around gender, sexuality, ethnicity or "race", and everyday life' (Mottier 2001, p. 332). As examples:

- Chapters 3 and 5 consider how 'welfare' mothers are singled out for particular forms of surveillance;
- Chapters 1 and 10 reflect on the impact of specific modes of governance on the lives of homosexual men and lesbians;
- Chapters 5 and 8 identify the uneven and disciplinary effects of specific forms of rule on Aboriginal people;
- Chapters 4, 6, 7, 9 and 10 share an interest in understanding the governmental influences that shape the lives we lead as parents, workers, students and researchers.

In these reflections, a WPR approach draws upon the interest of governmentality scholars in *forms of indirect rule* – referred to as 'government at a distance' (Miller and Rose 1990, p. 9). This perspective directs attention to the role played by institutions, agencies and 'knowledges', including but beyond the state, in governing processes. For example, in Chapter 3 we identify the proliferation of governmental agencies involved in governing welfare recipients. Chapter 6 notes the wide array of medical professionals who play a part in governing health practices. Chapters 9 and 10 identify educators and researchers as playing pivotal roles in governance objectives. These forms of rule are described as 'indirect' only in the sense that institutions of government are not directly involved. The impact on individuals' lives can be and often is both direct and punitive (see '81 Words', Chapter 10).

Following a governmentality perspective, a WPR approach sees value in identifying 'regimes of governance', though it tends to emphasise *hybrid* forms of rule rather than *ideal types*. It also emphasises the power involved in establishing particular forms of rule. This genealogical perspective (see Chapter 2) highlights the contingency of specific govern-*mentalities*. Noting that things could have been otherwise creates space for contestation (see O'Malley 2001).

In this vein, while acknowledging that key concepts are deeply embedded within long historical traditions of governmental practices and hence are difficult to challenge (see Dean 1999, p. 65), a focus on the politics involved in the shaping of meaning – a poststructuralist perspective – further destabilises problem representations we have cause to question. For example, the power involved in producing current dominant understandings of 'welfare dependency' (Chapter 3), 'problem gamblers' (Chapter 4) and 'irresponsible' citizens (Chapters 4, 5 and 6) is recognised as an important part of political processes.

The reference to 'problem representations *we have cause to question'*, signals the critical intent of a WPR approach to policy analysis. The suggestion here is that particular modes of rule have deleterious effects (**Q5**) that need to be uncovered and commented upon. To reduce or remove these effects, the possibility is raised that we may well need to be governed differently (see Pavlich 2001). Three ideas are central to this critique:

- ■ dividing practices that operate in current dominant modes of governance;
- ■ subjectification processes within current modes of governance that produce us as particular kinds of subjects; and,
- ■ lived effects that harm some and benefit others.

Dividing practices represent a major theme in the book, showing the relevance of a WPR approach for studying social relations. The book highlights the ways in which specific modes of governance set groups against each other, often in dichotomous ways, as a means of facilitating rule. For example:

- ■ Chapter 3 shows how the 'problem' of 'welfare dependency' sets 'dole bludgers' against 'tax-payers';
- ■ Chapter 4 notes how 'binge-drinkers' and 'problem gamblers' are contrasted with 'responsible' drinkers and gamblers;
- ■ Chapter 5 highlights how the behaviours of targeted minorities ('youth', Aboriginal peoples) are problematised, while suspect and illegal behaviours among the powerful are countenanced;
- ■ Chapters 7 and 9 encourage us to think about the role of education and immigration policies in marking specific groups within and without national borders as inadequate and/or as problematic – the *less* 'mobile' (in terms of seeking paid employment) who are seen to require 'lifelong learning', and the *excessively* 'mobile' ('illegal' migrants) who are seen to require containment.

As we are governed through these practices, the implication is the possible need to rethink policies that have these effects.

Studying subjectification processes helps to explain why this sort of rethinking may prove difficult. The argument here – considered in Question 5 of the approach and a concern throughout the book – is that policies have an influence upon how we come to think about ourselves and others. As the clearest example, Marginson (1997; see Chapter 9) talks about the way in which HECS produces the subjects it assumes – individuals concerned ultimately with securing a job that pays well in order to rid themselves of a HECS debt. Along similar lines the emphasis on individual responsibility in welfare policy (Chapter 3), drugs/alcohol and gambling policy (Chapter 4) and health policy (Chapter 6) privileges a particular kind of subject – one who is autonomous and independent, with little need of others – and hence incites us to think about ourselves as subjects of this kind.

'Changing behaviour'

In a 2007 publication the Australian Public Service Commission explicitly identifies behavioural change among citizens as a governmental objective. It identifies the 'rational choice model' as 'the behavioural change theory that underlies much public policy': 'People assess the choices before them in terms of costs and benefits and then select the choice that maximises their net benefits' (Australian Government 2007, p. 7).

- **What kind of a political subject is assumed in rational choice theory?**

- **Do you see any silences?**

A WPR approach urges us to think about the limitations ('limits') in this way of conceptualising human existence, and the lived effects that follow. It raises the possibility that we may not be happy with the individuals we (are encouraged to) become. Are there not aspects of a life worth living that are automatically discounted and indeed devalued in this presumption of individual autonomy and independence? Could not some of the growing concern about stress levels among young and older workers have some connection to this directive to become 'entrepreneurs of the self', calculating constantly about how best to acquire marketable 'human capital' and 'skills'? Could the lack of fit between our home and work lives, which is currently attracting so much attention, owe something to this imperative? Does not the emphasis on independence ignore our embodied interdependence over our lifespan and across borders (Beasley and Bacchi 2007)? If the answer to these questions is in the affirmative, policies that create (lack of) individual responsibility as the 'problem' have a good deal to answer for.

Of course, given our location within these identified modes of rule, it is not easy to stand back and reflect on them. However, it is not impossible to do so or a book such as this one could not have been written. By building in a directive to scrutinise our own proposals for change and the problem representations they produce, a WPR approach aims to create the conditions for systematic critical self-scrutiny, described in the book as reflexivity.

This range of issues is seldom raised in more conventional books on policy analysis. While there is no argument that a WPR approach is the *only* kind of policy analysis we need, there is a conviction that all approaches to policy, like all theoretically-informed analyses, are at their core political and have political effects. Consequently, these effects should be discussed. As a way to do this, I reflect briefly on the three 'cross-border' movements associated with a WPR approach to policy analysis:

- across national/international boundaries;
- across the boundaries of policy 'specialisms';
- across the government/non-government divide.

Current discussions about 'globalisation' might seem to capture or echo the first point about the need to rethink the nature of national/international boundaries. However, 'globalisation' tends to be talked about as if the two categories of 'national' and 'international' exist separately, and that what is at stake is relations *between* them. A WPR approach makes a different move. It broadens the field of analysis to *modes of governance* (drawing on governmentality studies) and therefore asks different sorts of questions. For example, in Chapter 7, we consider how assumptions about 'sovereign states' impact on the lived experience of the world's inhabitants, supporting a range of policies that penalise and punish people from outside some 'sovereign' space/s. As another example, we reflect on the way in which the current focus on international competitiveness (Chapter 9) lies behind policies like HECS and lifelong learning, policies that emphasise 'self-improvement'. The suggestion here is that a good deal can be learned about the ways in which the world works from comparing problem representations across space and time boundaries.

Similarly, the challenge to policy 'specialisms' raises new ways to think about policy. Noting that health policy is bound to fail, since at some stage we will all die (see Osborne 1997), for example, raises questions about the reasons we have a 'health policy' – surely an uncommon topic in social policy courses. Identifying how poverty issues and 'race' issues get turned into health issues challenges us to think about the consequences of this form of transposition. What is accomplished and what is hidden, for example, by focusing on the poor health of Aboriginal peoples? Does it depend on how the 'problem' is represented? What happens if racism is identified as a cause of poor health?

Our third 'cross-border' move – including but extending beyond the state to encompass the full array of institutions, agencies and 'knowledges' that influence forms of rule – creates a new agenda for policy studies. While some policy analysts direct attention to the nature of the relationship between the medical establishment (including psychology) and government policy, few consider the ways in which *psychological premises infiltrate and shape policy*. For example, psychological assumptions about fragile mental states underpin the *National Youth*

Suicide Prevention Strategy (Chapters 1 and 2). Assumptions about the nature of homosexuality — as in the *DSM*'s 1972 definition of homosexuality as 'sexual deviance' (Chapter 10) — serve to justify (rationalise) the exclusion of lesbian women from IVF services (see Activity on 'Access to reproductive technologies' in Chapter 1). Creating gamblers as 'pathological' (see Blaszczynski 2000; Chapter 4) supports a policy focus on counselling and 'rehabilitation' for 'problem gamblers'.

Psychology provides an easy target for this kind of analysis. It is more challenging to reflect on other forms of knowledge that we take for granted and that play a prominent role in supporting particular governance objectives. Chapter 5 considers how different criminal justice theories support particular approaches to governing crime. Along similar lines, Chapter 6 identifies links between competing perspectives on 'health' and health policy, while Chapter 10 draws on the work of McMillen (1996) to illustrate how specific interpretations of the nature and function of gambling serve to bolster particular policies. When we identify these forms of connection between academic disciplines and research, and government policy, two things are accomplished:

- ■ we see that there are indeed *competing* interpretations of social events, and hence *competing* 'knowledges';
- ■ we put a question mark over the 'truth' status of theoretical premises.

It follows that, since theories play a central role in how we are governed, it is necessary to reflect on how they *conceptualise* the 'problems' they purport to *address*. To this end, the book recommends subjecting competing theoretical perspectives to a WPR analysis.

This critical approach to theory raises some challenging issues for research practice. It calls upon researchers to scrutinise their own theoretical premises *as problem representations*, and to ask questions about the underlying assumptions and possible effects of these problem representations. It also raises questions about the relationship between research activity and government, a topic visited briefly in Chapter 6 and raised again in Chapter 10. A crucial question is asked: if 'problems' do not exist outside the ways in which they are thought about, who should set the 'problems' (i.e. questions or priorities) for research activity?

Speculation on the appropriate relationship between policy research and government has a long history. In a desire to achieve a degree of recognition and status for political science, there were attempts in the 1950s in the United States to produce policy studies as a *form of science* (see Lasswell 1951; see Activity on 'Policy Science' in Chapter 10). There remained concerns about the repercussions that would follow, however, if researchers became *too* dependent upon targeted government funding and, hence, potentially subject to government dictates for research directions. In this vein, Merton and Lerner (1951, p. 306) cautioned, 'So long as the social scientist continues to accept a role in which he (sic) does not question policies, state problems, and formulate alternatives, the more does he become routinized in the role of bureaucratic technician'.

The topic of 'uptake' of research, or research utilisation, continued to concern policy scholars through the 1970s and 1980s. There was recognition that, in order for research to be (considered) 'useful', it would need to fit 'realistic' political contexts. A compromise was struck. In order to produce 'usable knowledge', Lindblom and Cohen (1979, p. 64) acknowledged the need to invite 'users' (policy-makers and bureaucrats) to become involved as *advisers* in the setting of research priorities (see also Weiss 1978, p. 69).

In Chapter 6 we consider how this research-government relationship has evolved. Currently and increasingly governments set the questions ('problems') that researchers study and for which they are invited to provide 'evidence' about 'what works'. This trend reflects the growing reliance of researchers on targeted government funding (Bacchi 2008). In this situation it becomes difficult for researchers to put in question the 'problems' they are asked to 'address' – e.g. obesity, binge-drinking, problem gambling – or the concepts that have become unquestioned maxims, such as social capital (Australian Government 2007, p. 17) or social inclusion. The central contention in the book – that 'problems' do not exist outside the ways in which they are thought about – makes this trend deeply worrying. The potential to put designated policy priorities ('problems') and key terms in 'problem'-oriented research into question is increasingly limited, reminding us of Merton and Lerner's (1951, p. 306; see above) warning about becoming 'bureaucratic technicians'.

Nowhere is this trend clearer than in the current and growing popularity of evidence-based policy. Several places in the book illustrate the extent to which this paradigm is becoming difficult for researchers to resist (see Chapters 5, 6 and 10). This is a concern because the power to create the 'problems' (research questions, research priorities) for which 'evidence' is solicited tends to escape critical comment. As this book argues throughout, a great deal is at stake in the ways in which policies *represent* 'problems'. Hence, there appears to be a pressing need to challenge the growing tendency in the research community to provide 'evidence' for *pre-defined* 'problems', and a need to insist that the assumed shapes of those 'problems' ought to be opened up for discussion and debate. This thinking lies behind the assertion in the subtitle for this Conclusion, repeating Deleuze's (1994, p. 158) plea for a 'right to the problems'.

The intent behind a WPR approach then, through providing a methodology to contest assumed 'problems', is to support and give substance to Deleuze's suggestion. The approach cautions against any use of the term 'problem' which implies a given or fixed state, and which denies the *shaping* that goes on in the process of problematisation. It follows that the most effective way to generate critical thinking is, not through training students to *solve* 'problems', but through encouraging them to *put 'problems' into question* (see Chapter 10).

Is this shift from 'problem-*solving*' to 'problem-*questioning*' likely to occur in the current climate? Probably not. But at the least it should be possible to put in question the contemporary near hegemony of a 'problem-solving' paradigm. A WPR approach to policy analysis encourages such interrogation. The suggestion is that asking 'what's the problem represented to be?' will leaven, if you will, or counter-balance the fashionable weight accorded 'evidence'.

There is no suggestion here of a prescriptive program for change. With Foucault, the WPR approach does not propose *particular* policies. It consists, after all, of *questions*, not proposals. The hope, however, is that the chapters in the book indicate how the questions in the approach open up different and sometimes challenging reflections on current dominant modes of governance.

REFERENCES

AUSTRALIAN GOVERNMENT 2007, *Changing Behaviour: A Public Policy Perspective*, Australian Public Service Commission, <www.apsc.gov.au>, accessed 4 November 2008

BACCHI, C. 2008, 'The Politics of Research Management: Reflections on the Gap Between What We "Know" [about SDH] and What We Do', *Health Sociology Review*, vol. 17, no. 2, pp. 165–76.

BEASLEY, C. & BACCHI, C. 2007, 'Envisaging a New Politics for an Ethical Future: Beyond Trust, Care and Generosity – Towards an Ethic of "Social Flesh"', *Feminist Theory*, vol. 8, no. 3, pp. 279–98.

BLASZCZYNSKI, A. 2000, 'Pathways to Pathological Gambling: Identifying Typologies', *The Electronic Journal of Gambling Issues*, vol. 1, <www.camh.net>, accessed 20 June 2008.

DEAN, M. 1999, *Governmentality: Power and Rule in Modern Society*, Sage, London.

DELEUZE, G. 1994, *Difference and Repetition*, Trans. P. Patton, Columbia University Press, New York.

FOUCAULT, M. 1984, 'Polemics, Politics and Problematizations', based on an interview conducted by P. Rabinow, Trans. L. Davis, in *Essential Works of Foucault, Vol. 1: Ethics*, New Press, New York, <www.foucault.info>, accessed 9 August 2008.

GARLAND, D. 2001, *The Culture of Control: Crime and Social Order in Contemporary Society*, University of Chicago Press, Chicago.

LASSWELL, H. D. 1951, 'The Policy Orientation', in *The Policy Sciences: Recent Developments in Scope and Method*, eds D. Lerner and H. D. Lasswell, Stanford University Press, California.

LINDBLOM, C. E. & COHEN, D. K. 1979, *Usable Knowledge: Social Science and Social Problem Solving*, Yale University Press, New Haven.

MARGINSON, S. 1997, 'Subjects and Subjugation: The Economics of Education as Power-Knowledge', *Discourse: studies in the cultural politics of education*, vol. 18, no. 2, pp. 215–27.

McMILLEN, J. 1996, 'Understanding Gambling: History, Concepts and Theories', in *Gambling Cultures: Studies in history and interpretation*, ed. J. McMillen, Routledge, London.

MERTON, R. K. & LERNER, D. 1951, 'Social Scientists and Research Policy', in *The Policy Sciences: Recent Developments in Scope and Method*, eds D. Lerner and H. D. Lasswell, Stanford University Press, California.

MILLER, P. & ROSE, N. 1990, 'Governing Economic Life', *Economy and Society*, vol. 19, no. 1, pp. 1–31.

MOTTIER, V. 2001, 'Review Essay: Foucault Revisited: Recent Assessments of the Legacy', *Acta Sociologica*, vol. 44, pp. 329–36.

O'MALLEY, P. 2001, 'Genealogy, Systematisation and Resistance in "Advanced Liberalism"', in *Rethinking Law, Society and Governance: Foucault's Bequest*, eds G. Wickham & G. Pavlich, Hart Publishing, Portland, Oregon.

OSBORNE, T. 1997, 'On Health and Statecraft', in *Foucault, Health and Medicine*, eds A. Petersen & R. Bunton, Routledge, London.

PAVLICH, G. 2001, 'The Art of Critique or How Not to be Governed Thus', in *Rethinking Law, Society and Governance: Foucault's Bequest*, eds G. Wickham & G. Pavlich, Hart Publishing, Oregon.

ROSE, N. S. 2000, *Powers of Freedom: Reframing Political Thought*, 1st edition 1999, Cambridge University Press, Cambridge, UK.

WEISS, C. H. 1978, 'Improving the Linkage Between Social Research and Public Policy', in *Knowledge and Policy: The Uncertain Connection*, ed. L. E. Lynn, National Academy of Sciences, Washington.

Glossary

Archaeology: refers to the Foucauldian interest in the history of what could be thought; a form of inquiry that establishes the conditions under which certain statements are considered true and others false.

Assemblage: a term used by poststructural and governmentality scholars to signal a plurality of influences and unpredictability (contingency) in social relations; the term is commonly associated with the work of Gilles Deleuze and Felix Guattari (*A Thousand Plateaus: Capitalism and Schizophrenia*, Athlone Press, London, 1988).

Authorised choice: a term from Colebatch (see Chapter 10) describing an approach to policy that focuses on the decision-making of those who hold positions of power in the government. This approach is also called **comprehensive rationalism**.

Biopolitics (or *biopower*): a term used by Foucault to describe a form of politics that is directly concerned with administering the biological needs and capacities of citizens ('populations').

Chicago school: refers to a school of thought, associated with the faculty of the University of Chicago, which adheres to neoclassical economic views and emphasises non-intervention from government.

Comprehensive rationalism: an approach to policy that posits the government as an objective and rational decision-maker, making policy to regulate citizen behaviours.

Conceptual logics: meanings that are necessary to make a particular **problem representation** coherent; what is taken for granted in a specific **problematisation**; includes deep-seated epistemological and ontological assumptions.

Discourse: a group of related statements, signs and practices that *creates* the object/s and domains it purports to describe, giving those objects and domains status as 'truth' or 'knowledge'. Discourses set limits on what it is possible to say or think about the object/s they create, though they can and do contain tensions and contradictions that open up spaces for challenge and change.

Dividing practices: a term used by Foucault to describe practices that set some (marginalised) groups against other (mainstream) groups, and/or that set up divisions or tensions within political subjects. Attention to dividing practices offers insights into the ways in which governmental targeting of the behaviours of the socially marginal assists in regulating the wider population.

Endogenous: developing within; originating internally.

Epistême: Foucault used the term to refer to the set of relations in a specific epoch that ground specific knowledges and hence make possible what is considered to be 'truth'. The idea of epistêmes poses a challenge to a progressive, linear account of the history of ideas.

Epistemology: what we think we can know about the nature of things, i.e. about **ontology**.

Event: Foucault talks about 'events' as things that happened. They had a beginning and an end. History consists of multitudes of such happenings that take things in one direction rather than another. Recognising history as 'events' destabilises any notion of inevitable progress or linear evolution.

Exogenous: developing without; originating externally.

GATT (General Agreement on Tariffs and Trade): a set of rules, or treaty, put in place in 1948 by participating nations to reduce tariffs and other barriers to trade in goods and services. The functions of GATT were taken over in 1995 by the **World Trade Organization**.

Genealogy: a historical methodology, used by Foucault, which examines the twists and turns, the disjunctures or disconnections, in history. Genealogy emphasises the power dynamics in historical developments, destabilising accounts of the present as natural and inevitable.

Governance: in a Foucauldian sense the term evokes an understanding of rule that includes but that also extends beyond the state to encompass a wide range of groups, agencies and institutions, including professionals and the social sciences. This use of the term is not to be confused with the recent trend in international circles to talk about 'good governance', meaning to imply problems with a nation's or people's ability to govern or to sustain economic development and economic growth (see J. Jose 2007, 'Reframing the governance story', *Australian Journal of Political Science*, vol. 42, no. 3, pp. 455–70).

Governmental or political rationalities (modes of governance; modes of rule; rationalities of rule; diagrams of rule); the thought in or behind government; see **governmentality**.

Governmentality: best thought of as 'govern-*mentality*' (see Chapter 2). Used in a general sense to refer to the different kinds of thinking associated with particular approaches to governing, e.g. neoliberal, social, authoritarian. Used also in a more specific sense to refer to the form of rule that emerged in the late 18th century that focuses on 'population'.

Humanist: refers to the way in which humans were thought about in and after the 'Enlightenment'; a kind of 'essence' of humanity; what the 'human' is truly meant to be.

Ideological State Apparatuses: a term from Althusser that refers to the heterogeneous and dispersed institutions, including education and the family, through which ideology works (see L. Althusser 1971 [1970], 'Ideology and Ideological State Apparatuses', in L. Althusser, *Lenin and Philosophy and Other Essays*, Trans. B. Brewster, New Left Books, London).

International Monetary Fund (IMF): International organisation established in 1944 to manage international currency exchange.

Knowledge-power nexus: the ways in which **power** is involved in producing forms of knowledge, and in which knowledges exercise power or influence in shaping people's lives.

Limits: a term associated with poststructuralism in which no distinction is drawn between a core, or pure knowledge ('truth'), and its limits or boundaries. Hence, there are *only* limits, which are however seen as contingent and open to change. Critical analysis of limits allows us to reflect upon the limitations of our own thought and how issues could be thought differently.

Neoliberalism: a term used to describe the dominant governmental rationality (see **governmentality**) of the 1990s to the present; refers to a tendency to privilege market relations as a motif for thinking about all forms of human relationships.

Normalisation: the practices that create the 'normal subject' who is set off from 'others' (see **dividing practices**). By setting norms or standards of behaviour, normalisation has homogenising, and hence constricting, effects on what is considered to be appropriate and allowable. Norms are forms of regulation.

OECD (Organisation for Economic Co-operation and Development): an organisation of 30 market-based, high income countries with representative democratic institutions; a forum for the exchange of comparative information, experiences and policy ideas.

Ontology: what we believe about the nature of things; the study of the nature of existence.

Political rationalism: an approach to policy that challenges **comprehensive rationalism**. Attuned to value disputes, political rationalism sees a role for political analysts in assisting governments to manage these disputes. Not to be confused with **governmental/political rationalities**.

Poststructuralism: an intellectual tradition that emphasises fluidity and contestation in social thought and relations, and the politics involved in assigning meaning. There is a focus on how knowledge is produced and on how concepts change meaning over time and place. A key project is to expose the underlying assumptions of many Western norms, in particular the idea of the self as a coherent and singular entity (see **humanist**).

Power (as productive): an understanding of power as a positive force that makes things happen. This view of power signals that we are not governed *solely* through prohibitions; rather certain **discourses** make particular forms of rule and of being possible.

Problematistion: how something is put forward as a problem. Since policy proposals specify what needs to change, they are forms of problematisation, containing implicit representations of the character and causes of 'problems'.

Problem representations: the implied 'problems' in **problematisations**.

Reflexivity: critical reflection on the deep-seated assumptions and preconceptions found within one's own **problem representations** – the ways in which we characterise 'problems'.

Self-regulation: a mode of rule (or governance) that works *through* political subjects, encouraging them to behave in specific ways deemed desirable for social cohesion or economic development (see **normalisation**).

Social capital: a theory that, in its most basic form, links levels of community trust and social performance to measures of community organisational activity.

Social constructionism: an intellectual tradition that generally accepts that knowledge is a social creation.

Structured interaction: a term from Colebatch (see Chapter 10) that stresses the many and competing voices involved in defining policy 'problems' and deciding policy directions; also referred to as **political rationalism**.

Subject positions: those forms of subjectivity made available in discourses (e.g. the 'consumer', the 'caring' mother, the 'deviant', the 'problem gambler').

Superstructure: a key term in Marxist theory that includes political and legal institutions (law, the police, the government), as well as ideology (religious, moral, legal, political).

World Bank: Common name for the International Bank for Reconstruction and Development, established at the Bretton Woods Conference in 1944 to aid post-war reconstruction and development; supports development projects and structural adjustment programs in poor countries.

World Health Organization (WHO): one of the original agencies of the United Nations, set up in 1948 to coordinate international public health initiatives.

World Trade Organization (WTO): international organisation established in 1995 to supersede the General Agreement on Tariffs and Trade (**GATT**); makes and enforces rules for global trade by which members are bound to abide.

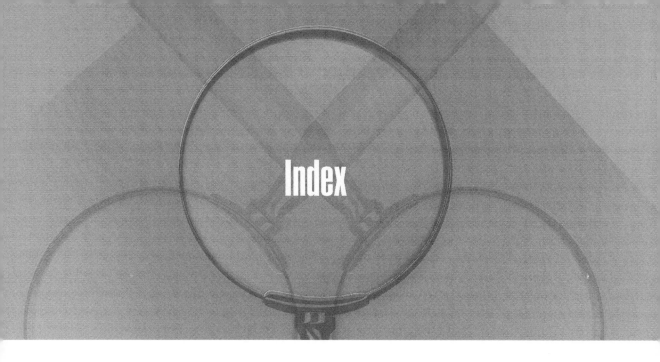

Index